THE LOEB CLASSICAL LIBRARY

FOUNDED BY JAMES LOEB, LL.D.

EDITED BY

†T. E. PAGE, C.H., LITT.D.

LIVY

X

BOOKS XXXV—XXXVII

LIVY

X

FROM XXXV–XXXVII

LIVY

WITH AN ENGLISH TRANSLATION BY
EVAN T. SAGE, Ph.D.
PROFESSOR OF LATIN AND HEAD OF THE DEPARTMENT OF
CLASSICS IN THE UNIVERSITY OF PITTSBURGH

IN FOURTEEN VOLUMES

X

BOOKS XXXV—XXXVII

CAMBRIDGE, MASSACHUSETTS
HARVARD UNIVERSITY PRESS
LONDON
WILLIAM HEINEMANN LTD
MCMLVIII

PA
6452
A2
1919
v.10

First printed 1935
Reprinted 1939, 1950, 1958

Printed in Great Britain

CONTENTS

CONTENTS

TRANSLATOR'S PREFACE

LITTLE need be added to the Translator's Preface of the preceding volume. My resources, problems, aims and methods of work are essentially those there described, and no significant additions to the literature have come to my attention. I content myself, therefore, with reference to the appropriate sections of the Preface of Volume IX.

Two points, however, may be mentioned. In two important particulars the Periocha differs from the continuous text. Livy (XXXV. xiv. 5–12) quotes the famous conversation between Africanus and Hannibal, with some apparent doubts as to its authenticity; the author of the Periocha is not so troubled. The difference in the account of the dedication of the temple of the Magna Mater is more serious. Livy (XXXVI. xxxvi. 4) says that it was dedicated by Brutus; the author of the Periocha assigns that distinction to Scipio Nasica. These variations raise the puzzling question of the relation of the Periochae to the continuous text, but I have not found space to discuss it at length.

The ever-troublesome problem of chronology becomes more serious in these Books. Livy seems happily unaware of it, but the translator with the most modest ambitions is painfully conscious of it while he recognizes his inability to solve it. It is

fortunate for him as for the Romans that inter-
calation was resorted to before matters grew worse.
I have devoted to this problem the minimum of
attention.

Maps 1 and 2, identical with the corresponding
maps in Volume IX, are the work of Mr. Foster.

I express my gratitude to him, as to my col-
leagues, Professor Adalaide J. Wegner and Dr. Nancy
Margaret Miller, for assistance at various points,
and to my son, Robert L. Sage, of the Oriental
Institute, University of Chicago, for aid, particularly
with the place-names of Asia Minor.

CONSPECTUS SIGLORUM

B = Codex Bambergensis M. IV. 9, s. 11.
F = Codex Bambergensis Q. IV. 27 (Theol. 99), s. 6.
M = Codex Moguntinus deperditus, s. 9 (?).
ς = Codices deteriores et editiones veteres (the
most important early editions are cited by
name).

INTRODUCTORY NOTE

In the Introductory Note to Volume IX I tried to picture with the maximum of simplicity the semi-anarchy prevailing in the eastern Mediterranean when Roman armies first showed themselves seriously in Greece. The Books contained in that volume give us the record of Rome's first large-scale contacts with the east, her defeat of Philip, the liberation of Greece, and her effort—which seems to me entirely genuine—to retire from Greece with clean hands.

There is no pause in Livy's narrative at the end of Book XXXIV, and no Roman of that time had the opportunity which I enjoy to recapitulate and to reflect on the course he was following. Nevertheless, it seems worth while to review the results of the defeat of Philip. The independent Asiatic states of Pergamum and Rhodes had co-operated with Rome but without compensation. Ptolemy had been friendly to Rome though he had not been called upon to demonstrate his loyalty in the field. Antiochus had shown unmistakable signs of his intentions by his attacks on the possessions of Ptolemy in Asia Minor and on the Greek cities of that region and by his territorial ambitions in Europe. Philip had been defeated but had suffered no territorial losses except in Greece. These were the major components of the empire of Alexander.

INTRODUCTORY NOTE

Within Greece there was no longer a pro-Macedonian party in any effective sense. The liberation of the Greek cities did not prevent attempts to coerce them into joining the Aetolian and Achaean Leagues which practically dominated Greece. Athens at this period relapsed into relative obscurity, emerging occasionally as a futile peace-maker. The half-hearted attempt of the Romans to destroy Nabis, tyrant of Sparta, made him the more ready to rise to the bait of the Aetolians.

While the Achaeans remained faithful to their Roman alliance, the Aetolians assumed the leadership in the effort to unite all the anti-Roman elements. Dissatisfied with their own meagre gains after Cynoscephalae and repeatedly offended by Flamininus, who had no disposition to be criticized, their discontent was generally known, and it was clear that their best policy was to seek the aid of Antiochus. The organization of Greece carried out under the direction of Flamininus had been aristocratic in character, and the Aetolians had much reason to count on the economic inequalities which were thus accentuated and on the violent party-spirit of the Greeks. They then undertook to fuse into one organic mass all the diversified elements which for conflicting reasons wished to end Roman influence in Greece and the east generally. Nabis and Antiochus were easily won over; Philip, surprisingly, would not join them; the Achaean League remained loyal to Rome, and if there were undercurrents of party strife within the Greek cities Livy is generally unconscious of them, and the pro-Roman parties, with the help of the Romans, were successful in suppressing their opponents.

INTRODUCTORY NOTE

A war between the Romans and Antiochus was probably inevitable even if the Aetolians had not taken the initiative. Antiochus had been allied with Philip against Ptolemy; he menaced Rome's friends in Rhodes and Pergamum; Rhodes was the potential champion of the Greek cities of Ionia; Hannibal was numbered among his counsellors. The most naïve reader cannot be surprised that Antiochus is the protagonist of the drama of this volume.

Whether Rome was willing to accept the part thrust upon her is an academic question. I cannot believe that she realized the possible consequences of her intervention in the larger eastern world, and the complexities of personal ambitions and internal politics made the realization impossible. Perhaps a disinterested and unambitious conqueror has at all times been an anachronism.

LIVY
FROM THE FOUNDING OF THE CITY

BOOK XXXV

T. LIVI

AB URBE CONDITA

LIBER XXXV

LIVY

FROM THE FOUNDING OF THE CITY

A.U.C.
561

I. PRINCIPIO anni quo haec gesta sunt, Sex. Digitius praetor in Hispania citeriore cum civitatibus iis, quae post profectionem M. Catonis permultae rebellaverant, crebra magis quam digna dictu proelia 2 fecit, et adeo pleraque adversa ut vix dimidium militum quam quod acceperat, successori tradiderit. 3 Nec dubium est quin omnis Hispania sublatura animos fuerit, ni alter praetor P. Cornelius Cn. F. Scipio trans Iberum multa secunda proelia fecisset, quo terrore non minus quinquaginta oppida ad eum 4 defecerunt. Praetor haec gesserat Scipio; idem 5 pro praetore Lusitanos, pervastata ulteriore provincia cum ingenti praeda domum redeuntes, in ipso itinere adgressus ab hora tertia diei ad octavam incerto eventu pugnavit, numero militum impar,

---

[1] For the assignment of Digitius to Hither Spain, see XXXIV. xliii. 7.

[2] For Cato's campaign in Spain, see XXXIV. xi–xxi; for his return and triumph, XXXIV. xlvi. 2.

[3] Scipio's appointment to Farther Spain was reported at XXXIV. xliii. 7; the term "propraetor" below is used to describe his status, probably informal, during the period

LIVY

FROM THE FOUNDING OF THE CITY

BOOK XXXV

I. In the beginning of the year in which these events occurred, Sextus Digitius, praetor in Hither Spain,[1] fought battles, numerous rather than memorable, with the tribes which had, in great numbers, revolted after the departure of Marcus Cato,[2] and most of these engagements were so unfortunate in result that he turned over to his successor barely half as many soldiers as he had received. Nor is there any doubt that all Spain would have taken courage to rebel had not the other praetor, Publius Cornelius Scipio, the son of Gnaeus,[3] fought many successful battles beyond the Ebro and so intimidated the natives that not less than fifty towns surrendered to him. These were Scipio's achievements as praetor; when he was propraetor he fell upon the Lusitani as they were returning home after plundering the farther province, laden with much spoil, while they were still on the march, and from the third hour of the day to the eighth maintained an indecisive action. He was unequal in number of

between the expiration of his term and the arrival of his successor, since no prorogation of his command is recorded.

3

LIVY

A.U.C.
561

6 superior aliis; nam et acie frequenti armatis adversus
longum et impeditum turba pecorum agmen et
recenti milite adversus fessos longo itinere concur-
7 rerat. Tertia namque vigilia exierant hostes; huic
nocturno itineri tres diurnae horae accesserant, nec
ulla quiete data laborem viae proelium exceperat.
8 Itaque principio pugnae vigoris aliquid in corporibus
animisque fuit, et turbaverant primo Romanos;
deinde aequata paulisper pugna est. In hoc discrimine ludos Iovi, si fudisset cecidissetque hostes,
9 propraetor[1] vovit. Tandem gradum acrius intulere
Romani, cessitque Lusitanus, deinde prorsus terga
dedit; et cum institissent fugientibus victores, ad
10 duodecim milia hostium sunt caesa, capti quingenti
quadraginta, omnes ferme equites, et signa militaria
capta centum triginta quattuor. De exercitu Ro-
11 mano septuaginta et tres amissi. Pugnatum haud
procul Ilipa urbe est; eo victorem opulentum praeda
exercitum P. Cornelius reduxit. Ea omnis ante
12 urbem exposita est, potestasque dominis suas res
cognoscendi facta est; cetera vendenda quaestori
data; quod inde refectum militi divisum.

II. Nondum ab Roma profectus erat C. Flaminius
2 praetor, cum haec in Hispania gerebantur. Itaque
adversae quam secundae res per ipsum amicosque

---

[1] propraetor *ed. Moguntina* 1518 : praetor *Bς*.

---

[1] The performance of this vow is recorded at XXXVI.
xxxvi. 1–2 (191 B.C.).
[2] This city is probably identical with that called Ἴλλιπα
μεγάλη by Ptolemy (II. iv. 13; cf. Plin. *N.H.* III. 11), on the
river Baetis. It is now Alcala del Rio.

troops, superior in all else; for with his troops in a compact body he had clashed with a column long drawn out and hindered by the great number of its pack-animals, and he fought with fresh troops against an enemy worn out by a long march. For they had set out during the third watch; three daylight hours had been added to their night march, and the battle had followed at once upon the labour of the journey, with no time given for repose. Accordingly, only at the outset of the fight did they retain some energy of mind and body, and at first they had thrown the Romans into confusion; later the battle became gradually more even. At this crisis the propraetor vowed games to Jupiter [1] if he should rout and slaughter the enemy. At length the Romans pressed on with greater vigour and the Lusitani gave way and finally fled; and while the victors pursued the fleeing foe, about twelve thousand of the enemy were killed, five hundred forty were taken prisoners, almost all cavalry, and one hundred thirty-four standards were captured. From the Roman army seventy-three were lost. The battle was fought not far from the city of Ilipa; [2] thither Publius Cornelius led the army flushed with victory and enriched with spoils. All the booty was exposed to view before the city, and the opportunity was afforded the owners of identifying their property; the rest was turned over to the quaestor to sell and the proceeds were divided among the soldiers.

II. Gaius Flaminius [3] had not yet left Rome when this happened in Spain. Therefore defeat rather than victory was the constant burden of the talk of

[3] Flaminius had been assigned to Hither Spain (XXXIV. lv. 6).

LIVY

3 eius magis sermonibus celebrabantur; et tempta-
verat, quoniam bellum ingens in provincia exarsisset,
et exiguas reliquias exercitus ab Sex. Digitio atque
eas ipsas [1] plenas pavoris ac fugae accepturus esset,
4 ut sibi unam ex urbanis legionibus decernerent, ad
quam cum militem ab se ipso scriptum ex senatus
consulto adiecisset, eligeret ex omni numero sex
5 milia et ducentos pedites, equites trecentos: ea se
legione—nam in Sex. Digiti exercitu haud multum
6 spei esse—rem gesturum. Seniores negare ad
rumores a privatis temere in gratiam magistratuum
confictos senatus consulta facienda esse; nisi quod
aut praetores ex provinciis scriberent aut legati
7 renuntiarent, nihil ratum haberi debere; si tumultus
in Hispania esset, placere tumultuarios milites extra
Italiam scribi a praetore. Mens ea senatus fuit ut
8 in Hispania tumultuarii milites legerentur. Valerius
Antias et in Siciliam navigasse dilectus causa C.
Flaminium scribit, et, ex Sicilia Hispaniam petentem,
tempestate in Africam delatum vagos milites de
9 exercitu P. Africani sacramento rogasse; his duarum
provinciarum dilectibus tertium in Hispania adiecisse.

III. Nec in Italia segnius Ligurum bellum crescebat. Pisas iam quadraginta [2] milibus hominum,
adfluente cotidie multitudine ad famam belli spemque

---

[1] eas ipsas ς: eas B.
[2] quadraginta edd. vett.: quadringentis Bς.

---

[1] The *urbanae legiones* were reserve troops, to be employed where need arose: cf. XXXIV. lvi. 4.
[2] The conduct of Flaminius with respect to the levies in Sicily and Africa appears to have been irregular, but there is no indication that the senate took cognizance of it, perhaps

him and his friends, and, since a great war had B.C. 1
flared up in the province and he was to take over
from Sextus Digitius the scanty remnants of his
army, and even these filled with panic and terror,
he had tried to induce them to decree to him
one of the city-legions,[1] and when he had added to
this the force which he had enlisted in accordance
with the decree of the senate, that he should choose
from the whole number six thousand two hundred
infantry and three hundred cavalry: with this
legion—for little confidence could be placed in the
army of Sextus Digitius—he would carry on the
campaign. The elders declared that no decree of
the senate should be passed on the basis of rumours
causelessly invented by private individuals to gratify
magistrates; unless either the praetors should send
reports from the provinces or their legates bring
word, nothing should be considered settled; if an
emergency existed in Spain, it was their will that
the praetor should enlist emergency troops outside
of Italy. It was the senate's intention that these
emergency troops should be raised in Spain. Valerius
Antias writes that Gaius Flaminius sailed also to
Sicily to conduct his levy and that on his way from
Sicily to Spain he was driven by a storm to Africa
and administered the oath to stragglers from the
army of Publius Africanus; that to the contingents
from these two provinces he added a third in Spain.[2]

III. Nor was the war with the Ligures in Italy
any slower to begin. Pisa was already besieged by
about forty thousand men, large numbers daily
pouring in by reason of the report of the war and in

because of the vagueness of their own phrase *extra Italiam*.
Scipio's soldiers had been in Africa since 201 B.C.

7

LIVY

praedae, circumsedebant. Minucius consul Arretium die quam edixerat [1] ad conveniendum militibus venit.
2 Inde quadrato agmine ad Pisas duxit, et cum hostes non plus mille passuum ab oppido trans fluvium movissent castra, consul urbem haud dubie servatam
3 adventu suo est ingressus. Postero die et ipse trans fluvium quingentos ferme passus ab hoste posuit castra. Inde levibus proeliis a populationibus agrum
4 sociorum tutabatur; in aciem exire non audebat novo milite et ex multis generibus hominum collecto necdum noto satis inter se, ut fidere alii aliis possent.
5 Ligures multitudine freti [2] et in aciem exibant, parati de summa rerum decernere, et abundantes militum numero passim multas manus per extrema
6 finium ad praedandum mittebant, et, cum coacta vis magna pecorum praedaeque esset, paratum erat praesidium, per quod [3] in castella eorum vicosque ageretur.

IV. Cum bellum Ligustinum ad Pisas constitisset, consul alter, L. Cornelius Merula, per extremos Ligurum fines exercitum in agrum Boiorum induxit, ubi longe alia belli ratio quam cum Liguribus erat.
2 Consul in aciem exibat, hostes pugnam detractabant; praedatumque, ubi nemo obviam exiret, discurrebant Romani, Boi diripi sua impune quam tuendo ea con-

[1] quam edixerat *Baumgarten-Crusius* : qua edixerat *B* : qua dixerat *M* : quem dixerat ς.
[2] freti ς : frequenti *B*.
[3] per quod ς : per quos *B*.

---

[1] Cf. XXXIV. lvi. 4.
[2] This is apparently the Auser river (Plin. *N.H.* III. 50), now the Serchio, which once emptied into the Arno near by.
[3] This statement is difficult to accept, in view of the fact that the major component of his force was the two *urbanae*

8

the hope of booty. The consul Minucius arrived at
Arretium on the day on which he had ordered the
troops to assemble.[1] Thence he led the force in a
hollow-square formation toward Pisa, and since the
enemy had moved their camp across the river,[2] no
more than a mile from the town, the consul marched
into the city that had without doubt been saved by
his arrival. The next day he too crossed the river
and encamped about five hundred paces from the
enemy. From this base he defended the allies'
country from ravage by fighting petty battles; he
did not dare to march out in battle-line with raw
troops, collected from many tribes and not yet well
enough known to one another to feel confidence in
their comrades.[3] The Ligures both marched out to
battle, trusting in their numbers and prepared to
risk a decisive engagement, and, since they had
abundance of men, sent out many parties to plunder
in all directions on the borders of the territory, and
when a large number of animals and much booty
had been collected, guards were available to conduct
them to their forts and villages.

IV. While the Ligurian war was at a standstill
around Pisa, the other consul, Lucius Cornelius
Merula, led his army through the farthest lands of
the Ligures into the country of the Boii, where the
war was conducted in a fashion far different from
that in the war with the Ligures. The consul
marched out to offer battle, the enemy declined to
engage; the Romans scattered to plunder when no one
confronted them, and the Boii preferred the devasta-

legiones of the year before : cf. the note to ii. 3 above. The
Romans, like modern commanders, stressed the necessity of
homogeneity and mutual confidence in combatant troops.

9

LIVY

3 serere certamen malebant. Postquam omnia ferro
ignique satis evastata erant consul agro hostium
excessit et ad Mutinam agmine incauto, ut inter
4 pacatos, ducebat. Boi ut egressum suis finibus
hostem sensere, sequebantur silenti agmine, locum
insidiis quaerentes. Nocte praetergressi castra Romana saltum, qua transeundum erat Romanis,
5 insederunt. Id cum parum occulte fecissent, consul,
qui multa nocte solitus erat movere castra, ne nox
terrorem in tumultuario proelio augeret, lucem
expectavit et, cum luce moveret, tamen turmam
6 equitum exploratum misit. Postquam relatum est,
quantae copiae et in quo[1] loco essent, totius agminis
sarcinas in medium coici iussit et triarios vallum
circumicere, cetero exercitu instructo ad hostem
7 accessit. Idem et Galli fecerunt, postquam apertas
esse insidias et recto ac iusto proelio, ubi vera vinceret
virtus, dimicandum viderunt.

V. Hora secunda ferme concursum est. Sinistra
sociorum ala et extraordinarii prima in acie pugnabant; praeerant duo consulares legati, M. Marcellus
2 et Ti.[2] Sempronius, prioris anni consul. Novus consul nunc ad prima signa erat, nunc legiones continebat

---

[1] et in quo ς: in quo B.
[2] Ti. *Sigonius*: t. B.

---

[1] The soldiers in the third line of the legionary battle-
formation.
[2] Cf. XXXI. xxi. 7; the *dextra ala* in this case was apparently
with the Roman legions : see sect. 6 below.
[3] These troops were not an organic part of the legion : cf.
XXXIV. xlvii. 4 and the note.
[4] Probably the consul of 196 B.C. (XXXIII. xxv. 4).
[5] Cf. XXXIV. xlii. 3.

tion of their lands without interference on their B.C. 193
part to the risk of a decisive battle while protecting
them. When everything had been sufficiently wasted
with sword and fire, the consul retired from the
enemy's country and marched toward Mutina, his
column taking no precautions as if it was traversing a
pacified country. When the Boii saw that the enemy
had withdrawn from their territory, they followed
stealthily, seeking a place for an ambush. At night
they passed the Roman camp and seized a defile
through which the Romans had to march. Since
their precautions for secrecy were insufficient, the
consul, who had been accustomed to break camp
late in the night, waited for daylight, that darkness
might not increase the terror from a sudden attack,
and, although he was moving by day, he nevertheless sent out a troop of cavalry to reconnoitre. When
word came back how strong the enemy was and
where he was stationed, he ordered the baggage of
the whole column brought into the midst and the
triarii [1] to construct a rampart around it, and with
the remainder of the army in battle-array marched
towards the enemy. The Gauls did the same when
they realized that their stratagem was discovered
and that they would have to fight in regular
and fair combat where constant courage would
conquer.

V. At about the second hour the battle began.
The left squadron [2] of the allies and the irregular
troops [3] were fighting in the front line; their commanders were two lieutenants of consular rank,
Marcus Marcellus [4] and Tiberius Sempronius,[5] consul
of the preceding year. The new consul was now with
the leading standards, now holding back the legions

11

LIVY

A.U.C.
561

in subsidiis, ne certaminis studio prius procurrerent
3 quam datum signum esset. Equites earum extra
aciem in locum patentem Q. et P. Minucios tribunos
militum educere iussit, unde, cum signum dedisset,
4 impetum ex aperto facerent. Haec agenti nuntius
venit a Ti. Sempronio Longo non sustinere extra-
5 ordinarios impetum Gallorum; et caesos permultos
esse et qui supersint partim labore partim metu
remisisse ardorem pugnae Legionem alteram ex
duabus, si videretur, summitteret, priusquam igno-
6 minia acciperetur. Secunda missa est legio et
extraordinarii recepti. Tum redintegrata est pugna,
cum et recens miles et frequens ordinibus legio
successisset. Et sinistra ala ex proelio subducta
7 est, dextra in primam aciem subiit. Sol ingenti
ardore torrebat minime patientia aestus Gallorum
corpora; densis tamen ordinibus nunc alii in alios,
nunc in scuta incumbentes sustinebant impetus
8 Romanorum. Quod ubi animadvertit consul, ad
perturbandos ordines eorum C. Livium Salinatorem,
qui praeerat alariis equitibus, quam concitatissimos
equos immittere iubet et legionarios equites in sub-
9 sidiis esse. Haec procella equestris primo confudit
et turbavit deinde dissipavit aciem Gallorum, non
10 tamen ut terga darent. Obstabant duces, hastilibus
caedentes terga trepidantium et redire in ordines
cogentes; sed interequitantes alarii non patiebantur.

---

[1] The phrase *ex aperto* does not repeat the idea of *in locum
patentem* above, but indicates that no ambuscade or masked
attack was planned for the cavalry.

[2] The manœuvre is that known as "passing through"
friendly troops, each unit moving through the intervals
separating the maniples of the corresponding element.

[3] Cf. xxiv. 6 below.

[4] That is, would not permit the enemy to reorganize their line.

in reserve, lest in their ardour for the fight they should rush forward before the signal was given. He ordered two military tribunes, Quintus and Publius Minucius, to lead the cavalry of these legions beyond the flanks of the battle-line into open ground, whence, when the signal was given, they were to attack from the open.[1] As he was thus engaged, a runner from Tiberius Sempronius Longus came to him, saying that the irregulars were not holding the Gallic attack and that many of them had been killed and that those who were left, partly as a result of their exertions, partly from fear, had lost their zest for fighting. He should send in, if he saw fit, one of the two legions before a disgraceful defeat was sustained. The second legion was sent forward and the irregular troops relieved.[2] Then the battle was restored, since fresh troops, a legion with full ranks, had entered the fight; and the left squadron was withdrawn from the battle and the right took its place in the battle-line. The sun with its fierce rays scorched the bodies of the Gauls, which were little capable of enduring heat; nevertheless, in dense ranks, resting now on one another, now on their shields, they withstood the attacks of the Romans. When the consul saw this, he ordered Gaius Livius Salinator,[3] who commanded the auxiliary cavalry, to charge at the utmost speed, the legionary cavalry to be in support. This storm of horsemen at first threw the battle-line of the Gauls into confusion and disorder, then scattered it, but without causing a rout. The captains prevented this, striking with their staffs the backs of the terror-stricken and forcing them back into the line, but the auxiliary cavalry, riding among them, would not allow this.[4] The

LIVY

11 Consul obtestabatur milites ut paulum adniterentur;
victoriam in manibus esse; dum turbatos et trepi-
dantes viderent, instarent; si restitui ordines sivissent,[1] integro rursus eos proelio et dubio[2] dimi-

12 caturos. Inferre vexillarios iussit signa. Omnes
conisi tandem averterunt hostem. Postquam terga
dabant et in fugam passim effundebantur, tum ad

13 persequendos eos legionarii equites immissi. Quattuordecim milia Boiorum eo die sunt caesa; vivi
capti mille nonaginta duo, equites septingenti viginti
unus, tres duces eorum, signa militaria ducenta

14 duodecim, carpenta sexaginta tria. Nec Romanis
incruenta victoria fuit; supra quinque milia militum,
ipsorum aut sociorum, amissa, centuriones tres et
viginti, praefecti socium quattuor et M. Genucius et
Q. et M. Marcii[3] tribuni militum secundae legionis.

VI. Eodem fere tempore duorum consulum litterae allatae sunt, L. Corneli de proelio ad Mutinam

2 cum Bois facto et Q. Minuci a Pisis: comitia suae
sortis esse; ceterum adeo suspensa omnia in Liguribus se habere, ut abscedi inde sine pernicie sociorum

3 et damno rei publicae non posset. Si ita videretur
patribus, mitterent ad collegam, ut is, qui profli-
gatum bellum haberet, ad comitia Romam rediret;

4 si id facere gravaretur, quod non suae sortis id
negotium esset, se quidem facturum quodcumque
senatus censuisset; sed etiam atque etiam viderent,

[1] sivissent ς : sinissent B.
[2] proelio et dubio FMς : om. B.
[3] et Q. et M. Marcii Drakenborch : q. et m. marci B : eques
et m. martius M.

---

[1] If both consuls were ordered away from Rome, it was
necessary for them to decide by lot which should return to
preside at the elections.

consul urged the troops to make a little more effort;
victory, he said, was in their grasp; they should
press on while they saw the enemy disordered and in
terror; if they permitted the ranks to be reformed
they would fight again a new and doubtful battle.
He ordered the standard-bearers to advance. All
joined in the effort and at last turned the enemy to
flight. As they were fleeing and scattering this way
and that in rout, at that moment the legionary
cavalry was let loose to pursue them. Fourteen
thousand of the Boii perished on that day; one
thousand and ninety-two were captured alive, seven
hundred and twenty-one cavalrymen, with three of
their commanders, two hundred and twelve standards
and sixty-three carts were taken. But for the
Romans the victory was not bloodless; more than
five thousand of the soldiers, Romans and allies, fell,
twenty-three centurions, four commanders of allies,
and Marcus Genucius and Quintus and Marcus
Marcius, military tribunes of the second legion.

VI. At about the same time letters from the two
consuls arrived at Rome, one from Lucius Cornelius
reporting the battle with the Boii near Mutina, the
other from Quintus Minucius from Pisa: the latter
said that it had fallen to his lot to preside at the
consular elections,[1] but so unsettled were conditions
generally among the Ligures that he could not
leave there without loss to the allies and danger to
the state. If it pleased the Fathers, they should
write to his colleague, who had finished his campaign, to return to Rome for the elections; if he
protested against doing this, because the task had
not fallen to him by lot, he would himself do the
senate's bidding; only let the senate consider again

15

ne magis e re publica esset interregnum iniri quam
5 ab se in eo statu relinqui provinciam. Senatus
C. Scribonio negotium dedit, ut duos legatos ex
ordine senatorio mitteret ad L. Cornelium consulem,
6 qui litteras collegae ad senatum missas deferrent ad
eum et nuntiarent senatum, ni is ad magistratus
subrogandos Romam veniret, potius quam Q. Minucium a bello integro avocaret, interregnum iniri
7 passurum. Missi legati renuntiarunt L. Cornelium
8 ad magistratus subrogandos Romam venturum. De
litteris L. Corneli, quas scripserat secundum proelium
9 cum Bois factum, disceptatio in senatu fuit, quia
privatim plerisque senatoribus legatus M. Claudius
scripserat fortunae populi Romani et militum virtuti
gratiam habendam, quod res bene gesta esset;
consulis opera et militum aliquantum amissum et
10 hostium exercitum, cuius delendi oblata fortuna
fuerit, elapsum: milites eo plures perisse, quod
tardius ex subsidiis, qui laborantibus opem ferrent,
successissent; hostes e manibus emissos, quod
equitibus legionariis et tardius datum signum esset
et persequi fugientes non licuisset.

---

¹ This device had rarely been resorted to in recent years.
Members of the senate were chosen in order to serve for five
days each, and the *interrex* (the name survived from the period
of the monarchy) either held the election or nominated another
interrex. Minucius' proposal probably had some political
motive, but the facts are unknown.

² The M. Marcellus of v. 1 above. Marcellus as consul had
fought the Gauls with indifferent success, although he had been
granted a triumph over the Insubres and Comenses (XXXIII.
xxxvii. 10). We have no means of verifying either the account
which Livy gives of the battle (which is on the whole sympathetic towards Cornelius) or Marcellus' less favourable
interpretation, which may have been inspired partly by

and again whether an interregnum [1] would not be more advantageous to the state than his absence from his province at such a time. The senate entrusted to Gaius Scribonius the task of sending two commissioners from the senatorial order to Lucius Cornelius the consul, to deliver to him the letter forwarded by his colleague to the senate, and to inform him that if he did not come to Rome to elect the magistrates the senate, rather than take Quintus Minucius away from an unfinished war, would suffer an interregnum to begin. The commissioners who were sent brought back the reply that Lucius Cornelius would come to Rome to choose the magistrates. Regarding the despatches of Lucius Cornelius, which he had written after he had fought the battle with the Boii, a controversy broke out in the senate because his lieutenant, Marcus Claudius,[2] had written privately to many senators that gratitude was due to the good fortune of the Roman people and the valour of the soldiers because the issue had been successful; but that by the action of the consul, both heavy losses of men had occurred and the army of the enemy had escaped, though there had been the opportunity to destroy it; the loss of men had been heavier since troops to replace the exhausted had come up too slowly from the reserve; the enemy had slipped from their hands both because the legionary cavalry had received their orders too late and because they had not been permitted to pursue the fleeing enemy.

jealousy, partly by political rivalry. This, however, did not prevent Cornelius from leaving him in command, although there was a hostile explanation of this action : cf. viii. 1–5 and the note below.

VII. De ea re nihil temere decerni placuit; ad
2 frequentiores consultatio dilata est; instabat enim
cura alia, quod civitas faenore laborabat et quod,
cum multis faenebribus legibus constricta avaritia
esset, via fraudis inita erat, ut in socios, qui non
tenerentur iis legibus, nomina transcriberent; ita
3 libero faenore obruebantur debitores. Cuius coer-
cendi cum ratio quaereretur, diem finiri placuit
Feralia quae proxime fuissent, ut, qui post eam
diem socii civibus Romanis credidissent pecunias
profiterentur, et ex ea die pecuniae creditae, quibus
4 debitor vellet legibus, ius creditori diceretur. Deinde
postquam professionibus detecta est magnitudo aeris
alieni per hanc fraudem contracti, M. Sempronius
tribunus plebis ex auctoritate patrum plebem rogavit,
5 plebesque scivit, ut cum sociis ac nomine Latino
creditae pecuniae ius idem quod cum civibus Romanis
esset. Haec in Italia domi militiaeque acta.
6   In Hispania nequaquam tantum belli fuit, quantum
7 auxerat fama. C. Flaminius in citeriore Hispania
oppidum Inluciam in Oretanis cepit, deinde in

---

¹ Creditors had found a device for collecting rates of interest
higher than those allowed by law (cf. VII. xvi. 1, etc.), by
transferring the ownership of accounts to subjects of allied
states, who thus became the real or fictitious lenders. The
procedure was to make suitable entries on the creditors'
ledgers. The legislation now adopted made such transactions
between citizens and allies matters of public record (and,
presumably, enforceable only when so recorded). Litigation
arising therefrom favoured the debtor, and the plebiscite of
Sempronius made the Roman code obligatory.

² The laws referred to formed parts of the *ius civile*, which
applied only to *cives* and was enforced by the *praetor urbanus*.
Cases to which allies were parties were tried before the
praetor peregrinus, and the provisions of the *ius civile* were not
binding.

VII. Regarding this matter, it was decreed that B.C. 193 no unconsidered action should be taken; the decision was postponed for a fuller meeting. This was due to the fact that another anxiety was weighing upon them—that the public was burdened by interest-payments,[1] and that, although greed was held in check by numerous laws governing usury, a way of evasion was opened because accounts were transferred to allies, who were not under the operation of these laws;[2] thus debtors were overwhelmed with unrestricted charges. When a method of curbing this practice was sought, it was determined that a day should be fixed, namely, the last occurrence of the festival of the Feralia,[3] that whatever allies had, after that date, loaned money to Roman citizens, should make a public statement to that effect, and that proceedings regarding money so loaned after that date should be governed by the laws of whichever state the debtor should elect. Then, after the greatness of the debt contracted by this evasion was revealed by these public declarations, Marcus Sempronius, tribune of the people, with the authorization of the senate proposed to the assembly, and the assembly voted, that the allies of the Latin confederacy should have the same law regarding the loan of money that applied to Roman citizens. Such were the events, civil and military, which took place in Italy.

In Spain the war was by no means so serious as the exaggerated report of it had been. Gaius Flaminius in Hither Spain captured the town of Inlucia in the land of the Oretani and then con-

---

[3] This festival was held on February 21.

LIVY

hibernacula [1] milites deduxit, et per hiemem proelia
aliquot nulla memoria digna adversus latronum
magis quam hostium excursiones vario tamen eventu
nec sine militum iactura sunt facta. Maiores gestae
8 res a M. Fulvio. Is apud Toletum oppidum cum
Vaccaeis Vettonibusque et Celtiberis signis collatis
dimicavit, exercitum earum gentium fudit fuga-
vitque, regem Hilernum vivum cepit.

VIII. Cum haec in Hispania gerebantur, comitiorum iam appetebat dies. Itaque L. Cornelius consul
2 relicto ad exercitum M. Claudio Romam venit. Is in
3 senatu cum de rebus ab se gestis disseruisset, quoque
statu provincia esset, questus est cum patribus con-
scriptis, quod tanto bello una secunda pugna tam
feliciter perfecto non esset habitus diis immortalibus
honos. Postulavit deinde, supplicationem simul
4 triumphumque decernerent. Prius tamen quam
relatio fieret, Q. Metellus, qui consul dictatorque
fuerat, litteras eodem tempore dixit et consulis
L. Corneli ad senatum et M. Marcelli ad magnam
partem senatorum adlatas esse inter se pugnantes,
5 eoque dilatam esse consultationem, ut praesentibus
auctoribus [2] earum litterarum disceptaretur. Itaque
expectasse sese ut consul, qui sciret ab legato suo
adversus se scriptum aliquid, cum ipsi veniendum
6 esset, deduceret eum secum Romam, cum etiam

---

[1] hibernacula *edd. vett.*: hiberna loca *B.*
[2] auctoribus ⌐: auribus *B.*

---

[1] His appointment to Farther Spain was recorded at
XXXIV. lv. 6.
[2] Metellus was consul in 206 B.C. (XXVIII. x. 2) and
dictator in 205 B.C. (XXIX. x. 2).

ducted the troops to their winter stations, and during
the winter fought several battles, unworthy of record,
against raiding parties of brigands rather than
soldiers, with varying results but not without the
loss of men. Greater things were done by Marcus
Fulvius.[1] Near the town of Toletum he engaged the
Vaccaei, the Vettones and the Celtiberi in pitched
battle, routed and put to flight the armies of these
tribes, and captured alive their king Hilernus.

VIII. While this was going on in Spain, the day
of the elections was drawing near. And so Lucius
Cornelius the consul left Marcus Claudius with the
army and returned to Rome. When he had discoursed in the senate about his achievements and
the condition in which his province was, he voiced a
complaint to the Fathers because, after so great a war
had been so successfully finished by a single victory,
no honour had been paid to the immortal gods. He
then demanded that they decree a thanksgiving and
a triumph at the same time. Before, however, the
formal motion was put, Quintus Metellus, who had
been consul and dictator,[2] said that letters had
arrived at the same time, addressed both to the
senate by Lucius Cornelius and to a great part of the
senators by Marcus Marcellus, that these reports
contradicted one another, and that a decision had
been postponed for the reason that the debate
might be held in the presence of the writers of
these letters. He had accordingly assumed that
the consul, who knew that something unfavourable
to himself had been written by his subordinate,
since he had himself to come to Rome, would bring
his lieutenant with him to the City, especially as it
would have been more correct to entrust the army

LIVY

verius esset Ti. Sempronio imperium habenti tradi
7 exercitum quam legato : nunc videri esse amotum [1]
de industria, qui, si [2] ea quae scripsisset praesens
diceret et arguere [3] coram et, si quid vani adferret,
argui posset, donec ad liquidum veritas explorata
8 esset. Itaque nihil eorum quae postularet consul
9 decernendum in praesentia censere. Cum pergeret
nihilo segnius referre ut supplicationes decerne-
rentur triumphantique sibi urbem invehi liceret,
M. et C. Titinii tribuni plebis se intercessuros si de
ea re fieret senatus consultum dixerunt.

IX. Censores erant priore anno creati Sex. Aelius
2 Paetus et C. Cornelius Cethegus. Cornelius lustrum
condidit. Censa sunt civium capita CXLIII DCCIV.
Aquae ingentes eo anno fuerunt [4] et Tiberis loca
3 plana urbis inundavit; circa portam Flumentanam
etiam collapsa quaedam ruinis sunt. Et porta
Caelimontana fulmine icta est, murusque circa

---

[1] videri esse amotum *ed. Frobeniana* 1535 : uidere se ad-
monitum *BFⱹ*.
[2] si *M. Mueller* : om. *B*.
[3] diceret et arguere *M. Mueller* : diceret arguere *BF*.
[4] fuerunt *edd. vett.* : fuerant *B*.

---

[1] Sempronius had been consul the preceding year and no
prorogation of his *imperium* is recorded; his successor had
arrived, and nothing is known to indicate that Metellus'
statement is accurate. Indeed, in v. 1 above Livy calls
Sempronius a *legatus*. On the basis of this scanty evidence
it seems that the criticism of Merula was unjustified. See
also the note on vi. 9 above.
[2] Cf. XXXIV. xliv. 4.
[3] This ceremony was the formal sacrifice and prayer which
marked the completion of the censors' tasks. The *lustrum*
was also the five-year period of the censors' term; it was

22

to Tiberius Sempronius, who had the *imperium*,[1] B.C. 193 than to a lieutenant: as matters stood, it seemed that he had wilfully kept away a man who, if he made in person the statement which he had made in writing, might both bring his charges openly and, supposing he asserted what was untrue, be himself charged, until the truth was clearly revealed. It was his proposal, therefore, that nothing which the consul demanded should be decreed for the present. When he pressed his claims with undiminished vigour, that the thanksgiving be voted and that he be allowed to ride into the City in triumph, Marcus and Gaius Titinius, tribunes of the people, declared that they would veto it if any decree of the senate were passed regarding the question.

IX. Censors had been elected the previous year, Sextus Aelius Paetus and Gaius Cornelius Cethegus.[2] Cornelius closed the *lustrum*.[3] The number of citizens rated was one hundred forty-three thousand seven hundred four.[4] There were great floods that year, and the Tiber overflowed the flat parts of the City; around the Porta Flumentana certain buildings even collapsed and fell. Also, the Porta Caelimontana was smitten by a thunderbolt and the wall in several places round about was struck by light-

customary for them to finish their business in a year and a half and thereafter to be inactive.

[4] While the MSS. give the number thus, some editors follow Pighius in prefixing an additional C to the numeral. The census reported in XXIX. xxxvii. 6 showed a population of 214,000 in 204 B.C.; in 188 B.C. (XXXVIII. xxxvi. 10) it was 258,318. The fluctuation is so great that the emendation is probably correct. I have, however, kept the reading of the MSS. despite the fact that numerals are notoriously liable to corruption.

LIVY

4 multis locis de caelo tactus; et Ariciae et Lanuvii et in [1] Aventino lapidibus pluit; et a Capua nuntiatum est examen vesparum ingens in forum advolasse et in Martis aede consedisse; eas collectas cum cura
5 et [2] igni crematas esse. Horum prodigiorum causa decemviri libros adire iussi, et novemdiale sacrum factum, et supplicatio indicta est atque urbs lustrata.
6 Iisdem diebus aediculam Victoriae Virginis prope aedem Victoriae M. Porcius Cato dedicavit biennio post quam vovit.

7 Eodem anno coloniam Latinam in castrum Frentinum triumviri deduxerunt A. Manlius Volso L. Apustius Fullo Q. [3] Aelius Tubero, cuius lege
8 deducebatur. Tria milia peditum iere, trecenti
9 equites, numerus exiguus pro copia agri. Dari potuere tricena [4] iugera in pedites, sexagena in equites. Apustio auctore tertia pars agri dempta est, quo postea si vellent novos colonos adscribere possent. Vicena iugera pedites, quadragena equites acceperunt.

X. In exitu iam annus erat, et ambitio magis quam umquam alias exarserat consularibus comitiis. Multi et potentes petebant patricii plebeique, P.

---

[1] in ed. *Lugdunensis* 1537 : *om. B.*
[2] et ed. *Frobeniana* 1531 : *om. B.*
[3] Q. *Sigonius*: p. *Bꝝ.*
[4] tricena *Glareanus* : *XL Bꝝ.*

---

[1] The Sibylline Books, as often : cf. XXXI. xii. 9 and the note.
[2] Two temples to Victoria are known, one on the Capitoline, one on the Palatine. Which is meant here is uncertain, and there is no other reference to Victoria Virgo. There is no record of the vow here mentioned.

ning; and at Aricia, at Lanuvium and on the Aven- B.C. 193
tine there were showers of stones; it was also reported from Capua that a great swarm of wasps had
flown into the forum and settled in the temple of
Mars; the wasps, it was said, were carefully collected
and consumed by fire. By reason of these prodigies
the decemvirs were directed to consult the Books,[1]
and a nine-day sacrifice was performed, a supplication
proclaimed, and the City purified. At the same time
a shrine to Victoria Virgo near the temple of Victory
was dedicated by Marcus Porcius Cato, two years
after he had vowed it.[2]

In the same year a Latin colony was established
at Castrum Frentinum[3] by the triumvirs Aulus
Manlius Volso, Lucius Apustius Fullo and Quintus
Aelius Tubero; by the law of the last-named the
colony was created. Three thousand infantry and
three hundred cavalry joined it, a small number
in proportion to the size of the tract. The allotments of land could have been thirty *iugera* per
infantryman and sixty per cavalryman. At the
suggestion of Apustius one-third of the land was
reserved, whereby they were enabled later to enroll
new colonists if they saw fit. Twenty *iugera* were
given to each infantryman, forty to each cavalryman.

X. It was now the end of the year, and can-
vassing at the consular election was more spirited
than ever before.[4] The candidates were many and

---

[3] This is probably the colony authorized *in agrum Thurinum*
(XXXIV. liii. 1), where the same commissioners are named.

[4] Probably for this reason we have an unusually detailed
account of the campaign and we get a clear impression of the
arguments employed.

LIVY

2 Cornelius Cn. filius Scipio, qui ex Hispania provincia nuper decesserat magnis rebus gestis, et L. Quinctius Flamininus, qui classi in Graecia praefuerat, et Cn.
3 Manlius Volso; hi patricii; plebei autem C. Laelius,
4 Cn. Domitius, C. Livius Salinator, M'.[1] Acilius. Sed omnium oculi in Quinctium Corneliumque coniecti; nam et in unum locum petebant ambo patricii, et rei militaris gloria recens utrumque commendabat.
5 Ceterum ante omnia certamen accendebant fratres candidatorum, duo clarissimi aetatis suae imperatores. Maior gloria Scipionis, et quo maior, eo propior invidiam; Quincti recentior, ut qui eo anno
6 triumphasset. Accedebat quod alter decimum iam prope annum adsiduus in oculis hominum fuerat, quae res minus verendos magnos homines ipsa satietate facit, consul iterum post devictum Hanni-
7 balem censorque fuerat; in Quinctio nova et recentia omnia ad gratiam erant; nihil nec petierat a populo
8 post triumphum nec adeptus erat. Pro fratre germano, non patrueli se petere aiebat, pro legato et

---

[1] M'. *Sigonius*: m. *Bⲋ.*

---

[1] The Licinian-Sextian legislation of 367 B.C. provided that one consul must be a plebeian and both might be. It was customary to elect one from each order.

[2] Cf. i. 3 ff. above.

[3] Cf. XXXII. xvi. 9, etc.

[4] He had been praetor in 195 B.C. (XXXIII. xlii. 7).

[5] Laelius was the most intimate friend of Scipio Africanus. He had entered politics late and had been praetor in 196 B.C. (XXXIII. xxiv. 2).

[6] He was praetor in 194 B.C. (XXXIV. xlii. 4).

[7] Probably, but not certainly, the man mentioned in v. 8 above.

[8] He had been plebeian aedile in 197 B.C. (XXXIII. xxv. 2). The circumstantial quality of Livy's details increases our confidence in his accuracy in the account of the campaign.

B.C. 193

influential, patricians and plebeians,[1] Publius Cornelius Scipio, the son of Gnaeus, who had recently returned from Spain after performing great deeds,[2] and Lucius Quinctius Flamininus, who had commanded the fleet in Greece,[3] and Gnaeus Manlius Volso;[4] these were the patricians; the plebeians now were Gaius Laelius,[5] Gnaeus Domitius,[6] Gaius Livius Salinator,[7] and Manius Acilius.[8] But the eyes of all men were turned upon Quinctius and Cornelius; for both were patricians, contending for one place, and recently-won military glory lent favour to each. But before all else, the brothers of the candidates [9] increased their rivalry, since they were the two most celebrated commanders of their age. The greater fame was Scipio's, and the greater it was, the more it was exposed to jealousy; that of Quinctius was fresher, inasmuch as he had triumphed that very year.[10] There was also the fact that the other had been for about ten years constantly in the public eye, a fact which renders prominent men less venerated from sheer surfeit of seeing them: he had been consul for the second time after the defeat of Hannibal and censor;[11] in the case of Quinctius, everything was new and fresh for winning favour; he had neither asked anything from the people since his triumph nor obtained anything. He said that he was campaigning for a real brother, not a cousin,

---

[9] Africanus and Nasica were actually cousins, but Roman nomenclature is sometimes slightly vague on such points. The Flaminini were real brothers, as the antithesis in sect. 8 (*fratre germano non patrueli*) shows.

[10] Cf. XXXIV. lii. 4 ff.

[11] His second consulship was in 194 B.C., his censorship in 198 B.C.

LIVY

participe administrandi belli; se terra fratrem mari
9 rem gessisse. His obtinuit ut praeferretur candidato
quem Africanus frater ducebat, quem Cornelia gens
Cornelio consule comitia habente, quem tantum
praeiudicium senatus, virum e civitate optimum
iudicatum, qui matrem Idaeam Pessinunte venientem
10 in urbem acciperet. L. Quinctius et Cn. Domitius
Ahenobarbus consules facti: adeo ne in plebeio
quidem consule, cum pro C. Laelio niteretur, Afri-
11 canus valuit. Postero die praetores creati L. Scribonius Libo M. Fulvius Centumalus A. Atilius
Serranus M. Baebius Tamphilus L. Valerius Tappo
Q. Salonius Sarra. Aedilitas insignis eo anno fuit
M. Aemilii Lepidi et L. Aemilii Pauli; multos
12 pecuarios damnarunt; ex ea pecunia clipea inaurata
in fastigio Iovis aedis posuerunt, porticum unam
extra portam Trigeminam, emporio ad Tiberim
adiecto, alteram a porta Fontinali[1] ad Martis aram,
qua in Campum iter esset, perduxerunt.

XI. Diu nihil in Liguribus dignum memoria
gestum erat; extremo eius anni bis in magnum
2 periculum res adducta est; nam et castra consulis
oppugnata aegre sunt defensa, et non ita multo
post per saltum angustum cum duceretur agmen
Romanum, ipsas fauces exercitus Ligurum insedit.

---

[1] a porta Fontinali *ed. Frobeniana* 1531 : ad portam fon-
tinalem *Bς*.

---

[1] Cf. XXIX. xiv. 8.
[2] I.e., for trespassing on public lands which they had not
leased: cf. e.g., XXXIII. xlii. 10.

for his lieutenant and a sharer in the conduct of the ^{B.C. 193} war; he on land, his brother on the sea, had conducted the operations. By such arguments he brought it to pass that his brother was preferred to the candidate whom his brother, Africanus, favoured, whom the Cornelian gens supported, while a consul Cornelius presided at the election, and who was honoured with so powerful a preliminary recommendation from the senate, which chose him as the best man of the state to receive the Idaean Mother when she came from Pessinus to Rome.[1] Lucius Quinctius and Gnaeus Domitius Ahenobarbus were chosen consuls: so little weight did Africanus have even in the selection of the plebeian consul, although he was working for Gaius Laelius. The next day the praetors were chosen, Lucius Scribonius Libo, Marcus Fulvius Centumalus, Aulus Atilius Serranus, Marcus Baebius Tamphilus, Lucius Valerius Tappo, Quintus Salonius Sarra. The aedileship of Marcus Aemilius Lepidus and Lucius Aemilius Paulus was notable that year; they condemned many grazers;[2] out of the fines they set up gilded shields on the roof of the temple of Jupiter, constructed one portico outside the Porta Trigemina, adding a wharf on the Tiber, and another portico from the Porta Fontinalis to the altar of Mars, where the way led into the Campus Martius.

XI. For a long time nothing worth recording occurred among the Ligures; but at the end of this year on two occasions situations of grave peril arose, for in the first place the consul's camp was assailed and with difficulty defended, and a little later, when the Roman column was being led through a narrow glade, the very exit was blocked by an army of

29

A.U.C. 561 3 Qua cum exitus non pateret, converso agmine redire
instituit consul. Et ab tergo fauces saltus occupatae[1]
a parte hostium erant, Caudinaeque cladis memoria
non animis modo, sed prope oculis obversabatur.
4 Numidas octingentos ferme equites inter auxilia
habebat. Eorum praefectus consuli pollicetur se
parte utra vellet cum suis erupturum, tantum uti
5 diceret, utra pars frequentior vicis esset;[2] in eos se
impetum facturum et nihil prius quam flammam
tectis iniecturum, ut is pavor cogeret Ligures excedere saltu quem obsiderent et discurrere ad opem
6 ferendam suis. Collaudatum eum consul spe praemiorum onerat. Numidae equos conscendunt et
obequitare stationibus hostium, neminem lacessentes,
7 coeperunt. Nihil primo adspectu contemptius: equi
hominesque paululi et graciles, discinctus et inermis
eques, praeterquam quod iacula secum portat, equi
8 sine frenis, deformis ipse cursus rigida cervice et
extento capite currentium. Hunc contemptum de
industria augentes labi ex equis et per ludibrium
9 spectaculo esse. Itaque qui primo intenti paratique
si lacesserentur in stationibus fuerant, iam inermes
10 sedentesque pars maxima spectabant. Numidae
adequitare, dein[3] refugere, sed propius saltum
paulatim evehi, velut quos impotentes regendi equi[4]
invitos efferrent. Postremo subditis calcaribus per

[1] occupatae ς: occupata *B*.
[2] vicis esset ς: vicisset *B*.
[3] adequitare dein *M*: dein *spat. rel. B*: adequitare et ς.
[4] equi *ed. Frobeniana* 1535: equos *B*.

---

[1] A Roman army had been entrapped in the pass of Caudium in 321 B.C. and had been captured and sent under the yoke.

the Ligures. Since the way there was not open, the consul began to move to the rear and retrace his steps. In the rear too the exit of the pass was closed by part of the enemy, and visions of the Caudine disaster [1] not only flitted through their minds but also appeared before their eyes. He had about eight hundred Numidian cavalry among the auxiliaries. Their commander promised the consul that he and his men would break through wherever he wished, if only the consul would inform him on which side the towns were more numerous; he would attack them and give his first attention to setting fire to the buildings, that the alarm might compel the Ligures to withdraw from the pass which they were holding and scatter to aid their friends. The consul praised him and loaded him with hopes of reward. The Numidians mounted their horses and began to ride up to the outposts of the enemy, attacking no one. At first nothing was more contemptible than their appearance: horses and men were tiny and gaunt; the riders unequipped and unarmed, except that they carried javelins with them; the horses without bridles, their very motion being the ugly gait of animals running with stiff necks and outstretched heads. Purposely making themselves more contemptible, they would fall from their horses and make themselves a spectacle to be jeered. So those who had been in the outposts, eager and ready if they should be attacked, now for the most part sat unarmed and watching the show. The Numidians kept riding up to them, then retiring, but coming gradually closer to the pass, like men incapable of controlling their horses and carried by them against their will. At last they applied their

LIVY

11 medias stationes hostium erupere, et in agrum
latiorem evecti omnia propinqua viae tecta incen-
dunt; proximo deinde vico inferunt ignem; ferro
12 flammaque omnia pervastant. Fumus primo con-
spectus deinde clamor trepidantium in vicis auditus,
13 postremo seniores puerique refugientes tumultum
in castris fecerunt. Itaque sine consilio, sine imperio
pro se quisque currere ad sua tutanda; momentoque
temporis castra relicta erant, et obsidione liberatus
consul quo intenderat pervenit.

XII. Sed neque Boi neque Hispani, cum quibus eo
anno bellatum erat, tam inimice infesti erant Romanis
2 quam Aetolorum gens. Ii post deportatos ex Graecia
exercitus primo in spe fuerant et Antiochum in
vacuam Europae possessionem venturum, nec Philip-
3 pum aut Nabim quieturos. Ubi nihil usquam moveri
viderunt, agitandum aliquid miscendumque rati, ne
cunctando senescerent consilia, concilium Naupactum
4 indixerunt. Ibi Thoas praetor eorum conquestus
iniurias Romanorum statumque Aetoliae, quod
omnium Graeciae gentium civitatiumque inhonoratis-
simi post eam victoriam essent, cuius causa ipsi

---

[1] Livy here turns to the Roman campaigns in the east, and
for his annalistic sources he substitutes Polybius. A settlement in Greece had been effected by Flamininus after the
defeat of Philip in 197 B.C., but the Aetolians had been from
the first dissatisfied with the arrangements (cf. XXXIV.
xxiii. 5 ff., etc.), and grasped every opportunity to unsettle the
minds of their neighbours. Their activity and its consequences are described in the following chapters.

[2] Livy here employs a legal phrase (*in vacuam possessionem
intrare*), used to express the act of taking possession of property which had no real or apparent owner (*dominus*). Greece
had been "liberated" by the Romans.

spurs and burst through the midst of the enemy's B.C. 193
outposts, and riding out into the more open country
set fire to all the buildings along the road; then
they hurled their torches upon the nearest village;
with sword and fire they ravaged everything. First
the smoke was seen, then the shouts of frightened
villagers were heard, and finally the fleeing elders
and children caused panic in the camp. And so
without design, without orders, each for himself
hurried to defend his own, and in a moment the
camp was abandoned and the consul, freed from
siege, arrived at his intended destination.

XII. But neither the Boii nor the Spaniards, with
whom war was carried on that year, were so hostile
and so dangerous to the Romans as the people of
the Aetolians.[1] After the evacuation of Greece by
the armies they had at first been in hopes that
Antiochus would come to occupy masterless Europe [2]
and that neither Philip [3] nor Nabis [4] would remain
quiet. When they saw that no movement was being
made, thinking that some agitation and confusion
should be caused, lest their scheming should become
feeble from lack of exercise, they called a council at
Naupactus.[5] There Thoas, their chief magistrate,
complained of the injuries inflicted by the Romans
and of the condition of Aetolia, because of all the
states and cities of Greece they were the least
honoured, after that victory for which they them-

[3] Philip was represented by the Aetolians as resentful at
his defeat.
[4] Nabis was tyrant or king, according to the point of view,
of Sparta.
[5] This council was held late in the fall of 194 B.C. or during
the following winter, and Livy is gathering up and summarizing
earlier events, preparatory to continuing the narrative.

LIVY

A.U.C.
561

5 fuissent, legatos censuit circa reges mittendos, qui
non solum temptarent animos eorum, sed suis
quemque stimulis moverent ad Romanum bellum.
6 Damocritus ad Nabim, Nicander ad Philippum,
Dicaearchus, frater praetoris, ad Antiochum est
7 missus. Tyranno Lacedaemonio Damocritus ademp-
tis maritimis civitatibus enervatam tyrannidem
dicere; inde militem, inde naves navalesque socios
habuisse; inclusum suis prope muris Achaeos videre
8 dominantes in Peloponneso; numquam habiturum
reciperandi sua occasionem, si eam quae tum esset
praetermisisset; et nullum exercitum Romanum in
Graecia esse, nec Gytheum [1] aut maritimos alios
Laconas dignam causam existimaturos Romanos, cur
9 legiones rursus in Graeciam transmittant. Haec ad
incitandum animum tyranni dicebantur ut, cum
Antiochus in Graeciam traiecisset, conscientia violatae
per sociorum iniurias Romanae amicitiae [2] con-
10 iungeret se cum Antiocho. Et Philippum Nicander
haud dissimili oratione incitabat; erat etiam maior
orationis materia, quo ex altiore fastigio rex quam
tyrannus detractus erat, quoque plures ademptae
11 res. Ad hoc vetusta regum Macedoniae fama per-
agratusque orbis terrarum victoriis eius gentis refere-
batur. Et tutum vel incepto vel eventu se consilium
12 adferre: nam neque ut ante se moveat Philippus,
quam Antiochus cum exercitu transierit in Graeciam,

---

[1] Gytheum *Gronovius*: propter cithelum *B*: propter
Gytheum ϛ.
[2] Romanae amicitiae *Sabellicus*: romae amicitias *Bϛ*.

---

[1] Polybius (XXI. xxxi) gives his name as Mnestas.
[2] In XXXIV. xxxv, Livy gives the terms of peace between
Rome and Nabis in 195 B.C. There the loss of the coast
towns is implied rather than expressly stated.

34

selves had been the chief cause, and proposed that B.C. 193 ambassadors should be sent around to the kings, who should not only sound out their sentiments but should rouse each, by proper inducements, to a Roman war. Damocritus was dispatched to Nabis, Nicander [1] to Philip, Dicaearchus, the praetor's brother, to Antiochus. To the Spartan tyrant Damocritus pointed out the weakening of the tyranny from the loss of the coast towns; [2] thence he had drawn soldiers, thence ships and naval allies; shut up, almost, within his own walls, he saw the Achaeans lording it in the Peloponnesus; he would never have a chance to recover his own if he let pass the one which then existed; there was, moreover, no Roman army in Greece; Gytheum and the other Spartan towns on the coast would not be considered by the Romans an adequate reason why they should again transport their legions to Greece. This was said to rouse the zeal of the tyrant, that, when Antiochus had crossed to Greece, the consciousness that the Roman friendship had been violated by the injuries done their allies might unite him with Antiochus. As to Philip, Nicander tried to provoke him by a somewhat similar argument; there was also more material for his persuasiveness, in proportion to the greater height from which the king had fallen, in comparison with the tyrant, and in proportion to the heavier losses he had suffered. In addition, he spoke of the ancient renown of the kings of Macedonia and the victorious progress of that race throughout the earth. He said, moreover, that the advice which he offered was safe, whether in the beginning or at the end: for he would not counsel Philip to move before Antiochus with his

LIVY

13 suadere et, qui sine Antiocho adversus Romanos
Aetolosque tam diu sustinuerit bellum, ei [1] adiuncto
Antiocho, sociis Aetolis, qui tum graviores hostes
quam Romani fuerint,[2] quibus tandem viribus re-
14 sistere Romanos posse? Adiciebat de duce Hannibale, nato adversus Romanos hoste, qui plures et
duces et milites eorum occidisset quam quot super-
15 essent. Haec Philippo Nicander; alia Dicaearchus
Antiocho; et omnium primum praedam de Philippo
Romanorum esse dicere, victoriam Aetolorum; et
aditum in Graeciam Romanis nullos alios quam
Aetolos dedisse, et ad vincendum vires eosdem [3]
16 praebuisse. Deinde quantas peditum equitumque
copias praebituri Antiocho ad bellum essent, quae
17 loca terrestribus copiis, quos portus maritimis. Tum
de Philippo et Nabide libero mendacio abutebatur:
paratum utrumque ad rebellandum esse, et primam
quamque occasionem reciperandi ea, quae bello
18 amisissent, arrepturos. Ita per totum simul orbem
terrarum Aetoli Romanis concitabant bellum.

XIII. Et reges tamen aut non moti aut tardius
moti sunt; Nabis exemplo circa omnes maritimos
vicos dimisit ad seditiones in iis miscendas, et alios
principum donis ad suam causam perduxit, alios pertinaciter in societate Romana manentes occidit.
2 Achaeis omnium maritimorum Laconum tuendorum
a T. Quinctio cura mandata erat. Itaque extemplo

---

[1] ei *ed. Frobeniana* 1535 : et *B.*
[2] quam Romani fuerint *ed. Moguntina* 1518 : cum romanis
fuerunt *B* : quam quam romani fuerant *M.*
[3] eosdem ς : eodem *B.*

---

[1] This statement is not confirmed by explicit testimony.
Technically, these cities, like the rest of Greece, were *socii*
of the Romans.

army should cross to Greece, and when he, who without Antiochus had so long sustained the war against the Romans and the Aetolians, was joined by Antiochus and had as allies the Aetolians, who had been at that time more dangerous foes than the Romans, with what strength, pray, could the Romans withstand him? He spoke further of the general Hannibal, born an enemy to the Romans, who had destroyed both their commanders and their soldiers in greater numbers than now remained. Such was Nicander's message to Philip; Dicaearchus approached Antiochus in another fashion, and first of all he said that the booty from Philip had become the Romans', the victory was the Aetolians'; none other than the Aetolians had given the Romans ingress to Greece and furnished them with the strength to conquer. Finally, he told Antiochus how great forces, infantry and cavalry, they would furnish him for the war, what stations for his land forces, what harbours for his navies. Then he employed a gratuitous lie regarding Philip and Nabis: each was ready to rebel and would seize the earliest opportunity to regain what he had lost in war. Thus throughout the whole world at once the Aetolians were arousing war against the Romans.

XIII. And the kings, nevertheless, either were unmoved or were moved too slowly; Nabis at once sent agents around all the maritime towns to stir up seditions in them, and some of the leading men he won over to his side by gifts, others, who stubbornly adhered to the Roman alliance, he put to death. The Achaeans had been entrusted with the responsibility for all maritime affairs in Sparta by Titus Quinctius.[1] So immediately they sent am-

LIVY

3 et ad tyrannum legatos miserunt, qui admonerent
foederis Romani denuntiarentque ne pacem quam
tantopere petisset turbaret, et auxilia ad Gytheum,
quod iam oppugnabatur ab tyranno, et Romam qui
ea nuntiarent legatos miserunt.

4 Antiochus rex, ea hieme Raphiae in Phoenice
Ptolomaeo regi Aegypti filia in matrimonium data,
cum Antiochiam se recepisset, per Ciliciam Tauro
monte superato extremo iam hiemis Ephesum per-
5 venit; inde principio veris, Antiocho filio misso in
Syriam ad custodiam ultimarum partium regni, ne
quid absente se ab tergo moveretur, ipse cum omnibus terrestribus copiis ad Pisidas, qui circa Sidam
6 incolunt, oppugnandos est profectus. Eo tempore
legati Romani P. Sulpicius et P. Villius, qui ad
Antiochum, sicut ante dictum est, missi erant, iussi
prius Eumenem adire Elaeam venere; inde Per-
7 gamum—ibi regia Eumenis fuit—escenderunt.[1] Cu-
pidus belli adversus Antiochum Eumenes erat,
gravem, si pax esset, accolam tanto potentiorem
regem credens, eundem, si motum bellum esset, non
magis parem Romanis fore quam Philippus fuisset,
8 et aut funditus sublatum iri, aut, si pax victo daretur,

---

[1] escenderunt *Jakob Gronovius* : descenderunt *B.*

---

[1] Livy makes no effort to report on the recent activities
of Antiochus, the last mention of whom, save for the reference
in the preceding chapter, was in XXXIV. lix. 8.

[2] This was apparently the winter of 194–193 B.C. Raphia
lay to the south-west of Gaza, on the coast between Cilicia
and Egypt, but not, strictly speaking, in Phoenicia.

[3] In XXXIV. lix. 8 the embassy consisted of Sulpicius,
Villius and P. Aelius; the last is not mentioned in this Book.
Sulpicius and Villius had commanded against Philip and were
frequently employed on missions in the east.

bassadors to the tyrant to remind him of the Roman treaty and to warn him not to disturb the peace which he had so earnestly sought, and sent reinforcements to Gytheum, which was now being besieged by the tyrant, and ambassadors to Rome to report these doings.

King Antiochus,[1] having given his daughter in marriage to King Ptolemy of Egypt at Raphia in Phoenicia during that winter,[2] when he had retired to Antioch, came by way of Cilicia, crossing the Taurus mountains well on towards the end of the winter, to Ephesus; thence at the beginning of spring, sending his son Antiochus into Syria to guard the remotest parts of his kingdom, lest any disturbance behind him should occur in his absence, he himself set out with all his land forces to attack the Pisidae who dwell around Sida. At that time the Roman commissioners, Publius Sulpicius and Publius Villius, who had been sent to Antiochus, as has already been stated,[3] having been ordered to visit Eumenes [4] first, came to Elaea; thence they climbed up to Pergamum, where Eumenes' capital was located. Eumenes was anxious for war against Antiochus, believing that a king so much more powerful than himself was a dangerous neighbour, if there was peace, and also that, if war should be provoked, he was no more likely to be a match for the Romans than Philip had been, and that either he would be utterly destroyed or, if peace were granted him after he had been defeated, much that was

---

[4] Eumenes had succeeded Attalus as king of Pergamum in 197 B.C. (XXXIII. xxi; xxxiv. 10). Elaea was the port of his capital of Pergamum, which lay inland on higher ground (hence *escenderunt*).

LIVY

multa illi detracta sibi accessura, ut facile deinde se
9 ab eo sine ullo auxilio Romano tueri posset. Etiam
si quid adversi casurum foret, satius esse Romanis
sociis quamcumque fortunam subire quam solum aut
imperium pati Antiochi aut abnuentem vi atque
10 armis cogi; ob haec, quantum auctoritate, quantum
consilio valebat, incitabat Romanos ad bellum.

XIV. Sulpicius aeger Pergami substitit; Villius
cum Pisidiae bello occupatum esse regem audisset,
Ephesum profectus, dum paucos ibi moratur dies,
2 dedit operam ut cum Hannibale, qui tum ibi forte
3 erat, saepe congrederetur, ut animum eius temptaret
et, si qua posset, metum demeret periculi quicquam
4 ei ab Romanis esse. Iis colloquiis aliud quidem
actum[1] nihil est, secutum tamen sua sponte est,
velut consilio petitum esset, ut vilior ob ea regi
Hannibal et suspectior ad omnia fieret.
5 Claudius, secutus Graecos Acilianos libros, P.
Africanum in ea fuisse legatione tradit eumque
Ephesi collocutum cum Hannibale, et sermonem

[1] aliud quidem actum *ed. Frobeniana* 1535: alii ut qui
tactum *B*.

---

[1] Frontiers were always vaguely defined in antiquity, as
was inevitable when precise geographical information was
scanty and maps practically unknown. The hopes of Eumenes
for territorial gains after the defeat of Antiochus were realized
in 188 B.C. (XXXVIII. xxxviii–xxxix).

[2] The flight of Hannibal from Carthage to Syria was reported in XXXIV. lx ff.

[3] The meaning of this phrase has been much debated, as
has also the identification of this Claudius with Claudius
Quadrigarius, who was one of the annalists used by Livy. I
see no objection to taking the phrase literally, that Acilius
(*ca.* 150 B.C.), who wrote a Roman history in Greek, was the
source of Claudius, whether he be Claudius Quadrigarius,
Claudius (Clodius) Licinus, or someone else. Nevertheless,

taken from Antiochus would fall to his own lot, so
that thenceforth he could easily defend himself
against Antiochus without any Roman aid. Even
if some misfortune should befall, it was better, he
thought, to endure whatever fate with the Romans
as allies than by himself either to submit to the
sovereignty of Antiochus or, if he refused, to be
compelled to do so by force of arms; for these
reasons with all his prestige and all his diplomatic
skill he urged the Romans to war.[1]

XIV. Sulpicius was ill and remained at Pergamum;
but Villius, when he learned that the king was involved in the war in Pisidia, set out for Ephesus, and
while he tarried there for a few days he saw to it
that he had frequent meetings with Hannibal,[2] who
happened to be there, that he might explore his
sentiments and, if it was in any way possible, dispel
his fear that any danger threatened him from the
Romans. By these conversations nothing else was
accomplished, yet it followed automatically, as if it
had been consciously sought, that Hannibal, by
reason of them, was less highly valued by the king
and was more an object of suspicion in all respects.

Claudius, following the Greek history of Acilius,[3]
reports that Publius Africanus was a member of
that embassy and that at Ephesus he conferred with
Hannibal, and he even relates one conversation:

the appearance of the same story in Appian (*Syr.* 10) suggests
that the actual source of both Livy and Appian is Polybius,
though the incident is not found in the extant portions of
Polybius. There is an additional difficulty in the fact that
Scipio was not, according to XXXIV. lix. 8, a member of
this embassy, but Livy has omitted much of the narrative
(cf. the note to xiii. 4 above), and there may have been other
embassies: cf. the note to sect. 12 below.

LIVY

6 unum etiam refert: quaerenti Africano, quem fuisse
7 maximum imperatorem Hannibal crederet, respondisse Alexandrum Macedonum regem, quod parva
manu innumerabiles exercitus fudisset quodque[1]
ultimas oras, quas visere supra spem humanam esset,
8 peragrasset. Quaerenti deinde quem secundum
poneret, Pyrrhum dixisse; castra metari primum
9 docuisse; ad hoc neminem elegantius loca cepisse,
praesidia disposuisse; artem etiam conciliandi sibi
homines eam habuisse, ut Italicae gentes regis
externi quam populi Romani, tam diu principis in
10 ea terra, imperium esse mallent. Exequenti quem
tertium duceret, haud dubie semet ipsum dixisse.
11 Tum risum obortum Scipioni, et subiecisse "Quidnam tu diceres, si me vicisses?" "Tum vero me"
inquit "et ante Alexandrum et ante Pyrrhum et
12 ante alios omnes imperatores esse." Et perplexum
Punico astu responsum et improvisum adsentationis

[1] quodque *ς* : quod *B*.

---

[1] This seems to refer to Alexander's expeditions to Arabia
and India.

[2] Pyrrhus' campaign in Italy was used to show the necessity
for the invasion of Greece in the Second Macedonian War:
cf. XXXI. vii. 8, etc.

[3] Neither Plutarch nor Appian confirms this; rather,
Plutarch (*Pyrr.* xvi. 5) says that Pyrrhus admired the skill
of the Romans in laying out camps : cf. the similar remark of
Philip, quoted by Livy at XXXI. xxxiv. 8.

[4] The story thus far is found, with slight changes, in
Appian (*Syr.* 10) and Plutarch (*Flamin.* xxi), although the
latter writer has another version (*Pyrr.* ix) in which he
names Pyrrhus, Scipio and Hannibal as the foremost commanders. An important item, omitted by Livy and Plutarch
but included by Appian, gives the reasons of Hannibal for

B.C. 193

when Africanus asked who, in Hannibal's opinion, was the greatest general, Hannibal named Alexander, the king of the Macedonians, because with a small force he had routed armies innumerable and because he had traversed the most distant regions, even to see which transcended human hopes.[1] To the next request, as to whom he would rank second, Hannibal selected Pyrrhus;[2] saying that he had been the first to teach the art of castrametation;[3] besides, no one had chosen his ground or placed his troops more discriminatingly; he possessed also the art of winning men over to him, so that the Italian peoples preferred the lordship of a foreign king to that of the Roman people, so long the master in that land. When he continued, asking whom Hannibal considered third, he named himself without hesitation. Then Scipio broke into a laugh and said, "What would you say if you had defeated me?" "Then, beyond doubt," he replied, "I should place myself both before Alexander and before Pyrrhus and before all other generals."[4] Both this response, with the unexpected turn given it by Punic cleverness,[5] and this unlooked-for kind

listing himself in third place. While the story is generally regarded to-day as apocryphal, the ranking as given by Livy may be genuine and represent Hannibal's considered judgment.

[5] Scipio's final question gives Hannibal an opening which he is quick to seize, for paying an indirect compliment to his conqueror. Appian also speaks of his "delicate flattery" of Scipio. Cf. also xlii. 8 below for another tribute to Hannibal's wit. An anecdote of him preserved by Cicero (de or. II. 75), on the other hand, represents him as distinctly lacking in tact in his remarks about a rhetorician.

LIVY

genus Scipionem movisse, quod e grege se imperatorum velut inaestimabilem secrevisset.

XV. Villius ab Epheso Apameam processit. Eo
et Antiochus audito legatorum Romanorum adventu
2 occurrit. Apameae congressis disceptatio eadem
ferme fuit quae Romae inter Quinctium et legatos
regis fuerat. Mors nuntiata Antiochi filii regis,
quem missum paulo ante dixeram in Syriam, diremit[1]
3 conloquia. Magnus luctus in regia fuit magnumque
eius iuvenis desiderium; id enim iam specimen sui
dederat ut, si vita longior contigisset, magni iustique
4 regis in eo indolem fuisse appareret. Quo carior
acceptiorque omnibus erat, eo mors eius suspectior
fuit, gravem successorem eum instare senectuti
suae patrem credentem per spadones quosdam,
talium ministeriis facinorum acceptos regibus, veneno
5 sustulisse. Eam quoque causam clandestino facinori
adiciebant, quod Seleuco filio Lysimachiam dedisset,
Antiocho quam similem daret sedem, ut procul ab se
honore eum quoque ablegaret, non habuisset.
6 Magni tamen luctus species per aliquot dies regiam
tenuit; legatusque Romanus ne alieno tempore
incommodus obversaretur, Pergamum concessit;
7 rex Ephesum omisso quod inchoaverat bello rediit.

---

[1] diremit _s_: dirimit _B_.

---

[1] The value of this story for characterizing purposes is
evident, and it would be pleasant if we could believe it.
Cf. also the final sentence of the note to XXXVII. xlv. 16
below.

[2] Cf. XXXIV. lvii–lix.

[3] Cf. xiii. 5 above.

[4] The apparent meaning is that the king wished to get rid
of his son, but could do so only by giving him a post of
responsibility and dignity, at such a distance that accepting
it amounted to going into exile.

of flattery, he says, stirred Scipio deeply, because
Hannibal had segregated him from all other commanders as one beyond estimation.[1]

XV. Villius proceeded from Ephesus to Apamea
and there Antiochus came when he learned of the
arrival of the Roman commissioners. At Apamea
there was almost the same debate that had taken
place in Rôme between Quinctius and the king's
ambassadors.[2] The announcement of the death of
Antiochus, the king's son, who, as I had said just
previously,[3] had been sent to Syria, broke off the
conference. There was great grief at the court and
great regret at the loss of the young man, for he
had already shown such revelations of himself that
it was clear that if longer life had been his fate the
character of a great and just king would have been
his. The dearer and more pleasing he was to all, the
more did his death cause a suspicion that his father,
believing that such a successor, following close upon
his own old age, would bring discredit upon him,
had, through the agency of certain eunuchs, who,
by their services in such crimes, commend themselves to kings, removed him by poison. They even
furnished a cause for this secret crime, that he had
given Lysimachia to his son Seleucus, but had not
had a similar capital to bestow upon Antiochus,
that he might banish him far from his presence even
while conferring a mark of honour upon him.[4] Nevertheless, a show of deep mourning filled the palace
for some days, and the Roman ambassador, not to
be an inconvenient visitor at an inopportune time,
withdrew to Pergamum. The king gave up the
war that he had undertaken and returned to Ephesus.
There, while the palace was closed during the

A.U.C.
561

Ibi per luctum regia clausa cum Minnione quodam,
qui princeps amicorum eius erat, secreta consilia
8 agitavit. Minnio, ignarus omnium externorum vires-
que aestimans regis ex rebus in Syria aut Asia gestis,
non causa modo superiorem esse Antiochum, quod
nihil aequi postularent Romani, sed bello quoque
9 superaturum credebat. Fugienti regi disceptationem
cum legatis, seu iam experto eam minus prosperam
seu maerore recenti confuso, professus Minnio se
quae pro causa essent dicturum persuasit, ut a
Pergamo accerserentur legati.

XVI. Iam convaluerat Sulpicius; itaque ambo
Ephesum venerunt. Rex a Minnione excusatus,
2 et absente eo agi res coepta est. Ibi praeparata
oratione Minnio " Specioso titulo " inquit " uti vos,
Romani, Graecarum civitatium liberandarum video,
sed facta vestrae orationi non conveniunt, et aliud
3 Antiocho iuris statuitis,[1] alio ipsi utimini. Qui
enim magis Zmyrnaei Lampsacenique Graeci sunt
quam Neapolitani et Regini et Tarentini, a quibus
stipendium, a quibus naves ex foedere exigitis?
4 Cur Syracusas atque in alias Siciliae Graecas urbes
praetorem quotannis cum imperio et virgis et securi-
bus mittitis? Nihil aliud profecto dicatis quam
5 armis superatis vos iis has leges imposuisse. Eandem
de Zmyrna, Lampsaco civitatibusque, quae Ioniae

---

[1] statuitis *Jakob Gronovius* : statuistis *Bϛ*.

---

[1] The argument of the Macedonian ambassadors in XXXI.
xxix should be compared.

mourning, the king continued secretly plotting with B.C. 193 one Minnio, who was the chief of his friends. Minnio, who was totally unacquainted with foreign affairs, and who judged the king's strength from events occurring in Syria or Asia, believed that Antiochus not only had a better cause, since the Roman demands were in no wise fair, but would conquer in war as well. When the king shunned a meeting with the commissioners, whether he had already found this debate unprofitable or because he was confused in mind by his recent grief, Minnio convinced him that he would say whatever was appropriate to the situation and that the commissioners should be summoned from Pergamum.

XVI. Sulpicius had now recovered, and so both came to Ephesus. Minnio apologized for the king's inability to be present, and in his absence the discussion began. Then Minnio opened the debate with a prepared speech. "I see, Romans," he said, "that you employ the plausible pretext of liberating Greek states, but your actions are inconsistent with your words, and you lay down one rule of conduct for Antiochus but yourselves follow another. For how are the people of Zmyrna and Lampsacus more Greek than the men of Naples or Rhegium or Tarentum, from whom you exact tribute, from whom you exact ships in accordance with treaty-stipulations? Why do Syracuse and other Greek cities of Sicily receive every year a praetor with the *imperium* and the rods and axes? Assuredly you make no other assertion than that you have imposed these conditions upon cities that have been conquered in battle.[1] Learn from Antiochus that the case is the same with Zmyrna and Lampsacus

aut Aeolidis sunt, causam ab Antiocho accipite.
6 Bello superatas a maioribus, stipendiarias ac vectigales
factas in antiquum ius [1] repetit; itaque ad haec ei
responderi velim, si ex aequo disceptatur et non
7 belli causa quaeritur." Ad ea Sulpicius " Fecit
verecunde " inquit " Antiochus, qui, si alia pro causa
eius non erant quae dicerentur quemlibet ista quam
8 se dicere maluit. Quid enim simile habet civitatium
earum quas comparasti causa? Ab Reginis et Nea-
politanis et Tarentinis, ex quo in nostram venerunt
potestatem, uno et perpetuo tenore iuris, semper
usurpato, numquam intermisso, quae ex foedere
9 debent exigimus. Potesne tandem dicere ut ii
populi non per se, non per alium quemquam foedus
10 mutaverint, sic Asiae civitates, ut semel venere in
maiorum Antiochi potestatem, in perpetua possessione regni vestri permansisse, et non alias earum in
Philippi, alias in Ptolomaei fuisse potestate, alias
per multos annos nullo ambigente libertatem usur-
11 passe? Nam si, quod [2] aliquando servierunt, tem-
porum iniquitate pressi, ius post tot saecula ad-
serendi eos in servitutem faciet, quid abest quin
12 actum nihil nobis sit, quod a Philippo liberavimus
Graeciam, et repetant posteri eius Corinthum Chalcidem Demetriadem et Thessalorum totam gentem?
13 Sed quid ego causam civitatium ago, quam ipsis

---

[1] in antiquum ius *ed. Frobeniana* 1535 : antiochum *B.*
[2] quod ⌐ : qui *B.*

and the cities which are in Ionia or Aeolis. Conquered in war by his forefathers[1] and made tributaries
and vassals, he restores them to their ancient status ;
therefore I wish that he be answered on these
points, if this is a discussion based on equity and
not a search for a pretext for war." To this Sulpicius
replied : " Antiochus has acted modestly, who, if
there is nothing else to be said on his behalf, has
preferred that anyone else should say this rather
than himself. What likeness is there in the status
of the states which you have mentioned? From
the people of Rhegium and Naples and Tarentum
we demand what they owe in accordance with the
treaty from the time they came under our sovereignty, with one unbroken continuity of right,
always recognized, never interrupted. Pray, can
you say that as those peoples have changed the
treaty neither through themselves nor through anyone else, so the Asian cities, when once they came
into the possession of Antiochus' forefathers, have
remained in the continuous possession of your empire, and that some have not passed under the
power of Philip, some into the hands of Ptolemy,
and some have enjoyed liberty with none to challenge
them? For if the fact that they have once been
slaves, constrained by the injustice of the times, is
to confer the right of reasserting control and forcing
them into slavery after so many generations, how
does this differ from saying that our labours have
been fruitless, in that we have freed Greece from
Philip and that his descendants may again demand
Corinth, Chalcis, Demetrias, and the whole state of
the Thessalians? But why do I plead the cause of

---

[1] See the note to sect. 13 below.

agentibus et nos et regem ipsum cognoscere aequius
est? "

XVII. Vocari deinde civitatium legationes iussit,
praeparatas iam ante et instructas ab Eumene, qui,
quantumcumque virium Antiocho decessisset, suo
2 id accessurum regno ducebat. Admissi plures, dum
suas quisque nunc querellas, nunc postulationes
inserit, et aequa iniquis miscent, ex disceptatione
altercationem fecerunt. Itaque nec remissa ulla
re nec impetrata, aeque ac venerant, omnium incerti
legati Romam redierunt.

3   Rex dimissis iis consilium de bello Romano habuit.
Ibi alius alio ferocius quia, quo quisque asperius ad-
4 versus Romanos locutus esset, eo spes gratiae maior
erat, alius superbiam postulatorum increpare, tamquam Nabidi victo, sic Antiocho, maximo Asiae
5 regum, imponentium leges; quamquam Nabidi
tamen dominationem in patria sua et patria Lacedae-
6 mone ¹ remissam, Antiocho si Zmyrna et Lampsacus
7 imperata faciant, indignum videri; alii parvas et

¹ patria Lacedaemone *Madvig* : patriam lacedaemonem *Bϛ*.

---

¹ While there is a manifest fallacy in the argument, from
our standpoint, it is sound from the Roman view-point.
Roman law recognized *possessio*, the unchallenged occupancy
of property for a certain definite period (cf. the note to xii.
2 above), as a means of acquiring a good title to it. The Greek
cities of Italy and Sicily, once conquered, had never effectively
established their independence or transferred their allegiance
to another state, *i.e.* had never challenged Roman *possessio*.
Zmyrna, Lampsacus, Miletus, Ephesus, and other cities on
the coast had at various times effectively asserted their
independence or transferred their allegiance after their conquest by Seleucus about 281 B.C. : cf. XXXIII. xxxviii-xl.
They had therefore challenged the *possessio* of Antiochus,
and this partially accidental circumstance constitutes the basis

these cities, which it is fairer that both we and the
king should learn from their own pleadings? " [1]

XVII. He then ordered the embassies of the cities
to be summoned, which had previously been made
ready and coached by Eumenes, who considered
that in whatsoever degree the strength of Antiochus
was diminished, by so much his own power would be
increased. These embassies, being admitted in
great numbers, while each one brought in now its
own complaints, now its demands, and all mingled
the just with the unjust, converted the meeting
from an orderly debate into a wrangle. And so,
with nothing conceded or gained, just as they had
come, the ambassadors, uncertain of everything,
returned to Rome.

When they had been dismissed the king held a
council regarding the Roman war. There each
tried to outdo the other in violence, since each
thought that he would win greater favour in proportion to the severity of his attitude towards the
Romans, while others assailed the insolence of their
demands, seeing that they were imposing terms
upon Antiochus the supreme monarch of Asia, just
as upon the conquered Nabis; and yet to Nabis
had been left the control in his own homeland and
in the country of Lacedaemon; while in the case of
Antiochus it seemed monstrous should Zmyrna and
Lampsacus do his bidding; others argued that these

for the distinction. A non-Roman might not accept the pre-
mise. Sulpicius is clear-headed enough to see that the acceptance of the position adopted by Antiochus would jeopardize
the liberation of Greece, for if Rome granted to the successors
of Seleucus the right of reconquest she would be compelled to
grant it also to the successors of Philip, and this would undo
her work in Greece and threaten her ascendancy.

51

LIVY

vix dictu dignas belli causas tanto regi eas civitates
esse; sed initium semper a parvis [1] iniusta imperandi
fieri, nisi crederent Persas, cum aquam terramque ab
Lacedaemoniis petierint, gleba terrae et haustu
8 aquae eguisse. Per similem temptationem a [2]
Romanis de duabus civitatibus agi; sed [3] alias
civitates, simul duas iugum exuisse vidissent, ad
9 liberatorem populum defecturas. Si non libertas
servitute potior sit, tamen omni [4] praesenti statu
spem cuique novandi res suas blandiorem esse.

XVIII. Alexander Acarnan in consilio erat;
2 Philippi quondam amicus, nuper relicto eo secutus
opulentiorem regiam Antiochi et tamquam peritus
Graeciae nec ignarus Romanorum in eum gradum
amicitiae regis ut consiliis quoque arcanis interesset
3 acceptus erat. Is, tamquam non utrum bellandum
esset necne consuleretur, sed ubi et qua ratione
bellum gereretur, victoriam se haud dubiam [5] proponere animo adfirmabat,[6] si in Europam transisset
rex et in aliqua Graeciae parte sedem bello cepisset.
4 Iam primum Aetolos, qui umbilicum Graeciae
incolerent, in armis eum inventurum, antesignanos
5 ad asperrima quaeque belli paratos; in duobus velut
cornibus Graeciae, Nabim a Peloponneso concitatu-

---

[1] a parvis ⌐: semper parvis B.
[2] a J. F. Gronovius: om. B.
[3] sed Crévier: et B⌐.   [4] omni Gelenius: omnem B.
[5] dubiam ⌐: dubie B.   [6] adfirmabat ⌐: firmabat B.

---

[1] These were the conventional symbols of submission,
demanded by the Persians, to whom the Seleucid kings
regarded themselves as successors.
[2] Servitus here, as elsewhere, does not necessarily imply
personal slavery, but only the political subordination of one

states were of small importance and scarcely worthy of B.C. 193
mention as causes of war for so great a king; but
always the beginnings of tyrannical rule were small,
unless one believed that the Persians, when they
demanded water and earth from the Spartans,[1] actually
needed a clod of soil or a sip of water. A like experi-
ment the Romans were attempting in the case of
the two cities; but other states, once they saw these
two throwing off the yoke, would revolt to the people
that would set them free. If liberty was not pre-
ferable to slavery,[2] nevertheless, no existing situation
was so attractive to anyone as the hope of a change
of circumstances.

XVIII. Alexander the Acarnanian was present at
this council; he had once been the friend of Philip, but
lately had left him and attached himself to the more
flourishing court of Antiochus and, as a man well
acquainted with Greece and not without knowledge of
the Romans, had advanced so far in the friendship
of the king that he was accepted as a member even
of secret councils. He, as if the question were not
whether there should be war or no, but where and
in what fashion the war should be conducted, asserted
that he foresaw in his mind a certain victory if the
king should have crossed to Europe and fixed the
seat of hostilities in some part of Greece. Even now,
at the beginning, he would find the Aetolians, who
dwelt in the navel of Greece, in arms, advanced
troops ready for the utmost hardships; on the two
wings of Greece, so to speak, Nabis from the Pelo-

community to another. The speaker here suggests that
campaigns for "liberty" might be nothing but attempts at
revolution for the sake of revolution and without reference to
the status from which escape is sought.

A.U.C.
561

rum omnia, repetentem Argivorum urbem, repetentem
6 maritimas civitates, quibus eum depulsum Romani
Lacedaemonis muris inclusissent, a Macedonia
Philippum, ubi primum bellicum cani audisset, arma
capturum: nosse se spiritus eius, nosse animum;
scire ferarum modo, quae claustris aut vinculis
teneantur, ingentes iam diu iras eum in pectore
7 volvere; meminisse etiam se, quotiens in bello
precari omnes deos solitus sit ut Antiochum sibi
darent adiutorem; cuius voti si compos nunc fiat,
8 nullam moram rebellandi facturum. Tantum non
cunctandum nec cessandum esse: in eo enim
victoriam verti si et loca opportuna et socii praeoc-
cuparentur. Hannibalem quoque sine mora mitten-
dum in Africam esse ad distringendos [1] Romanos.

XIX. Hannibal non adhibitus est in consilium,
propter colloquia cum Villio suspectus regi et in
nullo postea honore habitus. Primo eam contumeliam
2 tacitus tulit; deinde melius esse ratus et percunctari
causam repentinae alienationis et purgare se, tempore
apto quaesita simpliciter iracundiae causa auditaque
3 "pater Hamilcar" inquit "Antioche, parvum admodum me, cum sacrificaret, altaribus admotum
iureiurando adegit numquam amicum fore populi
4 Romani. Sub hoc sacramento sex et triginta annos
militavi; hoc me in pace patria mea expulit; hoc
patria extorrem in tuam regiam adduxit; hoc duce,

---

[1] distringendos *ed. Mediolanensis* 1505 : destringendos *B*.

---

[1] Alexander may have forgotten that Hannibal had been
banished from Carthage; he may also have meant that his
presence would rouse the people to recall him, or that he would
overawe his enemies with troops furnished by Antiochus.

[2] The same computation is found in XXX. xxxvii. 9.

ponnesus would cause universal confusion, trying to
recover the city of the Argives, trying to recover the
coast towns from which the Romans had ousted him
when they shut him up within the walls of Lacedaemon; from Macedonia Philip, the moment he heard
the trumpet sound, would take up arms; he was acquainted with his high spirits and with his temper;
he knew that like wild beasts which were confined in
cages or by chains he had long been turning over in
his mind wild passions; he himself, moreover, recalled
how often in the war Philip had been wont to
pray to the gods that they would grant him Antiochus
as an ally; if now he should attain the fulfilment of
his prayer, he would delay not one instant in rebelling.
Only let there be no delay or hesitation, for victory
turned upon the question whether suitable ground
and allies were secured in advance. Hannibal too
should be sent to Africa without delay in order to
distract the Romans.[1]

XIX. Hannibal had not been invited to this council,
being an object of suspicion to the king on account
of his conferences with Villius, and being held in no
honour after that. At first he endured this humilia-
tion in silence; then, thinking that it was better both
to inquire the reason for this sudden change of
attitude and to clear himself, he chose a suitable
time and frankly asked the reason for the king's
anger, and having heard it, he said, " My father
Hamilcar, Antiochus, led me, still a little boy, to the
altar when he was sacrificing and bound me by an
oath never to be a friend to the Roman people.
Under this oath I fought for six and thirty years [2];
this oath drove me from my fatherland in time of
peace; it brought me, an exile from my home, to

LIVY

si tu spem meam destitueris, ubicumque vires, ubi
arma esse sciam, inveniam, toto orbe terrarum
5 quaerens, aliquos Romanis hostes. Itaque si quibus
tuorum meis criminibus apud te crescere libet, aliam
6 materiam crescendi ex me quaerant. Odi[1] odioque
sum Romanis. Id me verum dicere pater Hamilcar
et dii testes sunt. Proinde cum de bello Romano
cogitabis, inter primos amicos Hannibalem habeto;
si qua res te ad pacem compellet, in id consilium
7 alium, cum quo deliberes, quaerito." Non movit
modo talis oratio regem, sed etiam reconciliavit
Hannibali. Ex consilio ita discessum est ut bellum
gereretur.

XX. Romae destinabant quidem sermonibus hostem Antiochum, sed nihildum ad id bellum praeter
2 animos parabant. Consulibus ambobus Italia[2] provincia decreta est ita ut inter se compararent sorti-
3 renturve uter comitiis eius anni praeesset; ad utrum
ea non pertineret cura, ut paratus esset si quo eum
4 extra Italiam opus esset ducere legiones. Huic
consuli permissum ut duas legiones scriberet novas
et socium Latini nominis viginti milia et equites octin-
5 gentos; alteri consuli duae legiones decretae quas
L. Cornelius consul superioris anni habuisset, et
socium ac Latini nominis ex eodem exercitu quin-
6 decim milia et equites quingenti. Q. Minucio cum

---

[1] odi *ed. Frobeniana* 1535 : om. *Bς*.
[2] Italia *ς* : ita *B*.

---

[1] The scene now changes to Rome, and the annalists are
more consistently employed as sources.
[2] These are the consuls whose election was reported at
x. 10 above.
[3] This action was due to the anticipation that war with
Antiochus would soon come.

your court; with it as my guiding principle, if you B.C. 193
disappoint my hopes, wherever I know that strength
and arms are found, searching throughout the whole
earth, I shall find some enemies of the Romans. And
so, whoever of your courtiers have a fancy to win
favour with you by insinuations against me, let
them choose another means of winning it at my
expense. I hate and am hateful to the Romans.
That I speak the truth my father Hamilcar and the
gods are witnesses. So long as you plan concerning
a war on Rome, consider Hannibal among your first
friends; if anything inclines you towards peace, seek
for that advice some other man with whom to
consult." This speech not only convinced the king
but reconciled him to Hannibal. The council broke
up with the decision that war should be begun.

XX. At Rome,[1] in talk at least, they had no B.C. 192
thoughts except for Antiochus as their enemy, but
as yet there were no preparations for war except in
their minds. To both consuls [2] Italy was decreed as
a province, with the qualification that they should
arrange between themselves or decide by lot which
should preside at the elections that year; the one
to whom that responsibility did not fall should be
prepared to lead the legions outside of Italy if any
need should arise anywhere.[3] This consul was
authorized to recruit two new legions and, from the
allies of the Latin confederacy, twenty thousand
infantry and eight hundred cavalry; to the other
consul were assigned the two legions which Lucius
Cornelius, consul of the preceding year, had commanded and, of the allies of the Latin confederacy
from the same army, fifteen thousand infantry and
five hundred cavalry. In the case of Quintus

LIVY

A.U.C.
562exercitu, quem in Liguribus habebat, prorogatum
imperium; additum, in supplementum ut quattuor
milia peditum Romanorum scriberentur, centum
quinquaginta equites, et sociis eodem quinque milia
peditum imperarentur, ducenti quinquaginta equites.
7 Cn. Domitio extra Italiam quo senatus censuisset
provincia evenit, L. Quinctio Gallia et comitia
8 habenda. Praetores [1] deinde provincias sortiti,
M. Fulvius Centumalus urbanam, L. Scribonius
Libo peregrinam, L. Valerius Tappo Siciliam, Q.
Salonius Sarra Sardiniam, M. Baebius Tamphilus
Hispaniam citeriorem, A. Atilius Serranus ulteriorem.
9 Sed his duobus primum senatus consulto, deinde
plebei etiam scito permutatae provinciae sunt:
10 Atilio classis et Macedonia, Baebio Brutti decreti.
11 Flaminio Fulvioque in Hispaniis prorogatum imperium. Atilio in Bruttios duae legiones decretae
quae priore anno urbanae fuissent, et ut sociis eodem
milia peditum quindecim imperarentur et quingenti
12 equites. Baebius Tamphilus triginta naves quinqueremes facere iussus et ex navalibus veteres
deducere si quae utiles essent, et scribere navales
socios; et consulibus imperatum, ut ei [2] duo milia
socium ac Latini nominis et mille Romanos darent
13 pedites. Hi duo praetores et duo exercitus, terrestris
navalisque, adversus Nabim aperte iam oppugnantem
14 socios populi Romani dicebantur parari; ceterum

---

[1] habenda. Praetores *ed. Frobeniana* 1535 : habita praetores
B.

[2] ut ei *ed. Frobeniana* 1535 : uti *B.*

---

[1] The procedure is not clear. Perhaps the senate induced
the tribunes to introduce the corrective measure.

[2] The names of Baebius and Atilius have been interchanged.

Minucius, along with the army which he had in B.C. 192
Liguria, his *imperium* was prolonged; it was added
that as reinforcements four thousand Roman infantry
should be enlisted and one hundred and fifty cavalry,
and the allies were ordered to furnish the same
general with five thousand infantry and two hundred
and fifty cavalry. Gnaeus Domitius received from the
lot a province outside Italy, wherever the senate
should decree; to Lucius Quinctius fell Gaul and the
holding of the elections. The praetors then drew
for their provinces, and Marcus Fulvius Centumalus
received the urban jurisdiction, Lucius Scribonius
Libo that between citizens and aliens, Lucius Valerius Tappo Sicily, Quintus Salonius Sarra Sardinia,
Marcus Baebius Tamphilus Hither Spain, Aulus
Atilius Serranus Farther Spain. But the provinces
of these two were changed first by the senate and
then by vote of the people also: to Atilius the fleet
and Macedonia were assigned, to Baebius the Brutti.[1]
The *imperium* of Flaminius and Fulvius in the Spanish
provinces was prolonged. To Atilius [2] for service
among the Brutti were assigned the two legions
which had been in reserve the year before, and it
was ordered that the allies should furnish him with
fifteen thousand infantry and five hundred cavalry.
Baebius Tamphilus was directed to build thirty
quinqueremes and to launch from the dockyards
whatever old ships were seaworthy, and to enlist
naval allies; the consuls were also directed to turn
over to him two thousand allies of the Latin confederacy and one thousand Roman infantry. These
two praetors and two armies, on land and sea, were
prepared, it was said, to operate against Nabis, who
was now openly attacking the allies of the Roman

59

legati ad Antiochum missi expectabantur, et priusquam ii redissent, vetuerat Cn. Domitium consulem
senatus [1] discedere ab urbe.

XXI. Praetoribus Fulvio et Scribonio, quibus ut
ius dicerent Romae provincia erat, negotium datum,
ut praeter eam classem, cui Baebius praefuturus
erat, centum quinqueremes pararent.[2]

2 Priusquam consul praetoresque in provincias proficiscerentur, supplicatio fuit prodigiorum causa.
3 Capram sex haedos uno fetu edidisse ex Piceno
nuntiatum est et Arreti puerum natum unimanum,
4 Amiterni terram pluvisse, Formiis portam murumque de caelo tacta et, quod maxime terrebat, consulis [3] Cn. Domiti bovem locutum " Roma, cave
5 tibi." Ceterorum prodigiorum causa supplicatum
est; bovem cum cura servari alique haruspices
iusserunt. Tiberis infestiore quam priore anno [4]
impetu illatus urbi duos pontes, aedificia multa,
6 maxime circa Flumentanam portam, evertit. Saxum
ingens, sive imbribus seu motu terrae leniore quam
ut alioqui sentiretur, labefactatum in vicum Iugarium
ex Capitolio procidit et multos oppressit. In agris
passim inundatis pecua ablata, villarum strages facta
est.
7 Priusquam L. Quinctius consul [5] in provinciam
perveniret, Q. Minucius in agro Pisano cum Liguribus

---

[1] consulem senatus 𝔰 : senatus consulem B.
[2] pararent 𝔰 : pararentur B.
[3] consulis *Pighius* : consulem 𝔰 : *om.* B.
[4] anno *T. Faber* : *om.* B.
[5] consul 𝔰 : procos. B.

---

[1] Cf. xiii. 1 above.
[2] These were the *pons Fabricius*, from the left bank to the
island, and the *pons Cestius*, from the island to the right bank.

people [1]; but the ambassadors sent to Antiochus B.C. 192 were awaited, and in the expectation of their return the senate had forbidden the consul Gnaeus Domitius to leave the City.

XXI. The praetors Fulvius and Scribonius, to whom had been allotted the province of administering justice in Rome, were instructed to make ready, in addition to the fleet which Baebius was to command, one hundred quinqueremes.

Before the consul and praetors set out for their provinces, a supplication was held by reason of prodigies. A she-goat was reported from Picenum to have given birth to six kids at one time, and at Arretium a boy with one hand was born, at Amiternum there was a shower of earth, at Formiae the wall and gate were struck by lightning, and, a thing which caused the greatest terror, at Rome a cow belonging to the consul Gnaeus Domitius spoke, saying, " Rome, for thyself beware." The period of prayer was held on account of the other portents; the *haruspices* ordered that the cow be carefully kept and fed. The Tiber, attacking the city with a more violent rush than the year before, swept away the two bridges [2] and many buildings, especially around the Porta Flumentana. A huge stone, dislodged either by the rains or by an earthquake too slight to be felt otherwise, fell into the *vicus Iugarius* [3] from the Capitoline and killed many people. In the flooded lands round about many cattle were washed away and damage was done to the farmhouses.

Before the consul Lucius Quinctius arrived in his province, Quintus Minucius, in the neighbourhood

[3] This street led southwards from the Forum at the base of the Capitoline.

signis collatis pugnavit; novem milia hostium occidit, ceteros fusos fugatosque in castra compulit. 8 Ea usque in noctem magno certamine oppugnata 9 defensaque sunt. Nocte clam profecti Ligures; prima luce vacua castra Romanus invasit; praedae minus inventum est quod subinde spolia agrorum 10 capta domos mittebant. Minucius nihil deinde laxamenti hostibus dedit; ex agro Pisano in Ligures profectus castella vicosque eorum[1] igni ferroque 11 pervastavit. Ibi praeda Etrusca quae missa a populatoribus fuerat repletus est miles Romanus.

XXII. Sub idem tempus legati ab regibus Romam 2 reverterunt; qui cum nihil quod satis maturam causam belli haberet, nisi adversus Lacedaemonium tyrannum, attulissent, quem et Achaei legati nuntiabant contra foedus maritimam oram Laconum oppugnare, Atilius praetor cum classe missus in 3 Graeciam est ad tuendos socios. Consules, quando nihil ab Antiocho instaret, proficisci ambo in provincias placuit. Domitius ab Arimino, qua proximum 4 fuit, Quinctius per Ligures in Boios venit. Duo consulum agmina diversa late agrum hostium pervastarunt. Primo equites eorum pauci cum praefectis, deinde universus senatus, postremo in quibus aut fortuna aliqua aut dignitas erat, ad mille quin5 genti ad consules transfugerunt. Et in utraque Hispania eo anno res prospere gestae; nam et C.

---

[1] eorum ⌐ : om. B.

---

[1] These kings were Eumenes and Antiochus; the commissioners seem to have had no instructions to visit Nabis, but they had picked up incidental information about him.

of Pisa, met the Ligures in a pitched battle; he killed B.C. 192
nine thousand of the enemy, routed and put to flight
the rest and drove them into their camp. This was
vigorously attacked and defended until nightfall.
By night the Ligures secretly withdrew and at daybreak the Romans entered the abandoned camp;
less booty was found there because the spoils from
the country were from time to time sent home.
Minucius then gave the enemy no rest; from
Pisan territory he marched into the land of the
Ligures and completely laid waste their citadels and
towns with fire and sword. There the booty of
Etruria, which had been sent on by the raiders, sated
the Roman soldiers.

XXII. About the same time the commissioners
returned from the kings [1] to Rome; when they had
no report to make which furnished a sufficiently
pressing cause for war, except against the Lacedae-
monian tyrant, whom the Achaean ambassadors
also reported to be attacking the Spartan coast in
contravention of the treaty, the praetor Atilius was
ordered to Greece with the fleet to defend the allies.
Both the consuls were directed to depart for their
provinces, since no action was imminent from Antiochus. Domitius by way of Ariminum, where the
way was most direct, Quinctius through Liguria,
came into the Boian territory. The columns of the
two consuls in different directions ravaged the land
of the enemy far and wide. At first a few of their
cavalry with their commanders, and then the senate
as a body, and finally all who possessed anything of
fortune or rank, to the number of fifteen hundred,
took refuge with the consuls. In both the Spanish
provinces as well things went prosperously this year, for

LIVY

Flaminius oppidum Licabrum munitum opulentum-
que vineis expugnavit et nobilem regulum Conri-
6 bilonem vivum cepit, et M. Fulvius proconsul cum
duobus exercitibus hostium duo secunda proelia
fecit, oppida duo Hispanorum, Vesceliam Helonem-
que, et castella multa expugnavit; alia voluntate ad
7 eum defecerunt. Tum in Oretanos progressus et ibi
duobus potitus oppidis, Noliba et Cusibi, ad Tagum
amnem ire pergit. Toletum ibi parva urbs erat, sed
8 loco munito. Eam cum oppugnaret, Vettonum
magnus exercitus Toletanis subsidio venit. Cum
iis signis collatis prospere pugnavit et fusis Vettonibus
operibus Toletum cepit.

XXIII. Ceterum eo tempore minus ea bella quae
gerebantur curae patribus erant quam expectatio
2 nondum coepti cum Antiocho belli. Nam etsi [1]
per legatos identidem omnia explorabantur,[2] tamen [3]
rumores temere sine ullis auctoribus orti multa falsa
3 veris miscebant. Inter quae adlatum erat, cum
in Aetoliam venisset Antiochus, extemplo classem
4 eum in Siciliam missurum. Itaque senatus, etsi
praetorem Atilium cum classe miserat in Graeciam,
5 tamen, quia non copiis modo sed etiam auctoritate
opus erat ad tenendos [4] sociorum animos, T. Quinctium et Cn. Octavium et Cn. Servilium et P. Villium
legatos in Graeciam misit et, ut M. Baebius ex

---

[1] etsi *ed. Moguntina* 1518 : et *B⁵*.
[2] explorabantur *ed. Moguntina* 1518 : expromebantur *B⁵*.
[3] tamen *ed. Moguntina* 1518 : et quod *B*.
[4] tenendos *T. Faber* : tuendos *B⁵*.

---

[1] Fulvius was actually a propraetor; it seems to have been
a trait of one annalist to call all Spanish governors proconsuls
regardless of rank. This habit has furnished scholars with a

Gaius Flaminius captured by storm the rich fortified B.C. 192 town of Licabrum and took alive the noble chieftain Conribilo, and Marcus Fulvius the proconsul [1] engaged with two armies of the enemy in two successful battles, captured two Spanish towns, Vescelia and Helo, and numerous forts; others voluntarily deserted to him. Then he marched against the Oretani, and after capturing two towns, Noliba and Cusibis, advanced to the river Tagus. There lay Toletum, a small town but on a naturally strong site. While he was besieging this city, a large force of the Vettones came to the aid of the Toletani. With them he fought successfully in a pitched battle, and after routing the Vettones he took Toletum by siege.[2]

XXIII. But at that time the wars which were going on caused less concern to the Fathers than the anticipation of the war with Antiochus which had not yet begun. For although everything was repeatedly investigated by commissioners, yet rumours, anonymous and groundlessly circulated, mingled much falsehood with the truth. Among them was the story that Antiochus, on his arrival in Aetolia, would immediately send a fleet to Sicily. Therefore the senate, although it had sent the praetor Atilius with a fleet to Greece, still, because there was need not only of military forces to influence the temper of the allies, but also of prestige, sent Titus Quinctius and Gnaeus Octavius and Gnaeus Servilius and Publius Villius as ambassadors to Greece, and decreed that Marcus Baebius should march his legions from

clue—often, unfortunately, overworked—to the separation of Livy's sources from one another.

[2] Cf. vii. 8 above for what may be the same incident as reported by another annalist.

LIVY

Bruttis ad Tarentum et Brundisium promoveret
legiones, decrevit, inde, si res posceret, in Macedon-
6 iam traiceret, et ut M. Fulvius praetor classem navium
viginti mitteret ad tuendam Siciliae oram, et ut [1]
7 cum imperio esset, qui classem eam duceret—duxit
L. Oppius Salinator, qui priore anno aedilis plebei
8 fuerat—et ut idem praetor L. Valerio collegae
scriberet periculum esse ne classis regis Antiochi
ex Aetolia in Siciliam traiceret: itaque placere
senatui ad eum exercitum quem haberet tumul-
tuariorum militum ad duodecim milia et quadringentos equites scriberet, quibus oram maritimam provinciae, qua vergeret in Graeciam, tueri posset.
9 Eum dilectum praetor non ex Sicilia ipsa tantum sed
ex circumiacentibus insulis habuit, oppidaque omnia
maritima, quae in Graeciam versa erant, praesidiis
10 firmavit. Addidit alimenta rumoribus [2] adventus
Attali, Eumenis fratris, qui nuntiavit, Antiochum
regem Hellespontum cum exercitu transisse, et
Aetolos ita se parare, ut sub adventum eius in armis
11 essent. Et Eumeni absenti et praesenti Attalo
gratiae actae, et aedes liberae locus lautia decreta,
et munera data, equi duo, bina equestria arma et
vasa argentea centum pondo et aurea viginti pondo.
XXIV. Cum alii atque alii nuntii bellum instare
adferrent, ad rem pertinere visum est consules

---

[1] et ut *ed. Frobeniana* 1535 : et Bϛ.
[2] alimenta rumoribus ϛ : alimentorum operibus *B*.

---

[1] The senate here seems to violate its own rule (see ii. 6
above) about acting on anonymous information. The emergency, however, was now greater and the rumours were
consistent with the reports of the ambassadors.

Bruttian territory to Tarentum and Brundisium, B.C. 192 thence, if the situation should demand it, should cross to Macedonia; that Marcus Fulvius the praetor should send a fleet of twenty vessels to defend the coast of Sicily; that he who commanded the fleet should have the *imperium* (the commander was Lucius Oppius Salinator, who had been plebeian aedile the previous year); that the same praetor should write to his colleague Lucius Valerius that there was danger that the fleet of King Antiochus would cross to Sicily from Aetolia, and that consequently the senate had resolved that in addition to the army which he had he should enlist an emergency force of about twelve thousand infantry and four hundred cavalry with which to defend the sea-coast of the province on the side which faced Greece.[1] This levy the praetor raised not only from Sicily proper but from the surrounding islands also, and all the towns on the coast which looked toward Greece he strengthened with garrisons. Further food was given to the rumours by the coming of Attalus, the brother of Eumenes, who brought the news that King Antiochus had crossed the Hellespont with his army and that the Aetolians were making such preparations that they would be in arms at his arrival. Both Eumenes who was absent and Attalus who was present were thanked, and a free lodging was given Attalus, a place of entertainment and gifts were presented to him—two horses, two suits of equestrian armour, silver vases of one hundred pounds weight and golden vases of twenty pounds.

XXIV. When one messenger after another kept reporting that the war was close at hand, it seemed important under the circumstances that the consuls

2 primo quoque tempore creari. Itaque senatus consultum factum est, ut M. Fulvius praetor litteras
extemplo ad consulem mitteret, quibus certior fieret
senatui placere, provincia exercituque tradito legatis
Romam reverti eum et ex itinere praemittere edictum,
3 quo comitia consulibus creandis ediceret. Paruit
iis litteris consul et praemisso edicto Romam venit.
4 Eo quoque anno magna ambitio fuit, quod patricii
tres in unum locum petierunt, P. Cornelius Cn. F.
Scipio, qui priore anno repulsam tulerat, et L.
5 Cornelius Scipio et Cn. Manlius Volso. P. Scipioni,
ut dilatum viro tali, non negatum honorem appareret,
consulatus datus est; additur ei de plebe collega
6 M'.[1] Acilius Glabrio. Postero die praetores creati L.
Aemilius Paulus M. Aemilius Lepidus M. Iunius
Brutus A. Cornelius Mammula C. Livius et L.
Oppius, utrique eorum Salinator cognomen erat;
Oppius is erat, qui classem viginti navium in Siciliam
7 duxerat. Interim, dum novi magistratus sortirentur
provincias, M. Baebius a Brundisio cum omnibus
copiis transire in Epirum est iussus et circa Apolloniam
8 copias continere, et M. Fulvio praetori urbano
negotium datum est ut quinqueremes novas quinquaginta faceret.

XXV. Et populus quidem Romanus ita se ad
2 omnes conatus Antiochi praeparabat; Nabis iam non

---

[1] M'. *Gruter*: m. *Bϛ.*

should be chosen at the first possible opportunity. Therefore a decree of the senate was passed to the effect that Marcus Fulvius the praetor should at once send despatches to the consul, in which he should be informed of the senate's desire that he should turn over his province and army to his lieutenants and return to Rome, and send ahead while on the road the edict in which he announced the election for the choice of consuls. The consul obeyed the message, and sending his edict ahead he came to Rome. In this year also there was a hotly-contested campaign, since three patricians were contending for one place—Publius Cornelius Scipio, the son of Gnaeus, who had suffered defeat the year before, and Lucius Cornelius Scipio and Gnaeus Manlius Volso. Publius Scipio, that it might seem in the case of so great a man that the honour was postponed but not refused, received one consulship; he was given as colleague from the plebeians Manius Acilius Glabrio. The next day the praetors were chosen— Lucius Aemilius Paulus, Marcus Aemilius Lepidus, Marcus Junius Brutus, Aulus Cornelius Mammula, Gaius Livius and Lucius Oppius, both of whom had the surname Salinator; it was Oppius who had led the fleet of twenty ships to Sicily. Meanwhile, until the new magistrates should cast lots for the provinces, Marcus Baebius was directed to cross with all his forces from Brundisium to Epirus and to hold his troops around Apollonia, and Marcus Fulvius the urban praetor was entrusted with the task of building fifty new quinqueremes.

XXV. And the Roman people, for its part, was thus making itself ready for any undertaking of Antiochus; Nabis by now was not putting off the

LIVY

differebat bellum, sed summa vi Gytheum oppugnabat et infestus Achaeis, quod miserant[1] obsessis
3 praesidium, agros eorum vastabat. Achaei non
antea ausi capessere bellum quam ab Roma revertis-
4 sent legati, ut quid senatui placeret scirent, post
reditum legatorum et Sicyonem concilium edixerunt
et legatos ad T. Quinctium miserunt qui consilium
5 ab eo peterent. In concilio omnium ad bellum
extemplo capessendum inclinatae sententiae erant;
litterae T. Quincti cunctationem iniecerunt, quibus
auctor erat praetorem classemque Romanam
6 expectandi. Cum principum alii in sententia per-
manerent, alii utendum eius quem ipsi consuluissent
consilio censerent, multitudo Philopoemenis senten-
7 tiam expectabat. Praetor is tum erat et omnes eo
tempore et prudentia et auctoritate anteibat. Is
praefatus bene comparatum apud Aetolos esse ne
praetor, cum de bello consuluisset, ipse sententiam
diceret, statuere quam primum ipsos quid vellent
8 iussit: praetorem decreta eorum cum fide et cura
exsecuturum adnisurumque ut, quantum in consilio
humano positum esset, nec pacis eos paeniteret nec
9 belli. Plus ea oratio momenti ad incitandos ad
bellum habuit quam si aperte suadendo cupiditatem
10 res gerendi ostendisset. Itaque ingenti consensu
bellum decretum est, tempus et ratio administrandi
11 eius libera praetori permissa. Philopoemen[2] praeterquam quod ita Quinctio placeret, et ipse existimabat

---

[1] miserant ς : miserat *B.*

[2] permissa. Philopoemen *Bekker*: permissa philopo eumenes
B.

---

[1] Philopoemen was one of Livy's heroes. He was now
strategus for the fourth time (Plut. *Philop.* xiv).

war but was besieging Gytheum with all his might, B.C. 192
and in his wrath at the Achaeans, because they had
sent aid to the besieged, was devastating their fields.
The Achaeans did not venture to begin hostilities
until their deputies had returned from Rome, that
they might know what was the will of the senate,
but after the return of the ambassadors they both
called a council at Sicyon and sent agents to Titus
Quinctius to ask advice from him. In the council
the votes of all were for an immediate beginning
of the war; the letter of Titus Quinctius caused some
hesitation, since in it he suggested that the praetor
and the Roman fleet should be awaited. When
some of the chiefs thought that they should abide
by their decision, while others argued that the advice
of him whom they themselves had consulted should
be followed, the multitude waited for the opinion of
Philopoemen.¹ He was then chief magistrate and
surpassed everyone at that time in wisdom and
influence. Beginning his speech by saying that it
was a good practice among the Aetolians that the
praetor, when he had put the question of war before
them, should not himself state his opinion, he bade
them to take as soon as possible what action they
wished: as praetor he would carry out their orders
faithfully and diligently and would strive, so far as this
depended on human wisdom, that they should not
regret either peace or war. This speech had more
weight in urging them to war than if he had, by openly
counselling it, revealed a desire to command. And
so with complete agreement the war was decreed,
and the time and method of prosecuting it left to the
discretion of the praetor. Philopoemen himself,
in addition to the fact that Quinctius wished it, also

71

LIVY

12 classem Romanam expectandam, quae a mari Gytheum tueri posset; sed metuens ne dilationem res
non[1] pateretur et non Gytheum solum sed praesidium
quoque missum ad tuendam urbem amitteretur,
naves Achaeorum deduxit.

XXVI. Comparaverat et tyrannus modicam classem
ad prohibenda si qua obsessis mari summitterentur
praesidia, tres tectas naves et lembos pristesque,
2 tradita vetere classe ex foedere Romanis. Harum
novarum navium agilitatem ut experiretur, simul
ut omnia satis apta ad certamen essent, provectos
in altum cotidie remigem militemque simulacris
navalis pugnae exercebat, in eo ratus verti spem
obsidionis, si praesidia maritima interclusisset.
3 Praetor Achaeorum sicut terrestrium certaminum
arte quemvis clarorum imperatorum vel usu vel
4 ingenio aequabat, ita rudis in re navali erat, Arcas,
mediterraneus homo, externorum etiam omnium,
nisi quod in Creta praefectus auxiliorum militaverat,
5 ignarus. Navis erat quadriremis vetus,[2] capta annis
LXXX ante, cum Crateri uxorem Nicaeam a Nau-
6 pacto Corinthum veheret. Huius fama motus[3]—
fuerat[4] enim nobile in classe regia quondam navi-
gium—deduci ab Aegio putrem iam admodum et
7 vetustate dilabentem iussit. Hac tum praetoria
nave praecedente classem, cum in ea Patrensis Tiso
praefectus classis veheretur, occurrerunt a Gytheo

[1] res non ⟨⟩ : res B.
[2] Navis erat quadriremis vetus ed. Frobeniana 1531 :
quadriremis vetus BM⟨⟩.
[3] fama motus ⟨⟩ : famosus B.
[4] fuerat ed. Frobeniana 1531 : venit ⟨⟩ : om. B.

---

[1] Crater was stepbrother of Antigonus Gonatas. This
incident is not mentioned elsewhere.

believed that he should wait for the Roman fleet
which could defend Gytheum by sea; but fearing
that the situation would not permit delay and that
both Gytheum and the garrison sent to defend the
city would be lost, he launched the ships of the
Achaeans.

XXVI. The tyrant also had prepared a fleet of modest
size to keep away any garrisons that might be sent
by sea to aid the beleaguered; three decked ships and
some smaller vessels and cutters, since his old fleet
had been surrendered to the Romans under the
treaty. That he might try the speed of these new
ships and that at the same time everything might be
made ready for battle, he daily sailed out into the
open water and drilled the oarsmen and marines in
mock naval engagements, thinking that the hope
for the siege depended on his ability to cut off
reinforcements coming by sea. While the praetor of
the Achaeans excelled, in his knowledge of fighting
on land, anyone you will of famous commanders,
either in experience or in aptitude, yet he was without experience in naval warfare, being an Arcadian,
a man from an inland country, unacquainted with the
practices of other countries, except that in Crete he
had served as a commander of auxiliaries. There
was an old ship, a quadrireme, captured eighty
years previously when it was transporting Nicaea,
the wife of Crater,[1] from Naupactus to Corinth.
Prompted by its reputation—for it had been in its
time a famous craft in the royal fleet—he ordered it
to be launched at Aegium although it was now quite
rotten and was falling to pieces from age. At this
time, with this flagship leading the fleet, with Tiso
of Patrae sailing in it as admiral of the fleet, the

LIVY

8 Laconum naves; et primo statim incursu ad novam
et firmam navem vetus, quae per se ipsa omnibus
compagibus aquam acciperet, divulsa est, captique
9 omnes, qui in nave erant. Cetera classis praetoria
nave amissa, quantum quaeque remis valuit fugerunt.
Ipse Philopoemen [1] in levi speculatoria nave fugit [2]
nec ante fugae finem, quam Patras ventum
10 est [3] fecit. Nihil ea res animum militaris viri et
multos experti casus imminuit; quin contra, si in
re navali, cuius esset ignarus, offendisset, eo plus in
ea, quorum usu calleret, spei nactus, breve id tyranno
gaudium se effecturum adfirmabat.

XXVII. Nabis cum prospera re elatus,[4] tum spem
etiam haud dubiam nactus nihil iam a mari periculi
fore, et terrestres aditus claudere opportune positis
2 praesidiis voluit. Tertia parte copiarum ab obsidione
3 Gythei abducta ad Pleias posuit castra; imminet is
locus et Leucis et Acriis, qua videbantur hostes
exercitum admoturi. Cum ibi stativa essent et
pauci tabernacula haberent, multitudo alia casas ex
harundine textas fronde, quae umbram modo prae-
4 beret, texissent,[5] priusquam in conspectum hostis
veniret, Philopoemen necopinantem eum improviso
5 genere belli adgredi statuit. Navigia parva in
stationem occultam agri Argivi contraxit; in ea
expeditos milites, caetratos plerosque, cum fundis et
6 iaculis et alio levi genere armaturae imposuit. Inde

---

[1] Philopoemen *ed. Frobeniana* 1535 : philipo eumenes *B*.
[2] fugit ς : fuit *BM*.
[3] est ς : sit *B*.
[4] prospera re elatus *Kreyssig* : prospere latus *M* : *om. B*.
[5] texissent *ed. Parisina* 1510 : erexisset *B*.

---

[1] Cf. XXXI. xxxvi. 1 and the note.

Spartan ships from Gytheum met them; and at the B.C. 192
first shock with a new and stout vessel, the old ship,
which even before had been taking in water through
every seam, broke up and everyone who sailed in it
was made prisoner. The rest of the fleet, when
their flagship was lost, fled as fast as the oars could
drive them. Philopoemen himself escaped in a light
scouting vessel and did not stop his flight until he
reached Patrae. In no wise did this mishap affect
the courage of this man, a soldier born and tried by
many vicissitudes; on the contrary, rather, if he had
failed in a naval battle, in which he was inexperienced,
he conceived the greater hope in respect to that in
the experience of which he excelled, and he asserted
that he would render the tyrant's joy of short
duration.

XXVII. Nabis, both gladdened by the victory and
filled also with the unquestioning hope that there
would no longer be any danger from the sea, wanted
to close the land approaches too by suitably-placed
guards. Withdrawing one-third of his troops from
the siege of Gytheum, he encamped near Pleiae;
this place threatens both Leuci and Acriae, where it
was evident that the enemy would bring up their
army. When he had placed his base there and only a
few had tents, but the rest of the throng had huts
woven out of reeds and thatched with leaves, which
offered nothing but shade, Philopoemen, before he
came in sight of the enemy, determined to attack him
unexpectedly with a new kind of warfare. He
collected small boats in a secret haven in Argive
territory; into them he loaded lightly-equipped
soldiers, mostly *caetrati*,[1] with slings and darts and
other kinds of light ordnance. Then, skirting the

littora legens cum ad propinquum castris hostium promunturium venisset, egressus callibus notis nocte Pleias pervenit et sopitis vigilibus ut in nullo pro- pinquo metu ignem casis ab omni parte castrorum
7 iniecit. Multi prius incendio absumpti sunt quam hostium adventum sentirent, et qui senserant nullam
8 opem ferre potuerunt. Ferro flammaque omnia absumpta; perpauci ex tam[1] ancipiti peste ad Gythe-
9 um in maiora castra perfugerunt. Ita perculsis hostibus Philopoemen protinus ad depopulandam
10 Tripolim Laconici agri, qui proximus finem Megalo- politarum est, duxit et magna vi pecorum hominum- que inde abrepta, priusquam a Gytheo tyrannus
11 praesidium agris mitteret, discessit. Inde Tegeam exercitu contracto concilioque eodem et Achaeis et sociis indicto, in quo et Epirotarum et Acarnanum
12 fuere principes, statuit, quoniam satis et suorum[2] a pudore maritimae ignominiae restituti animi et hostium conterriti essent, ad Lacedaemonem ducere, eo modo uno ratus ab obsidione Gythei hostem abduci
13 posse. Ad Caryas primum in hostium terra posuit castra. Eo ipso die Gytheum expugnatum est. Cuius rei ignarus Philopoemen castra ad Barnos- thenem—mons est decem milia passuum ab Lace-
14 daemone—promovit.[3] Et Nabis, recepto Gytheo cum expedito exercitu inde profectus, cum praeter Lacedaemonem raptim duxisset, Pyrrhi quae vocant

---

[1] ex tam *Bekker*: tam *B*: tamen ex tam *M*: tamen ς.
[2] et suorum *ed. Parisina* 1513: essent testes suorum *B*ς.
[3] promovit *ed. Lugdunensis* 1537: processit *B*ς.

---

[1] This was probably an irregular meeting, before which Philopoemen reported on his use of the discretion given him as commander (xxv. 10).
[2] This place lies to the north of Lacedaemon; another site of the same name was mentioned in XXXII. xiii. 2.

shore, when he came to a headland near the camp B.C. 192
of the enemy, he landed and travelling over familiar
trails by night came to Pleiae and, the sentinels
being asleep, like men in no immediate peril, hurled
firebrands upon the huts on every side of the camp.
Many were consumed by the flames before they knew
of the enemy's approach, and those who did know
of it were able to bring them no aid. With sword
and fire everything was destroyed; a very few
escaped from this two-fold destruction to Gytheum
and the larger camp. Having thus inflicted a defeat
upon the enemy, Philopoemen marched straight to
ravage Tripolis in Spartan territory, this being
nearest the borders of the Megalopolitae, and having
carried off thence a large number of animals and men
departed before the tyrant from Gytheum could
send guards over the land. Thence, having mustered
the army at Tegea and calling a council at the same
place,[1] of both Achaeans and allies, at which the
leading men of the Epirotes and Acarnanians were also
present, he determined, since on the one hand the
courage of his own men was restored after the shame
of the defeat on the sea, and on the other the enemy
was terrified, to lead the army against Lacedaemon,
thinking that in that way alone the enemy could be
drawn away from the siege of Gytheum. He first
pitched camp at Caryae in the enemy's country.
On that very day Gytheum was captured. Philopoemen, in ignorance of this fact, moved his camp
forward to Barnosthenes—this is a mountain ten miles
from Lacedaemon. And Nabis, having regained
Gytheum, left there with his army in light marching
order, and having speedily passed Lacedaemon,
occupied what they call the camp of Pyrrhus,[2]

LIVY

castra occupavit, quem peti locum ab Achaeis non
15 dubitabat. Inde hostibus occurrit. Obtinebant autem longo agmine propter angustias viae prope
quinque milia passuum; cogebatur agmen ab equitibus et maxima parte auxiliorum, quod existimabat
Philopoemen tyrannum mercennariis militibus, quibus plurimum fideret, ab tergo suos adgressurum.
16 Duae res simul inopinatae perculerunt eum, una
praeoccupatus quem petebat locus, altera, quod
primo agmini occurrisse hostem cernebat, ubi, cum
per loca confragosa iter esset, sine levis armaturae
praesidio signa ferri non videbat posse.

XXVIII. Erat autem Philopoemen praecipuae in
ducendo agmine locisque capiendis solertiae atque
usus, nec belli tantum temporibus, sed etiam in pace
2 ad id maxime animum exercuerat. Ubi iter quo-
piam faceret et ad difficilem transitu saltum venisset,
contemplatus ab omni parte loci naturam, cum solus
iret, secum ipse agitabat animo, cum comites haberet,
3 ab his quaerebat, si hostis eo loco apparuisset, quid,
si a fronte, quid, si ab latere hoc aut illo, quid, si ab
tergo adoriretur, capiendum consilii foret; posse [1]
instructos recta acie, posse inconditum [2] agmen et
4 tantummodo aptum viae occurrere. Quem locum
ipse capturus esset, cogitando aut quaerendo exeque-
batur, aut quot armatis aut quo genere armorum—

---

[1] posse ς : hos se B.
[2] inconditum ς : incognitum B.

a place that he did not doubt would be attacked by B.C. 192
the Achaeans. There he met the enemy. They
were now spread out over a stretch of about five
miles, their column being elongated on account of
the narrowness of the road; the rearguard was
composed of the cavalry and the mass of the auxiliaries, because Philopoemen thought that the tyrant
would attack him from the rear with his mercenary
troops, in whom he placed most confidence. Two
unexpected situations at one time filled him with
dismay: first, the fact that the place which he
sought had already been occupied; second, that he
saw the enemy confronting his van, where, since the
way led through rough country, he did not see how
the standards could be advanced without a screen of
light troops.

XXVIII. Philopoemen, however, was a man of
unusual astuteness and experience in leading troops
and choosing positions, and not only in war-times but
in peace as well he had trained his mind particularly
in these arts. When he was travelling anywhere
and had reached a pass difficult to get through,
viewing the character of the ground from every
angle, when he was travelling alone, he would
consider with himself, when he had companions,
he would ask them, if the enemy had shown himself
at that point, what plan should be adopted if he
attacked from the front, what if on this or that
flank, what if from the rear; it was possible to meet
him while drawn up in regular array, it was possible
to do so in a less orderly formation suited only to the
march. What ground he himself would occupy he
would try to determine, by reflecting or by asking
questions, or how many troops or what kind of

A.U.C.
562

plurimum enim interesse—usurus; quo impedimenta, quo sarcinas, quo turbam inermem reiceret;
5 quanto ea aut quali praesidio custodiret, et utrum
pergere, qua coepisset ire via, an eam, qua venisset,
6 repetere melius esset; castris quoque quem locum
caperet, quantum munimento amplecteretur loci,
qua opportuna aquatio, qua pabuli lignorumque
copia esset; qua postero die castra moventi tutum
7 maxime iter, quae forma agminis esset. His curis
cogitationibusque ita ab ineunte aetate animum
agitaverat ut nulla ei nova in tali re cogitatio esset.
8 Et tum omnium primum agmen constituit; dein
Cretenses auxiliares et quos Tarentinos vocabant
equites, binos secum trahentes equos, ad prima signa
misit et iussis equitibus subsequi super torrentem
9 unde aquari possent rupem occupavit; eo impedimenta omnia et calonum turbam collectam armatis
circumdedit et pro natura loci castra communivit;
tabernacula statuere in aspretis et inaequabili solo
10 difficile erat. Hostes quingentos passus aberant.
Ex eodem rivo utrique cum praesidio levis armaturae
aquati sunt; et priusquam qualia propinquis castris
solent contraheretur certamen, nox intervenit.
11 Postero die apparebat pugnandum pro aquatoribus
circa rivum esse. Nocte in valle a conspectu hostium

---

[1] It would be interesting to know where Livy found this
account of Philopoemen's self-administered course in minor
tactics. Plutarch (*Philop.* iv–v) tells practically the same
story, and adds that Evangelus and the histories of Alexander's
campaigns were his favourite reading, but that he preferred
terrain exercises to map problems (to use the current technical
terminology) and literary descriptions of battles.

weapons—for this was of the greatest importance— B.C. 192
he would use; where he would put the trains, where
the baggage, where the unarmed mass, with how
strong guards, and of what sort, he would protect
them, and whether it would be better to continue
by the way he had intended to go or to return the
way he had come; what place too he would choose
for his camp, how much space he would enclose in
the fortifications, where there was a suitable water-
supply and where were supplies of forage and wood;
where, when he moved his camp the next day, would
be his safest route, and what would be his order of
march. With such concerns and thoughts he had
from boyhood filled his mind, so that now no new
subject of consideration faced him at such a crisis.[1]
And at this time he first of all formed his column,
then he sent the Cretan auxiliaries and the cavalry
whom they call the Tarentini,[2] each leading two
horses with him, to the van, and ordering the cavalry
to follow he seized a cliff above a stream whence
they could get water; then he threw an armed guard
around all the baggage and the assembled throng
of camp followers and fortified the camp as the nature
of the ground required; it was difficult to pitch tents
on the rough and uneven ground. The enemy was
about five hundred paces away. Both sides, using
light-armed guards, drew water from the same
stream, but before a regular battle had begun, which
is the usual occurrence when camps are close together,
the night fell. It was clear that on the next day they
must fight at the stream in defence of the watering-
parties. At night, in a valley out of sight of the

[2] Whatever the origin of the name, these troops did not
come from Tarentum in Italy.

LIVY

aversa, quantum multitudinem locus occulere poterat, condidit caetratorum.

XXIX. Luce orta Cretensium levis armatura et Tarentini equites super torrentem proelium commiserunt; Telemnastus Cretensis popularibus suis, 2 equitibus Lycortas Megalopolitanus praeerat; Cretenses et hostium auxiliares, equitumque idem genus, Tarentini, praesidio aquatoribus erant.[1] Aliquamdiu dubium proelium fuit ut eodem ex parte utraque 3 hominum genere et armis paribus; procedente certamine et numero vicere tyranni auxiliares, et quia ita praeceptum a Philopoemene praefectis erat, ut modico edito proelio in fugam inclinarent hostemque ad locum insidiarum pertraherent. Effuse secuti fugientes per convallem plerique et vulnerati et interfecti sunt, priusquam occultum hostem vider-4 ent. Caetrati [2] ita quantum latitudo vallis patiebatur instructi sederant, ut facile per intervalla ordinum 5 fugientes suos acciperent. Consurgunt deinde ipsi integri, recentes, instructi; in hostes inordinatos, effusos, labore etiam et vulneribus fessos impetum 6 faciunt. Nec dubia victoria fuit: extemplo terga dedit tyranni miles et haud paulo concitatiore cursu quam secutus erat, fugiens in castra est compulsus. 7 Multi caesi captique in ea fuga sunt; et in castris quoque foret trepidatum, ni Philopoemen receptui

[1] erant 𝔰 : om. B.
[2] caetrati 𝔰 : certati B.

82

enemy, he placed as large a force of *caetrati* as the _{B.C. 192} place could conceal.

XXIX. When day broke the light-armed Cretans and the Tarentine cavalry began the battle on the banks of the river; Telemnastus the Cretan commanded his countrymen, Lycortas of Megalopolis the cavalry; the enemy also employed Cretan auxiliaries and cavalry of the same kind, that is, Tarentini, to protect their water-carriers. For a time the battle was doubtful, since the troops on both sides were of the same character and fought with similar equipment; as the fight went on the tyrant's auxiliaries gained the upper hand, both because they were superior in numbers and because Philopoemen had given his commanders specific instructions that after offering a fairly stiff resistance they should begin to retire and draw the enemy towards the place of the ambuscade. Following the retreating enemy headlong through the defile, many were wounded and slain before they spied the hidden foe. The *caetrati* had been resting in formation, so far as the width of the valley permitted, so that they easily permitted the fugitives to pass through the intervals in their ranks. Then they themselves arose, unwounded, fresh, in regular array; against an enemy in disorder, scattered, wearied alike by exertions and wounds, they made their charge. Nor was the issue in doubt, and at a rate no little faster than that of their pursuit the soldiers of the tyrant immediately fled and in their rout were driven into their camp. Many were killed and captured in this flight; and there would have been panic in the camp too had not Philopoemen ordered the recall sounded, in fear of the rough

A.U.C.
562

cani iussisset, loca magis confragosa et[1] quacumque temere processisset iniqua quam[2] hostem metuens.

8 Inde et ex fortuna pugnae et ex ingenio ducis coniectans, in quo tum is pavore esset, unum de 9 auxiliaribus specie transfugae mittit ad eum, qui pro comperto adferret Achaeos statuisse postero die ad Eurotan amnem, qui prope ipsis adfluit moenibus, progredi, ut intercluderent iter, ne aut tyrannus cum 10 vellet receptum ad urbem haberet, aut commeatus ab urbe in castra portarentur, simul et temptaturos, si quorum animi sollicitari ad defectionem a tyranno 11 possent. Non tam fidem dictis perfuga fecit quam perculso metu relinquendi castra causam probabilem 12 praebuit. Postero die Pythagoram cum auxiliaribus et equitatu stationem agere pro vallo iussit; ipse tamquam in aciem cum robore exercitus egressus signa ocius ferri ad urbem iussit.

XXX. Philopoemen postquam citatum agmen per angustam et proclivem viam duci raptim vidit, equitatum omnem et Cretensium auxiliares in stationem hostium quae pro castris erat emittit. 2 Illi ubi hostes adesse et a suis se desertos viderunt, 3 primo in castra recipere se conati sunt; deinde, postquam instructa acies tota Achaeorum admovebatur, metu ne cum ipsis castris caperentur, sequi suorum agmen aliquantum praegressum insistunt.

---

[1] et *ed. Frobeniana* 1535 : *om.* B.
[2] iniqua quam *ed. Frobeniana* 1531 : nequaquam Bⲋ.

---

[1] The walls of Nabis' city of Sparta.

and uneven ground where he had heedlessly advanced B.C. 192 rather than of the enemy.

Then, drawing inferences both from the outcome of the battle and from the character of the commander what his present fright must be, he sent to him one of the auxiliaries in the guise of a deserter, who reported it as an assured fact that the Achaeans would next day advance to the Eurotas river, which flowed almost beneath the very walls,[1] to block the road, that the tyrant might neither have a way to retreat into the city when he wished nor to transport supplies from the city to the camp, and that the Achaeans might make an effort to find out whether anyone could be influenced towards an inclination to desert the tyrant. The deserter did not so much produce confidence in his words as offer to a man stricken with terror a plausible excuse for abandoning his camp. The next day Nabis ordered Pythagoras with the auxiliaries and the cavalry to stand guard before the rampart; he himself, setting out with the main body of the army, as if to the battlefield, ordered the standards to proceed at quickened pace towards the city.

XXX. When Philopoemen saw that the rapidly-moving column was being hurriedly led over a narrow and steep road, he sent out all the cavalry and the Cretan auxiliaries against the guard of the enemy which was in front of the camp. When they saw the enemy approaching and themselves abandoned by their friends, they first tried to withdraw within the camp, then, when the whole battle-line of the Achaeans was moving forward, fearing that they would be captured camp and all, they decided to follow the column of their troops which was some

A.U.C.
562

4 Extemplo caetrati Achaeorum in castra impetum
faciunt et ea [1] diripiunt; ceteri ad persequendos
hostes ire pergunt. Erat iter tale, per quod vix [2]
tranquillum ab hostili metu agmen expediri posset;
5 ut vero ad postremos proelium ortum est, clamorque
terribilis ab tergo paventium ad prima signa est
perlatus, pro se quisque armis abiectis in circumiectas
itineri silvas diffugiunt, momentoque temporis
6 strage armorum saepta via est, maxime hastis, quae
pleraeque adversae cadentes velut vallo obiecto iter
7 impediebant. Philopoemen utcumque possent instare et persequi auxiliaribus iussis—utique enim
equitibus haud facilem futuram fugam—ipse gravius
agmen via patentiore ad Eurotan amnem deduxit.
8 Ibi castris sub occasum solis positis levem armaturam
quam ad persequendum reliquerat hostem opperie-
batur. Qui ubi prima vigilia venerunt, nuntiantes
tyrannum cum paucis ad urbem penetrasse, ceteram
multitudinem inermem toto sparsam vagari saltu,
9 corpora curare eos iubet; ipse ex cetera copia militum, qui quia priores in castra venerant, refecti
et cibo sumpto et modica quiete erant, delectos nihil
praeter gladios secum ferentes extemplo educit et
duarum portarum itineribus, quae Pharas quaeque
Barnosthenem ferunt, eos instruxit, qua ex fuga re-

[1] ea *Gronovius* : om. *B*.
[2] vix *ed. Moguntina* 1518 : via *B*.

---

[1] The context and the regular meaning of *adversus* require
this interpretation, but it is not easy to see how a spear,
dropped by a man in flight, would naturally fall with its point
facing the rear and its butt fixed in the ground. In XXXII.
xvii. 14 Livy compares the spear-points of the Macedonian
phalanx to a rampart. We may select as an explanation
excessive credulity, misunderstanding of the source, corruption

distance ahead. Straightway the Achaean *caetrati* assailed the camp and plundered it; the rest proceeded to pursue the enemy. The road was such that it could with difficulty be traversed by a column even if free from fear of an enemy; but when the battle began in the rear and a dreadful shout from panic-stricken men behind reached those in the van, each for himself threw away his weapons and plunged into the forests which lined the road, and in an instant the way was blocked by piles of arms, especially spears, many of which, falling with their points toward the enemy,[1] closed the road as if with a palisade placed in the way. Philopoemen ordered the auxiliaries to press on and follow wherever they could and—since the flight would not be easy, especially for the cavalry—himself conducted the heavier troops by a more open road toward the Eurotas river. There he pitched camp at sunset and waited for the lighter troops which he had left to pursue the enemy. When they arrived during the first watch, reporting that the tyrant with a few men had made their way into the city and the rest of the army was wandering without weapons hither and thither through all the woods, he ordered them to care for their bodies; he himself, out of the other body of troops who, because they had arrived in camp at an earlier hour, had been refreshed both by the food they had taken and by a brief rest, chose some, taking nothing with them but their swords, led them out at once and posted them at the roads from two gates which they call Pharae and Barnosthenes, where he thought the enemy would

in the text, or a miracle. Plutarch does not mention the incident.

LIVY

10 cepturos sese hostes credebat. Nec eum opinio
fefellit, nam Lacedaemonii, quoad lucis superfuit
quicquam, deviis callibus medio saltu recipiebant se;
primo vespere, ut lumina in castris hostium con-
spexere, e regione [1] eorum occultis semitis se tenue-
11 runt; ubi ea sunt praetergressi, iam tutum rati in
patentes vias descenderunt. Ibi excepti ab insidente
hoste passim ita multi caesi captique sunt ut vix
12 quarta pars de toto exercitu evaserit. Philopoemen
incluso tyranno in urbem insequentes dies prope
triginta vastandis agris Laconum absumpsit, de-
bilitatisque ac prope fractis tyranni viribus domum
rediit, aequantibus eum gloria rerum Achaeis im-
13 peratori Romano et, quod ad Laconum bellum
attineret, praeferentibus etiam.

XXXI. Dum inter Achaeos et tyrannum bellum
erat, legati Romanorum circuire sociorum urbes sol-
liciti, ne Aetoli partis alicuius animos ad Antiochum
2 avertissent. Minimum operae in Achaeis adeundis
consumpserunt, quos, quia Nabidi infesti erant, ad
3 cetera quoque satis fidos censebant esse. Athenas
primum, inde Chalcidem, inde in Thessaliam iere,
adlocutique concilio frequenti Thessalos Demetriadem iter flexere. Eo Magnetum concilium indictum
4 est. Accuratior ibi habenda oratio fuit, quod pars
principum alienati Romanis totique Antiochi et

---

[1] e regione ⑀ : regione *B*.

---

[1] Flamininus' campaign against Nabis (XXXIV. xxviii ff.)
had been inconclusive, and the favourable comparison of
Philopoemen to him was based on these campaigns, not on
the war with Philip. Justin (XXXI. iii. 4) tells the same
story.

return from the flight. Nor did his expectation deceive him, for the Lacedaemonians, as long as any light remained, kept to the paths invisible in the interior of the forest; when evening came and they saw the lights in the enemy's camp, they kept themselves to paths hidden from their direction; when they had passed the camp, thinking it was now safe, they went down into the open roads. There they were picked up by the enemy waiting all around, and so many were killed or captured that barely a fourth of the whole army escaped. Philopoemen, having shut up the tyrant in the city, spent about the ensuing thirty days in laying waste the fields of the Laconians, and having weakened and well-nigh broken the tyrant's power, returned home, the Achaeans equalizing him in the glory of his achievements with the Roman commander and, so far as the Spartan war was concerned, even placing him ahead.[1]

XXXI. While the war between the Achaeans and the tyrant was in progress, the Roman commissioners were going around the cities of the allies, being afraid that the Aetolians had turned the thoughts of some of the allies toward Antiochus. They spent the least effort in approaching the Achaeans, who, since they were hostile to Nabis, were, they felt certain, faithful enough in other relations as well. To Athens first, then to Chalcis, then to Thessaly they took their course, and after addressing the Thessalians in a full council they turned aside to Demetrias. There a council of the Magnetes had been called. It was necessary to employ more carefully-chosen language at this council because some of the chiefs were alienated from the Romans and wholly devoted

LIVY

5 Aetolorum erant, quia, cum reddi obsidem filium
Philippo adlatum esset stipendiumque impositum
remitti, inter cetera vana adlatum erat Demetria-
6 dem quoque ei reddituros Romanos esse. Id ne
fieret, Eurylochus, princeps Magnetum, factionisque
eius quidam omnia novari Aetolorum Antiochique
7 adventu malebant. Adversus eos ita disserendum
erat, ne timorem vanum iis demendo spes incisa
Philippum abalienaret, in quo plus ad omnia momenti
8 quam in Magnetibus esset. Illa tantum com-
memorata, cum totam Graeciam beneficio libertatis
obnoxiam Romanis esse tum eam civitatem prae-
9 cipue: ibi enim non praesidium modo Macedonum
fuisse, sed regiam exaedificatam, ut praesens semper
10 in oculis habendus esset dominus; ceterum nequiquam ea facta, si Aetoli Antiochum in Philippi
regiam adducerent, et novus et incognitus pro vetere
11 et experto habendus rex esset. Magnetarchen
summum magistratum vocant; is tum Eurylochus
erat, ac potestate ea fretus negavit dissimulandum
sibi et Magnetibus esse, quae fama vulgata de red-
12 denda Demetriade Philippo foret; id ne fieret,
omnia et conanda et audenda Magnetibus esse.
Et inter dicendi contentionem inconsultius evectus
proiecit tum quoque specie liberam Demetriadem
esse, re vera omnia ad nutum Romanorum fieri.

---

1 Livy does not mention any embassy to Philip at this
time and says nothing of any proposal to return his son until
191 B.C. (XXXVI. xxxv. 13), when Demetrius was restored
to his father. Diodorus (XXVIII. xvi), however, speaks
of an embassy which promised both these things to Philip.
The Magnetes, then, may have had some grounds for their
suspicions, as even Livy's language (note especially *spes
incisa* in sect. 7 below) indicates.

to Antiochus and the Aetolians because, when it was reported that Philip's son, who was a hostage, was being returned to him and the tribute which had been imposed remitted,[1] among other falsehoods it was said that Demetrias also would be given back to him by the Romans. To prevent this from happening, Eurylochus, the chief of the Magnetes, and some members of his party preferred that everything be thrown into confusion by the coming of Antiochus and the Aetolians. Against them such arguments had to be used that in taking from them their groundless fear the destruction of his hope might not alienate Philip, who was more important in every way than the Magnetes. The main facts were merely mentioned, that not only all Greece was indebted to the Romans for the blessing of liberty, but this state especially; for not only had there been a Macedonian garrison there, but a royal palace had been built, that their master in person might always be held before their eyes; but their liberation would prove to have been in vain if the Aetolians should install Antiochus in the palace of Philip and if they should have a new and unknown king in place of one who was old and tried. They call their chief magistrate the Magnetarch: Eurylochus then held the office, and relying on that authority he said that he and the Magnetes should not dissemble regarding the rumour that was in circulation that Demetrias was to be given back to Philip; to prevent that, the Magnetes would both try and venture anything. And, carried too far away in the passion of speaking, he threw out the remark that even then Demetrias was free in appearance, while in reality everything was done at the Romans' nod. At these

A.U.C.
562
13 Sub hanc vocem[1] fremitus variantis multitudinis
fuit partim adsensum[2] partim indignationem,[3] dicere
id ausum eum; Quinctius quidem adeo exarsit ira,
ut manus[4] ad caelum tendens deos testes ingrati ac
14 perfidi animi Magnetum invocaret. Hac voce per-
territis omnibus Zeno, ex principibus unus, magnae
cum ob eleganter actam vitam auctoritatis, tum
quod semper Romanorum haud dubie partis fuerat,
15 ab Quinctio legatisque aliis flens petit ne[5] unius
amentiam civitati adsignarent; suo quemque periculo furere; Magnetas non libertatem modo, sed
omnia quae hominibus sancta caraque sint T.
Quinctio et populo Romano debere; nihil quem-
16 quam ab diis immortalibus precari posse, quod non
Magnetes ab illis haberent, et in corpora sua citius
per furorem saevituros quam ut Romanam amicitiam
violarent.

XXXII. Huius orationem subsecutae multitudinis
preces sunt; Eurylochus ex concilio itineribus
occultis ad portam atque inde protinus in Aetoliam
2 profugit. Iam enim, et id magis in dies, Aetoli
defectionem nudabant, eoque ipso tempore forte
Thoas, princeps gentis, quem miserant ad Antiochum,
redierat inde Menippumque secum adduxerat regis
3 legatum. Qui, priusquam concilium iis daretur, im-
pleverant omnium aures terrestres navalesque copias
4 commemorando : ingentem vim peditum equitumque venire, ex India elephantos accitos, ante omnia,

---

[1] hanc vocem *ed. Moguntina* 1518 : hac voce *B.*
[2] adsensum ϛ : adsensu *B.*
[3] indignationem ϛ : indignatione *B.*
[4] manus ϛ : manum *B.*   [5] petit ne ϛ : petit *B.*

---

[1] Cf. xii. 4 above. His embassy to Antiochum has not been
mentioned.

B.C. 192

words there arose a shout from the crowd, some expressing agreement, some indignation that he should have dared to say this; Quinctius, indeed, was so inflamed with wrath that raising his hands to heaven he implored the gods to witness the ungrateful and treacherous spirit of the Magnetes. All were terrified by these words, and Zeno, one of the leading citizens, and possessed of great influence both because he pursued a seemly mode of life and because he had always indisputably belonged to the Roman party, with tears begged Quinctius and the other commissioners not to charge the insanity of one man against the community: each one was mad at his own peril; the Magnetes, he admitted, owed not merely their freedom but everything which man holds sacred and dear to Titus Quinctius and the Roman people; no man could pray to the immortal gods for anything which the Magnetes did not have from the Romans, and they would rather rage in madness against their own persons than violate the Roman friendship.

XXXII. His speech was followed by the prayers of the multitude; Eurylochus left the council by secret paths leading to the gate and thence fled straight into Aetolia. For now and more clearly every day the Aetolians were revealing their desertion, and at that very time it chanced that Thoas,[1] a leading man of the nation, whom they had sent to Antiochus, had returned from him and had brought with him Menippus as an ambassador from the king. They, before an audience was granted them, had filled the ears of all with talk about the land and naval forces: a huge contingent of infantry and cavalry was coming, elephants had been requisi-

LIVY

quo maxime credebant moveri multitudinis animos,
tantum advehi auri, ut ipsos emere Romanos posset.
5 Apparebat quid ea oratio in concilio motura esset;
nam et venisse eos et quae agerent omnia legatis
6 Romanis deferebantur; et quamquam prope abscisa
spes [1] erat, tamen non ab re esse Quinctio visum est
sociorum aliquos legatos interesse ei concilio, qui
admonerent Romanae societatis Aetolos, qui vocem
liberam mittere adversus regis legatum auderent.
7 Athenienses maxime in eam rem idonei visi sunt et
propter civitatis dignitatem et vetustam societatem
cum Aetolis. Ab iis Quinctius petit ut legatos ad
8 Panaetolicum concilium mitterent. Thoas primus
in eo concilio renuntiavit legationem. Menippus
post eum intromissus [2] optimum fuisse omnibus, qui
9 Graeciam Asiamque incolerent, ait, integris rebus
Philippi potuisse intervenire Antiochum : sua quemque habiturum fuisse, neque omnia sub nutum
10 dicionemque Romanam perventura. " Nunc quoque " inquit, " si modo vos quae inchoastis consilia
constanter perducitis ad exitum, poterit diis iuvantibus et Aetolis sociis Antiochus quamvis inclinatas
Graeciae res restituere in pristinam dignitatem.
11 Ea autem in libertate posita est, quae suis stat
12 viribus, non ex alieno arbitrio pendet." Athenienses, quibus primis post regiam legationem dicendi

---

[1] spes *Duker* : res *Bϛ*.
[2] intromissus *ϛ* : est intromissus *B*.

---

[1] There seems to be no record of an actual alliance between
the Athenians and the Aetolians, but the two states were
traditionally friendly : cf. XXXI. xxx. 11.
[2] This phrase seems to mean Philip and the individual
Greek states.

tioned from India, and before all—and by this they
believed that the mind of the crowd was especially
influenced—so much gold was being brought that
he could buy the Romans themselves. It was evident
what commotion such talk would cause in the
council; for both the fact that they had come and what
business brought them was all reported to the Roman
commissioners; and although hope was not entirely
cut off, nevertheless it seemed to Quinctius not to
be disadvantageous that some representatives of the
allies should attend the council, to remind the
Aetolians of the Roman alliance and to dare to speak
out freely against the ambassador of the king. The
Athenians seemed especially suitable for the purpose,
on account of the dignity of their state and in addition their ancient alliance with the Aetolians.[1]
Quinctius begged them to send delegates to the
Panaetolian council. Thoas was the first to speak
at that meeting, reporting on his mission. Menippus
was given audience after him and said that it would
have been best for all who lived in Greece and Asia
if Antiochus could have intervened while Philip's condition was unimpaired: each one[2] would have his
own and everything would not have become subject
to the nod and control of the Romans. "Even now,"
he said, "if only you steadfastly carry out to the
end the plans which you have formed, by the grace
of the gods and with the Aetolians as allies, Antiochus will be able to restore the affairs of Greece, however injured, to their former position. But this rests
on liberty, which exists by its own might and does
not depend on another's will." The Athenians, to
whom next after the king's ambassador had been
granted the opportunity of saying what they wished,

LIVY

quae vellent potestas facta est, mentione omni regis
praetermissa Romanae societatis Aetolos meritorumque[1] in universam Graeciam T. Quincti ad-
13 monuerunt: ne temere eam nimia celeritate con-
siliorum everterent; consilia calida et audacia prima
specie laeta, tractatu dura, eventu tristia esse.
Legatos Romanos, et in iis T. Quinctium, haud
14 procul inde abesse; dum integra omnia essent,
verbis potius de iis quae ambigerentur disceptarent
quam Asiam Europamque ad funestum armarent
bellum.

XXXIII. Multitudo avida novandi res Antiochi
tota erat, et ne admittendos quidem in concilium
Romanos censebant; principum maxime seniores
auctoritate obtinuerunt ut daretur iis concilium.
2 Hoc decretum Athenienses cum rettulissent, eundum
3 in Aetoliam Quinctio visum est: aut enim moturum
aliquid, aut omnes homines testes fore penes Aetolos
culpam belli esse, Romanos iusta ac prope necessaria
4 sumpturos arma. Postquam ventum est eo, Quinctius in concilio orsus a principio societatis Aetolorum
cum Romanis, et quotiens ab iis fides mota foederis
esset, pauca de iure civitatium de quibus ambi-
5 geretur disseruit: si quid tamen aequi se habere
arbitrarentur, quanto esse satius Romam mittere
6 legatos, seu disceptare seu rogare senatum mallent,

---

[1] meritorumque ς : meritorum *B*.

---

[1] In XXXIII. xiii. 11 Flamininus speaks of the alliance as
broken. It had not, so far as we can judge from Livy's narrative, been formally renewed, but it is convenient for the
Romans to regard it as even informally and tacitly in force
with the resumption of peaceful relations after the liberation
of Greece.

[2] Recalling the experience of the Aetolian embassy in 195

B.C. 192

omitting all mention of the king, reminded the Aetolians of the Roman alliance [1] and of the services rendered to all Greece by Titus Quinctius: they should not heedlessly, by too great haste in deciding, spoil all this; hot-headed and bold decisions were fair at first sight, hard to follow through, disastrous in result. The Roman commissioners, and among them Titus Quinctius, were not far away; before decisive action was taken, let them settle by words those matters which were in dispute rather than arm Asia and Europe for a fatal war.

XXXIII. The multitude was eager for a change and was all in favour of Antiochus, and they voted that the Romans should not even be admitted to the council; among the chiefs it was especially the elder men who by their influence secured them audience before the council. When the Athenians reported this vote, it seemed best to Quinctius that he should go to Aetolia: he would either cause them some uncertainty or all men would be witnesses that the responsibility for the war would rest with the Aetolians and that the Romans would take up arms with justice and almost from necessity. After his arrival there Quinctius in the council began with the origin of the alliance of the Aetolians with the Romans and how often the faith imposed by the treaty had been broken by them, and spoke briefly of the status of the cities about which there was debate: if, nevertheless, they considered that they had any just claim, how much better would it be to send ambassadors to Rome,[2] whether they preferred to arbitrate or to appeal to

B.C. (XXXIII. xlix. 8), one cannot blame the Aetolians for not being impressed by this argument.

LIVY

quam populum Romanum cum Antiocho lanistis
Aetolis non sine magno motu generis humani et
pernicie[1] Graeciae dimicare?[2] Nec ullos prius
cladem eius belli sensuros quam qui movissent.
7 Haec nequiquam velut vaticinatus Romanus. Thoas
deinde ceterique factionis eiusdem cum adsensu
8 omnium auditi pervicerunt ut ne dilato quidem
concilio et absentibus Romanis decretum fieret, quo
accerseretur Antiochus ad liberandam Graeciam
9 disceptandumque inter Aetolos et Romanos. Huic
tam superbo decreto addidit propriam contumeliam
Damocritus praetor eorum: nam cum[3] id ipsum
decretum posceret eum Quinctius, non veritus
10 maiestatem viri aliud in praesentia, quod magis
instaret, praevertendum sibi esse dixit; decretum
responsumque in Italia brevi castris super ripam
11 Tiberis positis daturum: tantus furor illo tempore
gentem Aetolorum, tantus magistratus eorum cepit.

XXXIV. Quinctius legatique Corinthum redierunt.
Inde, ut quaeque de Antiocho...[4] nihil per se ipsi
moti et sedentes expectare adventum viderentur
2 regis, concilium quidem universae gentis post dimis-

---

[1] pernicie ς : permittie B.
[2] dimicare ς : dimicaturo B : dimicature B².
[3] cum ed. Frobeniana 1535 : tum B.
[4] lacunam indicavit Weissenborn.

---

[1] My translation suggests part but not all of the Latin meta-
phor. The *lanistae* were the trainers of the gladiators, who
acted also in the capacity of the managers of modern prize-
fighters. Flamininus means that the Romans and Antiochus
are to be the gladiators and do the fighting; the Aetolians, as
the *lanistae* of both, will get the profits without undergoing
personal risk. To call them "umpires" or "marshals of the
lists" would inject other and even more erroneous ideas,

the senate, than for the Roman people to go to war B.C. 192
with Antiochus, the Aetolians being the match-
makers,[1] not without great disturbance to mankind
and the ruin of Greece. Nor would any experience
the calamity of this war sooner than those who had
caused it. This prophecy, as one might call it, of
the Roman was in vain. Thoas then and others of
the same party were heard with universal applause
and succeeded in carrying a motion, without even
adjourning the council or awaiting the departure of
the Romans, and by this decree Antiochus was
invited to liberate Greece and to arbitrate between
the Aetolians and the Romans. To this so insolent
vote a personal insult was added by their praetor
Damocritus : for when Quinctius asked for the actual
decree, he, showing no respect for the high position
of the man, replied that there was now a matter
which was more pressing which he had to attend to ;
the decree and the answer he would presently
deliver in Italy when his camp was pitched on the
banks of the Tiber :[2] such madness had at that time
seized the Aetolian people and such their magistrates.

XXXIV. Quinctius and the ambassadors returned
to Corinth. Then, as each message came from
Antiochus, that the Aetolians might not seem to
be doing nothing on their own account, but to be
sitting still waiting for the coming of the king,[3]
they held indeed no meeting of the entire people

since both imply disinterestedness and impartiality. For a
somewhat similar use of the word see Cicero, *Phil.* XIII. xl.

[2] Cf. XXXVI. xxiv. 12.

[3] The lacuna which seems to exist somewhere in this sentence (see the critical note) renders the meaning uncertain.
I have supplied what seems to be necessary for both thought
and syntax.

A.U.C.
562

sos Romanos non habuerunt, per apocletos autem—
ita vocant sanctius consilium; ex delectis constat
viris—id agitabant, quonam modo in Graecia res
3 novarentur. Inter omnes constabat in civitatibus
principes et optimum quemque Romanae societatis
esse et praesenti statu gaudere, multitudinem et
quorum res non ex sententia ipsorum essent omnia
4 novare velle. Aetoli consilium cum rei, tum spei[1]
quoque non audacis modo sed etiam impudentis
ceperunt, Demetriadem Chalcidem Lacedaemonem
5 occupandi. Singuli in singulas principes missi sunt,
Thoas Chalcidem, Alexamenus Lacedaemonem,
6 Diocles Demetriadem. Hunc exul Eurylochus, de
cuius fuga causaque fugae ante dictum est, quia
reditus in patriam nulla alia erat spes, adiuvit.
7 Litteris Eurylochi admoniti propinqui amicique et
qui eiusdem factionis erant liberos et coniugem eius
cum sordida veste, tenentes velamenta supplicum,
in[2] contionem frequentem acciverunt[3] singulos
universosque obtestantes ne insontem indemnatum
8 consenescere in exilio sinerent. Et simplices homines
misericordia et improbos seditiososque immiscendi

---

[1] cum rei tum spei *M. Müller* : uno die spei *Bç* : non dico
rei sed spei *M.*

[2] in *Madvig* : om. *B.*

[3] acciverunt *M. Müller* : adierunt *Bç* : adire iubent *M.*

---

[1] The institutions of Flamininus (see particularly XXXIV.
li. 6) had an aristocratic character, and the Aetolian interpretation of Greek sentiment is in all probability correct.
But no Roman who lived in the first century B.C. could say
"optimum quemque" without thinking of the political
connotations of the phrase in his own time. To such a person
the term implied both an "aristocrat" by birth or political
success and a political or economic "conservative." More-

after the dismissal of the Romans, but through the _{B.C. 192} *apocletes*—so they call their inner council: it consists of selected persons—they considered the question in what manner revolutions might be caused in all Greece. It was evident to all that in the cities the leading men and all the aristocracy [1] were in favour of the Roman alliance and were pleased with the present state of affairs, while the multitude and those whose affairs were not in the best condition desired a complete change. The Aetolians formed a plan not only bold but even shameless, both in its character and in its expectations, of seizing Demetrias, Chalcis,[2] and Lacedaemon. One of their chiefs was sent to each city, Thoas to Chalcis, Alexamenus to Lacedaemon, Diocles to Demetrias. The last was aided by the exile Eurylochus, of whose flight and its cause I have spoken above,[3] because he had no other hope of restoration to his home. Prompted by the letters of Eurylochus, his relatives and friends and those who belonged to the same party summoned his children and wife, dressed in mourning garb and carrying the badges of suppliants, into a crowded assembly, beseeching one and all not to permit a man, innocent and unjudged, to grow old in exile. And simple-minded men were moved by pity and wicked and seditious men by the hope of causing confusion by

over, to members of that party, but not necessarily to others, it was equivalent to "patriotic." My translation emphasizes what I believe was the Aetolian definition of the word : Livy and his contemporary readers no doubt believed that the true patriots among the Greeks were found in the pro-Roman party.

[2] These were two of the three "fetters of Greece" of XXXII. xxxvii. 4. The Aetolian strategy was skilful.

[3] Cf. xxxii. 1 above. No formal vote of exile is mentioned.

LIVY

res tumultu Aetolico spes movit. Ita [1] pro se quis-
9 que revocari iubebant. His praeparatis Diocles cum
omni equitatu—et erat tum praefectus equitum—
specie reducentis exulem hospitem profectus, die
ac nocte ingens iter emensus, cum milia sex ab urbe
abesset, prima luce tribus electis turmis, cetera
multitudine equitum subsequi iussa, praecessit.
10 Postquam portae appropinquabat, desilire omnes
ex equis iussit et loris ducere equos itineris maxime
modo solutis ordinibus, ut comitatus magis praefecti
11 videretur quam praesidium. Ibi una ex turmis ad
portam relicta, ne excludi subsequens equitatus
posset, media urbe ac per forum manu Eurylochum
tenens multis occurrentibus gratulantibusque domum
deduxit. Mox equitum plena urbs erat et loca
opportuna occupabantur; tum in domos missi qui
principes adversae factionis interficerent. Ita Demetrias Aetolorum facta est.

XXXV. Lacedaemone non urbi vis adferenda, sed
2 tyrannus dolo capiendus erat, quem spoliatum maritimis oppidis ab Romanis, tunc intra moenia etiam
Lacedaemonis ab Achaeis compulsum qui occupasset
occidere, eum totius gratiam rei apud Lacedaemonios
3 laturum. Causam mittendi ad eum habuerunt, quod
fatigabat precibus ut auxilia sibi, cum illis auctoribus
4 rebellasset, mitterentur. Mille pedites Alexameno

---

[1] ita *M. Müller*: om. *B.*

means of an Aetolian uprising. Thus each man for
himself favoured a vote of recall. After these preliminaries Diocles with all the cavalry—and he was
then the commander of the cavalry—setting out on
the pretext of conducting home his exiled friend,
completing a long march by day and night, when he
was six miles from the city, at daybreak led the way
with three picked troops, ordering the rest of the
cavalry to follow. When he was near the gate he
ordered them all to dismount and to lead their
horses by the reins, breaking ranks just as if on a
journey, that they might appear to be the commander's escort rather than an organized guard.
Then, leaving one troop at the gate, that the cavalry
in the rear might not be shut out, he conducted Eurylochus through the centre of the city and through
the market-place, clasping him by the hand, while
many men came up and congratulated him. Presently the city was full of troopers and the strategic
points were occupied; then soldiers were sent to
the houses to kill the leaders of the opposing party.
Thus Demetrias fell into the possession of the
Aetolians.

XXXV. At Lacedaemon the city was not to be
treated with violence but the tyrant taken by craft;
he had been stripped of the coast towns by the
Romans and shut up within the walls of Lacedaemon
itself by the Achaeans, and whoever took the
initiative in killing him would win the complete
gratitude of the Lacedaemonians. As a pretext for
sending men to him they had the fact that he was
wearying them with petitions that reinforcements
be sent to him, since it was at their instance that
he had rebelled. A thousand infantry were given

dati sunt et triginta delecti ex iuventute equites.
Iis a praetore Damocrito in consilio arcano gentis,
5 de quo ante dictum est, denuntiatur ne se ad bellum
Achaicum aut rem ullam, quam sua quisque opinione
praecipere posset, crederent missos esse; quidquid
Alexamenum res monuisset[1] subiti consilii capere,
ad id, quamvis inopinatum temerarium audax,
oboedienter exequendum parati essent ac pro eo
acciperent, tamquam ad id unum agendum missos
6 ab domo se scirent. Cum his ita praeparatis Alexamenus ad tyrannum venit, quem adveniens extemplo
7 spei implevit: Antiochum iam transisse in Europam,
mox in Graecia fore, terras maria armis viris completurum;[2] non cum Philippo rem esse credituros
Romanos; numerum iniri peditum equitumque ac
navium non posse; elephantorum aciem conspectu
8 ipso debellaturam. Aetolos toto suo exercitu paratos
esse venire Lacedaemonem, cum res poscat, sed
frequentes armatos ostendere advenienti regi voluisse.
9 Nabidi[3] et ipsi faciendum esse, ut quas haberet
copias non sineret sub tectis marcescere otio, sed
educeret et in armis decurrere cogeret, simul animos
10 acueret et corpora exerceret; consuetudine leviorem
laborem fore, et comitate ac benignitate ducis etiam
non iniucundum fieri posse. Educi inde frequenter

---

[1] monuisset *ed. Parisina* 1510 : monuisset et *B* : mouisset
*M*ς.
[2] completurum ς : inpleturum *B*.
[3] Nabidi *M. Müller* : Nabidi quoque *B*.

---

[1] That is, the thirty troopers.
[2] In xxxiv. 2 above.

Alexamenus and thirty troopers picked from the
youth. These [1] were given instructions by the
praetor Damocritus in the secret council of the
people which was mentioned above,[2] that they
should not believe themselves sent for the Achaean
war or for any other purpose that anyone could
arrive at by his own conjecture; whatever sudden
plan circumstances should prompt Alexamenus to
form, they should be prepared to follow obediently,
no matter how unexpected, rash and bold it might
be, and they should receive it as if they knew that
they had been sent from home to do that one thing.
With them, thus prepared, Alexamenus came to the
tyrant and by his coming immediately filled him
with hope: Antiochus, he said, had already crossed
into Europe, would soon be in Greece, and would
fill the lands and seas with arms and soldiers; the
Romans would realize that they were not dealing
with Philip; the number of infantry and cavalry
and ships could not be calculated; the line of
elephants by their very appearance would end the
war. The Aetolians with their entire army were
ready, he said, to come to Sparta when the situation
required, but that they had wished to display their full
strength to the king when he arrived. Nabis himself should also take such steps as not to permit
what troops he had to grow soft in idleness under
roofs, but should lead them out, force them to
march under arms and at the same time stimulate
their courage and train their bodies; as a result of
drill labour would be lighter, and through the
courtesy and consideration of their commander
could even become not unpleasant. From that time
on Nabis began to lead the troops out frequently into

ante urbem in campum ad Eurotan amnem coepere.
11 Satellites tyranni in media fere acie consistebant;
tyrannus cum tribus summum equitibus, inter quos
plerumque Alexamenus erat, ante signa vectabatur,
12 cornua extrema invisens; in dextro cornu Aetoli
erant, et qui ante auxiliares tyranni fuerant, et qui
13 venerant mille cum Alexameno. Fecerat sibi morem
Alexamenus nunc cum tyranno inter paucos ordines
circumeundi monendique eum quae in rem esse
14 videbantur, nunc in dextrum cornu ad suos adequi-
tandi, mox inde velut imperato, quod res poposcisset,
15 recipiendi se [1] ad tyrannum. Sed quem diem patrando facinori [2] statuerat, eo paulisper cum tyranno
16 vectatus cum ad suos concessisset, tum equitibus ab
domo secum missis " agenda " inquit " res est,
iuvenes, audendaque quam me duce impigre exequi
17 iussi estis; parate animos dextras, ne quis in eo
quod me viderit facientem, cesset; qui cunctatus
fuerit et suum consilium meo interponet, sciat sibi
reditum ad penates non esse." Horror cunctos
cepit, et meminerant cum quibus mandatis exissent.
18 Tyrannus ab laevo cornu veniebat; ponere hastas
equites Alexamenus iubet et se intueri; colligit et
ipse animum confusum tantae cogitatione rei. Postquam appropinquabat, impetum facit et transfixo
19 equo tyrannum deturbat; iacentem equites con-

---

[1] recipiendi se ς : recipiendi B.
[2] patrando facinori Aldus : patrandi facinoris ς : parando facinori B.

B.C. 192

the plain before the city along the Eurotas river.
The bodyguard of the tyrant was generally posted
in the centre of the line; the tyrant, with at most
three cavalrymen, of whom Alexamenus was usually
one, would ride in front of the standards, inspecting
the flanks to the end; the Aetolians were on the right
of the line, both those who had formerly been with
the tyrant and the thousand who had come with
Alexamenus. Alexamenus had established the habit
for himself now of riding around with the tyrant
with only a few attendants and of advising him
what seemed to be advantageous, now of riding off
to the right flank to his own men and then returning
to the tyrant as if he had given some order which
the situation demanded. But on the day which he
had chosen for the perpetration of the crime, when,
after riding for a while with the tyrant, he had
returned to his own men, he then addressed the
thirty troopers who had been sent from home with
him: "We must, young men, do and dare the deed
which you were ordered to perform strenuously
under my command; prepare your minds and hands
that no one may fail in what he sees me do; whoever shall hesitate and substitute his own plan for
mine shall know that he has no return to his own
home." Horror seized them all, and they remembered with what orders they had left home. The
tyrant was coming from the left wing; Alexamenus
ordered the cavalry to put their spears in rest and
to watch him; he himself also collected his thoughts,
disordered by his pondering over so great a deed.
When Nabis approached, he charged and piercing
his horse overthrew the tyrant; the troopers ran him
through as he lay on the ground; after many blows

LIVY

fodiunt; multis frustra in loricam ictibus datis
tandem in nudum corpus vulnera pervenerunt, et
priusquam a [1] media acie succurreretur, exspiravit.

XXXVI. Alexamenus cum omnibus Aetolis citato
2 gradu ad regiam occupandam pergit. Corporis
custodes, cum in oculis res gereretur, pavor primo
3 cepit; deinde, postquam abire Aetolorum agmen
videre, concurrunt ad relictum tyranni corpus, et
spectatorum turba ex custodibus vitae mortisque
4 ultoribus facta est. Nec movisset se quisquam, si
extemplo positis armis vocata in contionem multitudo fuisset et oratio habita tempori conveniens,
frequentes inde retenti in armis Aetoli sine iniuria
5 cuiusquam; sed, ut oportuit in consilio fraude
coepto, omnia in maturandam perniciem eorum, qui
6 fecerant, sunt acta. Dux regia inclusus diem ac
noctem in scrutandis thesauris tyranni absumpsit;
Aetoli velut capta urbe, quam liberasse videri vole-
7 bant, in praedam versi. Simul indignitas rei, simul [2]
contemptus animos Lacedaemoniis ad coeundum
fecit. Alii dicere exturbandos Aetolos et libertatem, cum restitui videretur [3] interceptam, repetendam; alii, ut caput agendae rei esset, regii
8 generis aliquem in speciem adsumendum. Laconicus

---

[1] a ed. *Frobeniana* 1531 : om. *B*.
[2] rei simul ed. *Frobeniana* 1535 : rei ac simul *Bϛ*.
[3] videretur ϛ videtur *B*.

had fallen vainly upon his armour the wounds at _{B.C. 192} last reached his unprotected body, and before aid could reach him from the centre of the line the tyrant was dead.

XXXVI. Alexamenus with all the Aetolians went off at full speed to take possession of the palace. The bodyguard, since the deed had been done before their eyes, was at first terror-stricken; then, after they saw the Aetolian column depart, they assembled around the abandoned body of the tyrant, and a crowd of spectators was formed out of the guardians of his life and the avengers of his death. Nor would anyone have stirred if the multitude had at once been summoned to lay aside their arms and attend an assembly and a speech been delivered suitable to the occasion, and thenceforth numerous Aetolians been kept under arms, without doing injury to anyone; but, as was fitting in plans undertaken with treachery, everything worked together to hasten the destruction of those who had committed the crime. Their leader shut himself up in the palace and spent a day and a night in going through the tyrant's treasures; the Aetolians, as if they had captured the city which they wished to seem to have set free, turned to plunder. Their shameless conduct and the contempt in which they were held combined to turn the thoughts of the Lacedaemonians towards unity of action. Some said that the Aetolians should be driven out and the liberty, lost at the moment when it seemed restored, should be regained; others, that there might be some head to the movement, thought that someone of the royal house should be brought forward as a symbol. There was a mere boy of the royal stock,

A.U.C.
562

eius stirpis erat puer admodum, eductus cum liberis
tyranni; eum in equum imponunt et armis arreptis
9 Aetolos vagos per urbem caedunt. Tum regiam
invadunt; ibi Alexamenum cum paucis resistentem
obtruncant. Aetoli circa Chalcioecon—Minervae
10 aereum est templum—congregati caeduntur; pauci
armis abiectis pars Tegeam pars Megalen polin
perfugiunt; ibi comprensi a magistratibus sub corona
venierunt.

XXXVII. Philopoemen audita caede tyranni profectus Lacedaemonem cum omnia turbata metu
2 invenisset, evocatis principibus et oratione habita,
qualis habenda Alexameno fuerat, societati Achaeo-
3 rum Lacedaemonios adiunxit, eo etiam facilius quod
ad idem forte tempus A. Atilius cum quattuor et
viginti quinqueremibus ad Gytheum accessit.
4 Iisdem diebus circa Chalcidem Thoas per Euthy-
midam principem, pulsum opibus eorum, qui Romanae
societatis erant, post T. Quinctii legatorumque[1]
5 adventum, et Herodorum, Cianum mercatorem, sed
potentem Chalcide propter divitias, praeparatis ad
proditionem iis, qui Euthymidae factionis erant,
nequaquam eandem[2] fortunam, qua Demetrias per
6 Eurylochum occupata erat, habuit. Euthymidas ab

[1] legatorumque ς : legatorum B.
[2] eandem ς : tandem B.

---

[1] The proper name *Laconicus* is not found elsewhere, and
Livy may have understood the adjective Λακωνικός as a noun;
it is also possible that the text is corrupt.
[2] The temple is said to have been so named (literally,
"bronze house") because the inner walls were decorated with
bronze reliefs : cf. Pausanias III. xvii. 3.
[3] These communities were Achaean and treated the
Aetolians as prisoners of war.

Laconicus,[1] brought up with the sons of the tyrant; B.C. 192 him they set upon a horse, and seizing their weapons they slaughtered the Aetolians as they straggled through the city. Next they attacked the palace. Alexamenus with a few companions resisted them there but was slain. The Aetolians gathered around the Chalcioecus [2]—this was a bronze temple to Minerva—were killed; a few threw away their arms and fled, some to Tegea, some to Megalopolis; there they were arrested by the magistrates and sold at auction.[3]

XXXVII. Philopoemen, who on hearing of the tyrant's death had set out for Lacedaemon, when he found everything in a confusion of terror, summoning the leading citizens and making a speech such as Alexamenus should have made, he joined the Lacedaemonians to the Achaean alliance,[4] with the greater ease because Aulus Atilius chanced at the same time to be approaching Gytheum with twenty-four quinqueremes.

During this period, in the neighbourhood of Chalcis, Thoas, through the agency of Euthymidas, one of the chiefs, who had been driven out by the influence of those who belonged to the Roman party, after the arrival of Titus Quinctius and the commissioners, and also with the aid of Herodorus, a merchant of Cios [5] but powerful at Chalcis on account of his wealth, having made ready for an uprising the men who were of the party of Euthymidas, did not by any means have the same good fortune that Eurylochus had enjoyed in gaining Demetrias. Euthymidas from Athens—he

---

[4] There is no record of any change in the Spartan constitution, and nothing more is heard of the boy on horseback.

[5] Herodorus was probably from Cios in Bithynia.

LIVY

Athenis—eum domicilio delegerat locum—Thebas
primum, hinc Salganea processit, Herodorus ad
7 Thronium. Inde haud procul in Maliaco sinu duo
milia peditum Thoas et [1] ducentos equites, onerarias
leves ad triginta habebat. Eas cum sexcentis peditibus Herodorus traicere in insulam Atalanten iussus,
8 ut inde, cum pedestres copias appropinquare iam
Aulidi atque Euripo sensisset, Chalcidem traiceret:
9 ipse ceteras copias nocturnis maxime itineribus,
quanta poterat celeritate, Chalcidem ducebat.

XXXVIII. Micythio et Xenoclides, penes quos
tum summa rerum pulso Euthymida Chalcide erat,
seu ipsi per se suspicati seu indicata re, primo pavidi
2 nihil usquam spei nisi in fuga ponebant; deinde
postquam resedit terror et prodi et deseri non
patriam modo sed etiam Romanorum societatem
3 cernebant, consilio tali animum adiecerunt. Sacrum
anniversarium eo forte tempore Eretriae Amaryn-
thidis Dianae erat, quod non popularium modo sed
4 Carystiorum etiam coetu celebratur. Eo miserunt
qui orarent Eretrienses Carystiosque, ut et suarum
fortunarum in eadem insula geniti misererentur et
Romanam societatem respicerent; ne sinerent
Aetolorum Chalcidem fieri; Euboeam habituros,
si Chalcidem habuissent; graves fuisse Macedonas
dominos; multo minus tolerabiles futuros Aetolos.
5 Romanorum maxime respectus civitates movit, et
6 virtutem nuper in bello et [2] in victoria iustitiam

[1] Thoas et *Crévier* : et thoas *B*.
[2] et *ed. Parisina* 1510 : om. *B*.

---

[1] Their official status is unknown.
[2] The festival may still have existed in Livy's time, but it
is also possible that the present tense of the verb is preserved
from the source.

had chosen this place for his home—went first to Thebes and then to Salganeus, and Herodorus to Thronium. Not far from there, in the Malian gulf, Thoas had two thousand infantry, two hundred cavalry, and about thirty light cargo-vessels. Herodorus was instructed to take these ships with six hundred infantry to the island of Atalante, so that from there, when he saw the infantry now approaching Aulis and Euripus, he might cross to Chalcis; Thoas himself led the rest of the troops, generally marching by night and with all possible speed, to Chalcis.

XXXVIII. Micythio and Xenoclides, in whose hands rested supreme power [1] after Euthymidas had been expelled from Chalcis, whether they formed their own suspicions or the plot was betrayed, at first were alarmed and placed no trust in anything but flight; then, when their terror subsided and they realized that they would be deserting and abandoning not only their country but also the Roman alliance, they increased their courage by the following scheme. It happened that at this time there was an annual festival at Eretria in honour of Diana Amarynthis, which crowds both of the natives and of the Carystii attend.[2] They sent there men to beg the people of Eretria and Carystus, born on the same island, to pity their plight and respect the Roman alliance; let them not permit Chalcis to become the property of the Aetolians; they would control Euboea if once they controlled Chalcis; the Macedonians had been hard to endure as masters; the Aetolians would be far less easy to bear. Regard for the Romans had especial influence with the states, which had recently had experience of both their valour in war and their justice and kindness in vic-

benignitatemque expertas. Itaque quod roboris in
iuventute erat utraque civitas armavit misitque.
7 Iis tuenda moenia Chalcidis oppidani cum tradi-
dissent, ipsi omnibus copiis transgressi Euripum ad
8 Salganea posuerunt castra. Inde caduceator primum,
deinde legati ad Aetolos missi percunctatum, quo
suo dicto factove socii atque amici ad se oppugnandos
9 venirent. Respondit Thoas, dux Aetolorum, non
ad oppugnandos sed ad liberandos ab Romanis
10 venire sese; splendidiore nunc eos catena, sed
multo graviore vinctos esse quam cum praesidium
Macedonum in arce habuissent. Se vero negare
Chalcidenses aut servire ulli aut praesidio cuiusquam
11 egere. Ita digressi ex colloquio legati ad suos;
Thoas et Aetoli, ut qui spem omnem in eo ut im-
12 proviso opprimerent, habuissent, ad iustum bellum
oppugnationemque urbis mari ac terra munitae
13 haudquaquam pares, domum rediere. Euthymidas
postquam castra popularium ad Salganea esse pro-
fectosque Aetolos audivit, et ipse a Thebis Athenas
14 rediit; et Herodorus cum per aliquot dies intentus
ab Atalante signum nequiquam expectasset, missa
speculatoria nave, ut quid morae esset sciret, postquam rem omissam ab sociis vidit, Thronium unde
venerat repetit.

XXXIX. Quinctius quoque his auditis, ab Corintho
veniens navibus, in Chalcidico Euripo Eumeni regi[1]
2 occurrit. Placuit quingentos milites praesidii causa

---

[1] Livy has not mentioned before the presence of Eumenes in
Greece.

tory. Therefore whatever strength in young men B.C. 192
each state had it armed and sent. When the townspeople had turned over to them the defence of the
walls of Chalcis, they themselves with all their forces
crossed the Euripus and pitched camp near Salganeus.
Thence first a herald and then ambassadors were
sent to the Aetolians to inquire what word or action
on their part had brought allies and friends to
attack them. Thoas, the Aetolian chieftain, replied
that they were coming, not to besiege them, but to
set them free from the Romans; now a more glitter-
ing chain, but a far heavier one, bound them than
when they had a Macedonian garrison in their
citadel. The Chalcidenses, however, denied that
they were slaves to any man or that they needed the
protection of anyone. So, leaving the conference,
the ambassadors returned to their people; Thoas
and the Aetolians, inasmuch as they had placed all
their hopes on the chance of catching them off
guard, since they were by no means equal to a
regular war and the siege of a city well fortified by
sea and land, returned home. After Euthymidas
learned that the camp of his countrymen had been
pitched at Salganea and that the Aetolians had gone,
he himself also returned from Thebes to Athens, and
Herodorus, after waiting several days in vain,
anxiously watching from Atalante for a signal,
sending out a scouting vessel to ascertain what was
causing the delay, when he learned that the attempt
had been abandoned by his allies, returned to
Thronium whence he had come.

XXXIX. Quinctius also, hearing of this, came from
Corinth by ship and in the Chalcidian Euripus met
King Eumenes.[1] It was decided that five hundred

A.U.C.
562

relinqui Chalcide ab Eumene rege, ipsum Athenas

3 ire. Quinctius quo profectus erat Demetriadem contendit, ratus Chalcidem liberatam momenti aliquid apud Magnetas ad repetendam societatem

4 Romanam facturam et, ut praesidii aliquid esset suae partis hominibus, Eunomo praetori Thessalorum scripsit, ut armaret iuventutem, et Villium [1] ad Demetriadem praemisit ad temptandos animos, non aliter, nisi pars aliqua inclinaret ad respectum

5 pristinae societatis, rem adgressurus. Villius quinqueremi nave ad ostium portus est invectus. Eo multitudo omnis Magnetum cum se effudisset, quaesivit Villius utrum ad amicos an ad hostes venisse

6 se mallent. Respondit Magnetarches Eurylochus ad amicos venisse eum; sed abstineret portu et sineret Magnetas in concordia et libertate esse nec per colloquii speciem multitudinem sollicitaret.

7 Altercatio inde, non sermo fuit, cum Romanus ut ingratos increparet Magnetas imminentesque praediceret clades, multitudo obstreperet nunc senatum nunc Quinctium accusando. Ita irrito incepto

8 Villius ad Quinctium sese recepit. At Quinctius nuntio ad praetorem misso, ut reduceret domum copias, ipse navibus Corinthum rediit.

XL. Abstulere me velut de spatio Graeciae res immixtae Romanis, non quia ipsas operae pretium

---

[1] Villium *edd. vett.* : *om. B.*

men should be left at Chalcis as a guard by King
Eumenes and that the king himself should go to
Athens. Quinctius hurried to Demetrias, for which
he had set out, in the belief that the liberation of
Chalcis would have some effect upon the Magnetes
in favour of renewing the Roman alliance and, that
there might be some protection for the men of his
party, he wrote to Eunomus, the praetor of the
Thessalians, that he should arm his young men,
and he sent Villius ahead to Demetrias, to test
their sentiments, without any intention of attempting any action unless some portion of them was
disposed to have regard for the former alliance.
Villius, in a ship of five banks of oars, sailed up to
the mouth of the harbour. When all the people of
the Magnetes had rushed there, Villius asked whether
they would prefer that he had come to friends
or to enemies. Eurylochus the Magnetarch replied
that he came to friends; but he should keep out of
the harbour and permit the Magnetes to live in
harmony and liberty and should not, under the
pretence of a conference, stir up the populace.
Then there was a violent argument, not a conversation, the Roman reproaching the Magnetes for ingratitude and foretelling impending disaster, the
crowd raising an uproar while accusing now the
senate and now Quinctius. So without accomplishing
anything Villius rejoined Quinctius. But Quinctius
sent a messenger to the praetor to lead his troops
back home and himself with his ships returned to
Corinth.

XL. I have been driven out of my course, so to say,
by blending events in Greece with those in Rome,
not because they were worth the effort of recording

A.U.C. 562 esset perscribere, sed quia causae cum Antiocho
2 fuerunt belli. Consulibus designatis—inde namque deverteram—L. Quinctius et Cn. Domitius consules in provincias profecti sunt, Quinctius in Ligures,
3 Domitius adversus Boios. Boi quieverunt, atque etiam senatus eorum cum liberis et praefecti cum equitatu—summa omnium mille et quingenti—con-
4 suli dediderunt se. Ab altero consule ager Ligurum late est vastatus castellaque aliquot capta, unde non praeda modo omnis generis cum captivis parta, sed recepti quoque aliquot cives sociique, qui in
5 hostium potestate fuerant. Eodem hoc anno Vibonem colonia deducta est ex senatus consulto plebique scito. Tria milia et septingenti pedites ierunt,
6 trecenti equites; triumviri deduxerunt eos Q. Naevius M. Minucius M. Furius Crassipes[1]; quina dena iugera agri data in singulos pedites sunt, duplex equiti. Bruttiorum proxime fuerat ager;
7 Brutti ceperant de Graecis. Romae per idem tempus duo maximi fuerunt terrores, diutinus alter, sed segnior: terra dies duodequadraginta movit; per totidem dies feriae in sollicitudine ac metu fuere;

[1] Crassipes *ed. Frobeniana* 1531: crassus *Bς*.

---

[1] This narrative is somewhat inconsistent with that previously given, and probably came from another source. In x. 10 the election of Quinctius and Domitius was reported; the assignment of provinces was postponed to xx. 2–7, to make room for the account of developments in the east. Their achievements in the provinces were summarily recorded in xxii. 3–4, with only slight variations from the later version, and at xxiv. 3 Quinctius returned to hold the elections at which Scipio and Glabrio were chosen consuls for 191 B.C. In this passage, however, Livy seems to keep both consuls in Rome until after the elections, forgetting that Domitius was

them, but because they were the origins of the war with Antiochus. When the consuls were elected— for this was the point at which I turned aside— Lucius Quinctius and Gnaeus Domitius departed to their provinces, Quinctius to the Ligures, Domitius against the Boii. The Boii remained quiet, and their senate with their children and the commanders with the cavalry—there were altogether fifteen hundred of them—even surrendered themselves to the consul. The other consul devastated the Ligurian country far and wide and captured some forts from which they not only secured plunder of all kinds, along with prisoners, but also recovered some citizens and allies who had been in the hands of the enemy.[1] In the same year a colony was established at Vibo in accordance with a decree of the senate and an enactment of the assembly. Three thousand seven hundred infantry went there and three hundred cavalrymen; the commission which established it consisted of Quintus Naevius, Marcus Minucius and Marcus Furius Crassipes; fifteen *iugera* of land were given to each infantryman and twice that to each cavalryman. The land had recently belonged to the Brutti; they in turn had taken it from the Greeks. At Rome in the same period there were two very serious alarms, one of longer duration but slower in its effect, for the earth trembled through thirty-eight days; for so many days there was a holiday spent in appre-

already in Gaul, according to the earlier account. He seems too to forget that the proconsul Minucius had been assigned to the Ligures (xx. 6). A further difference will be seen in the following sections: the source of chap. xxii went on to record events in Spain, and a possible duplication was pointed out in the note to xxii. 8; the source which Livy followed in chap. xl. continued with happenings at Rome.

LIVY

8 triduum[1] eius rei causa supplicatio habita est; ille
non pavor vanus, sed vera multorum clades fuit:
incendio a foro Boario orto diem noctemque aedificia
in Tiberim versa arsere, tabernaeque omnes cum
magni pretii mercibus conflagraverunt.

XLI. Iam fere in exitu annus erat, et in dies
magis[2] et fama de bello Antiochi et cura patribus
2 crescebat; itaque de provinciis designatorum magistratuum, quo intentiores essent omnes, agitari
3 coeptum est. Decrevere ut consulibus Italia et quo
senatus censuisset—eam[3] esse bellum adversus
Antiochum regem omnes sciebant—provinciae essent.
4 Cuius ea sors esset, quattuor milia peditum civium
Romanorum et trecenti equites, sex milia socium
Latini nominis cum quadringentis equitibus sunt
5 decreta. Eorum dilectum habere L. Quinctius consul iussus, ne quid moraretur quo minus consul novus
quo senatus censuisset extemplo proficisci posse.
6 Item de provinciis praetorum decretum est,[4] prima
ut sors duae, urbanaque[5] et inter cives ac peregrinos
iurisdictio esset, secunda Brutti, tertia classis, ut
navigaret quo senatus censuisset, quarta Sicilia,
7 quinta Sardinia, sexta Hispania ulterior. Imperatum praeterea L. Quinctio consuli est ut duas

---

[1] triduum *Siesbye* : in triduum *B*.
[2] magis *edd. vett.* : magna *B*.
[3] eam *Madvig* : iam *Bꝛ*.
[4] decretum est ꝛ : decretum *B*.
[5] urbanaque ꝛ : urbana *B*.

---

[1] This " cattle-market " lay between the Circus Maximus
and the Tiber.
[2] The continued presence of Quinctius in Rome is more
consistent with the account in xxiv. 2 than with that in xl. 2.

hension and fear; by reason of this occurrence a B.C. 192 three-day period of prayer was held; the other was no idle panic but actual destruction to many: a fire broke out in the Forum Boarium,[1] and for a day and a night the buildings facing the Tiber burned, and all the shops with merchandise of great value were consumed.

XLI. The year was now almost at an end and the talk about the war with Antiochus and the concern of the Fathers were growing greater and greater from day to day; in order, therefore, that all might be more attentive to duty, the question of provinces for the magistrates-elect began to be considered. They decreed that for the consuls Italy and wherever the senate ordered—that this province would be the war against King Antiochus was known to everyone— should be the provinces. The one to whom the latter lot fell was authorized to enlist four thousand Roman citizens for the infantry and three hundred cavalry and six thousand allies of the Latin confederacy with four hundred cavalry. The enrolment of these troops Lucius Quinctius the consul [2] was ordered to undertake, that nothing might delay the new consul from going at once to whatever place the senate should have ordered. Moreover, regarding the provinces of the praetors, it was decided that the first lot should cover the two jurisdictions, that between citizens and that between citizens and aliens, the second the Brutti, the third the fleet, to sail wherever the senate should have directed, the fourth Sicily, the fifth Sardinia, the sixth Farther Spain.[3] Instructions were also given to Lucius Quinctius the consul to

[3] The other provinces would be governed by proconsuls or propraetors, who are not here designated.

LIVY

legiones civium Romanorum novas conscriberet et
socium ac Latini nominis viginti milia peditum
et octingentos equites. Eum exercitum praetori cui
Brutti provincia evenisset decreverunt.

8 Aedes duae Iovis eo anno in Capitolio dedicatae
sunt; voverat L. Furius Purpurio praetor Gallico bello
unam, alteram consul; dedicavit Q. Marcius Ralla
9 duumvir. Iudicia in faeneratores eo anno multa
severe sunt facta accusantibus privatos aedilibus
10 curulibus M. Tuccio et P. Iunio Bruto. De multa
damnatorum quadrigae inauratae in Capitolio positae,
et in cella Iovis supra fastigium aediculae et duodecim clupea inaurata, et iidem porticum extra
portam Trigeminam inter lignarios fecerunt.

XLII. Intentis in apparatum novi belli Romanis
2 ne ab Antiocho quidem cessabatur. Tres eum civitates tenebant, Zmyrna et Alexandria Troas et
Lampsacus, quas neque vi expugnare ad eam diem
poterat neque condicionibus in amicitiam perlicere,
neque ab tergo relinquere traiciens ipse in Europam
volebat. Tenuit eum et de Hannibale deliberatio.
3 Et primo naves apertae, quas cum eo missurus in
4 Africam fuerat, moratae sunt; deinde an omnino
mittendus esset, consultatio mota est, maxime a
Thoante Aetolo, qui omnibus in Graecia tumultu

---

[1] Cf. XXXIV. liii. 7 and the note. The account of these
temples and of the career of Furius is badly confused.

[2] These prosecutions may have been laid under the Sem-
pronian legislation mentioned at vii. 5 above.

[3] The segregation of industries in Rome made it possible
to use such terms as addresses, since nothing more accurate
existed : cf. *inter falcarios* in Cicero, *Cat.* I. 8.

[4] Zmyrna and Lampsacus were mentioned in xvi. 3 as cities
which Antiochus was trying to recover; Alexandria Troas

raise two new legions of Roman citizens and from the allies of the Latin confederacy twenty thousand infantry and eight hundred cavalry. This army was decreed to the praetor to whom the Brutti should have been allotted as a province.

Two temples to Jupiter were dedicated that year on the Capitoline; Lucius Furius Purpurio [1] had vowed one while praetor in the Gallic war, the other while consul; the dedication was performed by Quintus Marcius Ralla the duumvir. Many prosecutions that year were directed against usurers,[2] the curule aediles Marcus Tuccius and Publius Junius Brutus bringing charges against private citizens. From the fines imposed on the condemned, gilded four-horse chariots were set up on the Capitoline and in the inner room of the temple of Jupiter, above the roof of the shrine, twelve gilded shields were also placed, and the same men built a portico outside the Porta Trigemina in the wood-dealers' quarter.[3]

XLII. While the Romans were concentrating on the preparations for the new war, there was no idleness on the part of Antiochus either. Three cities were detaining him, Zmyrna and Alexandria Troas and Lampsacus,[4] which he had up to that time been able neither to take by assault nor to win over to friendship by negotiations, nor was he willing to leave them in his rear when he crossed to Greece. The question of Hannibal also detained him. And at first the open ships which he had planned to send with him to Africa were delayed; then the question whether he should be sent at all was raised, particularly by Thoas the Aetolian, who, after everything

was one of the other cities of xvi. 6 above. The events now related belong to the period 192–191 B.C.

A.U.C.
562

completis Demetriadem adferebat in potestate esse
5 et, quibus mendaciis de rege, multiplicando verbis
copias eius, erexerat multorum in Graecia animos,
iisdem et regis spem inflabat: omnium votis eum
accersi, concursum ad littora futurum, unde classem
6 regiam prospexissent. Hic idem ausus de Hannibale
est movere sententiam prope iam certam regis.
Nam neque dimittendam partem navium a classe
7 regia censebat, neque, si mittendae naves forent,
minus quemquam ei classi quam Hannibalem prae-
8 ficiendum: exulem illum et Poenum esse, cui mille
in dies nova consilia vel fortuna sua vel ingenium
9 possit facere, et ipsam eam gloriam belli, qua velut
dote Hannibal concilietur, nimiam in praefecto regio
esse. Regem conspici, regem unum ducem, unum
10 imperatorem videri debere. Si classem, si exercitum
amittat Hannibal, idem damni fore ac si per alium
ducem amittantur; si quid prospere eveniat, Hanni-
11 balis eam, non Antiochi gloriam fore; si vero universo
bello vincendi Romanos fortuna detur, quam spem
esse sub rege victurum Hannibalem, uni subiectum,
12 qui patriam prope[1] non tulerit? Non ita se a
iuventa eum gessisse, spe animoque complexum orbis
terrarum imperium, ut in senectute dominum laturus
videatur. Nihil opus esse regi duce Hannibale;

---

[1] patriam prope ς: patriam B.

---

[1] The rhetoric of Thoas gives him some neat balances,
exulem : fortuna; *Poenum : ingenium*, and furnishes Livy
with another chance to play upon his favourite theme, *Punica
fides.*

in Greece had been thrown into confusion, brought word that Demetrias was in his power, and with lies like those about the king, with which, multiplying his forces in his harangues, he had roused the passions of many in Greece, he excited the hopes of the king also : the prayers of all were calling him, there would be a rush to the shore from which they could catch glimpses of the royal fleet. This same man dared to try to change the king's decision about Hannibal, now almost fully determined. For he said that part of the ships should by no means be detached from the royal fleet, nor, if ships should be sent, was any man less fit than Hannibal to be placed in command : he was an exile and a Carthaginian, to whom either his own luck or his wit could suggest a thousand new schemes a day,[1] and Hannibal's military fame endowed him with a distinction which was out of place in a mere officer of a king. The king, he said, ought to be the centre of interest, ought to be regarded as the single leader, the single general. If Hannibal should lose a fleet or an army, the loss would be the same as if they were lost by any other leader ; if any success were attained, to Hannibal, not to Antiochus, would the credit accrue ; but if in the whole war the fortune of conquering the Romans should be vouchsafed them, what hope was there that Hannibal would live under a king, subject to an individual, when he had practically failed to endure the rule of his own country ? He had not conducted himself from youth up, cherishing in his hopes and thoughts the sovereignty of the world, in such a way that in his old age he would be ready, as it seemed, to suffer a master. The king, he concluded, had no need of Hannibal as a commander ; as a companion

LIVY

13 comite et consiliario eodem ad bellum uti posse.
14 Modicum fructum ex ingenio tali neque gravem
neque inutilem fore; si summa petantur, et dantem
et accipientem praegravatura.

XLIII. Nulla ingenia tam prona ad invidiam sunt
quam eorum qui genus ac fortunam suam animis non
aequant, quia virtutem et bonum alienum oderunt.
Extemplo consilium mittendi Hannibalis, quod unum
in principio belli utiliter cogitatum erat, abiectum
2 est. Demetriadis maxime defectione ab Romanis
ad Aetolos elatus non ultra differre profectionem in
3 Graeciam constituit. Priusquam solveret naves,
Ilium a mari escendit,[1] ut Minervae sacrificaret.
Inde ad classem regressus proficiscitur quadraginta
tectis [2] navibus, apertis sexaginta, et ducentae onerariae cum omnis generis commeatu bellicoque alio
4 apparatu sequebantur. Imbrum primo insulam
tenuit; inde Sciathum traiecit; ubi collectis in alto
quae dissipatae erant navibus ad Pteleum primum
5 continentis venit. Ibi Eurylochus ei Magnetarches
principesque Magnetum ab Demetriade occurrerunt,
quorum frequentia laetus die postero in portum urbis
navibus est invectus; copias haud procul inde exposuit.
6 Decem milia peditum fuere et quingenti equites, sex
elephanti, vix ad Graeciam nudam occupandam satis
copiarum, nedum ad sustinendum Romanum bellum.

---

[1] escendit ς : descendit B.
[2] tectis ed. Mediolanensis 1505 : lectis B.

---

[1] Nepos (Hannibal viii. 1) asserts that Hannibal was actually
sent to Africa, but without a fleet. Speculation as to the facts
and as to the consequences if Hannibal had been able to draw
Carthage into the war is interesting but fruitless.
[2] After the extravagances of the earlier reports, the small
size of the expeditionary force which actually landed must
have seemed an anticlimax to others than Antiochus (xliv. 4)

and as an adviser he could use such a man for the war. A moderate employment of such talents would be neither dangerous nor unprofitable; if the greatest use of them were made, it would ruin both the giver and the receiver.

XLIII. No dispositions are so prone to envy as those of men whose abilities do not correspond to their birth and fortune, because they hate excellence and good qualities in another. Immediately the plan of sending Hannibal, which was the only good thing thought of at the beginning of the war, was laid aside.[1] The king, especially rejoiced at the revolt of Demetrias from the Romans to the Aetolians, decided not to postpone longer his departure for Greece. Before he set sail he went up from the coast to Ilium to offer sacrifice to Minerva. Thence he returned and departed with forty decked and sixty open vessels, while two hundred cargo-ships, with all kinds of supplies and equipment for war, followed. He first steered for the island of Imbros; thence crossed to Sciathos; there he first collected the ships that had been scattered in the open sea and arrived at Pteleum, the first point on the mainland. There Eurylochus the Magnetarch and the chiefs of the Magnetes from Demetrias met him, and rejoicing at their number on the next day he sailed into the harbour of the city with his fleet; his troops he landed not far away. There were ten thousand infantry and five hundred cavalry and six elephants, a force scarcely sufficient to take possession of Greece if it were undefended, not to mention the necessity of resistance to the Romans.[2]

and Flamininus (xlix. 9), and it is strange that Livy makes no further mention of the subject.

LIVY

7 Aetoli, postquam Demetriadem venisse Antiochum
adlatum est, concilio indicto decretum quo accerse-
8 rent eum fecerunt. Iam profectus ab Demetriade
rex, quia ita decreturos sciebat, Phalara in sinum
9 Maliacum processerat. Inde decreto accepto Lamiam venit, exceptus ingenti favore multitudinis cum
plausibus clamoribusque et quibus aliis laetitia effusa
vulgi significatur.[1]

XLIV. In concilium ut ventum est, aegre a
Phaenea praetore principibusque aliis introductus
2 facto silentio dicere orsus rex. Prima eius oratio fuit
excusantis,[2] quod tanto minoribus spe atque opinione
3 omnium copiis venisset. Id suae impensae erga eos
voluntatis maximum debere indicium esse, quod
nec paratus satis ulla re et tempore ad navigandum
immaturo vocantibus legatis eorum haud gravate
obsecutus esset credidissetque, cum se vidissent
Aetoli, omnia vel in se uno posita praesidia existi-
4 maturos esse. Ceterum eorum quoque se, quorum
expectatio destituta in praesentia videatur, spem
5 abunde expleturum: nam simul primum anni tempus navigabile praebuisset mare, omnem se Graeciam
armis viris equis,[3] omnem oram maritimam classibus
6 completurum, nec impensae nec labori nec periculo
parsurum, donec depulso cervicibus eorum imperio
Romano liberam vere Graeciam atque in ea principes
7 Aetolos fecisset. Cum exercitibus commeatus quo-

---

[1] vulgi significatur *Aldus*: vulgo significatur *Bς*: signifi-
cabatur volgi *M*.
[2] excusantis *ed. Moguntina* 1518: primo excusantis *B*.
[3] equis *ed. Frobeniana* 1535: equisque *Bς*.

---

[1] The phrase indicates that Antiochus crossed the Aegean
in the fall (of 192 B.C.), after the storms had begun, instead of
waiting for the next spring.

The Aetolians, after it was reported that Antiochus B.C. 192
had arrived at Demetrias, called a council and confirmed the decree by which they had invited him.
The king had already left Demetrias, knowing that
they would vote thus, and had come to Phalara on
the Malian gulf.   Thence, after receiving the decree,
he came to Lamia and was welcomed with great
enthusiasm on the part of the populace, with hand-
clappings and shouts and the other demonstrations
with which the unrestrained joy of a crowd is
expressed.

XLIV. When they came to the council, silence
being with difficulty obtained, the king was introduced by Phaeneas the praetor and the other chiefs
and began to speak.   The opening of his speech was
an apology because he had come with forces so much
smaller than everyone had hoped and expected.
This, he said, should be the best proof of the good-
will which he felt for them, because, although not
fully prepared in any respect and at a premature
time [1] for sailing, at the summons of their ambassadors he had obeyed without objection and had
believed that when the Aetolians saw him they would
consider that all their hope of safety depended on
himself alone.   But the hopes, even of those whose
expectations seemed disappointed for the moment,
he would realize to the full: for as soon as the early
season of the year made the sea navigable he would
fill all Greece with arms, men, horses, the whole sea-
coast with ships, and would spare no expense nor toil
nor danger until, with the Roman yoke removed from
their necks, he had made Greece free in truth and
the Aetolians the foremost people in the land.   With
the armies, supplies of every kind also would come

que omnis generis ex Asia venturos; in praesentia curae esse Aetolis debere, ut copia frumenti suis et annona tolerabilis rerum aliarum suppeditetur.

XLV. In hanc sententiam rex cum magno omnium 2 adsensu locutus discessit. Post discessum regis inter duos principes Aetolorum, Phaeneam et Thoantem, 3 contentio fuit. Phaeneas reconciliatore pacis et disceptatore de iis quae in controversia cum populo Romano essent utendum potius Antiocho censebat 4 quam duce belli: adventum eius et maiestatem ad verecundiam faciendam Romanis vim maiorem habituram quam arma; multa homines, ne bellare necesse sit, voluntate remittere, quae bello et armis cogi 5 non possint. Thoas negare paci studere Phaeneam, sed discutere apparatum belli velle, ut taedio et impetus relanguescat regis et Romani tempus ad 6 comparandum habeant: nihil enim aequi ab Romanis impetrari posse totiens legationibus missis Romam, totiens cum ipso Quinctio disceptando satis expertum esse, nec nisi abscisa omni spe auxilium Antiochi 7 imploraturos fuisse. Quo celerius spe omnium oblato non esse elanguescendum, sed orandum potius regem ut, quoniam, quod maximum fuerit, ipse vindex Graeciae venerit, copias quoque terrestres 8 navalesque accersat. Armatum regem aliquid impetraturum; inermem non pro Aetolis modo, sed ne pro se quidem ipso momenti ullius futurum apud

---

[1] With unusual politeness, Thoas refrains from calling Phaeneas a pro-Roman.

from Asia; in the meantime the responsibility should B.C. 192
rest upon the Aetolians of supplying him with
abundance of grain for his men and with other things
at a fair price.

XLV. Having spoken thus amid loud applause
from all, the king left the meeting. After the
withdrawal of the king an argument arose between
two chiefs of the Aetolians, Phaeneas and Thoas.
Phaeneas thought that they should use Antiochus
as a restorer of peace and as an arbitrator in those
matters which were in dispute with the Roman
people rather than as a leader in war: his arrival and
his majesty would be more effectual than arms in
causing the Romans to observe moderation; men, to
avoid the necessity of fighting, would make many
voluntary concessions which they could not be compelled to make by war and arms. Thoas asserted
that Phaeneas was not interested in peace but was
trying to delay preparations for war, that through
weariness the energy of the king might relax and
also that the Romans might have time for preparation: it was well established by sending so many
embassies to Rome and holding so many conferences
with Quinctius himself, that no justice could be
obtained from the Romans, nor would they have asked
aid from Antiochus if all hope had not been lost.[1]
Since this aid had arrived sooner than anyone
expected, there should be, he said, no diminution of
effort, but rather the king should be asked, since he
had come in person as the avenger of Greece, which
was the all-important thing, to summon also his
military and naval forces. The king in arms would
obtain something; unarmed, he would not have the
slightest influence with the Romans, either for the

LIVY

9 Romanos. Haec vicit sententia, imperatoremque
regem appellandum censuerunt et triginta principes,
cum quibus si qua vellet consultaret, delegerunt.

XLVI. Ita dimisso concilio multitudo omnis in
2 suas civitates dilapsa est; rex postero die cum
apocletis eorum unde bellum ordiretur, consultabat.
Optimum visum est Chalcidem, frustra ab Aetolis
nuper temptatam, primum adgredi; et celeritate
magis in eam rem quam magno conatu et apparatu
3 opus esse. Itaque cum mille peditibus rex qui ab
Demetriade secuti erant profectus per Phocidem
est, et alio itinere principes Aetoli iuniorum paucis
evocatis ad Chaeroniam occurrerunt et decem navi-
4 bus constratis secuti sunt. Rex ad Salganea castris
positis navibus ipse cum principibus Aetolorum
Euripum traiecit, et, cum haud procul portu egressus
esset, magistratus quoque Chalcidensium et principes
ante portam processerunt. Pauci utrimque ad col-
5 loquium congressi sunt. Aetoli magno opere suadere
ut salva Romanorum amicitia regem quoque adsu-
6 merent socium atque amicum: neque enim eum
inferendi belli, sed liberandae Graeciae causa in
Europam traiecisse, et liberandae re,[1] non verbis
7 et simulatione, quod fecissent Romani; nihil autem
utilius Graeciae civitatibus esse quam utramque
complecti amicitiam; ita enim ab utriusque iniuria
tutas [2] alterius semper praesidio et fiducia fore.
8 Nam si non recepissent regem, viderent, quid patiendum iis extemplo foret, cum Romanorum procul
auxilium, hostis Antiochus, cui resistere suis viribus

---

[1] et liberandae re *Drakenborch*: liberanda re *B*: et re
liberandae *M*: liberandae re ς.
[2] tutas *Duker*: tutan *B*.

Aetolians or even for himself. This opinion prevailed, B.C. 192 and they voted that the king should be named commander-in-chief and chose thirty of the leaders with whom, if he wished, he could consult.

XLVI. The council being thus adjourned, the people all scattered to their own cities; the king next day consulted the *apocletes* as to where the war should begin. It seemed best first to attack Chalcis, on which an attempt had recently been made in vain by the Aetolians; and it was agreed that speed was more necessary for this purpose than great strength or preparation. The king therefore with a thousand infantry who had come with him from Demetrias set out through Phocis and by another road the chiefs of the Aetolians, calling out a few of their young men, hastened to Chaeronia and followed in ten decked ships. The king himself encamped at Salganeus and crossed the Euripus by boat with the Aetolian chiefs and, since he had disembarked not far from the harbour, the magistrates of the Chalcidenses also and the foremost citizens came out before the gate. A few from each side met for a conference. The Aetolians urged them strongly while retaining the Roman friendship to take the king also as an ally and friend: for he had not come to Europe to make war but to free Greece, and to free it in reality, not in words and pretence, as the Romans had done; nothing, moreover, was more useful to the Greek cities than to embrace both friendships, for thus they would always be guarded by the protection and good faith of the one from the injustice of the other. For if they did not receive the king, they would see at once what they would have to endure, when Roman aid was far away and Antiochus, an enemy whom they

9 non possent, ante portas esset. Ad haec Micythio, unus ex principibus, mirari se dixit ad quos liberandos Antiochus relicto regno suo in Europam traiecisset:
10 nullam enim civitatem se in Graecia nosse quae aut praesidium habeat, aut stipendium Romanis pendat, aut foedere iniquo adligata quas nolit leges patiatur:
11 itaque Chalcidenses neque vindice libertatis ullo egere, cum liberi sint, neque praesidio, cum pacem eiusdem populi Romani beneficio et libertatem
12 habeant. Amicitiam regis non aspernari nec ipsorum Aetolorum. Id primum eos pro amicis facturos, si
13 insula excedant[1] atque abeant: nam ipsis certum esse non modo non recipere moenibus, sed ne societatem quidem ullam pacisci nisi ex auctoritate Romanorum.

XLVII. Haec renuntiata regi ad naves ubi restiterat cum essent, in praesentia—neque enim iis[2] venerat copiis ut vi[3] agere quicquam posset—reverti
2 Demetriadem placuit. Ibi, quoniam primum vanum inceptum evasisset, consultare cum Aetolis rex, quid deinde fieret. Placuit Boeotos[4] Achaeos Amynan-
3 drum regem Athamanum temptare. Boeotorum gentem aversam ab Romanis iam inde a Brachyllae morte et quae secuta eam fuerant, censebant;
4 Achaeorum Philopoemenem principem aemulatione gloriae in bello Laconum infestum invisumque esse

---

[1] excedant ς : cedant B.
[2] iis ς : his B.
[3] vi ς : vel B.
[4] Boeotos *Perizonius* : om. B.

---

[1] Micythio claims for Chalcis all the normal characteristics of a free state; the final sentence of the chapter is not inconsistent, since Chalcis was at liberty to make any alliance it chose, but would voluntarily submit to Rome's judgment on such matters.

could not withstand by their own might, was at their B.C. 192
gates. At this Micythio, one of the chiefs, said that
he wondered for whose liberation Antiochus had left
his own kingdom and crossed to Europe : for he knew
no state in Greece which had a garrison or paid
tribute to the Romans or suffered, under the compulsion of an unfair treaty, laws which it did not wish[1] ;
therefore the people of Chalcis needed neither any
champion of their liberty, since they were free, nor
any protection, since by the kindness of the same
Roman people they enjoyed peace along with liberty.
They did not reject, he said, the friendship of the king
nor that of the Aetolians themselves. In their
capacity as friends their first act would be to retire
from the island and go away : for they were determined not only not to admit them within the walls,
but not to conclude any alliance even except in
accordance with the authorization of the Romans.

XLVII. When this answer had been conveyed to
the king at the ships where he had stayed, for the
present—for he had not come with such strength
that he could undertake any forcible measures—it
was decided to return to Demetrias. There, since
their first venture had proved fruitless, the king
consulted with the Aetolians what should be done
next. It was agreed to try the Boeotians, the
Achaeans, and Amynander, king of the Athamanes.
They believed that the Boeotians had been unfriendly to the Romans ever since the death of
Brachyllas and the events which followed[2] ; they
thought that the Achaean magistrate Philopoemen,
since he had become a rival in fame as a result of the
war in Lacedaemon, was hostile to and hated ·by

[2] Cf. XXXIII. xxviii. 1 ff.

135

A.U.C.
562

5 Quinctio credebant. Amynander uxorem Apamam,
filiam Alexandri cuiusdam Megalopolitani, habebat,
qui se oriundum a magno Alexandro ferens filiis
duobus Philippum atque[1] Alexandrum et filiae
6 Apamam nomina imposuerat; quam regiis iunctam[2]
nuptiis maior ex fratribus Philippus secutus in Atha-
7 maniam fuerat. Hunc forte ingenio vanum Aetoli
et Antiochus impulerant in spem Macedoniae regni,
quod is vere regum stirpis esset, si Amynandrum
8 Athamanesque Antiocho coniunxisset. Et ea vani-
tas promissorum non apud Philippum modo sed
etiam apud Amynandrum valuit.

XLVIII. In Achaia legatis Antiochi Aetolorumque
coram T. Quinctio Aegii datum est concilium.
2 Antiochi legatus prior quam Aetoli est auditus. Is,
ut plerique, quos opes regiae alunt, vaniloquus maria
3 terrasque inani sonitu verborum complevit: equitum
innumerabilem vim traici Hellesponto in Europam,
partim loricatos, quos cataphractos vocant, partim
sagittis ex equo utentes et, a quo nihil satis tecti sit,
4 averso refugientes equo certius figentes. His[3] eques-
tribus copiis quamquam vel totius Europae exercitus
in unum coacti obrui possent, adiciebat multiplices
5 copias peditum, et nominibus quoque gentium vix
fando auditis terrebat, Dahas Medos Elymaeosque
6 et Cadusios appellans. Navalium vero copiarum,

---

[1] atque ς : et B.
[2] regiis iunctam Koch : regis inclutam BM.   [3] his ς : iis B.

---

[1] Cf. xxx. 12–13 above. Plutarch (*Philop.* xv) traces their
jealousy to this same cause, but his chronology is confused.
[2] Amynander had been an ally of the Romans against
Philip (XXXI. xxviii. 1), but may have felt slighted in the
re-arrangements following the peace (XXXIII. xxxiv. 11).

Quinctius.[1] Amynander [2] had as wife Apama,[3]
daughter of one Alexander of Megalopolis, who,
boasting descent from Alexander the Great, had
given to his two sons the names of Philip and Alexander and to his daughter that of Apama; when she
was joined in royal wedlock her elder brother Philip
followed her to Athamania. Since he happened to
be vain in character, the Aetolians and Antiochus
had induced him to hope for the throne of Macedonia, being, as they told him, truly of the stock
of kings, if he allied Amynander and the Athamanes
with Antiochus. And this vain promise availed not
only with Philip but also with Amynander.

XLVIII. In Achaea a hearing before the council
was granted the representatives of Antiochus and
the Aetolians in the presence of Titus Quinctius at
Aegium. The ambassador of Antiochus was heard
before the Aetolians. He, a boaster like most who
are maintained by a king's power, filled seas and
lands with an empty sound of words: an uncountable
number of cavalry was crossing the Hellespont into
Europe, partly equipped with breastplates—these
they call the *cataphracti*—partly those who use arrows
from horseback, and as a result of which there is no
protection against them, since they aimed quite
accurately backwards while fleeing on their horses.
Although by these forces of cavalry the armies even
of all Europe, collected in one body, could be overwhelmed, he added army after army of infantry, and
he caused terror when they heard names of tribes
besides, scarcely known by name, talking of Dahae,[4]
Medes, Elymaeans and Cadusians. As to the naval

---

[3] Apama was the wife of Seleucus I, but the name is not
known as characteristically a family-name among the descendants of Philip of Macedon.

[4] The Dahae were Scythians: cf. Plin. *N.H.* VI. 50.

quas nulli portus capere in Graecia possent, dextrum cornu Sidonios et Tyrios, sinistrum Aradios et ex Pamphylia Sidetas tenere, quas gentes nullae 7 umquam nec arte nec virtute navali aequassent. Iam pecuniam, iam alios belli apparatus referre supervacaneum esse: scire ipsos abundasse auro semper regna Asiae. Itaque non cum Philippo nec Hannibale rem futuram Romanis, principe altero unius civitatis, altero Macedoniae tantum regni finibus incluso, sed cum magno Asiae totius partisque 8 Europae rege. Eum tamen, quamquam ab ultimis orientis terminis ad liberandam Graeciam veniat, nihil postulare ab Achaeis, in quo fides eorum adversus Romanos, priores socios atque amicos, 9 laedatur: non enim ut secum adversus eos arma capiant, sed ut neutri parti sese coniungant petere. Pacem utrique parti, quod medios deceat amicos, 10 optent; bello se non interponant. Idem ferme et Aetolorum legatus Archidamus petit[1] ut, quae facillima et tutissima esset, quietem praestarent, spectatoresque belli fortunarum alienarum eventum sine ullo discrimine rerum suarum opperirentur. 11 Provectus deinde est intemperantia linguae in maledicta nunc communiter Romanorum, nunc proprie 12 ipsius Quinctii, ingratos appellans et exprobrans non victoriam modo de Philippo virtute Aetolorum partam sed etiam salutem, ipsumque et exercitum 13 sua opera servatos. Quo enim illum umquam imperatoris functum officio esse? Auspicantem

---

[1] petit ς: peti B.

forces, moreover, which no harbours in Greece could
shelter, the right wing was held by men of Sidon and
Tyre, the left by Aradii and Sidetes from Pamphylia,
which races none had ever equalled either in skill
or in courage in naval combat. At this time to
speak of money, at this time to speak of other
equipment for war, he said was useless: they themselves were aware that the kingdoms of Asia had
always been rich in gold. Therefore the Romans
would not have to do with Philip or Hannibal, the one
the chief of a single state, the other confined only
within the bounds of the Macedonian kingdom, but
with the mighty lord of all Asia and part of Europe.
Nevertheless, although he came from the farthest
parts of the east to liberate Greece, he demanded
nothing of the Achaeans by which their loyalty to the
Romans, who had priority as allies and friends, would
be diminished: for he did not ask that they should
take up arms on his side against the Romans, but that
they should ally themselves with neither side. Let
them wish for peace for both parties, as was befitting
the friends of both; let them take no part in war.
About the same request was made by the Aetolian
ambassador Archidamus, that they maintain peace,
which was the easiest and safest course, and as
onlookers at the war let them await the outcome of
others' destinies without any risk to their own cause.
Then he was carried away by the vehemence of his
language to the point of insulting now the Romans
generally, now Quinctius himself specifically, calling
them ingrates and taunting him with the remark
that not only the victory over Philip but Quinctius'
own safety had been gained by the valour of the
Aetolians, and when, he demanded, had Quinctius
ever performed the functions of a commander?

A.U.C.
562

immolantemque et vota nuncupantem sacrificuli vatis modo in acie vidisse, cum ipse corpus suum pro eo telis hostium obiceret.

XLIX. Ad ea Quinctius, coram quibus magis quam apud quos verba faceret, dicere Archidamum rationem
2 habuisse: Achaeos enim probe scire Aetolorum omnem ferociam in verbis non in factis esse, et in conciliis magis contionibusque quam in acie apparere:
3 itaque parvi Achaeorum existimationem, quibus notos esse se scirent, fecisse; legatis regis et per eos
4 absenti regi eum se iactasse. Quod si quis antea ignorasset quae res Antiochum et Aetolos con- iunxisset, ex legatorum sermone potuisse apparere, mentiendo in vicem iactandoque vires quas non haberent, inflasse vana spe atque inflatos esse,
5 " dum hi ab se victum Philippum, sua virtute pro- tectos Romanos et, quae modo audiebatis, narrant vos ceterasque civitates et gentes suam sectam esse secuturos, rex contra peditum equitumque nubes
6 iactat et consternit maria classibus suis. Est autem res simillima cenae Chalcidensis hospitis mei, et hominis [1] boni et sciti convivatoris, apud quem solstitiali tempore comiter accepti cum miraremur, unde illi eo tempore anni tam varia et multa venatio,
7 homo non quam isti [2] sunt gloriosus renidens condi-

---

[1] et hominis *Weissenborn* : hominis et *B⌐*.
[2] isti ⌐ : iusti *B* : ut isti *M*.

---

[1] Livy does not mention this in his description of Cynos- cephalae, but Polybius (XVIII. xxi. 5) gives Archidamus credit for conspicuous courage there, omitting the slurs on Flamininus.
[2] This was the summer solstice, when game was out of season.

Taking auspices and sacrificing and performing vows like a poor sacrificing priest—thus had he seen Quinctius in the battle, while he himself was exposing his person in behalf of Quinctius to the weapons of the enemy.[1]

XLIX. To this Quinctius replied that Archidamus had considered in whose presence he was speaking rather than whom he was addressing: for the Achaeans knew well that all the fierceness of the Aetolians consisted in words and not in actions, and was seen in councils and assemblies more than in battle: therefore Archidamus took small account of the opinion of the Achaeans, to whom he realized that the Aetolians were known; it was for the benefit of the king's ambassadors and through them of the king that he had boasted thus. But if anyone had been ignorant before what cause had brought Antiochus and the Aetolians together, it could now be clear from the speeches of their delegates that by an exchange of lies and of boasts of strength which they did not possess they filled one another's minds, and in turn were filled, with groundless hopes. "While they are saying that by them Philip was defeated and by their valour the Romans were preserved, and, as you just heard, that you and the other cities and peoples will follow in their path, the king on the other hand is boasting of his clouds of infantry and cavalry and is hiding the sea beneath his fleet. But the whole affair is very like a dinner given by a friend of mine in Chalcis, both an excellent man and a witty table-companion, and when we were entertained at his house at the time of the solstice,[2] and were wondering where at that time of the year he found so much game and of so many kinds, this man, not boasting in the manner

LIVY

mentis ait varietatem illam et speciem ferinae carnis
ex mansueto sue factam." Hoc dici apte in copias
8 regis, quae paulo ante iactatae sint,[1] posse: varia
enim genera armorum et multa nomina gentium
inauditarum, Dahas et Medos et Cadusios et Ely-
maeos, Suros omnes esse, haud paulo mancipiorum
melius propter servilia ingenia quam militum genus.
9 " Et utinam subicere vestris oculis, Achaei, possem
concursationem regis magni ab Demetriade nunc
Lamiam in concilium Aetolorum nunc Chalcidem;
10 videretis vix duarum male plenarum legiuncularum
instar in castris regis; videretis regem nunc mendi-
11 cantem prope frumentum ab Aetolis, quod militi
admetiatur, nunc mutuas pecunias faenore in stipendium [2] quaerentem, nunc ad portas Chalcidis stantem
et mox, inde exclusum, nihil aliud quam Aulide atque
Euripo spectatis in Aetoliam redeuntem. Male
crediderunt et Antiochus Aetolis et Aetoli regiae
12 vanitati: quo minus vos decipi debetis, sed expertae
potius [3] spectataeque Romanorum fidei credere.
13 Nam quod optimum esse dicunt,[4] non interponi vos
bello, nihil immo tam alienum rebus vestris est;
quippe sine gratia sine dignitate praemium victoris
eritis."

L. Nec absurde adversus utrosque respondisse
visus est, et facile erat orationem apud faventes
2 aequis auribus accipi. Nulla enim nec disceptatio

---

[1] sint *ed. Frobeniana* 1531 : sunt *Bς*.
[2] in stipendium *ς* : stipendium *B*.
[3] potius *Mς* : tocius *B*.
[4] dicunt *ς* : dicant *B*.

of our opponents, said with a smile that by seasoning B.C. 192 these varied forms of wild game had been made out of tame swine." This, he said, could be well applied to the forces of the king, about which there had been so much bragging a little while ago; the different kinds of weapons, the many names of unheard-of peoples, Dahae and Medes and Cadusians and Elymaeans —these were all Syrians, far better fitted to be slaves, on account of their servile dispositions, than to be a race of warriors. " And would that I could, Achaeans, set before your eyes the frantic rush of the great king from Demetrias, now to Lamia for the council of the Aetolians, now to Chalcis; you would scarcely find the like of two poor legions of reduced strength in the camp of the king; you would see the king now almost begging food from the Aetolians to be distributed to his troops, now seeking the loan of funds on interest for their pay, now standing before the gates of Chalcis and presently, shut out from there, having done nothing more than look at Aulis and the Euripus, going back to Aetolia. Foolishly have they trusted, both Antiochus in the Aetolians and the Aetolians in the vainglory of the king: the less should you be deceived, but you should place your trust rather in the tried and known protection of the Romans. For as to what they say is best, that you should not take any part in the war, nothing, on the contrary, is so inconsistent with your interests; yes, disregarded and discredited you will be the prize of the conqueror."

L. Not without point did he appear to have answered both parties, and it was easy for his speech to be received with favouring ears by men who were on his side. For there was no debate or doubt that

LIVY

A.U.C.
562 nec dubitatio fuit quin omnes eosdem genti Achaeorum hostes et amicos, quos populus Romanus
censuisset, iudicarent, bellumque et Antiocho et
3 Aetolis nuntiari iuberent. Auxilia etiam quo censuit
Quinctius, quingentorum militum Chalcidem, quin-
4 gentorum Piraeum extemplo miserunt. Erat enim [1]
haud procul seditione Athenis res trahentibus ad
Antiochum quibusdam spe largitionum venalem
pretio multitudinem, donec ab iis, qui Romanae
partis erant, Quinctius est accitus, et accusante
Leonte quodam Apollodorus auctor defectionis
damnatus atque in exilium est eiectus.

5 Et ab Achaeis quidem cum tristi responso legatio
ad regem rediit; Boeoti nihil certi responderunt:
cum Antiochus in Boeotiam venisset, tum quid sibi
faciendum esset se deliberaturos esse.

6 Antiochus cum ad Chalcidis praesidium et Achaeos
et Eumenem regem misisse audisset, maturandum
ratus, ut et praevenirent sui et venientes si possent
7 exciperent, Menippum cum tribus ferme milibus
militum et omni classe Polyxenidan mittit, ipse
paucos post dies sex milia suorum militum et ex ea
copia quae Lamiae repente colligi potuit non ita
8 multos Aetolos ducit. Achaei quingenti et ab [2] Eumene rege modicum auxilium missum duce Xenoclide
Chalcidensi nondum obsessis itineribus tuto trans-
9 gressi Euripum Chalcidem pervenerunt; Romani

---

[1] enim ⌐ : autem *B.*
[2] et ab *Gronovius* : ab *B.*

---

[1] Livy has said nothing about this Roman detachment, and
does not explain whether they came from the fleet or from the
army of Baebius (cf. xxiv. 7 above); the latter is more probable,
considering the direction of their march.

they would pronounce judgment that the people of
the Achaeans would hold as enemies and friends the
same whom the Roman people held as such, and that
they would order war declared on Antiochus and the
Aetolians. Auxiliaries also, as Quinctius advised,
five hundred soldiers to Chalcis and five hundred to
Piraeus, were at once sent. For there was at Athens
a situation not much different from a rebellion, since
some people, from the hope of bribes, were trying to
win by money the venal multitude over to the side
of Antiochus, until Quinctius was summoned by those
who were of the Roman faction, and on the accusation
of a certain Leon, Apollodorus, the author of the
sedition, was convicted and driven into exile.

And the Achaeans indeed gave the ambassadors
an unsympathetic answer to take back to the king;
the Boeotians made no positive response: when
Antiochus should have come to Boeotia, then, they
said, they would consider what course of action they
should adopt.

When Antiochus heard that garrisons had been
sent to Chalcis by both the Achaeans and King
Eumenes, he thought that his men should make haste
to anticipate them and if possible meet them on their
arrival, and he sent Menippus with about three
thousand soldiers and Polyxenidas with the entire
fleet, and a few days later he too led six thousand of
his own troops and some few of the Aetolians from
such forces as could be mustered on short notice
at Lamia. The five hundred Achaeans and a
small force sent by King Eumenes, with Xenoclides
of Chalcis as their leader, the roads being not yet
closed, crossed the Euripus in safety and arrived in
Chalcis; the Roman soldiers,[1] these too about five

A.U.C.
562

milites, quingenti ferme et ipsi, cum iam Menippus
castra ante Salganea ad Hermaeum, qua transitus ex
Boeotia in Euboeam insulam est, haberet, venerunt.
10 Micythio erat cum iis, legatus ab Chalcide ad Quinctium ad id ipsum praesidium petendum missus.
11 Qui, postquam ab hostibus obsessas fauces vidit,
omisso ad Aulidem itinere Delium convertit, ut inde
in Euboeam transmissurus.

LI. Templum est Apollinis Delium, imminens
mari; quinque milia passuum ab Tanagra abest;
minus quattuor milium inde [1] in proxima Euboeae
2 est mari traiectus. Ubi et in fano lucoque ea
religione et eo iure sancto, quo sunt templa, quae [2]
asyla Graeci appellant, et nondum aut indicto bello
aut ita commisso, ut strictos gladios aut sanguinem
3 usquam factum audissent, cum per magnum otium
milites alii ad spectaculum templi lucique versi, alii
in littore inermes vagarentur, magna pars per agros
4 lignatum pabulatumque dilapsa esset, repente
Menippus palatos passim adgressus cecidit,[3] ad
quinquaginta vivos cepit; perpauci [4] effugerunt, in
quibus Micythio parva oneraria nave exceptus.
5 Ea res Quinctio Romanisque sicut iactura militum
molesta, ita ad ius inferendi Antiocho belli adiecisse

---

[1] quattuor milium inde *ed. Frobeniana* 1531 : IIII inde
B : quattuor inde milium ⟨ς⟩.
[2] quo sunt templa quae *ed. Frobeniana* 1531 : quoque sunt
templa *B*.
[3] cecidit *edd. vett.* : eos cecidit *B* : CCC cecidit *Madvig* :
locum mendosum esse vidit Crévier.
[4] perpauci ⟨ς⟩ : pauci *B*.

---

[1] Rome had not formally declared war, although the
Achaeans had done so (comparing 1, 2 and 5 above). Whether
the presence of these soldiers here on this errand constituted
a tacit recognition that a state of war existed is debatable.

hundred in number, arrived when Menippus already had his camp before Salganeus near the Hermaeum, where there is a crossing from Boeotia to the island of Euboea. Micythio was with them, sent from Chalcis to Quinctius to request that very garrison. When he saw that the pass was held by the enemy, he abandoned the march to Aulis and turned toward Delium, planning to cross from there to Euboea.

LI. Delium is a temple of Apollo, overlooking the sea; it is five miles away from Tanagra; the crossing by sea from there to the nearest parts of Euboea is less than four miles. Not only were they in a shrine and sacred grove, of so religious a character, and under the law of sanctuary which protects those temples which the Greeks call "asylums," but also the war had as yet been neither declared [1] nor brought to such an issue that they had seen swords drawn or blood shed anywhere, while the soldiers were wandering around completely at ease, some going to see the temple and the grove, some strolling along the shore unarmed, and a great part scattering through the country in quest of wood and forage; suddenly Menippus fell upon them as they straggled here and there and slew them,[2] and captured about fifty alive; a very few got away, among them Micythio, who was picked up by a small trading-vessel. Just as the loss of the soldiers was annoying to Quinctius and the Romans, so too the affair seemed to have given some further justification for

---

[2] A numeral has dropped out of the text. Some editors supply *trecentos*, to leave some survivors (in addition to the fifty prisoners and the "very few" mentioned in the next clause) to garrison the fort mentioned in sect. 7 below.

LIVY

6 aliquantum videbatur. Antiochus admoto ad Aulidem exercitu, cum rursus oratores partim ex suis
partim Aetolos Chalcidem misisset, qui eadem illa
quae nuper cum minis gravioribus agerent, nequiquam contra Micythione et Xenoclide tendentibus
7 facile tenuit ut portae sibi aperirentur. Qui Romanae
partis erant sub adventum regis urbe excesserunt.
Achaeorum et Eumenis milites Salganea tenebant,
et in Euripo castellum Romani milites pauci custodiae
8 causa loci[1] communiebant. Salganea Menippus,
rex ipse castellum Euripi oppugnare est adortus.
Priores Achaei et Eumenis milites pacti ut sine
fraude liceret abire, praesidio excesserunt; pertina-
9 cius Romani Euripum tuebantur. Hi quoque tamen,[2]
cum terra marique obsiderentur et iam machinas
tormentaque adportari viderent, non tulere obsidio-
10 nem. Cum id, quod caput erat Euboeae, teneret
rex, ne ceterae quidem insulae eius urbes imperium
abnuerunt; magnoque principio sibi orsus bellum
videbatur, quod tanta insula et tot opportunae urbes
in suam dicionem venissent.

---

[1] loci *ed. Frobeniana* 1535 : locum *Bϛ*.
[2] tamen *ed. Frobeniana* 1535 : iam *Bϛ*.

declaring war on Antiochus. Antiochus moved his B.C. 192 army up to Aulis, and when he had again sent ambassadors to Chalcis, some of his own people and some Aetolians, who urged in more threatening language the same course they had recently advised, although Micythio and Xenoclides vainly strove against it, he easily gained his point that the gates should be opened to him. Those of the Roman party left the city at the approach of the king. The soldiers of the Achaeans and Eumenes held Salganeus, and on the Euripus a few Roman soldiers built a fort to guard the place. Menippus attacked Salganeus, the king himself began to attack the fort on the Euripus. The Achaeans and the soldiers of Eumenes were the first to bargain that they be allowed to depart under safeguard and left their post; with greater stubbornness the Romans tried to hold the Euripus. Nevertheless, even they, when they were besieged by land and sea and saw the engines and artillery being moved forward, did not withstand the siege. Since the king held this, which was the chief city of Euboea, the other cities of the island did not disobey his orders, and he seemed to himself to have made an important start to the war in the fact that so great an island and so many well-situated cities had come under his sway.

LIBRI XXXV PERIOCHA

P. Scipio Africanus legatus ad Antiochum missus Ephesi cum Hannibale, qui se Antiocho adiunxerat, collocutus est ut, si fieri posset, metum ei quem ex populo Romano conceperat eximeret. Inter alia cum quaereret quem fuisse maximum imperatorem Hannibal crederet, respondit Alexandrum, Macedonum regem, quod parva manu innumerabiles exercitus fudisset quodque ultimas oras, quas visere supra spem humanam esset, peragrasset. Quaerenti deinde quem secundum poneret, Pyrrhum, inquit, castra metari primum docuisse, ad hoc neminem loca elegantius cepisse, praesidia disposuisse. Exsequenti quem tertium diceret, semet ipsum dixit. Ridens Scipio : " Quidnam tu diceres " inquit " si me vicisses ? " " Tunc vero me " inquit " et ante Alexandrum et ante Pyrrhum et ante alios posuissem." Inter alia prodigia quae plurima fuisse traduntur, bovem Cn. Domitii consulis locutam " Roma, cave tibi " refertur. Nabis, Lacedaemoniorum tyrannus, incitatus ab Aetolis, qui et Philippum et Antiochum ad inferendum bellum populo Romano sollicitabant,[1] a populo Romano descivit, sed bello [2] adversus Philopoemenen, Achaeorum praetorem, gesto ab Aetolis interfectus est. Aetoli quoque ab amicitia populi Romani defecerunt. Cum societate iuncta Antiochus, Syriae rex, bellum Graeciae intulisset, complures urbes occupavit, inter quas Chalcidem et totam Euboeam. Res praeterea in Liguribus gestas et adparatum belli ab Antiocho continet.

[1] sollicitabant *cd. princeps* : sollicitabat *codd.*
[2] descivit sed bello *Rossbach* : desciuisse et bellum *NP.*

SUMMARY OF BOOK XXXV

Publius Scipio Africanus, sent on an embassy to Antiochus, at Ephesus conversed with Hannibal, who had associated himself with Antiochus, in order that, if it were possible, he should take from him the fear which he felt of the Roman people. Among other things, when he asked whom Hannibal considered the greatest general, he named Alexander, king of the Macedonians, because with a small force he had defeated armies uncountable and because he had traversed the farthest countries, to see which was beyond human hopes. When Scipio asked whom he ranked second, he said that Pyrrhus had been the first to teach the art of castrametation, and besides no one had chosen his ground or placed his troops more skilfully. Continuing as to whom he would place third, he named himself there. Scipio then asked with a smile, " What would you say if you had defeated me ? " " Then, in truth," he replied, " I should have ranked myself ahead of Alexander, ahead of Pyrrhus and ahead of all other generals." Among other prodigies, which are reported to have been very numerous, it is said that a cow belonging to Gnaeus Domitius exclaimed, " Rome, for thyself beware." Nabis, tyrant of the Spartans, provoked by the Aetolians, who were inciting both Philip and Antiochus to make war upon the Roman people, rebelled against the Roman people, but waging war against Philopoemen, the chief of the Achaeans, was killed by the Aetolians. The Aetolians also abandoned the friendship of the Roman people. Antiochus, when he had joined in alliance with them and had begun war in Greece, occupied several cities, among them Chalcis and all Euboea. The book contains in addition the narrative of events among the Ligures and the preparations of Antiochus for war.

151

BOOK XXXVI

LIBER XXXVI

I. P. CORNELIUM CN. filium Scipionem et
M'. Acilium Glabrionem consules inito magistratu
2 patres, priusquam de provinciis agerent, res divinas
facere maioribus hostiis iusserunt in omnibus fanis,
in quibus lectisternium maiorem partem anni fieri
solet, precarique, quod senatus de novo bello in
animo haberet, ut ea res senatui populoque Romano
3 bene atque feliciter eveniret. Ea omnia sacrificia
laeta fuerunt, primisque hostiis perlitatum est, et ita
haruspices responderunt, eo bello terminos populi
Romani propagari, victoriam ac triumphum ostendi.
4 Haec cum renuntiata essent, solutis religione animis
5 patres rogationem ad populum ferri iusserunt, vellent
iuberentne cum Antiocho rege, quique eius sectam
secuti essent, bellum iniri; si ea perlata rogatio esset,
tum, si ita videretur consulibus, rem integram ad
6 senatum referrent. P. Cornelius eam rogationem
pertulit; tum senatus decrevit, ut consules Italiam

---

[1] For their election cf. XXXV. xxiv. 5.

[2] The *lectisternium* was a festival at which the images of
the gods were exposed on couches (hence *lecti-*) on the streets
and were served with food.

[3] For the formula cf. XXXI. v. 4.

[4] The entrails of the victims were inspected; if the first
animal sacrificed did not yield a favourable result the ceremony was repeated until good omens were secured.

[5] For the formula cf. XXXI. vi. 1.

BOOK XXXVI

I. PUBLIUS CORNELIUS SCIPIO, the son of Gnaeus, B.C. 191 and Manius Acilius Glabrio [1] were inaugurated consuls, and were directed by the Fathers, before they took up the question of provinces, to perform sacrifices with full-grown victims at all the shrines at which the *lectisternium* [2] was customarily celebrated throughout the greater part of the year, and to offer prayer that what the senate had in mind regarding the new war might turn out well and successfully for the senate and the Roman people.[3] All these sacrifices were favourable and good omens were obtained from the first victims,[4] and the interpretation of the *haruspices* was this, that in this war the boundaries of the Roman people were being enlarged and that victory and a triumph were foreshadowed. When this had been reported, the Fathers, their minds freed of religious scruples, directed that the question be proposed to the assembly, whether they wished and ordered [5] war to be entered upon with King Antiochus and those who had followed his path; [6] if this motion should be adopted, then, if the consuls saw fit, they should lay the whole question before the senate. Publius Cornelius carried the motion; the senate then decreed that the consuls should cast lots for the

---

[6] Cf. XXXV. xlix. 5; the alliterative phrase has a half-proverbial sound.

LIVY

et Graeciam provincias sortirentur; cui Graecia
evenisset, ut praeter eum numerum militum, quem
L. Quinctius consul in eam provinciam ex auctoritate
7 senatus scripsisset imperassetve,[1] ut eum exercitum
acciperet,[2] quem M. Baebius praetor anno priore ex
8 senatus consulto in Macedoniam traiecisset; et extra
Italiam permissum ut, si res postulasset, auxilia ab
sociis ne supra quinque milium numerum acciperet.
L. Quinctium superioris anni consulem legari ad id
9 bellum placuit. Alter consul, cui Italia provincia
evenisset, cum Bois iussus bellum gerere utro exercitu
mallet ex duobus quos superiores consules habuissent,
alterum ut mitteret Romam, eaeque urbanae legiones
essent paratae quo senatus censuisset.

II. His ita in senatu, incerto[3] ad id, quae cuiusque[4]
provincia foret, decretis, tum demum sortiri consules
placuit. Acilio Graecia, Cornelio Italia evenit.
2 Certa deinde sorte senatus consultum factum est,
quod populus Romanus eo tempore duellum iussisset

---

[1] imperassetue ut ⟂ : imperasset uelut B.
[2] acciperet ed. Moguntina 1518 : acciperet et B.
[3] incerto ad Koch : ad B.
[4] quae cuiusque Ruperti : cuius B : quod cuius ⟂.

---

[1] In XXXV. xli. 3 one province was left undetermined;
the conduct of the war against Antiochus is now specifically
named as that province, though the designation "Greece"
is somewhat vague. (Livy's method separates events which
probably were close together in time. In XXXV. xxiv. the
imminence of the war demanded an early election; in XXXV.
xli. the question of the provinces was under consideration, but
the decision is reported only here.)
[2] Cf. XXXV. xli. 5.   [3] Cf. XXXV. xxiv. 7.
[4] Nothing more is heard of this proposal, and in xvii. 1
two other *legati* are mentioned. It has been reported (in
XXXV. xxiii. 5) that Titus Quinctius was one of five *legati*

provinces of Italy and Greece[1]; the one to whom B.C. 191
Greece should be allotted was instructed, in addition
to that number of troops which the consul Lucius
Quinctius had enlisted or levied for service in that
province in accordance with the action of the senate,[2]
to take over the army which Marcus Baebius[3] the
praetor had the year before transported to Macedonia
with the authorization of the senate; he was permitted also, if the situation required it, to accept from
the allies outside of Italy for auxiliaries not to exceed
five thousand men. It was the senate's pleasure that
Lucius Quinctius, the consul of the preceding year,
should be taken to this war as a lieutenant.[4] The
other consul, to whom Italy should have fallen as a
province, was ordered to carry on war with the Boii,
using whichever he preferred of the two armies which
the preceding consuls had had, and to send the other
to Rome, and that these, as reserve legions,[5] should
be ready to move wherever the senate should direct.

II. These decrees having been enacted in the
senate, and it being up to this time uncertain which
province would be assigned to which consul, it was
then at length decided that the consuls should cast
lots. To Acilius fell Greece, to Cornelius Italy.
The drawing being concluded, a decree of the senate
was then passed that, since the Roman people had

sent to Greece to exercise *auctoritas*, and Plutarch (*Flamininus*
xvii) speaks of him as legatus to Acilius. It is therefore
probable that the sources confused the two Quinctii and that
thus the tradition came into existence that one of them had
been *legatus* to Acilius.

[5] The *urbanae legiones* were normally new troops. The
drafts for the year had been heavy, and, since Minucius also
was in Gaul (XXXV. xx. 6), the forces there seemed sufficient.
This gave Rome a mobile reserve of veterans.

esse cum rege Antiocho, quique sub imperio eius
essent, ut eius rei causa supplicationem imperarent
consules, utique M'. Acilius consul ludos magnos Iovi
3 voveret et dona ad omnia pulvinaria. Id votum in
haec verba praeeunte P. Licinio pontifice maximo
consul nuncupavit: " Si duellum quod cum rege
Antiocho sumi populus iussit, id ex sententia senatus
4 populique Romani confectum erit, tum tibi, Iuppiter,
populus Romanus ludos magnos dies decem continuos
faciet, donaque ad omnia pulvinaria dabuntur de
5 pecunia, quantam senatus decreverit. Quisquis
magistratus eos ludos quando ubique faxit, hi ludi
recte facti donaque data recte sunto." Supplicatio
inde ab duobus consulibus edicta per biduum fuit.
6 Consulibus sortitis provincias extemplo et praetores
sortiti sunt. M. Iunio Bruto iurisdictio utraque
evenit, A. Cornelio Mammulae Brutti, M. Aemilio
Lepido Sicilia, L. Oppio Salinatori Sardinia, C. Livio
Salinatori classis, L. Aemilio Paulo Hispania ulterior.
7 His ita exercitus decreti: A. Cornelio novi milites,
conscripti priore anno ex senatus consulto a L.
Quinctio consule, dati sunt, iussusque tueri omnem
8 oram circa Tarentum Brundisiumque. L. Aemilio
Paulo in ulteriorem Hispaniam, praeter eum exercitum quem a M. Fulvio proconsule accepturus esset,

---

[1] The archaic form *duellum* is especially appropriate to
such formulae.
[2] Cf. IV. xxvii. 1.
[3] The selection of these praetorian provinces was reported
at XXXV. xli. 6.   [4] Cf. XXXV. xli. 7.

at that time ordered that there be war [1] with King B.C. 191
Antiochus and those who were under his authority,
the consuls should proclaim a period of prayer for
the success of this undertaking, and that the consul
Manius Acilius should vow the great games [2] to Jupiter
and gifts at all the banquet-tables of the gods. This
vow, at the dictation of Publius Licinius the high
priest, the consul made in the following form: " If
the war which the people has ordered to be undertaken with King Antiochus shall have been finished
to the satisfaction of the senate and the Roman
people, then in your honour, Jupiter, the Roman
people will perform the Great Games for ten consecu-
tive days and gifts will be offered at all the banquet-
tables, of whatever value the senate shall determine.
Whatever magistrate shall celebrate these games,
at whatever time and place, let these games be
regarded as duly celebrated and the gifts as duly
offered." Then the period of prayer was proclaimed
by both consuls, to continue for two days.

The consuls having drawn for their provinces, the
praetors too at once cast lots. Marcus Junius
Brutus received the two jurisdictions, Aulus Cornelius
Mammula the Brutti, Marcus Aemilius Lepidus
Sicily, Lucius Oppius Salinator Sardinia, Gaius
Livius Salinator the fleet, Lucius Aemilius Paulus
Farther Spain.[3] Troops were assigned to them thus:
to Aulus Cornelius were given the new troops raised
the year before by Lucius Quinctius the consul
under the decree of the senate,[4] and he was ordered
to defend the whole coast in the vicinity of Tarentum
and Brundisium. To Lucius Aemilius Paulus, for
service in Farther Spain, authority was given to
raise, in addition to the army which he was to take

LIVY

decretum est ut novorum militum tria milia duceret
et trecentos equites, ita ut in iis duae partes socium
Latini nominis, tertia civium Romanorum esset.
9 Idem supplementi ad C. Flaminium, cui imperium
prorogabatur, in Hispaniam citeriorem[1] est missum.
10 M. Aemilius Lepidus ab L. Valerio, cui successurus
esset, simul provinciam exercitumque accipere iussus;
11 L. Valerium, si ita videretur, pro praetore in provincia
retinere et provinciam ita dividere ut una ab Agri-
gento ad Pachynum esset, altera a Pachyno Tyndare-
um; eam[2] maritimam oram L. Valerius viginti
12 navibus longis custodiret. Eidem praetori mandatum ut duas decumas frumenti exigeret; id ad
mare comportandum devehendumque in Graeciam
13 curaret. Idem L. Oppio de alteris decumis exigendis
in Sardinia imperatum; ceterum non in Graeciam
14 sed Romam id frumentum portari placere. C. Livius
praetor, cui classis evenerat, triginta navibus paratis
traicere in Graeciam primo quoque tempore iussus,
15 et ab Atilio naves accipere. Veteres naves, quae in
navalibus erant, ut reficeret et armaret, M. Iunio
praetori negotium datum est, et in[3] eam classem
socios navales libertinos legeret.
   III. Legati terni in Africam ad Carthaginienses
et in[4] Numidiam ad frumentum rogandum quod in

---

[1] citeriorem ς: ulteriorem B.
[2] eam ed. Moguntina 1518: cum B.
[3] et in ed. Frobeniana 1535: in Bς: ut in M.
[4] et in ς: in B.

---

[1] Cf. XXXV. ii.
[2] This arrangement provides for the defence of the vulnerable southern and eastern coasts. Less concern is felt
regarding the interior.

over from Marcus Fulvius the proconsul, three B.C. 191
thousand new infantry and three hundred cavalry,
on this basis, that two-thirds should be allies of the
Latin confederacy and one-third Roman citizens.
The same reinforcement was sent to Gaius Flaminius,[1] whose *imperium* was prolonged, for Nearer
Spain. Marcus Aemilius Lepidus was directed to
take over both province and army from Lucius
Valerius, whom he was to succeed; if he desired, he
should keep Lucius Valerius in the province as
propraetor and should divide the province in such a
way that one part should extend from Agrigentum
to Pachynum, the other from Pachynum to Tyn-
dareus;[2] this coast Lucius Valerius was to guard
with twenty warships. The same praetor was
instructed to requisition two tithes[3] of grain; he
was to see to its collection on the coast and its trans-
portation to Greece. The same order was given to
Lucius Oppius regarding collecting a second tithe in
Sardinia; this grain, however, they wished transported not to Greece but to Rome. Gaius Livius
the praetor, to whom the fleet had been allotted,
was instructed to prepare thirty ships and cross to
Greece at the earliest opportunity and to take over
the fleet from Atilius. The refitting and equipping
of the old ships which were in the yards was assigned
to Marcus Junius the praetor, and the enrolment of
freedmen as naval allies.[4]

III. Commissioners were sent to Africa, three
each to the Carthaginians and to Numidia, to solicit

[3] Sicily and Sardinia paid their tributes on the tithe system,
probably on the basis of the pre-Roman legislation of Hiero.
Rome in such cases probably paid for the second tithe.

[4] Service on the sea was less honourable than service on
land: cf. XXXII. xxiii. 9. Roman citizens were usually exempt.

LIVY

Graeciam portaretur missi, pro quo pretium solveret
populus Romanus.   Adeoque in apparatum curamque
2 eius belli civitas intenta fuit ut P. Cornelius consul
3 ediceret, qui senatores essent quibusque in senatu
sententiam dicere liceret, quique minores magistratus
essent, ne quis eorum longius ab urbe Roma abiret
quam unde eo die redire posset, neve uno tempore
4 quinque senatores ab urbe Roma abessent. In
comparanda impigre classe C. Livium praetorem
contentio orta cum colonis maritimis paulisper
5 tenuit. Nam cum cogerentur in classem, tribunos
plebi appellarunt; ab iis ad senatum reiecti sunt.
Senatus ita ut ad unum omnes consentirent, decrevit
6 vacationem rei navalis eis colonis non esse. Ostia
et Fregenae et Castrum Novum et Pyrgi et Antium
et Tarracina et Minturnae et Sinuessa fuerunt, quae
7 cum praetore de vacatione certarunt.[1]   Consul deinde
M'. Acilius ex senatus consulto ad collegium fetialium
rettulit, ipsine utique regi Antiocho indiceretur
bellum, an satis esset ad praesidium aliquod eius
8 nuntiari,[2] et num Aetolis quoque separatim indici
iuberent bellum, et num prius societas et amicitia
eis [3] renuntianda esset quam bellum indicendum.
9 Fetiales responderunt iam ante sese, cum de Philippo

----

[1] certarunt ς : certarent B.
[2] nuntiari *Kreyssig* : nuntiaret B : nuntiaretur M.
[3] et amicitia eis ς : eis et amicitia B.

----

[1] Persons who had held the offices which conferred eligibility
to sit in the senate but had not yet been formally admitted
by the censors were granted in the interim the *ius sententiam
dicendi.*
[2] Here, as in XXXV. xxxiii. 4, it is assumed that the alliance
with the Aetolians was in effect, even though there is no mention of any formal renewal after the war with Philip.   There

grain to be shipped to Greece, for which the Roman B.C. 191
people would pay. And so absorbed was the state
in the preparation and provision for this war that
Publius Cornelius the consul issued an edict to the
effect that, of those who were senators and those who
had the right to vote in the senate [1] and those who
held the lesser offices, no one should be so far distant
from the city of Rome that he could not return the
same day, and that five senators should not be away
from Rome at one time. In his zealous collection
of a fleet Gaius Livius was delayed for a while by a
dispute which arose with the colonists on the coast.
For when they were drafted for naval service they
appealed to the tribunes of the people; by them they
were referred to the senate. With such unanimity
that all the members to a man agreed, the senate
voted that no exemptions from naval service should
be granted to these colonists. Ostia, Fregenae, Castrum Novum, Pyrgi, Antium, Terracina, Minturnae
and Sinuessa were the colonies which disputed with
the praetor over exemptions. Then the consul
Manius Acilius, with the authorization of the senate,
laid the question before the college of fetials whether
the declaration of war should be delivered to King
Antiochus himself directly or whether it sufficed that
it be proclaimed at some of his military stations;
and also whether they ordered the war to be formally
announced to the Aetolians independently, and
whether the alliance and friendship with them
should be formally broken off before the declaration
of war.[2] The fetials replied that they had already

is also no record of any declaration of war upon the Aetolians,
except as they were included among the partisans of Antiochus
(i. 5 above).

A.U.C.
563

consulerentur, decrevisse nihil referre, ipsi coram an
10 ad praesidium nuntiaretur; amicitiam renuntiatam
videri, cum legatis totiens repetentibus res nec reddi
11 nec satisfieri aequum censuissent; Aetolos ultro sibi
bellum indixisse, cum Demetriadem, sociorum urbem,
12 per vim occupassent, Chalcidem terra marique
oppugnatum issent, regem Antiochum in Europam
ad bellum populo Romano inferendum traduxissent,
13 Omnibus iam satis comparatis M'. Acilius consul
edixit ut quos L. Quinctius milites conscripsisset et
quos sociis nominique Latino imperasset, quos secum
in provinciam ire oporteret, et tribuni militum
legionis primae et tertiae, ut ii omnes [1] Brundisium
14 idibus Mais convenirent.[2] Ipse a. d. quintum nonas
Maias paludatus urbe egressus est. Per eosdem
dies et praetores in provincias profecti sunt.

IV. Sub idem tempus legati ab duobus regibus,
Philippo et Ptolomaeo, Aegypti rege, Romam
venerunt, Philippo pollicente ad bellum auxilia et

---

[1] ut ii omnes *Weissenborn* : uti homines *B* : uti omnes ς.
[2] conuenirent ς : conuenissent *B*.

---

[1] Cf. XXXI. viii. 3.
[2] The etiquette of declarations of war was a special function
of the fetials, and the importance of proper ceremonial was
very great, not only because of the Roman fondness for punc-
tiliousness but because of their desire to have justice and the
gods on their side. The traditional form of the fetial ritual—
probably little changed in later times—is described by Livy
in I. xxxii; it put especial stress on the demand for restitution
(*res repetere*) of stolen property, as would be natural in early
times. The same phraseology is used here : the immediate
cause for complaint on Rome's part was Antiochus' attempt
to recover the Greek cities on the Asian coast (XXXV. xvi. 3).
The "restitution" demanded of him was the abandonment of
the attempt to take away their liberties. The Aetolians were
involved with him in this offence.

earlier decided, when they were consulted regarding B.C. 191
Philip,[1] that it made no difference whether the
declaration was delivered to him in person or at a
military post; the friendship seemed to be already
broken off since they had voted that restitution had
not been made after ambassadors had so often demanded it nor fair satisfaction given;[2] the Aetolians
had taken the initiative in declaring war upon them
when they had seized Demetrias, a city belonging
to the allies, by violence, had proceeded to invest
Chalcis by land and sea, and had invited King
Antiochus to Europe to make war upon the Roman
people.[3] All arrangements having been satisfactorily
made, the consul Manius Acilius issued an edict to
the soldiers whom Lucius Quinctius had enlisted and
those whom he had requisitioned from the allies of
the Latin confederacy, whom he was to take with
him to his province, and to the military tribunes [4] of
the first and the third legions, that they should all
assemble at Brundisium on the Ides of May. He
himself left the City in uniform on the fifth day
before the Nones of May. About the same time
the praetors too set out for their provinces.

IV. About the same time ambassadors arrived in
Rome from two kings, Philip and Ptolemy,[5] King
of Egypt; Philip promised aid and money and grain

---

[3] These actions on the part of the Aetolians were good
enough causes for war, even though they were not, literally,
the specific offences contemplated by the fetial institution.
Possibly these overt acts justified the Romans in omitting
a formal declaration of war upon them.

[4] The military tribunes were elected by the assembly
(XXVII. xxxvi. 14).

[5] Ptolemy was the son-in-law of Antiochus (XXXV. xiii. 4).

LIVY

2 pecuniam et frumentum; ab Ptolomaeo etiam mille
pondo auri, viginti milia[1] pondo argenti adlata.
3 Nihil eius acceptum; gratiae regibus actae; et cum
uterque se cum omnibus copiis in Aetoliam venturum
belloque interfuturum polliceretur, Ptolomaeo id
4 remissum; Philippi legatis responsum gratum eum
senatui populoque Romano facturum, si M'. Acilio
5 consuli non defuisset. Item ab Carthaginiensibus
et Masinissa rege legati venerunt. Carthaginienses
tritici modium D milia,[2] hordei quingenta ad exercitum, dimidium eius Romam apportaturos polliciti;
6 id ut ab se munus Romani acciperent, petere sese, et
7 classem suo[3] sumptu comparaturos, et stipendium,
quod pluribus pensionibus in multos annos deberent,
8 praesens omne daturos; Masinissae legati quingenta
milia modium tritici, trecenta hordei ad exercitum
in Graeciam, Romam trecenta milia modium[4] tritici,
ducenta quinquaginta hordei, equites quingentos,
elephantos viginti regem ad M'. Acilium consulem
9 missurum. De frumento utrisque responsum, ita
usurum eo populum Romanum, si pretium acciperent;
de classe Carthaginiensibus remissum, praeterquam

---

[1] viginti milia *ed. Frobeniana* 1535 : .XX. *B.*
[2] modium .D. milia *M. Müller* : modium .D. *B* : modia
mille *M* : modium mille ⴝ.
[3] suo *Duker* : suorum suo *B.*
[4] trecenta milia modium ⴝ : .CCC. modium *B* : trecenta
modia *M.*

---

[1] The quantity is doubtful (see the critical note). I have
followed what seems to be the most trustworthy authority.
[2] The treaty of peace with Carthage provided for annual
payments of tribute for fifty years (XXX. xxxvii. 5; Polybius
XV. xviii). The Carthaginians were prepared to pay at

for the war; from Ptolemy also was brought the B.C. 191 sum of a thousand pounds of gold and twenty thousand pounds of silver. None of these gifts was accepted; thanks were expressed to the kings, and when each of them promised to come with all his forces to Aetolia and participate in the war, Ptolemy was excused from this; to the ambassadors of Philip the answer was given that it would be acceptable to the senate and the Roman people if he did not fail the consul Manius Acilius. Ambassadors also came from the Carthaginians and King Masinissa. The Carthaginians promised five hundred [1] thousand *modii* of wheat and five hundred thousand *modii* of barley, and offered to transport half of it to Rome; they begged the Romans to accept it as a gift from them and they said that they would prepare a fleet at their own expense and would pay at once in a lump sum the tribute which they owed in successive instalments over a term of years.[2] The ambassadors of Masinissa promised that the king would send five hundred thousand *modii* of wheat and three hundred thousand of barley to Greece for the army, three hundred thousand *modii* of wheat and two hundred fifty thousand of barley to Rome, and five hundred cavalry and twenty elephants to Manius Acilius the consul. Regarding the grain, the answer was given both that the Roman people would use the grain if they would accept pay for it; the Carthaginians were released from their promise about the fleet, except with respect to the ships which they owed under

once the entire balance. The financial reforms introduced by Hannibal (XXXIII. xlvii. 1-2) had apparently been effective.

LIVY

si quid navium ex foedere deberent; de pecunia item responsum, nullam ante diem accepturos.

V. Cum haec Romae agebantur, Chalcide Antiochus, ne cessaret per hibernorum tempus, partim ipse sollicitabat civitatium animos mittendis legatis, partim ultro ad eum veniebant, sicut Epirotae communi gentis consensu et Elei[1] e Peloponneso venerunt.
2 Elei auxilium adversus Achaeos petebant, quos post bellum non ex sua sententia indictum Antiocho primum civitati suae arma illaturos credebant.[2]
3 Mille iis pedites cum duce Cretensi Euphane sunt missi. Epirotarum legatio erat minime in partem ullam liberi aut simplicis animi; apud regem gratiam initam volebant cum eo, ut caverent, ne quid
4 offenderent Romanos. Petebant enim ne se temere in causam deduceret, expositos adversus Italiam pro omni Graecia et primos impetus Romanorum excep-
5 turos; sed si ipse posset terrestribus navalibusque copiis praesidere Epiro, cupide eum omnes Epirotas et urbibus et portibus suis accepturos; si id non

---

[1] et Elei *Sabellicus* : ex pelei *B* : et pelei ς.
[2] credebant *ed. Parmensis* 1480 : *om. B.*

---

[1] The sources quoted in the preceding note say nothing of any obligation to furnish ships to Rome, aside from the surrender of vessels on hand at the close of the war. However, we see from xliv. 5 below that there were Carthaginian ships in the fleet of Livius in the east.
[2] Editors are disagreed as to the interpretation of this somewhat ungracious reply. Some say that Rome feared to lose her hold on Carthage; it is pleasanter to believe with others that Rome wanted to give the impression to Carthage as to Philip, both of whom seem exceedingly generous, that she was able with her own resources to meet even an emergency of this magnitude. It would be interesting to know whether

the treaty;[1] as to the money also, the reply was B.C. 191
that they would accept none before it was due.[2]

V. While this was going on at Rome, Antiochus
at Chalcis, not to waste the winter in idleness,[3]
sometimes was himself stirring up the minds of the
states by sending embassies, sometimes was receiving
delegations voluntarily sent to him, as, for instance,
the Epirotes, who came with the unanimous approval
of the people, and the men of Elis from the Peloponnesus. The Elei were asking aid against the
Achaeans, who, they thought, would attack their city
first after declaring a war on Antiochus of which the
Elei disapproved.[4] A thousand infantry were sent
to them under command of Euphanes the Cretan.
The embassy of the Epirotes showed no outspoken
and plain inclination to either side; they were
trying to curry favour with the king, meanwhile
avoiding giving any offence to the Romans. For
they asked that he should not heedlessly involve
them in the affair,[5] being placed face to face with
Italy, in the forefront of Greece and fated to receive
the first attacks of the Romans. But if he himself
could stand guard over Epirus with his armies and
fleets, all the Epirotes would eagerly receive him
in cities and harbours alike; if he could not, they

these recent enemies were simply politic or were really as
well-disposed as their offers of help indicates.

[3] Livy now resumes the narrative of events in the east,
interrupted at the end of Book XXXV. The winter referred
to is that of 192–191 B.C.

[4] To judge by other casual references, such as Plutarch
(*Cato* xii) and the hints in XXXV. 1, Greece was in a state of
great unrest at this time, although Livy minimizes the trouble.

[5] Polybius (XX. iii.) is more explicit, defining *causa* as the
war itself.

LIVY

posset, deprecari ne se nudos atque inermes Romano
6 bello obiceret. Hac legatione id agi apparebat, ut
sive, quod magis credebant, abstinuisset Epiro,
integra sibi omnia apud exercitus Romanos essent,
conciliata satis apud regem gratia, quod accepturi
7 fuissent venientem, sive venisset, sic quoque spes
veniae ab Romanis foret, quos non expectato longin-
quo ab se auxilio praesentis viribus succubuissent.
8 Huic tam perplexae legationi quia non satis in
promptu erat quid responderet, legatos se missurum
ad eos dixit qui de iis, quae ad illos seque communiter pertinerent, loquerentur.

VI. In Boeotiam ipse profectus est, causas in
speciem irae adversus Romanos eas quas ante dixi
habentem, Brachyllae necem et bellum a Quinctio
Coroneae propter Romanorum militum caedes illatum,
2 re vera per multa iam saecula publice privatimque
labante egregia quondam disciplina gentis et multorum eo statu, qui diuturnus esse sine mutatione
3 rerum non posset. Obviam effusis undique Boeotiae
principibus Thebas venit. Ibi in concilio gentis,
quamquam et ad Delium impetu in praesidium

---

[1] One can hardly blame the Epirotes for trying to guard
themselves against any contingency. Apollonia, the usual
port of debarkation of the Romans, lay just to the north, and
Roman armies would soon be passing through their country
(we know little of the whereabouts of the army brought over
by Baebius). On the other hand, if the strength of Antiochus
in any degree equalled the large forces promised by him, he
would probably not hesitate to cut loose from his bases and
try to locate the theatre of operations on the west coast.

[2] Cf. XXXV. xlvii. 3 and the note.

[3] Livy probably has in mind the period of Theban greatness
under Pelopidas and Epaminondas.

[4] Polybius (XX. iv. ff.) gives a more depressing picture of
conditions in Boeotia. As the Aetolians had seen (XXXV.

begged that he should not make them, naked and B.C. 191
unarmed, bear the brunt of the Roman war. It was
clear that the object of the embassy was that either,
if, as they rather believed, he kept away from Epirus,
they might not be committed to anything in the eyes
of the Roman armies, though they had well established their position with the king, since they had
been ready to receive him if he came, or, if he did
come, that thus there would be the hope of pardon
from the Romans because, not expecting from them
aid which was so far away, they had yielded to the
might of the king who was so close at hand.[1] Since
there was no sufficiently obvious reply to such an
equivocal proposal, he said that he would send
ambassadors to them to confer with them concerning
the questions which pertained to them and himself
alike.

VI. He himself proceeded to Boeotia, which had
as apparent causes for anger at the Romans those
occurrences which I mentioned before,[2] the murder
of Brachyllas and the campaign carried on by
Quinctius at Coronea by reason of the slaughtering
of the Roman soldiers, while in fact the discipline[3]
in which that people was once eminent, in public
and private, had for many years now been degenerat-
ing, and the condition of many was such that it could
not last without a change of circumstances.[4] With
the chiefs of Boeotia coming out in crowds to meet
him, he arrived in Thebes. There in the council of
the people, although he had, both by the attack
made on the Roman garrison at Delium[5] and by the

xxxiv. 3), economic distress prepared many for any sort of
political change : cf. XLII. xxx. 4.

[5] Cf. XXXV. li.

LIVY

Romanum facto et ad Chalcidem commiserat nec
parvis nec dubiis principiis bellum, tamen eandem
4 orationem est exorsus,[1] qua in colloquio primo ad
Chalcidem quaque per legatos in concilio Achaeorum
usus erat, ut amicitiam secum institui,[2] non bellum
indici Romanis postularet. Neminem quid ageretur
5 fallebat; decretum tamen sub leni verborum praetextu[3] pro rege adversus Romanos factum est.
6 Hac quoque gente adiuncta Chalcidem regressus,
praemissis inde litteris, ut Demetriadem convenirent
principes Aetolorum, cum quibus de summa rerum
deliberaret, navibus eo ad diem indictum concilio
7 venit. Et Amynander, accitus ad consultandum ex
Athamania, et Hannibal Poenus, iam diu non adhi-
8 bitus, interfuit ei consilio. Consultatum de Thessalorum gente est, quorum omnibus qui aderant
9 voluntas temptanda videbatur. In eo modo diversae
sententiae erant, quod alii extemplo agendum, alii
ex hieme, quae tum ferme media erat, differendum in
veris principium, et alii legatos tantummodo mitten-
10 dos, alii[4] cum omnibus copiis eundum censebant
terrendosque metu, si cunctarentur.

VII. Cum circa hanc fere consultationem disceptatio omnis verteretur, Hannibal nominatim

---

[1] est exorsus *Kreyssig* : exorsus *B*.
[2] institui ς : constitui *B*.
[3] praetextu ς : praetexto *B*.
[4] alii ς : et alii *B*.

---

[1] Cf. XXXV. xxxvi. 5 ff.   [2] Cf. XXXV. xlviii. 8–9.
[3] The precise terms of the decree are uncertain : perhaps
it declared Boeotia neutral but lent encouragement to Antiochus.
[4] In XXXV. xix. 7 the reconciliation of Hannibal and Antiochus was described; later the arguments of Thoas (XXXV.
xlii. 6–14) were more effective.

capture of Chalcis, acts which were neither unim- B.C. 191
portant nor uncertain, engaged in war, he nevertheless began the same speech that he had used in
the first conference at Chalcis [1] and that he had
delivered through his delegates [2] in the council of
the Achaeans, to wit, that he asked that they make
a treaty of friendship with him, not that they
declare war on the Romans. No one was deceived
as to what was going on; nevertheless, a decree
was passed, under a cloak of mild verbiage, in
favour of the king and against the Romans.[3]

Having won over this people also, he returned to
Chalcis, sending in advance letters to summon to
Demetrias the chiefs of the Aetolians, with whom
he could take counsel regarding the general policy,
and himself arrived there by boat on the day appointed
for the conference. Amynander also, summoned
from Athamania to take part in the deliberations,
and Hannibal the Carthaginian, who for a long
time past had not been called in,[4] attended the
council. The question for consideration had to do
with the Thessalian people, whose intentions, as all
who were present agreed, should be ascertained.
In the matter of procedure there were different
opinions, some favouring immediate action, others
thinking that they should postpone doing anything
from the winter, which was now half gone, to the
beginning of spring, while some thought that
ambassadors only should be sent and others that he
should go with his entire force and terrorize them
if they hesitated.

VII. Since the whole debate centred practically
on this one question, Hannibal, appealed to by
name for his opinion, turned the king and all who

173

LIVY

interrogatus sententiam in universi belli cogitationem
regem atque eos, qui aderant, tali oratione avertit.
2 " Si ex quo traiecimus in Graeciam, adhibitus essem
in consilium, cum de Euboea deque Achaeis et de [1]
Boeotia agebatur, eandem sententiam dixissem quam
3 hodie cum de Thessalis agitur dicam. Ante omnia
Philippum et Macedonas in societatem belli [2] qua-
4 cumque ratione censeo deducendos esse. Nam quod
ad Euboeam Boeotosque et Thessalos attinet, cui
dubium est quin, ut quibus nullae suae vires sint,
praesentibus adulando semper, quem metum in
consilio habeant, eodem ad impetrandam veniam
5 utantur, simul ac Romanum exercitum in Graecia
viderint, ad consuetum imperium se avertant, nec
iis noxiae futurum sit, quod, cum Romani procul
abessent, vim tuam praesentis exercitusque tui
6 experiri noluerint [3]? Quanto igitur prius potiusque
est Philippum nobis coniungere quam hos? Cui, [4]
si semel in causam descenderit, nihil integri futurum
sit, [5] quique eas vires adferat, quae non accessio
tantum ad Romanum esse bellum, sed per se ipsae
7 nuper sustinere potuerint Romanos. Hoc ego
adiuncto—absit verbo invidia—qui dubitare de
eventu possim, cum, quibus adversus Philippum

[1] et de ς : de B : deque M.
[2] in societatem belli *ed. Frobeniana* 1535 : belli in societatem Bς.
[3] noluerint ς : noluerunt B.
[4] cui *edd. vett.* : qui Bς.
[5] futurum sit ς : futuri sint B.

---

[1] The speech of Hannibal is also reported by Appian (*Syr.*
14), and both versions are probably derived from Polybius.
[2] A *causa integra* was one which left the person concerned
free to choose his course of action. An alliance between

174

were present to the consideration of the war as a
whole, by a speech of the following character: [1]
" If I had been invited to the council from the time
we crossed to Greece, when the question concerned
Euboea or the Achaeans or Boeotia, I should have
expressed the same opinion as to-day when we are
discussing the Thessalians. Before anything else, I
vote that Philip and the Macedonians be drawn, in
any possible way, into a military alliance. For as
to Euboea and the Boeotians and the Thessalians,
who doubts that they, possessing no strength of
their own, are ever fawning upon those who are close
at hand, and will use the same fearfulness which they
display in the council as a means of winning pardon,
and that, as soon as they see the Roman army in
Greece, they will turn back to their accustomed
masters and that they will suffer no harm because,
when the Romans were far away, they were unwilling to test, face to face, the strength of you and
your army? How much greater priority and
preference should we give to allying ourselves with
Philip rather than with them? He, if once he joins
our cause, will have no choice left, [2] and he can
contribute that strength which will be not merely
an additional resource for the Roman war, but one
which by itself alone was able recently to withstand
the Romans. With this reinforcement—may I say
so without offence [3]—how can I doubt the result
when I see that those very men with whose

Philip and Antiochus would at once commit Philip to war
with Rome, and so leave *nihil integri* to him.

[3] The term *invidia* always suggests " casting the evil eye
upon " the person or act involved. Here proud words were
held to provoke the jealousy of the powers above, and
Hannibal is deprecating this *invidia*.

LIVY

8 valuerint Romani, iis nunc fore videam, ut ipsi
oppugnentur? Aetoli, qui Philippum, quod inter
omnes constat, vicerunt, cum Philippo adversus
9 Romanos pugnabunt; Amynander atque Athamanum
gens, quorum secundum Aetolos plurima fuit opera
10 in eo bello, nobiscum stabunt; Philippus tum te
quieto totam molem sustinebat belli; nunc duo
maximi reges Asiae Europaeque viribus adversus
unum populum, ut meam utramque fortunam taceam,
patrum certe aetate ne uni quidem Epirotarum regi
parem (qui quid[1] tandem erat[2] vobiscum com-
11 paratus?) geretis bellum. Quae igitur res mihi
fiduciam praebet coniungi nobis Philippum posse?
Una, communis utilitas, quae societatis maximum
12 vinculum est; altera, auctores vos Aetoli. Vester
enim legatus hic Thoas inter cetera quae ad excien-
dum in Graeciam Antiochum dicere est solitus, ante
omnia hoc semper affirmavit, fremere Philippum et
aegre pati sub specie pacis leges servitutis sibi
13 impositas. Ille quidem ferae[3] bestiae vinctae aut
clausae et refringere claustra cupienti regis iram
verbis aequabat. Cuius si talis animus est, solvamus
nos eius vincula et claustra refringamus, ut erumpere
14 diu coercitam iram in hostes communes possit. Quod
si nihil eum legatio nostra moverit, at nos, quoniam
nobis eum adiungere non possumus, ne hostibus
15 nostris ille adiungi possit, caveamus. Seleucus filius
tuus Lysimachiae est; qui si eo exercitu quem
secum habet, per Thraciam proxima Macedoniae

---

[1] qui quid *Doujat*: quicquid *B*: quid *M*: quidquid *ς*.
[2] erat *Madvig*: erit *Mς*: om. *B*.
[3] ferae *ed. Frobeniana* 1535: ut ferae *Bς*.

---

[1] In XXXV. xviii. 6 this figure is attributed to Alexander
the Acarnanian.

assistance the Romans prevailed over Philip will B.C. 191 now be overwhelming the Romans themselves? The Aetolians who, as all agree, defeated Philip, will fight with Philip against the Romans; Amynander and the nation of the Athamanes, whose services in that war were the greatest after those of the Aetolians, will stand with us; Philip then, when you were inactive, bore the whole burden of the war; now you, the two mightiest kings of Asia and Europe, will wage war against one people which, not to speak of my own twofold experience, in the time of our fathers at least could not contend even against one king of Epirus—and how could he be compared with you? What cause, then, convinces me that Philip can be allied with us? First, the common profit, which is the firmest bond in an alliance; second, the assurances of you Aetolians. For your representative, Thoas here, among other reasons which he was wont to use to attract Antiochus to Greece, continually made this assertion before all else, that Philip was enraged and that he found it hard to bear the laws of slavery imposed upon him under the guise of peace. Indeed in his speech he likened the king in his wrath to a wild beast chained or shut up and trying to break his bonds.[1] If such is his temper, let us break his chains and tear away his bars, that he may let loose his long-restrained passion upon the common enemy. But if our embassy to him does not move him, let us at least, since we cannot unite him with ourselves, see to it that he does not make common cause with our foes. Your son Seleucus is at Lysimachia; if with that army which he has with him he shall begin to move through Thrace and devastate the adjacent portions of Macedonia, he

A.U.C.
563

16 coeperit depopulari, facile ab auxilio ferendo Romanis Philippum ad sua potissimum tuenda avertet. De Philippo meam sententiam habes; de ratione universi belli quid sentirem, iam ab initio non ignorasti. Quod si tum auditus forem, non in Euboea Chalcidem captam et castellum Euripi expugnatum Romani,[1] sed Etruriam Ligurumque et Galliae Cisalpinae oram bello ardere, et, qui maximus iis

17 terror est, Hannibalem in Italia esse audirent. Nunc quoque accersas censeo omnes navales terrestresque copias; sequantur classem onerariae cum commeatibus; nam hic sicut ad belli munera pauci sumus, sic nimis multi pro inopia commeatuum.

18 Cum omnes tuas contraxeris vires, divisa classe partem Corcyrae in statione habebis, ne transitus

19 Romanis liber ac tutus pateat, partem ad litus Italiae, quod Sardiniam Africamque spectat, traicies; ipse cum omnibus terrestribus copiis in Bullinum agrum

20 procedes; inde Graeciae praesidebis, et speciem Romanis traiecturum te praebens et, si res poposcerit, traiecturus. Haec suadeo, qui ut non omnis peritissimus sim belli, cum Romanis certe bellare bonis

21 malisque meis didici. In quae consilium dedi, in eadem nec infidelem nec segnem operam polliceor. Dii approbent eam sententiam quae tibi optima visa fuerit."

VIII. Haec ferme Hannibalis oratio fuit; quam laudarunt magis in praesentia qui aderant, quam

----

[1] romani ς: romanis B: a romanis M.

----

[1] Bullis (Byllis) was a town on the Illyrian coast not far from Apollonia.

will easily turn Philip from sending aid to the Romans
to the more important task of defending his own
possessions. As to Philip you have my views; even
from the first you have not been ignorant of my
opinion as to the strategy of the war as a whole. If
I had been listened to then, the Romans would not
now be hearing that Chalcis in Euboea was captured
and a fort on the Euripus, but that Etruria and the
coasts of Liguria and Cisalpine Gaul were aflame
with war and—this is what they dread beyond
everything else—that Hannibal is in Italy. Now too
I vote that you summon all your forces on land and
sea; let cargo-boats follow with supplies, for, as we
are few here for the tasks of war, so we are too many
in proportion to our shortage of supplies. When
you have assembled all your strength, you will
divide your fleet, keeping part on guard near Corcyra,
that free and safe passage may not be open to the
Romans, and sending part across to the coast of
Italy which faces Sardinia and Africa; you yourself
will go ahead with all your armies to the territory of
Bullis;[1] thence you will stand guard over Greece
and offer to the Romans the appearance of being
about to cross, and, if the situation shall demand it,
will actually cross. This is the advice I give, I who,
though I am not well versed in every kind of war,
with the Romans at least have learned to fight from
my own successes and failures. For this same
programme which I have advised I promise aid
neither faithless nor reluctant. May the gods
approve that proposal which shall have seemed to
you the best."

VIII. This was in purport the speech of Hannibal;
those who were present applauded it for the moment

LIVY

rebus ipsis exsecuti sunt; nihil enim eorum factum est, nisi quod ad classem copiasque accersendas ex
2 Asia Polyxenidam misit. Legati Larisam ad concilium Thessalorum sunt missi, et Aetolis Amynandroque dies ad conveniendum exercitui Pheras est dictus; eodem et rex cum suis copiis confestim venit.
3 Ubi dum opperitur Amynandrum atque Aetolos, Philippum Megalopolitanum cum duobus milibus hominum ad legenda ossa Macedonum circa Cynos-
4 cephalas, ubi debellatum erat cum Philippo, misit, sive ab ipso, quaerente sibi commendationem ad Macedonum gentem et invidiam regi, quod insepultos milites reliquisset, monitus, sive ab insita regibus vanitate ad consilium specie amplum, re inane animo
5 adiecto. Tumulus est in unum ossibus quae passim strata[1] erant coacervatis factus, qui nullam gratiam ad Macedonas, odium ingens ad Philippum movit.
6 Itaque qui ad id tempus fortunam esset habiturus in consilio, is extemplo ad M. Baebium propraetorem misit, Antiochum in Thessaliam impetum fecisse; si videretur ei, moveret ex hibernis; se obviam processurum, ut, quid agendum esset, consultarent.

IX. Antiocho ad Pheras iam castra habenti, ubi coniunxerant ei se[2] Aetoli et Amynander, legati ab Larisa venerunt quaerentes quod ob factum dic-
2 tumve[3] Thessalorum bello lacesseret eos, simul

---

[1] strata 𝖘 : tracta B.   [2] ei se 𝖘 : eis B.
[3] ob factum dictumue 𝖘 : ob hoc factum dictumque B.

---

[1] For this Philip and his aspirations to the Macedonian throne, see XXXV. xlvii. 5–8. The identity of names introduces unnecessary confusion into the passage.
[2] Philip had decided to await developments before adopting any course of action; his resentment at Antiochus now leads him to join forces with the Romans.

B.C. 191

rather than adopted it in actual decisions; for
nothing of these things was done, save that he sent
Polyxenidas to summon the fleet and troops from
Asia. Ambassadors were sent to Larisa to the
council of the Thessalians, and a day was fixed for
the Aetolians and Amynander to hold the muster of
the army at Pherae; the king also with his troops
came with speed to the same place. While he was
waiting there for Amynander and the Aetolians, he
sent Philip of Megalopolis with two thousand men
to collect the bones of the Macedonians around
Cynoscephalae, where the decisive battle with Philip
was fought, whether he was prompted by Philip of
Megalopolis,[1] who was seeking for himself some
recommendation to the people of the Macedonians
and unpopularity for the king because he had left
his soldiers unburied, or whether, with the native
vanity of kings, he turned his thoughts to a plan
attractive in appearance but useless in fact. A
burial mound was erected by gathering together
the bones which were scattered everywhere, but
among the Macedonians it caused no gratitude and
in King Philip an immense resentment. And so
he, who up to that time had decided to take fortune
as the guide to his policy,[2] at once wrote to Marcus
Baebius the propraetor to say that Antiochus had
invaded Thessaly; if it seemed wise to Baebius he
should move from winter quarters; he himself would
come to meet him to consult what should be done.

IX. While Antiochus was in camp at Pherae,
where the Aetolians and Amynander had joined
him, ambassadors from Larisa came asking for what
deed or word of the Thessalians he was assailing them
with war, and likewise asking that he should with-

LIVY

orantes ut remoto exercitu per legatos, si quid ei
3 videretur, secum disceptaret. Eodem tempore quin
gentos armatos duce Hippolocho Pheras in praesidium
miserunt; ii exclusi aditu, iam omnia itinera obsiden-
4 tibus regiis, Scotusam se receperunt. Legatis
Larisaeorum rex clementer respondit, non belli
faciendi sed tuendae et stabiliendae libertatis
5 Thessalorum causa se Thessaliam intrasse. Similia
his qui cum Pheraeis ageret, missus; cui nullo dato
responso Pheraei ipsi legatum ad regem principem
6 civitatis Pausaniam miserunt. Qui cum haud dis-
similia iis, ut in causa pari, quae pro Chalcidensibus
in colloquio ad Euripi fretum dicta erant, quaedam
7 etiam ferocius egisset, rex etiam atque etiam delibe-
rare eos iussos, ne id consilii caperent, cuius, dum in
futurum nimis cauti et providi essent, extemplo
8 paeniteret, dimisit. Haec renuntiata Pheras legatio
cum esset, ne paulum quidem dubitarunt quin pro
fide erga Romanos, quidquid fors belli tulisset, pate-
9 rentur. Itaque et hi summa ope parabant se ad
urbem defendendam, et rex ab omni parte simul
oppugnare moenia est adgressus et, ut qui satis
10 intellegeret—neque enim dubium erat—in eventu
eius urbis positum esse quam primam adgressus esset,
aut sperni deinde ab universa gente Thessalorum aut
timeri se, omnem undique terrorem obsessis iniecit.

---

[1] Probably the conference reported at XXXV. xxxviii. 8 ff.

draw his army and discuss with them through B.C. 191
ambassadors whatever seemed to him worth considering. At the same time they sent five hundred
armed men under command of Hippolochus as a
garrison for Pherae; they were prevented from
entering, all the roads being now blocked by the
king's forces, and retired to Scotusa. The king responded mildly to the ambassadors of the Larisaeans,
that he had entered Thessaly not to make war but
to defend and assure the liberty of the Thessalians.
A delegate was sent to conduct similar negotiations
with the people of Pherae; giving him no answer,
the Pheraeans themselves sent to the king Pausanias,
their chief magistrate. When he had with a good
deal of vigour presented certain arguments not
unlike those which, in a similar situation, had been
used on behalf of the Chalcidians in the conference
at the strait of Euripus,[1] the king, bidding them
again and again to ponder and not to adopt any
plan of which, while being too cautious and thought-
ful for the future, they would at once repent,
dismissed him. When this mission was reported at
Pherae, they did not even for a brief period doubt
that they should, for the sake of their loyalty to the
Romans, endure whatever the fortune of war might
bring. And so both the Pheraeans were preparing
with all their might to defend their city and the
king was attempting to assault the town from every
side at once, and, since he clearly understood—for
there was no question about it—that it depended
on the fate of this city which he attacked first,
whether he should thenceforth be either scorned or
feared by the whole nation of the Thessalians, he
brought every form of terror to bear from all sides

183

A.U.C.
563

11 Primum impetum oppugnationis satis constanter
sustinuerunt; dein cum multi propugnantes caderent
12 aut vulnerarentur, labare animi coeperunt. Revocat
deinde castigationibus principum ad perseverandum
in proposito, relicto exteriore circulo muri, deficienti-
bus iam copiis in interiorem partem urbis concesserunt cui[1] brevior orbis munitionis circumiectus erat
postremo victi malis, cum timerent, ne vi captis nulla
13 apud victorem venia esset, dediderunt sese. Nihil
deinde[2] moratus rex quattuor milia[3] armatorum
dum recens terror esset, Scotusam misit. Nec ibi
mora deditionis est facta cernentibus Pheraeorum
14 recens exemplum, qui, quod pertinaciter primo
abnuerant, malo domiti tandem fecissent; cum ipsa
urbe Hippolochus Larisaeorumque deditum est
15 praesidium. Dimissi ab rege inviolati omnes, quod
eam rem magni momenti futuram rex ad conciliandos
Larisaeorum animos credebat.

X. Intra decimum diem quam[4] Pheras venerat,
his perfectis Crannonem profectus cum toto exercitu
2 primo adventu cepit. Inde Cierium et Metropolim
et iis circumiecta castella recepit; omniaque iam
regionis eius praeter Atracem et Gyrtonem in
3 potestate erant. Tunc aggredi Larisam constituit
ratus vel terrore ceterarum expugnatarum vel beneficio praesidii dimissi vel exemplo tot civitatium
dedentium sese non ultra in pertinacia mansuros.

---

[1] cui ⵕ : quibus B.
[2] deinde ⵕ : inde B.
[3] quattuor milia ⵕ : .IIII. B : mille trecentos M.
[4] quam ⵕ : quod B.

---

[1] It is uncertain which of two towns of this name is meant:
one was near Cierium, the other near Atrax.

upon the besieged. The first brunt of the attack
they bore with sufficient resolution; then, when
many of the defenders had fallen or were wounded,
their courage began to fail. Recalled then by the
reproofs of their captains to persevere in their
purpose, leaving the outer line of wall as their
strength was now diminishing, they retired into the
inner quarter of the city, which was surrounded
by a rampart less long than the other; finally,
overcome by their misfortunes and feeling that no
quarter would be given by the conqueror if they
were taken fighting, they surrendered. Then the
king without delay, while the terror was still new,
sent four thousand troops to Scotusa. There was
no delay there in surrendering when they considered the recent case of the Pheraeans, who had
finally, conquered by their ills, done what they had
at first tenaciously refused to do; with the city itself
Hippolochus and the garrison of Larisaeans were
surrendered. All were released without injury by
the king, because this act, in the king's opinion,
would have great weight in winning the sympathies
of the Larisaeans.

X. All this was accomplished within ten days after
his arrival at Pherae, and going to Crannon with his
entire army he captured it as soon as he reached it.
Then he took Cierium and Metropolis [1] and the forts
around them; and everything in that region except
Atrax and Gyrto was in his power. Then he decided
to attack Larisa, thinking that either from the fear
inspired by the capture of the other towns or by their
gratitude at the release of their garrison or from
the example of so many other states that had submitted they would not continue long in their stubborn

4 Elephantis agi ante signa terroris causa iussis quadrato agmine ad urbem incessit, ut incerti fluctuarentur
animi magnae partis Larisaeorum inter metum
praesentem hostium et verecundiam absentium [1]
5 sociorum. Per eosdem dies Amynander cum Athamanum iuventute occupat Pellinaeum, et Menippus
cum tribus milibus peditum Aetolorum et ducentis
equitibus in Perrhaebiam profectus Malloeam et
Cyretias vi cepit et [2] depopulatus est agrum Tripoli-
6 tanum. His raptim peractis Larisam ad regem
redeunt; consultanti quidnam agendum de Larisa
7 esset, supervenerunt. Ibi in diversum sententiae
tendebant aliis vim adhibendam et non differendum
censentibus, quin operibus ac machinis simul undique
moenia aggrederetur urbis sitae in plano, aperto et [3]
8 campestri undique aditu, aliis nunc vires [4] urbis
nequaquam Pheris conferendae memorantibus, nunc
hiemem et tempus anni nulli bellicae rei, minime
9 obsidioni atque oppugnationi urbium aptum. Incerto
regi inter spem metumque legati a Pharsalo, qui ad
dedendam urbem suam forte venerant, animos
10 auxerunt. M. Baebius interim cum Philippo in
Dassaretiis congressus Ap. Claudium ex communi
consilio ad praesidium Larisae misit, qui per Macedoniam magnis itineribus in iugum montium, quod
11 super Gonnos est, pervenit. Oppidum Gonni viginti
milia ab Larisa abest, in ipsis faucibus saltus, quae

---

[1] absentium ς : absentem B.
[2] cepit et Weissenborn : cepit Bς.
[3] aperto et Duker : apertae Bς.
[4] nunc uires ς : nunc cuius res B : tunc uires M.

---

[1] These are the foothills of Mount Olympus. The town of
Gonni commanded the western approaches to Tempe.

resistance. Ordering the elephants to be driven B.C. 191 before the standards to inspire fear, he marched up to the town in a hollow square, so that the thoughts of a great part of the Larisaeans wavered doubtfully between immediate fear of the enemy and respect for their distant allies. About the same time Amynander with all the youth of the Athamanes took possession of Pellinacium, and Menippus with three thousand Aetolian infantry and two hundred cavalry marched into Perrhaebia, took Malloea and Cyretiae by storm and laid waste the fields of Tripolis. Having done all this with speed, they returned to the king at Larisa; they arrived there while he was considering what he should do about Larisa. There opinions turned different ways, some urging that they ought to employ force and not to delay assaulting with siege-works and artillery from all sides at once, upon the walls of a town lying in a plain open and level to approach from any direction, others reminding him now that the strength of this city was by no means to be compared with that of Pherae, now that it was winter and a time unsuited to all military operations and particularly to the siege and storming of cities. While the king was wavering between hope and fear, ambassadors from Pharsalus, who by chance had come to surrender their city, gave him new courage. In the meantime Marcus Baebius had met Philip in the country of the Dassaretii, and as a result of the agreement of the two he sent Appius Claudius to the defence of Larisa, and he came by forced marching through Macedonia to the ridge of mountains [1] which lies above Gonni. The town of Gonni is twenty miles from Larisa, situated at the very entrance to the defile which

LIVY

Tempe appellantur, situm. Ibi castra metatus latius
quam pro copiis et plures quam quot satis in usum
erant ignes cum accendisset, speciem, quam quae-
sierat, hosti fecit omnem ibi Romanum exercitum
12 cum rege Philippo esse. Itaque hiemem instare [1]
apud suos causatus rex unum tantum moratus diem
ab Larisa recessit et Demetriadem rediit, Aetolique
13 et Athamanes in suos receperunt se fines. Appius
etsi cuius rei causa missus erat, solutam cernebat
obsidionem, tamen Larisam ad confirmandos in
14 reliquum sociorum animos descendit; duplexque
laetitia erat, quod et hostes excesserant finibus, et
intra moenia praesidium Romanum cernebant.

XI. Rex Chalcidem a Demetriade, amore captus
virginis Chalcidensis, Cleoptolemi filiae, cum patrem
primo allegando, deinde coram ipse rogando fati-
2 gasset, invitum se gravioris fortunae condicioni
illigantem, tandem impetrata re tamquam in media
pace nuptias celebrat [2] et reliquum [3] hiemis, oblitus
quantas simul duas res suscepisset, bellum Romanum
et Graeciam liberandam, omissa omnium rerum cura,
in conviviis et vinum sequentibus voluptatibus ac
deinde ex fatigatione magis quam satietate earum
3 in somno traduxit. Eadem omnes praefectos regios,

***

[1] instare ς : stare B.
[2] celebrat ς : celebrabat B.
[3] reliquum (relicum) ς : relictum B.

***

[1] Polybius (XX. viii.) adds other details, that Antiochus
was now fifty years old, that Cleoptolemus was a man of rank,
and that his daughter, whom Antiochus named Euboea, was
of extraordinary beauty, and that she escaped to Ephesus
after the defeat at Thermopylae. On the other hand, he says

they call Tempe. When he had laid out a camp
there too large in proportion to the size of his force
and built more fires than were necessary for practical
purposes, he created in the enemy the impression
he had desired, that the whole Roman army with
King Philip was there. So the king, using as a
pretext to his men the approach of winter, delayed
only one day and retired from Larisa and withdrew
to Demetrias, and the Aetolians and Athamanes
returned to their own countries. Although Appius
saw that the siege had been raised, which had been
the purpose of his coming, he yet went down to
Larisa to reassure the minds of the allies for the
future; and there was double joy, both because the
enemy had left their country and because they saw
a Roman garrison within the walls.

XI. From Demetrias the king went on to Chalcis,
having fallen in love with a young woman of Chalcis,
the daughter of Cleoptolemus,[1] and when he had
worn her father out first by sending messengers, then
by personal requests delivered verbally, the father
being reluctant to entangle himself in a match which
promised too great difficulties, at length he gained
his point, and as if in the midst of peace he celebrated
his nuptials and for the rest of the winter, forgetful
of the magnitude of the two tasks he had undertaken,
the Roman war and the liberation of Greece, laying
aside the responsibility for everything he engaged in
banquets and the delights which follow wine and then,
from weariness rather than satiety of these pleasures,
he gave himself over to sleep. This same habit of
easy living seized all the king's prefects who were

nothing of the reluctance of her father to permit the match, and
he makes less of the unsuitability of Antiochus' conduct.

A.U.C.
563

qui ubique, ad Boeotiam maxime, praepositi hibernis
erant, cepit luxuria; in eandem et milites effusi sunt,
nec quisquam eorum aut arma induit [1] aut stationem
4 aut vigilias servavit aut quicquam, quod militaris
5 operis aut muneris esset, fecit. Itaque principio veris,
cum per Phocidem Chaeroneam, quo convenire
omnem undique exercitum iusserat, venisset, facile
animadvertit nihilo severiore disciplina milites quam
6 ducem hibernasse. Alexandrum inde Acarnana et
Menippum Macedonem Stratum [2] Aetoliae copias
ducere iussit; ipse Delphis sacrificio Apollini facto
7 Naupactum processit. Consilio [3] principum Aetoliae
habito via, quae praeter Calydonem et Lysimachiam
fert ad Stratum,[4] suis qui per Maliacum sinum
8 veniebant occurrit. Ibi Mnasilochus princeps Acarnanum, multis emptus donis, non ipse solum gentem
regi conciliabat, sed Clytum etiam praetorem, penes
quem tum summa potestas erat, in suam sententiam
9 adduxerat. Is cum Leucadios, quod Acarnaniae
caput est, non facile ad defectionem posse cerneret
impelli propter metum Romanae classis, quae cum
Atilio quaeque [5] circa Cephallaniam erat, arte [6] eos
10 est aggressus. Nam cum in concilio dixisset tuenda
mediterranea Acarnaniae esse et omnibus qui arma
ferrent exeundum ad Medionem et Thyrreum, ne ab
11 Antiocho aut Aetolis occuparentur, fuere qui dicerent

---

[1] induit ς : induxit B. [2] stratum ς : magistratum B.
[3] consilio J. *Gronovius* : concilio Bς.
[4] ad stratum ς : astratum B.
[5] quaeque *Weissenborn* : quae B : quaeue ς.
[6] arte ς : ante B.

---

[1] In iii. 14 above the narrative of events in Rome was brought
up to May. The account of events in Greece is now abreast
of it.

in command of the winter camps everywhere, espe- cially in Boeotia; the soldiers too fell into the same way of life, nor did one of them put on his armour or walk his post or perform sentinel-duty or do anything else which pertained to the tasks and duties of a soldier. And so at the beginning of spring,[1] when he had come by way of Phocis to Chaeronea, where he had ordered the whole army to assemble from all its stations, he readily perceived that the soldiers had spent the winter under no sterner discipline than their commander. Then he ordered Alexander the Acarnanian and Menippus the Macedonian to conduct their troops to Stratus in Aetolia; he himself offered sacrifice to Apollo at Delphi and proceeded to Naupactus. Having held a conference with the Aetolian chiefs, on the road which leads past Calydon and Lysimachia to Stratus, he met his own men who were marching by way of the Malian gulf. There Mnasilochus, a leading Acarnanian, purchased by many gifts, did not merely by his own efforts win over the people to the king's side, but even brought Clytus the praetor, who at that time held the chief magistracy, over to his own opinion. When he saw that the people of Leucas, this being the principal city of Acarnania, could not easily be induced to rebel, because of their fear of the Roman fleet which was with Atilius and which was off Cephallania, he attacked them by guile. For when he had said in the council that the interior portions of Acarnania should be defended and that all who could bear arms should repair to Medio and Thyrreum, that these towns might not be captured by Antiochus or the Aetolians, there were some who argued that it was unnecessary that all should be called out as for a

191

nihil attinere omnes tumultuose concitari, satis esse
quingentorum hominum praesidium. Eam iuventutem nactus, trecentis Medione, ducentis Thyrrei [1] in
praesidio positis, id agebat ut pro obsidibus futuri
venirent in potestatem regis.

XII. Per eosdem [2] dies legati regis Medionem
venerunt; quibus auditis cum in contione, quidnam
respondendum regi esset, consultaretur, et alii
2 manendum in Romana societate, alii non asper-
nandam amicitiam regis censerent, media visa est
3 Clyti sententia eoque accepta, ut ad regem mitterent
legatos peterentque ab eo ut Medionios super tanta
4 re consultare in concilio Acarnanum pateretur. In
eam legationem Mnasilochus et qui eius factionis
erant de industria coniecti, clam missis qui regem
admovere copias iuberent ipsi terebant tempus.
5 Itaque vixdum iis egressis legatis Antiochus in
finibus et mox ad portas erat, et trepidantibus, qui
expertes proditionis fuerant, tumultuoseque iuventutem ad arma vocantibus ab Clyto et Mnasilocho in
6 urbem est inductus; et aliis sua voluntate ad-
fluentibus metu coacti etiam, qui [3] dissentiebant, ad
regem convenerunt. Quos [4] placida oratione territos
cum permulsisset, ad spem vulgatae clementiae
7 aliquot populi Acarnaniae defecerunt. Thyrreum a
Medione profectus est Mnasilocho eodem et legatis

[1] trecentis medione ducentis thyrrei ϛ : praesentis medio
deducentis turri B.
[2] eosdem ϛ : eos B.
[3] qui ϛ : quod B.
[4] quos ϛ : quod B.

major emergency, but that a garrison of five hundred B.C. 191 men was adequate. Obtaining this number of young men and placing three hundred at Medio and two hundred at Thyrreum as garrisons, he so conducted matters that these might fall into the hands of the king to serve as hostages.

XII. About this time the ambassadors of the king reached Medio; when they had been heard and the general assembly was debating the question of what answer should be given the king, and some urged that they should abide by the Roman alliance and others that the friendship of the king should not be disdained, the opinion of Clytus seemed to take the middle course and was therefore adopted, that they should send ambassadors to the king and ask him to permit the people of Medio to deliberate on so important a matter in the council of the Acarnanians. Mnasilochus and those who belonged to his faction were deliberately thrust into this embassy, and sending secret messages to the king to urge him to move his army forward, they themselves wasted time. Accordingly, when the ambassadors had barely set out, Antiochus was already at the frontier and soon before the gates, and while those who were without knowledge of the treachery were in panic and were excitedly calling the youth to arms, he was admitted into the city by Clytus and Mnasilochus; and as some flocked to him voluntarily, those who disagreed also, under the compulsion of fear, joined the king. When he had pacified the terror-stricken by a kindly speech, several states of Acarnania went over to him, attracted by the hope of his well-known clemency. He proceeded to Thyrreum from Medio, sending ahead the same Mnasilochus

A.U.C.
563

praemissis. Ceterum detecta Medione fraus cau-
8 tiores, non timidiores Thyrreenses fecit; dato enim [1]
haud perplexo responso, nullam se novam societatem
nisi ex auctoritate imperatorum Romanorum accepturos, portisque [2] clausis armatos in muris disposuerunt.
9 Et peropportune ad confirmandos Acarnanum animos
Cn. Octavius missus a Quinctio, cum praesidium et
paucas naves ab A. Postumio, qui ab Atilio legato
10 Cephallaniae praepositus fuerat, accepisset, Leucadem
venit implevitque spei socios M'. Acilium consulem
iam cum legionibus mare traiecisse et in Thessalia
11 castra Romana esse. Hunc rumorem [3] quia similem
veri tempus anni maturum iam ad navigandum
faciebat, rex praesidio Medione imposito et in quibusdam aliis Acarnaniae oppidis Thyrreo abscessit
et per Aetoliae ac Phocidis urbes Chalcidem rediit.

XIII. Sub idem tempus M. Baebius et Philippus
rex, iam ante per hiemem in Dassaretiis congressi,
cum Ap. Claudium, ut obsidione Larisam eximeret, in
2 Thessaliam misissent, quia id tempus rebus gerendis
immaturum erat, in hiberna regressi, principio veris
3 coniunctis copiis in Thessaliam descenderunt. In
Acarnania tum Antiochus erat. Advenientes Philippus Malloeam Perrhaebiae, Baebius Phacium est
adgressus; quo primo prope impetu capto Phaestum
4 eadem celeritate capit. Inde Atracem cum se
recepisset, Cyretias hinc et Eritium occupat, prae-

---

[1] dato enim ϛ : dato B.
[2] portisque ϛ : portis B.
[3] rumorem ϛ : cruorem B.

---

[1] Atilius would normally be called *propraetor*, as is Baebius
in viii. 6 above, since both were waiting for their successors.

and the ambassadors. But the treachery disclosed B.C. 191 at Medio made the people of Thyrreum more cautious, not more fearful; giving an answer quite free from ambiguity, to the effect that they would enter upon no new alliance except with the authorization of the Roman commanders, they closed the gates and disposed guards along the walls. And, very fortunately for the reassurance of the minds of the Acarnanians, Gnaeus Octavius, sent by Quinctius, when he had received an escort and a few ships from Aulus Postumius, who had been placed in command at Cephallania by Atilius the lieutenant,[1] came to Leucas and filled the allies with the hope that the consul Manius Acilius with the legions had already crossed the sea and that there was a Roman camp in Thessaly. Since this rumour was rendered plausible by the fact that the season of the year was now suitable for navigation, the king left garrisons at Medio and certain other towns in Acarnania, went away from Thyrreum and returned by way of the cities in Aetolia and Phocis to Chalcis.

XIII. About the same time Marcus Baebius and King Philip, who had already previously met in the country of the Dassaretii, when they had sent Appius Claudius into Thessaly to raise the siege of Larisa, and, because the time seemed too early for active campaigning, had returned to their winter quarters, at the beginning of spring joined their forces and marched down into Thessaly. Antiochus was then in Acarnania. When they arrived, Philip attacked Malloea in Perrhaebia, and Baebius Phacium; when this fell at the first assault Baebius took Phaestum with the same speed. When he had turned back from there to Atrax, he next occupied Cyretiae

sidiisque per recepta oppida dispositis Philippo rursus
5 obsidenti Malloeam se coniungit. Sub adventum [1]
Romani exercitus seu ad metum virium seu ad spem
veniae cum dedidissent sese, ad ea recipienda oppida,
quae Athamanes occupaverant, uno agmine ierunt.
6 Erant autem haec: Aeginium Ericinium Gomphi
7 Silana Tricca Meliboea Phaloria. Inde Pellinaeum,
ubi Philippus Megalopolitanus cum quingentis
peditibus et equitibus quadraginta in praesidio erat,
circumsidunt et, priusquam oppugnarent, mittunt ad
Philippum qui monerent ne vim ultimam experiri
8 vellet. Quibus ille satis ferociter respondit vel
Romanis vel Thessalis se crediturum fuisse, in Philippi
9 se potestatem commissurum non esse. Postquam
apparuit vi agendum, quia videbatur et Limnaeum
eodem tempore oppugnari posse, regem ad Limnaeum ire placuit, Baebius restitit ad Pellinaeum
oppugnandum.

XIV. Per eos forte dies M'. Acilius consul cum
viginti [2] milibus peditum, duobus milibus equitum,
quindecim elephantis mari traiecto pedestres copias
Larisam ducere tribunos militum iussit; ipse cum
2 equitatu Limnaeum ad Philippum venit. Adventu

---

[1] aduentum *ed. Moguntina* 1518 : aduentu *B.*
[2] viginti *J. F. Gronovius* : .X. *B.*

---

[1] These towns, so far as they can be located, were on the
western borders of Thessaly. Cf. x. 5 above.
[2] That is, King Philip, who naturally resented his name-
sake's aspirations.
[3] Cf. iii. 13 above. It is not easy to account for these
troops. In XXXV. xli. 4 the senate authorized 10,000
infantry and 700 cavalry for this campaign, in addition to the
two legions commanded by Baebius, but these legions were still

and Eritium, and establishing garrisons in the towns B.C. 191 he had recovered he rejoined Philip, who was still engaged in the siege of Malloea. When at the coming of the Roman army the people of Malloea had surrendered, whether through fear of Roman might or in the hope of pardon, Baebius and Philip moved in one column to retake the towns which the Athamanes had occupied. These were the following: Aeginium, Ericinium, Gomphi, Silana, Tricca, Meliboea, Phaloria.[1] Then Pellinaeum, where Philip of Megalopolis with five hundred infantry and forty cavalry was in the garrison, was surrounded, and before they stormed it they sent to Philip to advise him not to wish to try resistance to the last. To this he replied with sufficient vehemence that he would entrust himself either to the Romans or to the Thessalians but would not put himself in the power of Philip.[2] When it was evident that force must be employed, because it seemed that Limnaeum could be stormed at the same time, it was decided that the king should go to Limnaeum while Baebius remained to attack Pellinaeum.

XIV. During this time, as it happened, Manius Acilius the consul crossed the sea with twenty thousand infantry, two thousand cavalry, and fifteen elephants,[3] and ordered the military tribunes to lead the infantry to Larisa; he himself with the cavalry went to Philip at Limnaeum. The arrival of the

at Pellinaeum. The 5,000 allies from Greece were probably not included. The elephants may be part of the twenty promised by Masinissa (iv. 8 above). The loss of this portion of the text of Polybius increases the difficulty, but he is probably the source of this passage, since Appian (*Syr.* 17) agrees generally with Livy. Acilius probably disembarked at Apollonia and marched down the western coast of Epirus.

LIVY

consulis deditio sine cunctatione est facta, traditumque [1] praesidium regium et cum iis Athamanes.
3 Ab Limnaeo Pellinaeum consul proficiscitur. Ibi
primi Athamanes tradiderunt sese, deinde et
4 Philippus Megalopolitanus; cui decedenti [2] praesidio
cum obvius forte fuisset Philippus rex, ad ludibrium
regem eum consalutari iussit, ipse congressus fratrem
haud sane decoro maiestati [3] suae ioco appellavit.
5 Deductus inde ad consulem custodiri iussus est [4] et
haud ita multo post in vinculis Romam missus.
Cetera multitudo Athamanum aut militum Antiochi
regis, quae in praesidiis deditorum per eos dies oppidorum fuerat, Philippo tradita regi est; fuere autem
6 ad quattuor milia [5] hominum. Consul Larisam est
profectus, ibi de summa belli consultaturus. In
itinere ab Cierio et Metropoli legati tradentes urbes
7 suas occurrerunt. Philippus Athamanum praecipue
captivis indulgenter habitis, ut per eos conciliaret
gentem, nactus spem Athamaniae potiendae exer-
8 citum eo duxit praemissis in civitates captivis. Et
illi magnam auctoritatem apud populares habuerunt
clementiam erga se regis munificentiamque com-
9 memorantes, et Amynander, cuius praesentis
maiestas aliquos in fide continuisset, veritus ne
traderetur Philippo iam pridem hosti et Romanis
merito tunc propter defectionem infensis, cum
coniuge ac liberis regno excessit Ambraciamque se
contulit; ita Athamania omnis in ius dicionemque

---

[1] traditumque *ς* : traditum *B.*
[2] decedenti *ς* : descendenti *B.*
[3] maiestati *ed. Parisina* 1513 : maiestatis *Bς.*
[4] iussus est *Ussing* : iussus *B.*
[5] quattuor milia *edd.* : .IIII. *B* : tria milia *ς.*

---

[1] The same propensity was criticized at XXXII. xxxiv. 3.

consul caused surrender to be offered without delay, B.C. 191 and the royal garrison was handed over and along with them the Athamanes. From Limnaeum the consul went to Pellinaeum. There the Athamanes first gave themselves up, then Philip of Megalopolis; when by chance King Philip encountered him as he was leaving the garrison, he ordered him hailed as king in mockery, and meeting him face to face, he greeted him as " brother," a jest by no means befitting his dignity.[1] Conducted then before the consul, he was ordered to be placed under guard, and a little later was sent to Rome in chains. The rest of the people of the Athamanes or of the soldiers of King Antiochus who had been in the garrisons of the towns surrendered at this period were delivered to King Philip: they numbered now about four thousand men. The consul proceeded to Larisa, there to hold a council regarding the general conduct of the war. On the way ambassadors came from Cierium and Metropolis surrendering their cities. Philip treated with especial kindness the prisoners of the Athamanes, that through them he might win over the tribe, and entertaining the hope of gaining possession of Athamania, he led his army thither, sending the captives ahead to their cities. And they had great influence with their fellow-citizens, recalling the kindness and generosity of the king towards them, and Amynander, who, had he been present, might by his majesty have kept some to their allegiance, fearing that he would be delivered to Philip, long his enemy, or to the Romans, at that time justly angered because of his desertion, left the kingdom with his wife and children and took refuge in Ambracia; thus all Athamania came under the

10 Philippi concessit. Consul ad reficienda maxime
iumenta, quae et navigatione et postea itineribus
fatigata erant, paucos Larisae moratus dies, velut
renovato modica quiete exercitu Crannonem est
11 progressus. Venienti Pharsalus et Scotusa et Pherae
quaeque in eis praesidia Antiochi erant deduntur.
Ex iis interrogatis, qui manere secum vellent, mille
volentes Philippo tradit, ceteros inermes Deme-
12 triadem remittit. Proernam inde recepit et quae
circa eam[1] castella erant. Ducere tum porro in
sinum Maliacum coepit. Appropinquanti faucibus
super quas siti Thaumaci sunt, deserta urbe iuventus
omnis armata silvas et itinera insedit et in agmen
13 Romanum ex superioribus locis incursavit. Consul
primo misit[2] qui ex propinquo colloquentes deter-
rerent eos a tali furore; postquam perseverare in
incepto vidit, tribuno cum duorum signorum militibus
circummisso interclusit ad urbem iter armatis,
14 vacuamque eam cepit. Tum clamore ab tergo
captae urbis audito refugientium undique ex silvis
15 insidiatorum caedes facta est. Ab Thaumacis altero
die consul ad Spercheum amnem pervenit, inde
Hypataeorum agros vastavit.

XV. Cum haec agebantur, Chalcide erat Antiochus,
iam tum cernens nihil se ex Graecia praeter amoena
2 Chalcide hiberna et infames nuptias petisse. Tunc
Aetolorum vana promissa incusare et Thoantem,

---

[1] circa eam ς : circa ea B.
[2] consul primo misit *Madvig* : primo missi Bς : consul
primo mittere M.

---

[1] Cf. XXXII. iv. 1–4.
[2] The Romans have now recovered practically all the towns
taken by Antiochus, as a comparison of place-names shows.

sovereignty and power of Philip. The consul, to B.C. 191
rest the pack-animals which had been exhausted
both by the voyage and by the later marching,
delayed a few days at Larisa, and with an army
renewed, so to speak, by a brief rest, proceeded to
Crannon. On his journey Pharsalus and Scotusa and
Pherae and the garrisons of Antiochus which were
in them were surrendered. Questioning them as
to who were willing to stay with him, he handed
over to Philip a thousand volunteers and sent the
rest unarmed back to Demetrias. Next he took
Proerna and the forts surrounding it. Then he
began to lead the army straight towards the Malian
gulf. As he drew near the pass above which
Thaumaci¹ is situated, the young men left the town,
armed themselves and attacked the Roman column
from the higher ground. At first the consul sent
men to try, by talking to them at close quarters, to
deter them from so insane a course; when he saw
that they persisted in their purpose, he sent a tribune
with the soldiers of two maniples by a roundabout
way, closed the road to the city against the soldiers,
and captured the undefended town. Then when
they heard the shouts from the captured city behind
them there was a slaughter by the troops in ambush,
as the enemy fled in all directions from the forests.
From Thaumaci on the second day the consul came
to the Spercheus river and then laid waste the lands
of the Hypataeans.²

XV. While this was going on Antiochus was at
Chalcis, now at last perceiving that he had gained
nothing from Greece except a pleasant winter at
Chalcis and a shameful marriage. Then he began
to blame the false promises of the Aetolians and

LIVY

A.U.C.
563

Hannibalem vero non ut prudentem tantum virum sed prope vatem omnium, quae tum evenirent, admirari. Ne tamen temere coepta segnitia insuper everteret, nuntios in Aetoliam misit ut omni con-

3 tracta iuventute convenirent Lamiam;[1] et ipse eo decem milia fere peditum ex iis, qui postea venerant

4 ex Asia, expleta et equites quingentos duxit. Quo[2] cum aliquanto pauciores quam umquam antea convenissent, et principes tantummodo cum paucis clientibus essent, atque ii dicerent omnia sedulo ab se facta ut quam plurimos ex civitatibus suis evo-

5 carent; nec auctoritate nec gratia nec imperio adversus detractantes militiam valuisse, destitutus undique et ab suis, qui morabantur in Asia, et ab sociis, qui ea[3] in quorum spem vocaverant non praestabant, intra saltum Thermopylarum sese

6 recepit. Id iugum, sicut Appennini dorso Italia

7 dividitur, ita mediam Graeciam dirimit. Ante saltum Thermopylarum in septentrionem versa Epirus et Perrhaebia et Magnesia et Thessalia est et

8 Phthiotae Achaei et sinus Maliacus; intra[4] fauces ad meridiem vergunt Aetoliae pars maior et Acarnania et cum Locride Phocis et Boeotia adiunctaque insula Euboea et excurrente in altum velut pro-

---

[1] Lamiam *Duker*: iam Bς.   [2] quo ς: quod B.
[3] ea ς: eam B.   [4] intra ς: infra B.

---

[1] Livy here transfers to Greece a Roman institution of which there is no other trace in Greece. The precise status of these dependents is then uncertain.
[2] At this distance of time and space, the war with Antiochus so far seems to have the character of comic opera: the extravagant promises of Antiochus and the Aetolians; the insignificant forces; the childish hesitation and frequent

to censure Thoas, but Hannibal he admired as not
only a wise man but as little less than a prophet of
all that was happening. Yet, not to risk still
more his rash enterprise by his own inactivity, he
sent messages to Aetolia that they should assemble
all their youth and meet at Lamia; and he too led
there about ten thousand infantry, including replacements from those who had later arrived from
Asia, and five hundred cavalry. When a somewhat
smaller number than ever before had assembled
there, only the chiefs, in fact, with a few clients,[1]
and these explained that they had worked with all
diligence to call out the largest possible numbers
from their cities, but had prevailed by neither influence nor persuasion nor right of command against
the shirkers of military service, then, abandoned on all
sides, both by his own subjects, who were tarrying
in Asia, and by his allies, who were not fulfilling the
promises by the hope of which they had invited
him, he retired within the pass of Thermopylae.[2]
This ridge, just as Italy is cut in two by the backbone
of the Apennines, divides Greece. In front of the
pass of Thermopylae, facing the north, are Epirus
and Perrhaebia and Magnesia and Thessaly and
Phthiotic Achaea and the Malian gulf; within the
pass towards the south lie the larger part of Aetolia
and Acarnania and Phocis with Locris and Boeotia
with the island of Euboea adjoining it and, on a
sort of promontory running out into the sea, the

changes of plan; the feeble discipline; the burlesque scene
of the marriage; the futile conquest of Thessaly; the in-
glorious retirement to the site of one of the most splendid
events in ancient history. Rome must almost have repented
of her elaborate preparations.

munturio Attica terra et sita ab tergo [1] Pelopon-
9 nesus. Hoc iugum ab Leucate et mari ad occidentem
verso per Aetoliam ad alterum mare orienti obiectum
tendens ea aspreta rupesque interiectas habet, ut
non modo exercitus sed ne expediti quidem facile
10 ullas ad transitum calles inveniant. Extremos ad
orientem montes Oetam vocant, quorum quod altis-
simum est Callidromon appellatur, in cuius valle ad
Maliacum sinum vergente iter est non latius quam
11 sexaginta passus. Haec una militaris via est, qua
traduci exercitus, si non prohibeantur, possint.[2]
12 Ideo Pylae et ab aliis, quia calidae aquae in ipsis
faucibus sunt, Thermopylae locus appellatur, nobilis
Lacedaemoniorum adversus Persas morte magis
memorabili quam pugna.

XVI. Haudquaquam pari tum animo Antiochus
intra portas loci eius castris positis munitionibus insuper saltum impediebat et, cum duplici vallo fossaque
2 et muro etiam, qua res postulabat, ex multa copia
3 passim iacentium lapidum permunisset omnia, satis
fidens numquam ea vim [3] Romanum exercitum facturum, Aetolos ex quattuor milibus—tot enim
convenerant—partim ad Heracleam praesidio ob-
4 tinendam, quae ante ipsas fauces posita est, partim
Hypatam mittit, et Heracleam haud dubius consulem

---

[1] et sita ab tergo *M. Müller*: sita ab tergo et *B.*
[2] possint *ς*: possent *B.*   [3] uim *ς*: uiam *B.*

---

[1] Livy conceives of the pass as the terminus of a mountain
barrier crossing Greece in a west-east direction. With reference
to that barrier he places the principal geographical subdivisions.
His comparison with the Apennines is graphic but misleading,
since the geographical importance of the two ranges is quite
unlike; the historical importance of Thermopylae is no doubt
responsible. The pass begins here to figure in Roman history

Attic land, and lying behind it the Peloponnesus. B.C. 191
This range, taking its course from Leucas and the
sea on the west and continuing through Aetolia to
the other sea on the east, has such thickets and
scattered cliffs that not even individuals travelling
light, not to mention armies, can easily find paths
by which to cross. The mountains on the extreme
east they call Oeta, the highest of which is named
Callidromum, in the valley of which, where it slopes
down to the Malian gulf, there is a road not wider
than sixty paces. This is the one military road
where an army can pass if there is no resistance.[1]
For that reason the place is called Pylae and by
others, because there are warm springs within the
pass itself, Thermopylae,[2] and it is renowned for
the death of the Lacedaemonians as they opposed
the Persians, more memorable than the battle.

XVI. With a spirit wholly unlike theirs at that
time, Antiochus pitched his camp within the "Gates"
to the place and besides blocked the pass with
fortifications, and when he had strengthened everything with a double wall and ditch and, where the
situation demanded, with a rampart constructed
out of the great quantity of stones which were
scattered all about, confident that the Roman army
would never force a passage, of the four thousand
Aetolians—for so many had assembled—he sent
part to hold Heraclea with a garrison, part to Hypata,[3]
being both certain that the consul would attack

and this geographical excursus is therefore pertinent, though
not in Livy's ordinary manner.

[2] "Pylae" means literally "Gates," "Thermopylae"
"Hot Gates."

[3] Heraclea lay west-south-west of the pass, Hypata west-
north-west.

LIVY

oppugnaturum, et iam multis nuntiantibus circa
5 Hypatam omnia evastari. Consul depopulatus Hy-
patensem primo deinde Heracleensem agrum, inutili
utrobique auxilio Aetolorum, in ipsis faucibus prope
fontes calidarum aquarum adversus regem posuit
castra. Aetolorum utraeque manus Heracleam sese
6 incluserunt. Antiochum, cui[1] priusquam hostem
cerneret satis omnia permunita et praesidiis obsaepta
videbantur, timor incessit, ne quas per imminentia
7 iuga calles inveniret ad transitum Romanus; nam
et Lacedaemonios quondam ita a Persis circuitos
fama erat, et nuper Philippum ab iisdem Romanis;
8 itaque nuntium Heracleam ad Aetolos mittit, ut
hanc saltem sibi operam eo bello praestarent, ut
vertices circa montium occuparent obsiderentque, ne
9 qua transire Romani possent. Hoc nuntio audito dis-
sensio inter Aetolos orta est. Pars imperio paren-
10 dum regis atque eundum censebant, pars subsis-
tendum Heracleae ad utramque fortunam, ut, sive
victus ab consule rex esset, in expedito haberent
integras copias ad opem propinquis ferendam civitatibus suis, sive vinceret, ut dissipatos in fugam
11 Romanos persequerentur. Utraque pars non mansit
modo in sententia sua, sed etiam exsecuta est consilium: duo milia Heracleae substiterunt; duo
trifariam divisa Callidromum et Rhoduntiam et
Tichiunta—haec nomina cacuminibus sunt—occu-
pavere.

XVII. Consul postquam insessa superiora loca ab

---

[1] cui ʃ : qui *B.*

---

[1] At the Aous river (XXXII. xii. 4).

Heraclea and informed by many messengers that all B.C. 191
the country around Hypata was being devastated.
The consul, having first ravaged the fields of Hypata
and then of Heraclea, the aid of the Aetolians being
useless to both, encamped within the pass itself
near the springs of hot water facing the king.
Both contingents of Aetolians shut themselves up
in Heraclea. Antiochus, to whom, before he saw
the enemy, everything seemed well fortified and
guarded by posts, was terror-stricken lest the Roman
should find trails somewhere over the overhanging
cliffs to permit their passage; for the story was
that so the Lacedaemonians were once surrounded
by the Persians, and recently Philip [1] by the Romans
themselves; so he sent a runner to the Aetolians
in Heraclea that they should render at least so
much service to him in this war as to seize and hold
the mountain-tops round about, that the Romans
might find no way to cross. On hearing this message
a disagreement arose among the Aetolians. Part
thought that they should obey the king's order and
go, part that they should wait at Heraclea for either
turn of fortune, that, if the king were defeated by
the consul, they might have fresh troops in readiness to bring aid to their cities, but if he conquered,
that they might pursue the Romans when scattered
in flight. Each party not only adhered to its
own opinion but acted on its own decision: two
thousand remained at Heraclea; two thousand,
separating into three detachments, occupied Callidromum and Rhoduntia and Tichius—these are
names of peaks.

XVII. When the consul saw that the higher
ground was held by the Aetolians, he sent Marcus

LIVY

Aetolis vidit, M. Porcium Catonem et L. Valerium
Flaccum consulares legatos cum binis milibus delectorum peditum ad castella Aetolorum, Flaccum in Rhoduntiam et Tichiunta, Catonem in Callidromum mittit.
2 Ipse, priusquam ad hostem copias admoveret, vocatos
in contionem milites paucis est adlocutus. "Plerosque omnium ordinum, milites, inter vos esse video,
qui in hac [1] eadem provincia T. Quincti ductu
3 auspicioque militaveritis. Macedonico bello inex-
superabilior saltus ad amnem Aoum fuit [2] quam hic;
4 quippe portae sunt hae,[3] et unus inter [4] duo maria
clausis omnibus velut naturalis transitus est; munitiones et locis opportunioribus tunc fuerunt et
validiores impositae; exercitus hostium ille et
numero maior et militum genere aliquanto melior;
5 quippe illic Macedones Thracesque et Illyrii erant,
ferocissimae omnes gentes, hic Syri et Asiatici
Graeci [5] sunt, vilissima genera hominum et servituti
6 nata; rex ille bellicosissimus et exercitatus iam inde [6]
ab iuventa finitimis Thracum atque Illyriorum et
circa omnium accolarum bellis, hic, ut aliam omnem
7 vitam sileam, is est,[7] qui cum ad inferendum populo
Romano bellum ex Asia in Europam transisset,
nihil memorabilius toto tempore hibernorum gesserit,

[1] in hac ⲋ: hac *B*.   [2] fuit ⲋ: fui in *B*.
[3] hae ⲋ: haec *B*.   [4] inter ⲋ: in *B*.
    [5] graeci ⲋ: regis *B*.
    [6] inde *ed. Parisina* 1513: ille *B*ⲋ.
    [7] is est *ed. Frobeniana* 1535: est *B*.

---

[1] The rank of Cato is uncertain. Cicero (*Cato maior* 32)
calls him a *tribunus militaris*, but the term *consularis legatus*
is frequent in Livy (*e.g.* XXXV. v. 1) and is more appropriate
here.

Porcius Cato [1] and Lucius Valerius Flaccus, lieutenants of consular rank, with two thousand picked
men each, against the strong points of the Aetolians,
Flaccus to Rhoduntia and Tichius, Cato to Callidromum. He himself, before he moved his troops
forward against the enemy, called the soldiers to
an assembly and harangued them briefly: " I see
that most among you, soldiers, are men of all ranks,
who fought in this same province under the leadership and auspices of Titus Quinctius. In the Macedonian war the pass of Aous was more difficult to
traverse than this; for surely this is a gate and the
one natural aisle, so to speak, between the two seas,
all other ways being closed; [2] the fortifications were
then both more suitably situated and more strongly
constructed; that hostile army was both larger in
numbers and composed of a somewhat better grade
of soldiers; there, as you know, there were Macedonians and Thracians and Illyrians, all most warlike nations, here Syrians and Asiatic Greeks, the
most worthless peoples among mankind and born
for slavery; that king was most devoted to war and
trained from youth up in wars with the neighbouring
Thracians and Illyrians and all the inhabitants round
about; here, to pass over in silence all the rest of
his career, is one who, after crossing from Asia to
Europe to make war upon the Roman people, did
nothing more worthy of note during the whole season
of the winter than for love's sake to marry a woman

---

[2] The speaker seems to mean that Thermopylae was the
only north-south gateway which could be found between the
Aegean sea to the east and the Ionian sea to the west. For
rhetorical reasons he regards the pass as a gateway that can
be forced open rather than as a barrier that can be kept closed.

quam quod amoris causa ex domo privata et obscuri
etiam inter populares generis uxorem duxit, et novus
8 maritus, velut saginatus nuptialibus cenis, ad pugnam
processit. Summa virium speique eius in Aetolis
fuit, gente vanissima et ingratissima, ut vos prius
9 experti estis, nunc Antiochus experitur. Nam nec
venerunt frequentes, nec contineri in castris potuerunt, et in seditione ipsi inter sese sunt et, cum
Hypatam tuendam Heracleamque depoposcissent,
neutram tutati [1] refugerunt in iuga montium, pars
10 Heracleae incluserunt sese. Rex ipse confessus
nusquam aequo campo non modo congredi se ad
pugnam audere, sed ne castra quidem in aperto
ponere, relicta omni ante se regione ea, quam se
nobis ac Philippo ademisse gloriabatur, condidit se [2]
intra rupes, ne ante fauces quidem saltus, ut quondam
11 Lacedaemonios fama est, sed intra penitus retractis
castris; quod quantum interest ad timorem osten-
dendum, an muris urbis alicuius obsidendum sese
12 incluserit? Sed neque Antiochum tuebuntur angustiae, nec Aetolos vertices illi quos ceperunt.
Satis undique provisum atque praecautum est, ne
quid adversus vos in pugna praeter hostis esset.
13 Illud proponere animo vestro debetis, non vos pro
Graeciae libertate tantum dimicare, quamquam is
quoque egregius titulus esset, liberatam [3] a Philippo
ante nunc ab Aetolis et ab Antiocho liberare, neque
ea tantum in praemium vestrum cessura, quae nunc
14 in regiis [4] castris sunt, sed illum quoque omnem

---

[1] neutram tutati ς : neutra mutati B.
[2] condidit se ς : condidisse B.
[3] liberatam ς : liberam B.   [4] regiis ς : regis B.

---

[1] I.e., Thessaly; in xv. 7 above Livy speaks of Thessaly as
lying " in front of " (ante) Thermopylae.

B.C. 191

from a private home, of a family obscure and even common, and the new bridegroom, stuffed, let me say, with wedding feasts, went forth to battle. The substance of his strength and hope is in the Aetolians, a most boastful and ungrateful race, as you have learned before this and as Antiochus is now learning. For neither did they come in great numbers nor could they be kept in camp, and they are even at odds with one another, and although they had demanded the guardianship of Hypata and Heraclea, they defended neither, but some fled to the mountain-tops and some shut themselves up in Heraclea. The king himself, confessing that he not only does not dare to trust himself to battle on level ground anywhere but does not even venture to encamp in the open, abandoning all that country in front of him[1] which he boasted he had taken from us and from Philip, has shut himself up within the cliffs, not even placing his camp in front of the entrance to the pass, as they say the Spartans once did, but withdrawing it deep inside; and how does this differ, as an exhibition of fear, from shutting himself up to be besieged within the walls of some city? But neither the narrow defile will protect Antiochus nor the heights which they have seized the Aetolians. Sufficient care and precaution have been taken on every side to prevent your facing any peril except the enemy. You should hold this thought before your minds, that you are fighting not merely for the liberty of Greece, although this is a noble cause to defend, but to set free a people, formerly freed from Philip, now from the Aetolians and Antiochus, nor will your reward consist only of those things which are in the king's camp, but all that equipment too which is daily

LIVY

apparatum, qui in dies ab Epheso expectatur, praedae futurum, Asiam deinde Syriamque et omnia usque ad ortum solis ditissima regna Romano imperio
15 aperturos. Quid deinde [1] aberit quin ab Gadibus ad mare rubrum Oceano fines terminemus, qui orbem terrarum amplexu finit, et omne humanum genus
16 secundum deos nomen Romanum veneretur? In haec tanta praemia dignos parate animos, ut crastino die bene iuvantibus diis acie decernamus."

XVIII. Ab hac contione dimissi milites, priusquam corpora curarent, arma telaque [2] parant. Luce prima signo pugnae proposito instruit aciem consul,
2 arta fronte, ad naturam et angustias loci. Rex, postquam signa hostium conspexit, et ipse copias educit. Levis armaturae partem ante vallum in primo locavit, tum Macedonum robur, quos sarisophorus appellabant, velut firmamentum circa ipsas
3 munitiones constituit. His ab sinistro cornu iaculatorum sagittariorumque et funditorum manum sub ipsis radicibus montis posuit, ut ex altiore loco nuda
4 latera hostium incesserent. Ab dextro Macedonibus ad ipsum munimentorum finem, qua [3] loca usque ad mare invia palustri limo et voraginibus claudunt, elephantos cum adsueto praesidio posuit, post eos equites, tum modico intervallo relicto ceteras copias

[1] deinde ς : inde B.
[2] arma telaque ς : arma tela B.
[3] qua ς : quae B.

---

[1] Appian and Plutarch report no such speech, and it was probably not found in Polybius.

[2] The successors of Alexander all used the phalanx formation, which in this case was presumably made up of Syrians: cf. XXXVII. xl. 1.

expected from Ephesus will be booty, and thereafter Asia and Syria and the treasure-laden realms
right up to the sunrise will be opened to Roman
rule. What then will be lacking, that we shall not
bound our empire by the ocean from Gades to the
Red Sea, that ocean which holds the earth in its
embrace, and that the whole human race will not
reverence the Roman name next after the gods?
Make your minds ready to deserve such great rewards, that to-morrow with the good aid of the gods
we may fight it out in battle-line." [1]

XVIII. After this assembly the soldiers were dismissed, and before they saw to their bodily needs
they made ready their armour and arms. At daybreak the battle-signal was displayed and the consul
deployed his forces on a narrow front, according to
the nature and limits of the position. When the king
saw the standards of the enemy he too led out his
troops. Part of his light-armed troops he placed
before the rampart in the front line, then he drew
up the main body of the Macedonians,[2] whom they
call *sarisophori*,[3] as a bulwark around the fortification
itself. Next to them on the left flank he placed a
detachment of dart-throwers and archers and slingers
at the very base of the mountain, to harass the
exposed flank of the enemy from the higher ground.
On the right, next to the Macedonians, at the very
end of the fortification, where the ground, impassable
as far as the sea, closed it in with swampy mud and
quicksands, he stationed the elephants with their
usual guard and behind them the cavalry; then, a
short distance to the rear, the rest of his troops in

---

[3] Literally, "lancers," armed with the heavy Macedonian
sarisa.

5 in secunda acie. Macedones pro [1] vallo locati primo
facile sustinebant Romanos, temptantes ab omni
parte aditus, multum adiuvantibus, qui ex loco
superiore fundis velut nimbum glandes et sagittas
6 simul ac iacula ingerebant; deinde, ut maior nec
iam toleranda vis hostium inferebat se, pulsi loco
intra munimenta subductis ordinibus concesserunt;
inde ex vallo prope alterum vallum hastis prae se
7 obiectis fecerunt. Et ita modica altitudo valli erat,
ut et locum superiorem suis ad pugnandum praeberet,
et propter longitudinem hastarum subiectum haberet
8 hostem. Multi temere subeuntes vallum transfixi
sunt; et aut incepto irrito recessissent aut plures
cecidissent,[2] ni M. Porcius ab iugo Callidromi deiectis
inde Aetolis et magna ex parte caesis—incautos
enim et plerosque sopitos oppresserat—super imminentem castris collem apparuisset.

XIX. Flacco non eadem fortuna ad Tichiunta et
Rhoduntiam, nequiquam subire ad ea castella conato,
2 fuerat. Macedones quique alii in castris regiis
erant [3] primo, dum procul nihil aliud quam turba et
agmen apparebat, Aetolos credere visa procul pugna
3 subsidio venire; ceterum, ut primum signaque et
arma ex propinquo cognita errorem [4] aperuerunt,

[1] pro ς : prae B.
[2] cecidissent ς : occidissent B.
[3] regiis erant ed. Frobeniana 1535 : regis erant B : fuerant
regiis M : fuerant regis ς.
[4] cognita errorem ς : cognitae prore B.

[1] Plutarch (Cato xiii. ff.) gives a much more picturesque
account of this episode, with greater emphasis upon Cato.

the second line. The Macedonians standing in front
of the rampart at first easily held off the Romans,
who were trying the approaches from every direction, with much assistance from those who from the
higher ground were hurling a veritable cloud of
missiles from their slings as well as darts and arrows
at the same time; then, as a greater and more
irresistible pressure was placed upon them by the
enemy, driven from their places they gradually
withdrew their ranks and fell back inside the fortifications; thence from the rampart they almost made
another rampart of the spears held out in front of
them. And the height of the rampart was so moderate
that it both offered its defenders higher ground from
which to fight and held the enemy within thrusting-
distance below them on account of the length of
the spears. Many who rashly drew near the rampart
were run through; and either they would have withdrawn with their task unaccomplished or more would
have perished had not Marcus Porcius, having dislodged the Aetolians from the heights of Callidromum and killed a large part of them—for he had
caught them off their guard and many of them
asleep—shown himself on the hill which overlooked
the camp.[1]

XIX. Flaccus did not enjoy the same fortune at
Tichius and Rhoduntia, having tried in vain to get
up to those forts. The Macedonians and the others
who were in the king's camp at first, while there
was nothing visible in the distance except a crowd
and a column, believed that the Aetolians had seen
the battle from afar and were coming to their assistance; but as soon as the standards and arms, recognized close at hand, revealed their mistake, such

A.U.C.
563

tantus repente pavor omnes cepit ut abiectis armis
4 fugerent. Et munimenta sequentes impedierunt, et [1]
angustiae vallis, per quam sequendi erant, et maxime
omnium quod elephanti novissimi agminis erant,
quos pedes aegre praeterire, eques nullo poterat
modo timentibus equis tumultumque inter se
5 maiorem quam in proelio edentibus; aliquantum
temporis et direptio castrorum tenuit; Scarpheam
6 tamen eo die consecuti sunt hostem. Multis in ipso
itinere caesis captisque, non equis virisque tantum,
sed etiam elephantis, quos capere non potuerant,[2]
7 interfectis, in castra reverterunt; quae temptata eo
die inter ipsum pugnae tempus ab Aetolis, Heracleam obtinentibus praesidio, sine ullo haud parum
8 audacis incepti effectu fuerant. Consul noctis inse-
quentis tertia vigilia praemisso equitatu ad persequendum hostem, signa legionum luce prima movit.
9 Aliquantum viae praeceperat rex, ut qui non ante
quam Elatiae ab effuso [3] constiterit cursu; ubi
primum reliquiis [4] pugnaeque et fugae collectis, cum
perexigua [5] manu semiermium militum Chalcidem se
10 recepit. Romanus equitatus ipsum quidem regem
Elatiae adsecutus non est; magnam partem agminis
aut lassitudine subsistentes aut errore, ut qui sine
ducibus per ignota itinera fugerent, dissipatos op-
11 presserunt; nec praeter quingentos, qui circa regem
fuerunt, ex toto exercitu quisquam effugit, etiam ex

[1] et ⌠ : om. B.   [2] potuerant ⌠ : poterant B.
[3] ab effuso ed. Frobeniana 1535 : a confuso B⌠.
[4] reliquiis ⌠ : reliquis B.
[5] perexigua ⌠ : rex exigua B.

terror all at once seized them that they threw away B.C. 191
their arms and fled. Both the walls and the narrowness of the valley through which they had to pass
hindered the pursuers, and most of all the fact that
the elephants brought up the rear, and these the
infantry could pass only with difficulty and the cavalry
not at all, since the horses were frightened and
caused greater disturbance in their own ranks than
in the battle; some time was also consumed in the
plundering of the camp; nevertheless, they pursued
the enemy that day as far as Scarphea. They not
only killed and captured many, men and horses, on
the way, but also killed the elephants which they
could not take, and returned to camp; this had been
attacked during the time the battle was going on
by the Aetolians who were holding Heraclea with
their garrison, but without any results commensurate
with the considerable boldness of the undertaking.
During the third watch of the next night the consul
sent on the cavalry to pursue the enemy and at
daybreak advanced the legionary standards. The king
had gone a considerable distance ahead, inasmuch as
he had not ceased his headlong flight until he reached
Elatia; there, as soon as he collected the scanty
leavings of the battle and the flight, with a little
band of half-armed men he withdrew to Chalcis.
The Roman cavalry did not overtake the king himself
at Elatia; but a great part of the column, stopping
either from weariness or because they had lost their
way, as was natural for men fleeing without guides
over strange roads, was dispersed and destroyed;
nor did anyone out of the whole army escape with
the exception of five hundred who were with the
king, a small number even out of the ten thousand

decem milibus militum, quos[1] Polybio auctore
traiecisse secum regem in Graeciam scripsimus,
12 exiguus numerus; quid,[2] si Antiati Valerio credamus
sexaginta milia militum fuisse in regio exercitu
scribenti, quadraginta inde milia cecidisse, supra
quinque milia capta cum signis militaribus ducentis
triginta? Romanorum centum quinquaginta in ipso
certamine pugnae, ab incursu Aetolorum se tuentes
non plus quinquaginta interfecti sunt.

XX. Consule per Phocidem et Boeotiam exercitum
ducente consciae defectionis civitates cum velamentis
ante portas stabant metu, ne hostiliter diriperentur.
2 Ceterum per omnes dies haud secus quam in pacato[3]
agro sine vexatione ullius rei agmen processit, donec
3 in agrum Coroneum ventum est. Ibi statua regis
Antiochi posita in templo Minervae Itoniae[4] iram
accendit, permissumque militi est ut circumiectum
templo agrum popularetur; dein cogitatio animum
subit, cum communi decreto Boeotorum posita esset
statua, indignum esse in unum Coronensem agrum
4 saevire. Revocato extemplo milite finis populandi
factus; castigati tantum verbis Boeoti ob ingratum
in tantis tamque recentibus beneficiis animum erga
Romanos.
5 Inter ipsum pugnae tempus decem naves regiae
cum praefecto Isidoro ad Thronium in sinu Maliaco
stabant. Eo gravis vulneribus Alexander Acarnan,
nuntius adversae pugnae, cum perfugisset, trepidae

---

[1] quos ς : quod B.   [2] quid ς : quod B.
[3] in pacato edd. vett. : pacato B.
[4] Itoniae J. F. Gronovius : itonaeae M : om. Bς.

---

[1] Cf. XXXV. xliii. 6. Livy does not take into account the
replacements who came over later (xv. 3 above.)

soldiers who, as I have written [1] on the authority of B.C. 191 Polybius, the king had brought with him to Greece; what if we were to believe Valerius Antias, who writes that there were sixty thousand men in the king's army, that forty thousand of them were killed and more than five thousand captured along with two hundred thirty military standards. One hundred fifty Romans perished in the actual shock of the battle, and from those who defended themselves against the attack of the Aetolians not more than fifty were killed.

XX. As the consul led the army through Phocis and Boeotia, the citizens, conscious of their rebellion, were standing before the gates holding badges of supplication, in fear that they would be plundered like enemies. But during all these days the column marched just as if they were passing through a peaceful country, doing no injury to anyone, until they came to the territory of Coronea. There a statue of King Antiochus, set up in the temple of Athena Itonia, enkindled the consul's wrath, and the soldiers were permitted to devastate the land around the temple; then the thought came to his mind that since the statue had been set up by a general decree of the Boeotians it was improper to vent his wrath on the territory of Coronea alone. The soldiers were at once recalled and an end put to the pillaging; the Boeotians received only a verbal reproof for their ingratitude to the Romans after such notable and recent acts of kindness.

Just at the time of the battle ten of the king's ships with the prefect Isidorus were moored at Thronium in the Malian gulf. Alexander the Acarnanian, arriving there sorely wounded, with news of

inde recenti terrore naves Cenaeum Euboeae petie-
6 runt. Ibi mortuus sepultusque Alexander. Tres,
quae ex Asia profectae eundem portum tenuerant,
naves audita exercitus clade Ephesum redierunt.
Isidorus ab Cenaeo Demetriadem, si forte eo deferret
7 fuga regem, traiecit. Per eosdem dies A. Atilius
praefectus Romanae classis magnos regios commeatus
iam fretum, quod ad Andrum insulam est, praeter-
8 vectos excepit; alias mersit, alias cepit naves; quae
novissimi agminis erant cursum in Asiam verterunt.
Atilius Piraeum unde profectus erat cum agmine
captivarum navium revectus magnam vim frumenti
et Atheniensibus et aliis eiusdem regionis sociis divisit.

XXI. Antiochus sub adventum consulis a Chalcide profectus Tenum primo tenuit, inde Ephesum
2 transmisit. Consuli Chalcidem venienti portae patu-
erunt, cum appropinquante eo Aristoteles praefectus
3 regis urbe excessisset. Et ceterae urbes in Euboea
sine certamine traditae; post paucosque dies omnibus
perpacatis sine ullius noxa urbis exercitus Thermopylas reductus, multo [1] modestia post victoriam quam

---

[1] multo ς : multa B.

---

[1] By this Livy probably means the narrow stretch of water
between Andros and Euboea.
[2] In the light of the narrative that has just preceded the
leisurely progress of the consul after the battle is hard to
explain or defend. A more relentless pursuit by the cavalry,
reinforced with light infantry, and liaison with the fleet of
Atilius, which was operating off the eastern coast, might
easily have resulted in the capture of the king and the final
termination of the war. Instead of following the coast route
after the battle, Glabrio marched well inland, with no apparent
motive, and the time he thus consumed (note especially
per omnes dies in xx. 1 above) gave the king the opportunity
to reach Chalcis, reorganize the remnant of his forces, and

the defeat, the ships at once made for Cenaeum in B.C. 191 Euboea, panic-stricken with fear. There Alexander died and was buried. Three ships which had set out from Asia and put in to the same harbour, learning of the slaughter of the army, returned to Ephesus. Isidorus from Cenaeum crossed to Demetrias, on the chance that the flight had taken the king that way. About this time Aulus Atilius, the commander of the Roman fleet, fell in with a great quantity of stores belonging to the king which had now crossed the strait [1] which lies near the island of Andros; some ships he sank, others he captured; those which were in the rear turned their course towards Asia. Atilius with his convoy of captured ships returned to Piraeus whence he had sailed, and distributed a great quantity of grain among both the Athenians and the other allies in the same vicinity.

XXI. Antiochus, at the approach of the consul,[2] left Chalcis and first proceeded to Tenos, then crossed to Ephesus. When the consul arrived at Chalcis the gates stood open, since at his approach Aristoteles, the king's prefect, had left the city. And the other cities of Euboea were given up without a struggle; and a few days later everything was quiet and the army was led back to Thermopylae doing no injury to any city, their moderate conduct after the victory being far more worthy of praise

make good his escape. We should remember that communications were slow and uncertain for both sides and information scanty and unreliable. It should also be pointed out that Livy shows no sign that he considers Acilius delinquent in any way, and there is no mention of any criticism on this ground a year later, when he was sharply criticized for other things (XXXVII. lvii. 10–15).

4 ipsa victoria laudabilior. Inde consul M. Catonem,
per quem quae gesta essent senatus populusque Ro-
5 manus haud dubio auctore sciret, Romam misit. Is a
Creusa—Thespiensium emporium est, in intimo sinu
Corinthiaco retractum—Patras Achaiae petit; a
Patris Corcyram usque Aetoliae atque Acarnaniae
littora legit, atque ita ad Hydruntum Italiae traicit.
6 Quinto die inde pedestri itinere Romam ingenti cursu
pervenit. Ante lucem ingressus urbem a porta ad
7 praetorem M. Iunium iter intendit. Is prima luce in
senatum vocavit; quo L. Cornelius Scipio, aliquot
diebus ante a consule dimissus, cum adveniens
audisset praegressum Catonem in senatu esse, super-
8 venit exponenti quae gesta essent. Duo inde legati
iussu senatus in contionem sunt producti, atque ibi
eadem quae in senatu de rebus in Aetolia gestis
9 exposuerunt. Supplicatio in triduum decreta est et
ut quadraginta hostiis maioribus praetor, quibus diis
10 ei videretur, sacrificaret. Per eosdem dies et M.
Fulvius Nobilior, qui biennio ante praetor in Hispaniam erat profectus, ovans urbem est ingressus;
11 argenti bigati prae se tulit centum triginta milia et

---

[1] These details might almost have been taken from some
eulogistic biography (or autobiography?) of Cato: cf. the
note to XXXIV. xxi. 8. The account in Plutarch (*Cato* xiv)
differs in several respects. According to it Cato was sent
immediately after the battle, that he might be the first to
report his own achievements; the route was different but the
five-day land journey is the same; there is no mention of
Scipio.

[2] Scipio had been defeated in the consular election for this
year (XXXV. xxiv. 4) but was elected for the following year
(xlv. 9 below). There is no other reference to his presence in

than the actual victory. Then the consul sent
Marcus Cato to Rome, that from him, a thoroughly
trustworthy source, the senate and the Roman
people might learn what had happened. From
Creusa—this is the trading-port of the Thespians,
lying deep in the Corinthian gulf—he made for
Patrae in Achaea; from Patrae he skirted the shores
of Aetolia and Acarnania right up to Corcyra and
thence crossed to Hydruntum in Italy. On the fifth
day from there in hurried progress by land he arrived
in Rome. Entering the City before daybreak he went
from the gate straight to the praetor Marcus Junius.[1]
Junius at daybreak summoned the senate; Lucius
Cornelius Scipio,[2] who had been sent on some days
before by the consul, learning on his arrival that
Cato had reached there first and was in the senate,
came in while he was recounting what had happened. Then the two legates by order of the senate
were taken before the assembly and there told the
same story as in the senate about the events in
Aetolia. A period of thanksgiving for three days
was proclaimed and the praetor was ordered to
sacrifice forty full-grown victims to whatever gods
he saw fit. About the same time too Marcus
Fulvius Nobilior,[3] who two years before had as
praetor set out for Spain, entered the City in ovation;
he carried in his procession one hundred and thirty
thousand silver coins stamped with the two-horse
chariot, and in addition to the minted money twelve

Greece, and Livy may have confused his visit to Rome with
one of Publius Scipio to announce a victory in Gaul (xxxix.
4 below).

[3] For his appointment to Spain see XXXIV. lv. 6; cf. also
xxxix. 1 below.

extra numeratum duodecim milia pondo argenti, auri
pondo centum viginti septem.

XXII. Acilius consul ab Thermopylis Heracleam
ad Aetolos praemisit ut tunc saltem, experti regiam
vanitatem, resipiscerent traditaque Heraclea cogi-
tarent de petenda ab senatu seu furoris sui seu
2 erroris venia.   Et ceteras Graeciae civitates defecisse
eo bello ab optime meritis Romanis; sed quia post
fugam regis, cuius fiducia officio decessissent,[1] non
addidissent pertinaciam culpae, in fidem receptas
3 esse; Aetolos quoque, quamquam non secuti sint
regem, sed accersierint, et duces [2] belli, non socii
fuerint, si paenitere possint, posse et incolumes esse.
4 Ad ea cum pacati nihil responderetur, appareretque
armis rem gerendam et rege superato bellum
Aetolicum integrum restare, castra ab Thermopylis
ad Heracleam movit, eoque ipso die, ut situm
nosceret urbis, ab omni parte equo moenia est
5 circumvectus.   Heraclea sita est in radicibus Oetae
montis, ipsa in campo, arcem imminentem loco alto
6 et undique praecipiti habet.   Contemplatus omnia
quae noscenda erant, quattuor simul locis aggredi
7 urbem constituit.   A flumine Asopo, qua et gymnasium est, L. Valerium operibus atque oppugnationi
praeposuit; partem extra muros, quae [3] frequentius
prope quam in urbe habitabatur, Ti. Sempronio
8 Longo oppugnandam dedit; e regione sinus Maliaci,

---

[1] decessissent ⸝: decessisset B.
[2] et duces ⸝: duces B.
[3] partem extra muros quae Madvig: arcem extra muros
quae M: om. B⸝.

thousand pounds of silver and one hundred and B.C. 191 twenty-seven pounds of gold.

XXII. The consul Acilius dispatched agents from Thermopylae to the Aetolians at Heraclea that then at least, having made trial of the king's unreliability, they might regain their senses, surrender Heraclea, and take counsel about asking pardon from the senate for their madness or, if they preferred, their mistake. Other states of Greece too in that war, he said, had revolted from the Romans who deserved so well of them, but because, after the flight of the king, from confidence in whom they had thrown off their allegiance, they had not added stubbornness to their fault, they had been received into alliance; the Aetolians also, though they had not followed the king but had summoned him, and had been the leaders in the war and not allies, if they could repent, could likewise be saved. When they gave no pacific reply to this, and it was evident that he must have recourse to arms, and that after the defeat of the king the Aetolian war remained as before, he moved camp from Thermopylae to Heraclea, and on the same day, to reconnoitre the site of the city, he rode on horseback around the walls on every side. Heraclea is situated at the foot of Mount Oeta, and the town proper was in a plain, with a citadel that overhung it, in a position lofty and steep on every side. In the direction of the Asopus river, where there is also a gymnasium, he put Lucius Valerius in charge of the works and the assault; the quarters outside the walls, which were almost more densely populated than the city itself, he gave to Tiberius Sempronius Longus to attack; on the side towards the Malian gulf, which had a

quae [1] aditum haud facilem pars habebat, M. Baebium, ab altero amniculo [2] quem Melana vocant,
adversus Dianae templum Ap. Claudium opposuit.
9 Horum magno certamine intra paucos dies turres
arietesque et alius omnis apparatus oppugnandarum
10 urbium perficitur. Et cum ager Heracleensis paluster
omnis frequensque proceris arboribus benigne ad
omne genus operum materiam suppeditabat, tum,
11 quia refugerant intra moenia Aetoli, deserta quae in
vestibulo urbis erant, tecta in varios usus non tigna
modo et tabulas sed laterem quoque et caementa et
saxa variae magnitudinis praebebant.

XXIII. Et Romani quidem operibus magis quam
armis urbem oppugnabant, Aetoli contra armis se
2 tuebantur. Nam cum ariete quaterentur muri, non
laqueis, ut solet,[3] exceptos declinabant ictus, sed
armati frequentes erumpebant,[4] quidam ignes etiam,
3 quos aggeribus inicerent, ferebant. Fornices quoque
in muro erant apti ad excurrendum,[5] et ipsi, cum pro
dirutis reficerent muros, crebriores eos ut pluribus
4 erumperetur in hostem locis faciebant. Hoc primis
diebus, dum integrae vires erant, et frequentes et
impigre [6] fecerunt; in dies deinde pauciores et
5 segnius. Etenim cum multis urgerentur rebus,

[1] e regione sinus Maliaci quae *Weissenborn* : et regione
mella quoque *B* : a sino maliaco quae *M* : et regione malea
quoque *ς*.

[2] amniculo *ed. Frobeniana* 1535 : angulo *Bς* : amnis latere
M.

[3] solet *ς* : solent *BM*.

[4] erumpebant *J. F. Gronovius* : om. *B*

[5] excurrendum *ς* : currendum *B*.

[6] et inpigre *ς* : inpigre *B*.

[1] These zones are, respectively, on the east, south-east (?),
north-east and west sides of the city.

B.C. 191

rather difficult approach, he placed Marcus Baebius, and at another little stream, which they call Melas, facing the temple of Artemis, he stationed Appius Claudius.[1] With great rivalry on their part, within a few days towers and battering-rams and all the other engines for attacking cities were prepared. And while the lands of Heraclea, all marshy and abounding in tall trees, made generous provision of materials for every kind of device, then too, because the Aetolians had taken refuge within the walls, the deserted houses in the entrance to the city offered them, for their various needs, not only beams and planks but brick and cement and stones of different sizes.

XXIII. And the Romans for their part conducted the siege with engines rather than by personal combat; the Aetolians, on the contrary, defended themselves by arms. For when the battering-rams shook the walls they did not, in the usual fashion, try to ward off the blows by catching the rams in nooses,[2] but made frequent armed sallies, and some carried firebrands also, to throw against the works. There were also arches in the walls suitable for sally-ports, and they themselves, as they built new walls to replace those that were destroyed, left more numerous openings to permit sallies against the enemy in more directions. In the early days, while they were fresh in strength, they did this both frequently and stoutly; day by day then their attacks grew fewer and more half-hearted. For although many difficulties beset them, nothing wore

[2] A recognized device for defence against battering-rams was to slip nooses over their heads and so dismount the rams or at least divert their blows.

LIVY

nulla eos res aeque ac vigiliae conficiebant, Romanis
in magna copia militum succedentibus aliis in
stationem aliorum, Aetolos propter paucitatem eos-
6 dem dies noctesque adsiduo labore urente. Per
quattuor et viginti dies, ita ut nullum tempus vacuum
dimicatione esset, adversus quattuor e partibus simul
oppugnantem hostem nocturnus diurno continuatus
7 labor est. Cum fatigatos iam Aetolos sciret consul
et ex spatio [1] temporis et quod ita transfugae
8 adfirmabant, tale consilium init. Media nocte
receptui signum dedit et ab oppugnatione simul
milites omnes deductos usque ad diei tertiam horam
9 quietos in castris tenuit; inde coepta oppugnatio ad
mediam rursus noctem perducta est,[2] intermissa
10 deinde usque ad tertiam diei horam. Fatigationem
rati esse causam Aetoli non continuandae oppugnationis, quae et ipsos adfecerat, ubi Romanis datum
receptui signum esset, velut ipsi quoque [3] revocati
pro se quisque ex stationibus decedebant, nec ante
tertiam diei horam armati in muris apparebant.

XXIV. Consul cum nocte media intermisisset
oppugnationem, quarta vigilia rursus ab tribus
2 partibus summa vi adgressus, ab una Ti.[4] Sem-
pronium tenere intentos milites signumque expectare
iussit, ad ea [5] in nocturno tumultu, unde clamor
exaudiretur, haud dubie ratus hostes concursuros.
3 Aetoli pars sopiti adfecta labore ac vigiliis corpora ex
somno moliebantur, pars vigilantes adhuc ad [6]
4 strepitum pugnantium in tenebris currunt. Hostes

---

[1] ex spatio *Novak* : expectatio *B* : expectatione ς.
[2] perducta est ς : perductae sunt *B*.
[3] ipsi quoque ς : spe hac *B*.
[4] Ti. *Sigonius* : t. *M* : om. *B*ς.
[5] ea ς : eam *B*.   [6] adhuc ad *Gelenius* : ad hunc *B*.

them down so much as loss of sleep; the Romans,
with their wealth of men, sent relief after relief
to the posts, while the Aetolians, on account of
their small number, were tortured by constant toil
falling to the same men day and night. For four-
and-twenty days, so that no time was free from
fighting, against an enemy attacking from four sides
at once, nightly toil was joined to daily labour.
When the consul saw that the Aetolians were now
weary, judging both by the lapse of time and by
the testimony of deserters, he formed the following
plan. At midnight he gave the signal for the recall,
and withdrawing all his men from the works, until
the third hour of the day he kept them quiet in
camp; then the siege was begun and continued
again until midnight and then interrupted until the
third hour of the day. The Aetolians thought that
the cause of interrupting operations was weariness,
which had troubled them too, and when the recall
was sounded for the Romans, as if they too were
summoned, each for himself left his post, nor did
they show themselves in arms on the walls until the
third hour of the day.

XXIV. When the consul had stopped the siege at
midnight, during the fourth watch he again launched
a furious attack from three sides, ordering Tiberius
Sempronius on one side to hold his men alert and
await orders, thinking that without doubt, in a
night alarm, the enemy would rush to the point from
which the noise was heard. Part of the Aetolians
who had been sleeping were rousing themselves,
exhausted by toil and loss of sleep, part, who were
still awake, rushed in the dark towards the shouts
of the fighters. Some of the enemy were trying to

A.U.C.
563

partim per ruinas iacentis muri transcendere conantur,
partim scalis ascensus temptant, adversus quos
undique ad opem ferendam concurrunt Aetoli.
5 Pars una, in qua aedificia extra urbem erant, neque
defenditur neque oppugnatur; sed qui oppugnarent
intenti signum expectabant; defensor nemo aderat.
6 Iam dilucescebat, cum signum consul dedit; et sine
ullo certamine partim per semirutos, partim scalis [1]
integros muros transcendere. Simul clamor, index
capti oppidi, est exauditus; undique Aetoli desertis
7 stationibus in arcem fugiunt. Oppidum victores
permissu consulis diripiunt, non tam ab ira nec ab
odio quam ut miles, coercitus in tot receptis ex
potestate hostium urbibus, aliquo tandem loco
8 fructum victoriae sentiret. Revocatos inde a medio
ferme die milites cum in duas divisisset partes, unam
radicibus montium circumduci ad rupem iussit,
quae fastigio altitudinis par,[2] media valle velut
9 abrupta erat ab arce; sed adeo prope geminata
cacumina eorum montium sunt, ut ex vertice altero
conici tela in arcem possint;[3] cum dimidia parte
militum consul ab urbe escensurus [4] in arcem signum
ab iis qui ab tergo in rupem evasuri erant expectabat.
10 Non tulere qui in arce erant Aetoli primum eorum
qui rupem ceperant clamorem, deinde impetum ab
urbe Romanorum et fractis [5] iam animis et nulla ibi
praeparata re ad obsidionem diutius tolerandam,

---

[1] partim per semirutos, partim scalis *Weissenborn* : partim
scalis *B* : partim per erutos partim scalis *M*.
[2] par ϛ : pars *B*.
[3] possint ϛ : possent *BM*.
[4] consul ab urbe escensurus *J. F. Gronovius* : consul ab
urbe descensurus *Bϛ* : excessurus consul ab urbe *M*.
[5] et fractis *ed. Parisina* 1513 : ex fractis *B* : effractis ϛ.

climb over the fallen ruins of the wall, some attempting to get up by means of ladders, and against them
the Aetolians rushed from all sides to bring aid.
The one side, on which there were buildings outside
the city, was neither defended nor attacked; but
men to attack it were waiting, eager for the signal;
there was no one to defend it. It was now growing
light when the consul gave the signal; and without any
opposition some climbed over the half-fallen walls,
others with ladders surmounted the uninjured sections. At the same moment the shout which testifies
that a city has been taken was heard; the Aetolians
from all sides left their posts and fled to the citadel.
The victors, with the permission of the consul,
plundered the city, not so much from any wrath or
hatred as that the soldiers, restrained in the case of
so many cities recovered from the enemy, might in
some place at last see the fruits of victory. The
soldiers were then recalled at about midday, and
when he had divided them into two parts he ordered
one to be led around at the foot of the mountain to
a cliff which, being about its equal in height, was
cut off from the citadel by, as it were, a valley lying
between them; but the summits of the two heights
were so close together that from the other crest
weapons could be hurled into the citadel; with the
other half of the troops the consul intended to
climb the citadel from the town and was waiting
for the signal from those who were to come out on
the cliff from the rear. The Aetolians who were in
the citadel did not endure first the shout of the
party which had taken the cliff, then the attack of
the Romans from the town, being now both broken
in spirit and unprepared with anything necessary to

231

LIVY

11 utpote congregatis [1] feminis puerisque et imbelli alia
turba in arcem, quae vix capere, nedum tueri multitudinem tantam posset. Itaque ad primum impetum
12 abiectis armis dediderunt sese. Traditus [2] inter
ceteros princeps Aetolorum Damocritus est, qui
principio belli decretum Aetolorum, quo accersendum
Antiochum censuerant, T. Quinctio poscenti respon-
derat, in Italia daturum, cum castra ibi Aetoli
posuissent. Ob eam ferociam maius victoribus
gaudium traditus fuit.

XXV. Eodem tempore, quo Romani Heracleam,
Philippus Lamiam ex composito oppugnabat,[3] circa
Thermopylas cum consule redeunte ex Boeotia, ut
victoriam ipsi populoque Romano gratularetur excu-
saretque, quod morbo impeditus bello non inter-
2 fuisset, congressus. Inde diversi ad duas simul
3 oppugnandas urbes profecti. Intersunt septem
ferme milia passuum; et quia Lamia cum [4] posita
in tumulo est, tum regionem maxime Oetae spectat,
oppido quam breve intervallum videtur, et omnia in
4 conspectu sunt. Cum enixe, velut proposito certamine, Romani Macedonesque diem ac noctem aut
in operibus aut in proeliis essent, hoc maior difficultas
Macedonibus erat, quod Romani aggere et vineis
et omnibus supra terram operibus, subter Macedones

---

[1] congregatis ς : congregandis B.
[2] traditus edd. vett. : traditum B.
[3] oppugnabat ς : oppugnabant BM.
[4] cum ed. Frobeniana 1535 : om. B.

---

[1] Cf. XXXV. xxxiii. 9–10, and for his death, XXXVII.
xlvi. 5.

B.C. 191

resist any longer an attack there, especially since the women and children and the other non-combatants had collected in the citadel, which could scarce hold the defenders and still less protect so great a crowd. And so at the first assault they threw down their arms and surrendered. Among those thus given up was Damocritus, the chief of the Aetolians, who, at the beginning of hostilities, when Titus Quinctius had asked for the decree of the Aetolians by which they had voted to invite Antiochus, had replied that he would give it to him in Italy when they had encamped there.[1] By reason of this violent disposition his surrender was a greater pleasure to the victors.

XXV. At the same time that the Romans were attacking Heraclea, Philip by agreement was besieging Lamia, having met the consul near Thermopylae when he returned from Boeotia, to congratulate him and the Roman people upon his victory and to apologize because as a result of illness he had not been present at the battle. Then they separated to attack the two cities at the same time. They are about seven miles apart, and because Lamia both lies on a hill and commands a view especially over the region of Oeta, the distance seems exceedingly [2] short and everything is in sight. While the Romans and the Macedonians, as if competing for a prize, were strenuously engaged day and night either on the siege-works or in fighting, the task of the Macedonians was the more difficult because the Romans were fighting with a terrace and mantlets and all their works above ground, the Macedonians

---

[2] Both *oppido* and *quam* are colloquial intensives, and the combination of the two seems not to occur before Livy.

A.U.C.
563

cuniculis oppugnabant, et in asperis locis silex paene
5 impenetrabilis ferro occurrebat. Et cum parum
procederet inceptum, per colloquia principum oppi-
6 danos temptabat rex ut urbem dederent,[1] haud dubius
quin si prius Heraclea capta foret, Romanis se potius
quam sibi dedituri essent, suamque gratiam consul in
7 obsidione liberanda facturus esset. Nec eum opinio
est frustrata; confestim enim ab Heraclea capta
nuntius venit ut oppugnatione absisteret: aequius
esse Romanos milites, qui acie dimicassent cum
8 Aetolis, praemia victoriae habere. Ita recessum ab
Lamia est, et propinquae clade urbis ipsi, ne quid
simile paterentur, effugerunt.

XXVI. Paucis priusquam Heraclea caperetur diebus Aetoli concilio Hypatam coacto legatos ad An-
2 tiochum miserunt, inter quos et Thoas idem, qui et
antea, missus est. Mandata erant ut ab rege peterent, primum ut ipse coactis rursus terrestribus
3 navalibusque[2] copiis in Graeciam traiceret, deinde,
si qua ipsum teneret res, ut pecuniam et auxilia
mitteret; id cum ad dignitatem eius fidemque
pertinere,[3] non prodi socios, tum etiam ad incolumi-
tatem regni, ne sineret Romanos vacuos omni cura,
4 cum Aetolorum gentem sustulissent, omnibus copiis
5 in Asiam traicere.[4] Vera erant quae dicebantur;

---

[1] dederent ⟨⟩: decederent B.
[2] naualibusque ⟨⟩: naualibus B.
[3] pertinere *Aldus*: pertineret B⟨⟩.
[4] traicere ⟨⟩: traiceret B.

---

[1] Philip showed no signs of resentment at this treatment
until 185 B.C. (XXXIX. xxiii. 9), when it was one of his
grievances.

234

with tunnels underground, and in the rough spots
flint, almost unworkable with iron, met them. And
since they were making little progress, the king,
through conferences with their chiefs, tried to induce
the townspeople to surrender the city, not doubting
that if Heraclea were captured first they would
submit to the Romans in preference to him and that
the consul would take the credit to himself in raising
the siege. Nor was he deceived in this opinion;
for immediately after the taking of Heraclea the
message came that he should abandon the siege:
it was fairer that the Roman soldiers, who had
fought in the battle-line with the Aetolians, should
enjoy the rewards of victory.[1] So he retired from
Lamia and, after the misfortune of a neighbouring
city, the people escaped suffering a similar fate.[2]

XXVI. A few days before Heraclea was taken the
Aetolians held a council at Hypata and sent ambassadors to Antiochus, among whom was again the
same Thoas who had been sent there before. Their
instructions were that they should ask the king,
first, that he should again collect all his forces on
land and sea and cross to Greece; secondly, if anything detained him, that he should send money and
reinforcements; that his allies be not deserted concerned not only his dignity and loyalty but the
safety of his kingdom; that he should not permit
the Romans, free from all worry after they had
destroyed the Aetolian people, to cross with all
their forces to Asia. What they said was true; and

---

[2] The natural inference from the consul's message would
be that the Roman army would at once take up the siege,
but this was not done and Lamia was not taken until the next
year (XXXVII. v. 3).

A.U.C.
563

eo magis regem moverunt. Itaque in praesentia
pecuniam, quae ad usus belli necessaria erat, legatis
dedit; auxilia terrestria navaliaque affirmavit mis-
6 surum. Thoantem unum ex legatis retinuit, et
ipsum haud invitum morantem, ut exactor praesens
promissorum adesset.

XXVII. Ceterum Heraclea capta fregit tandem
2 animos Aetolorum, et paucos [1] post dies quam ad
bellum renovandum acciendumque regem in Asiam
miserant legatos, abiectis belli consiliis pacis petendae
3 oratores ad consulem miserunt. Quos dicere exorsos
consul interfatus, cum alia sibi praevertenda esse
dixisset, redire Hypatam eos datis dierum decem
indutiis et L. Valerio Flacco cum iis misso iussit
eique, quae secum acturi fuissent, exponere, et si
4 qua vellent alia. Hypatam ut est ventum, principes
Aetolorum apud Flaccum concilium habuerunt con-
sultantes, quonam agendum modo apud consulem
5 foret. Parantibus iis antiqua iura foederum ordiri
meritaque in populum Romanum absistere iis Flaccus
6 iussit, quae ipsi violassent ac rupissent; confessionem
iis culpae magis profuturam et totam in preces
orationem versam; nec enim in causa [2] ipsorum, sed
in populi Romani clementia [3] spem salutis positam
7 esse; et se [4] suppliciter agentibus iis adfuturum [5]
et apud consulem et Romae in senatu; eo quoque
8 enim mittendos fore legatos. Haec una via omnibus

---

[1] paucos *Drakenborch* : ad paucos *Bς*.
[2] causa *ς* : causam *B*.
[3] clementia *ς* : clementiam *B*.
[4] se *ed. Frobeniana* 1535 : *om. B*.
[5] adfuturum *ς* : profuturum *B*.

for that reason it impressed the king more. Therefore for the moment he gave the ambassadors the
money which was needed for the expenses of the
war; he assured them that he would send military
and naval assistance. Thoas, one of the ambassadors,
he kept with him; he remained there not at all
against his will, that someone might be at hand to
demand the fulfilment of the promises.

XXVII. But the capture of Heraclea finally broke
the spirit of the Aetolians, and a few days after
they had sent ambassadors to Asia to renew the war
and summon the king, they laid aside their warlike
designs and sent delegates to the consul to beg for
peace. The consul broke in when they had begun
to speak, saying that he had more important matters
to attend to, and ordered them to return to Hypata,
granting them a truce of ten days and sending
Lucius Valerius Flaccus with them, telling them to
state to him the matters they had planned to discuss
with himself and anything else they desired. When
they reached Hypata the chiefs of the Aetolians
held a meeting with Flaccus, considering in what
manner they should plead with the consul. They
were preparing to begin with their ancient treaty
relations and their services to the Roman people,
when Flaccus bade them cease to mention what
they had themselves violated and broken; a con-
fession of wrongdoing would avail them more and a
speech devoted entirely to prayers; for not on their
own cause but on the clemency of the Roman people
did their hopes of safety depend; he too would
support them if they should plead like suppliants
both before the consul and with the senate at Rome;
for there too ambassadors should be sent. This

A.U.C.
563

ad salutem visa est, ut in fidem se permitteren
Romanorum; ita enim et illis [1] violandi supplice
verecundiam se imposituros, et ipsos nihilo minu
suae potestatis fore, si quid melius fortuna ostendis
set.

XXVIII. Postquam ad consulem ventum est
Phaeneas legationis princeps longam orationem e
varie ad mitigandam iram victoris compositam ita
ad extremum finivit, ut diceret Aetolos se suaque
2 omnia fidei populi Romani permittere. Id consul ub
audivit, " etiam atque etiam videte " inquit, " Aetoli
ut ita permittatis." Tum decretum Phaeneas, in
3 quo id [2] diserte scriptum erat, ostendit. " Quando
ergo " inquit " ita permittitis, postulo, ut [3] mihi
Dicaearchum civem vestrum et Menestam Epirotam"
—Naupactum is cum praesidio ingressus ad defectionem compulerat—" et Amynandrum cum principibus Athamanum, quorum consilio ab nobis defecistis,
4 sine mora dedatis." Prope dicentem interfatus
Romanum " non in servitutem " inquit, " sed in
fidem tuam nos tradidimus, et certum habeo te [4]

---

[1] illis *edd. vett.* : illi *B*ς.
[2] in quo id *ed. Frobeniana* 1535 : in id quod *B* : in id quo ς.
[3] ut *ed. Moguntina* 1518 : id *B*ς.
[4] habeo te *ed. Frobeniana* 1535 : habeo *B* : te habeo ς.

---

[1] There was then a mental reservation in the submission
of the Aetolians which was consistent enough with Greek
institutions: it bound the Romans to show them the consideration due to suppliants, but left the Aetolians free to break
off the relations when an opportunity presented itself. One
wonders how much of this Flaccus understood and accepted
as part of the proposal. On the other hand, as Polybius
(XX. ix) shows, the Aetolians did not understand that to the
Romans *in fidem se permittere* meant complete and un-
conditional surrender. In consequence the two parties are at

eemed to all of them the only way to safety, that
they should entrust themselves to the good faith of
the Romans; for that by so doing they would at
once render the Romans ashamed to do violence to
suppliants and themselves no less be absolutely free
should fortune offer them anything better.

XXVIII. When they came before the consul,
Phaeneas, the leader of the embassy, spoke at
length and with manifold devices with which to
soften the heart of the conqueror and concluded by
saying that the Aetolians entrusted themselves and
all their possessions to the good faith of the Roman
people. When the consul heard this he replied,
" Consider again and again, Aetolians, whether you
are submitting on these conditions." Then Phaeneas
displayed the decree in which this was explicitly
stated in writing.[1] " Since, then," the consul said,
" you are submitting on these terms, I demand that
Dicaearchus your fellow-citizen and Menestas of
Epirus "—he had entered Naupactus with a garrison
and compelled it to revolt—" and Amynander with
the chiefs of the Athamanes, by whose advice you
revolted from us,[2] be delivered to me without delay."
He interrupted while the Roman was still speaking:
" We have not delivered ourselves into slavery but
have entrusted ourselves to your good faith,[3] and I

cross purposes in the following debate until the national
definitions are made clear.

[2] From XXXV. xlvii. 5–8 it appears that Acilius is mis-
informed about the conduct of the Athamanes. In any case
Amynander himself was beyond the reach of the Aetolians
(xiv. 9 above).

[3] This is the Aetolian interpretation of the phrase, which
put the Romans on their honour to treat them as suppliants,
but bound the Aetolians by no obligation.

A.U.C.
563

imprudentia labi, qui nobis imperes, quae mori
5 Graecorum non sint." Ad ea consul " nec hercule
inquit " magnopere nunc curo quid Aetoli satis e
more Graecorum factum esse censeant, dum eg
more Romano imperium inhibeam in deditos mod
6 decreto suo, ante armis victos; itaque, ni propere fit
quod impero, vinciri vos iam iubebo." Adfer
catenas et circumsistere lictores iussit. Tum
fracta Phaeneae ferocia Aetolisque aliis est, e
7 tandem cuius condicionis essent senserunt, e
Phaeneas se quidem et qui adsint Aetolorum scir
facienda esse quae imperentur dixit, sed ad decer
nenda ea concilio[2] Aetolorum opus esse; ad i
8 petere ut decem dierum indutias daret. Petent
Flacco pro Aetolis indutiae datae, et Hypatan
reditum est. Ubi cum in consilio delectorum, quo
apocletos[3] vocant, Phaeneas, et quae imperarentur e
9 quae ipsis[4] prope accidissent, exposuisset, ingemue
runt quidem principes condicioni[5] suae, parendun
tamen victori censebant et ex omnibus oppidis con
vocandos Aetolos ad concilium.

XXIX. Postquam vero coacta omnis multitud
eadem illa audivit, adeo saevitia imperii atqu
indignitate animi exasperati sunt ut, si in pac
fuissent, illo impetu irae concitari potuerint a

---

[1] tum ⸝: cum B.
[2] concilio ⸝: consilio B.
[3] apocletos ⸝: apoclestos B.
[4] ipsis ⸝: ipsi B.
[5] condicioni ed. Frobeniana 1535 : condicionis B⸝.

---

[1] This is the Roman interpretation of the same phrase.

feel sure that you err from ignorance in giving us orders which are inconsistent with the customs of the Greeks." To this the consul replied: " Nor, by Hercules, do I care very much what the Aetolians regard as properly consistent with the customs of the Greeks, since I, in the Roman way, am delivering an order to men who a moment ago surrendered[1] by their own decree and had previously been conquered by armed force; therefore, unless my order is immediately executed I shall at once order you to be put in chains." He directed the chains to be brought and the lictors to stand by. Then the haughty spirit of Phaeneas was broken and that of the other Aetolians, and they finally perceived in what condition they were, and Phaeneas said that he and those of the Aetolians who were present knew that they would have to do what was commanded, but that to confirm the decree a council of the Aetolians was necessary; for that purpose he requested that a truce for ten days be granted them. When Flaccus supported the request on behalf of the Aetolians the truce was granted and they returned to Hypata. There, when in the select council which they call the *apocletes* Phaeneas explained both what they were ordered to do and what they had almost experienced, the chiefs indeed groaned at their situation, yet recognized that they must obey their conqueror and that the Aetolians from all the towns must be summoned to a council.

XXIX. But after the assembled multitude had heard the same narrative, anger at the order and a sense of unjust treatment so inflamed their minds that, if they had been at peace, they would by that onset of passion have been provoked to war.

A.U.C.
563

2 bellum. Ad iram accedebat et difficultas eorum
quae imperarentur (quonam modo enim utique re

3 gem Amynandrum se tradere posse?) et spes fort
oblata, quod Nicander eo ipso tempore ab rege An
tiocho veniens implevit expectatione vana multitu

4 dinem, terra marique ingens parari bellum. Duo
decimo is die quam conscenderat navem, in Aetolian
perfecta legatione rediens Phalara in sinu Maliac

5 tenuit. Inde Lamiam pecuniam cum devexisset
ipse cum expeditis prima vespera inter Macedonun
Romanaque castra medio agro, dum Hypatam noti
callibus petit, in stationem incidit Macedonun
deductusque ad regem est nondum convivio dimisso

6 Quod ubi nuntiatum est, velut hospitis, non hosti
adventu motus Philippus accumbere eum epulariqu

7 iussit, atque inde dimissis aliis, solum retentum

8 ipsum quidem de se timere quicquam vetuit, Aeto
lorum prava consilia atque in ipsorum capu
semper recidentia accusavit, qui primum Romanos

9 deinde Antiochum in Graeciam adduxissent. Se
praeteritorum, quae magis reprehendi quam corrig
possint, oblitum se non facturum, ut insultet adversi

10 rebus eorum; Aetolos quoque finire tandem adversu
se odia debere, et Nicandrum privatim [1] eius diei, qu

11 servatus a se foret, meminisse. Ita datis qui i
tutum eum prosequerentur, Hypatam Nicande
consultantibus de pace Romana supervenit.

---

[1] priuatim ς : priuatum B.

Added to their wrath was also the difficulty of the
orders (for how, in any case, could they possibly
hand over King Amynander?) and the hope which by
chance offered itself because just at that time
Nicander, coming from King Antiochus, filled the
multitude with the idle expectation that a great war
was preparing on land and sea. On the twelfth day
after he had embarked he returned to Aetolia after
completing his mission and put in at Phalara on the
Malian gulf. When he had brought the money from
there to Lamia and he with his companions travelling
light was passing at nightfall across the fields between the Macedonian and Roman camps, seeking
Hypata over familiar paths, he encountered a picket
of Macedonians and was conducted to the king,
whose dinner-party had not yet broken up. When
this was announced Philip, behaving as if a guest,
not an enemy, had arrived, bade him recline and
dine and then, dismissing the others and keeping
him alone, forbade his guest to have any fear of
himself, and blamed the Aetolians for the evil
counsels which had brought first the Romans and
then Antiochus to Greece, counsels ever fated to
recoil upon their own heads. But forgetting the
past, which could be criticized more easily than
corrected, he would not act in such a way as to
trample upon them in their misfortunes; the
Aetolians too should at length end their quarrel
with him, and Nicander personally should remember
the day on which his life had been spared by him.
So he provided him with an escort to conduct him
to a place of safety, and Nicander proceeded
to Hypata and found them deliberating about the
Roman peace.

XXX. M'. Acilius vendita aut concessa militi circa
Heracleam praeda, postquam nec Hypatae pacata
consilia[1] esse, et Naupactum concurrisse Aetolos
ut inde totum impetum belli sustinerent, audivit
2 praemisso Ap. Claudio cum quattuor milibus militum
ad occupanda iuga, qua difficiles transitus montium
3 erant, ipse Oetam escendit Herculique sacrificium
fecit in eo loco quem Pyram, quod ibi mortale corpus
eius dei sit crematum, appellant. Inde toto exercitu
profectus reliquum iter satis expedito agmine fecit
4 ut ad Coracem ventum est—mons est altissimus inter
Callipolim et Naupactum—ibi et iumenta multa ex
agmine praecipitata cum ipsis oneribus sunt et ho-
5 mines vexati; et facile apparebat quam cum inerti
hoste res esset, qui tam impeditum saltum nullo
6 praesidio, ut clauderet transitum, insedisset. Tum
quoque vexato exercitu ad Naupactum descendit, et
uno castello adversus arcem posito ceteras partes
urbis divisis copiis pro situ moenium circumsedit.
Nec minus operis laborisque ea oppugnatio quam
Heracleae habuit.

XXXI. Eodem tempore et Messene in Peloponneso ab Achaeis, quod concilii eorum recusaret esse,
2 oppugnari coepta est. Duae[2] civitates, Messene et
Elis, extra concilium Achaicum erant; cum Aetolis
3 sentiebant. Elei tamen post fugatum ex Graecia
Antiochum legatis Achaeorum lenius responderant:

---

[1] consilia 5 : concilia B.
[2] duae 5 : et duae B.

---

[1] Literally, "funeral pile."
[2] For their embassy to Antiochus and their anticipations
of trouble with the Achaeans, see v. 1–2 above.

XXX. Manius Acilius, having sold or given to the soldiers the booty around Heraclea, when he heard that no pacific counsels were being taken at Hypata but that the Aetolians had assembled at Naupactus, that from there they might endure the whole violence of the war, sent Appius Claudius in advance with four thousand men to hold the ridges where the crossing of the mountains was difficult and himself climbed Oeta and offered sacrifice to Hercules at the place which they call Pyra,[1] since there the mortal body of the god had been burned. Then setting out with the entire army he finished the rest of the journey with fairly easy marching; when he came to Corax—this is a very high mountain between Callipolis and Naupactus—there both many animals from the train plunged to the bottom of the gorge, loads and all, and the men were in difficulties; and it was easily seen with how careless an enemy they had to deal, who had not held so difficult a pass with any kind of guard to prevent their crossing. Then too, though his army had suffered, he marched down to Naupactus, and establishing one fort over against the citadel he, dividing his forces as the situation of the walls required, surrounded the other sections of the city. Nor did this siege involve any less toil and labour than that of Heraclea.

XXXI. At the same time too Messene in the Peloponnesus began to be besieged by the Achaeans because it refused to join their league. Two cities, Messene and Elis, were outside the Achaean council; their sympathies were with the Aetolians. The Eleans, however, after Antiochus was driven from Greece,[2] responded more moderately to the am-

LIVY

dimisso praesidio regio cogitaturos se quid [1] sibi
4 faciendum esset; Messenii sine responso dimissis
legatis moverant bellum, trepidique rerum suarum,
5 cum iam ager effuso exercitu passim ureretur castra-
que prope urbem poni viderent, legatos Chalcidem
ad T. Quinctium, auctorem libertatis, miserunt, qui
nuntiarent Messenios Romanis, non Achaeis et
6 aperire portas et dedere urbem paratos esse. Auditis
legatis extemplo profectus Quinctius a Megalopoli
ad Diophanen praetorem Achaeorum misit, qui
extemplo reducere eum a Messene exercitum et
7 venire ad se iuberet. Dicto paruit Diophanes et
soluta obsidione expeditus ipse praegressus agmen
circa Andaniam, parvum oppidum inter Megalopolim
8 Messenenque positum, Quinctio occurrit; et cum
causas oppugnationis exponeret, castigatum leniter,
quod tantam rem sine auctoritate sua conatus esset,
dimittere exercitum iussit nec pacem omnium bono
9 partam turbare. Messeniis imperavit ut exules
reducerent et Achaeorum concilii essent; si qua
haberent de quibus aut recusare aut in posterum
10 caveri sibi vellent, Corinthum ad se venirent; Diophanen concilium Achaeorum extemplo sibi praebere

---

¹ se quid ς : quid *B*.

---

¹ The Achaeans were trying to induce these two cities
voluntarily to join them or, if necessary, to coerce them.
² Livy does not mention it, but a short time before
Philopoemen had released Messene from the domination of
Nabis (Pausanias IV. xxix. 4); it had probably favoured
Antiochus. Cities within Achaean territory but not members
of the League were of course constant menaces to the League.
³ Diophanes had succeeded Philopoemen as Achaean
strategus in the fall of 191 B.C.
⁴ Quinctius had no authority from any source, Roman or
Greek, to issue orders to the Greeks. He based his actions

ambassadors of the Achaeans:[1] if the royal garrison were withdrawn they would consider what they should do; the Messenians,[2] on the other hand, had dismissed the ambassadors unanswered and had begun war, but fearful for their cause when their crops were being burned everywhere by a wide-ranging army and they saw the camp established near the city, they sent ambassadors to Chalcis to Titus Quinctius, the source of their liberty, to say that the Messenians were ready to open their gates and surrender their city to the Romans, not the Achaeans. Having listened to the ambassadors Quinctius, setting out at once from Megalopolis, sent a messenger to Diophanes, praetor of the Achaeans,[3] to order him to withdraw his army at once from Messene and to report to him. Diophanes obeyed the summons, and raising the siege and himself travelling light, preceded the column and near Andania, a little town located between Megalopolis and Messene, met Quinctius; and when he had explained the reason for the siege, Quinctius reproached him gently because he had undertaken so important a matter without his authorization,[4] and ordered him to disband his army and not to disturb the peace secured to the advantage of everyone. He instructed the Messenians to recall their exiles and join the council of the Achaeans; if they had any matters about which they wished to raise objections or to take precautions for themselves against future contingencies, they should come to him at Corinth; Diophanes he directed to give him an immediate opportunity to meet the Achaean

in his prestige and his peculiar position as the liberator of Greece, and they were rarely challenged by the Greek states.

A.U.C.
563

iussit. Ibi de Zacyntho intercepta per fraudem
insula questus postulavit, ut restitueretur Romanis
11 Philippi Macedonum regis Zacynthus fuerat; eam
mercedem Amynandro dederat, ut per Athamaniam
ducere exercitum in superiorem partem Aetoliae
liceret, qua expeditione fractis animis Aetolos com-
12 pulit ad petendam pacem. Amynander Philippum
Megalopolitanum insulae praefecit; postea per
bellum, quo se Antiocho adversus Romanos con-
iunxit, Philippo ad munera belli revocato Hieroclem
Agrigentinum successorem misit.

XXXII. Is post fugam ab Thermopylis Antiocho
Amynandrumque a Philippo Athamania pulsum,
missis ultro ad Diophanen praetorem Achaeorum
nuntiis pecunia pactus [1] insulam Achaeis tradidit.
2 Id praemium belli suum esse aequum censebant
Romani : non enim M'. Acilium consulem legionesque
Romanas Diophani et Achaeis ad Thermopylas
3 pugnasse. Diophanes adversus haec purgare interdum [3] sese gentemque, interdum de iure facti dis-
4 serere. Quidam Achaeorum et initio eam se rem
aspernatos testabantur et tunc pertinaciam increpita-

---

[1] pactus ς : pactis B.
[2] tradidit ς : tradit B.
[3] purgare interdum *aut* interdum purgare ς : purgare B.

---

[1] Now that Rome was permanently involved in the east
Zacynthos had a certain strategic value, since it was important
to have all possible naval bases closed to foreign powers.
Rome had occupied it in 211 B.C. (XXVI. xxiv. 15), but in
some manner it had passed into Philip's possession. Livy
relates its subsequent history in the following sections. For
some reason Quinctius makes no mention of Rome's earlier
interest.

ouncil. There he complained about the island of B.C. 191
Zacynthos,¹ which had been wrongfully occupied,
and demanded that it be restored to the Romans.
Zacynthos had formerly belonged to Philip, king of
the Macedonians; he had ceded it to Amynander
as a bribe to induce him to permit Philip to lead
his army through Athamania into the upper part of
Aetolia, on the expedition ² by which he had broken
the spirits of the Aetolians and forced them to seek
peace. Amynander had appointed Philip of Megalopolis governor of the island; later, during the war
in which he joined Antiochus against the Romans,
he had recalled Philip for military duties and sent
Hierocles of Agrigentum to succeed him.

XXXII. He, after the flight of Antiochus from
Thermopylae and the expulsion of Amynander from
Athamania by Philip, had at his own instance sent
ambassadors to Diophanes, praetor of the Achaeans,
had made a bargain for money, and transferred the
island to the Achaeans. That it should be their
prize of war seemed fair to the Romans: for, they
said, Manius Acilius the consul and the Roman
legions had not fought for Diophanes and the
Achaeans at Thermopylae.³ Diophanes in reply
sometimes defended himself and the state, sometimes argued the legal aspects of the case. Some
of the Achaeans both bore witness that from the
beginning they had objected to the proceeding and
at this time taunted the praetor for his persistence;

² In 207 B.C. (XXVIII. vii. 14) or 205 B.C. (XXIX. xii. 1).
³ Quinctius may have spoken more frankly than he realized
or intended on this occasion, but the Greeks themselves were
rapidly making the Roman position as disinterested liberators
untenable.

bant praetoris; auctoribusque iis decretum est, u
5 T. Quinctio ea res permitteretur. Erat Quinctiu
sicut adversantibus asper, ita, si cederes, iden
placabilis. Omissa contentione vocis vultusque " s
utilem " inquit " possessionem eius insulae censeren
Achaeis esse, auctor essem senatui populoqu
6 Romano ut eam vos habere sinerent [1]; ceterum sicu
testudinem, ubi collecta in suum tegumen est, tutan
ad omnes ictus video esse, ubi exserit [2] partes aliquas
quodcumque nudavit,[3] obnoxium atque infirmun
habere, haud dissimiliter vos, Achaei, clausos undiqu
7 mari, quae intra Peloponnesi sunt terminos,[4] ea e
8 iungere vobis et iuncta tueri facile, simul aviditat
plura amplectendi hinc excedatis, nuda vobis omnia
quae extra sint, et exposita ad omnes ictus esse.'
9 Adsentienti omni concilio nec Diophane ultra tender
auso Zacynthus Romanis traditur.

XXXIII. Per idem tempus Philippus rex profi
ciscentem consulem ad Naupactum percunctatus, si s
interim quae defecissent ab societate Romana urbe
2 recipere vellet, permittente eo ad Demetriaden
copias admovit haud ignarus, quanta ibi tum turbati
3 esset. Destituti enim ab omni spe, cum desertos s
ab Antiocho, spem nullam in Aetolis esse cernerent
dies noctesque aut Philippi hostis adventum au
infestiorem etiam, quo iustius irati erant, Romanorun

---

[1] sinerent ς : sineret B.
[2] exserit ς : exiret B.
[3] nudavit ed. Frobeniana 1535 : nudabit B.
[4] sunt terminos ed. Frobeniana 1531 : est termino Bς.

---

[1] Practically the same story, though with a different con
text, is told by Plutarch (Flamininus xvii).
[2] Flamininus was fond of homely and graphic similes
cf. XXXV. xlix. 6-7, which is also related by Plutarch (l.c.).

and on their motion it was voted that the question be referred to Titus Quinctius. Although Quinctius was harsh in the face of opposition, yet, if you gave in to him, he was also easy to please. Banishing all signs of passion from voice and expression, he said, " If I believed that the possession of the island was useful to you, Achaeans, I should urge upon the senate and the Roman people that they permit you to keep it; but like a tortoise,[1] which I see to be secure against all attacks when it has all its parts drawn up inside its shell, but when it sticks any part out it has that member which is exposed weak and open to injury, in no different fashion you, Achaeans, shut in on all sides by the sea, can both easily unite to yourselves anything within the boundaries of the Peloponnesus, and, when thus united, easily defend it, but as soon as in your desire for larger acquisitions you overstep those limits, I see that all the parts which lie outside are unprotected and vulnerable to every blow."[2] The whole council assenting and Diophanes not daring to struggle longer, Zacynthos was ceded to the Romans.

XXXIII. About the same time King Philip, as the consul was leaving for Naupactus, asked him whether he wished meanwhile to recover the cities that had abandoned the Roman alliance, and with his consent moved his troops towards Demetrias, well knowing what confusion reigned there. For, abandoned by all hope, when they saw themselves deserted by Antiochus, with no prospect of help from the Aetolians, by day and night they looked for the arrival either of Philip, an enemy, or of the Romans, even more hostile in proportion to their

LIVY

4 expectabant.[1] Turba erat ibi incondita [2] regiorum,
qui primo pauci in praesidio relicti, postea plures,
plerique inermes, ex proelio adverso fuga delati,
nec virium nec animi satis ad obsidionem tolerandam
5 habebant; itaque praemissis a Philippo, qui [3] spem
impetrabilis veniae ostendebant, responderunt patere
6 portas regi. Ad primum eius ingressum principum
quidam urbe excesserunt, Eurylochus mortem sibi
conscivit. Antiochi milites—sic enim pacti erant—
per Macedoniam Thraeciamque prosequentibus
Macedonibus, ne quis eos violaret, Lysimachiam
7 deducti sunt. Erant et paucae naves Demetriade,
quibus praeerat Isidorus; eae quoque cum praefecto
suo dimissae sunt. Inde Dolopiam et Aperantiam
et Perrhaebiae quasdam civitates recipit.

XXXIV. Dum haec a Philippo geruntur, T. Quinctius recepta Zacyntho ab Achaico concilio Nau-
2 pactum traiecit, quae iam per duos menses—et iam
prope excidium erat—oppugnabatur, et si [4] capta vi
foret, omne nomen ibi Aetolorum ad internecionem
3 videbatur venturum. Ceterum quamquam merito
iratus erat Aetolis, quod solos obtrectasse gloriae
suae cum liberaret Graeciam meminerat, et nihil
auctoritate sua motos esse, cum quae tum maxime
accidebant [5] casura praemonens a furioso incepto

[1] expectabant *ed. Frobeniana* 1531 : expectarent *B⸀*.
[2] turba erat ibi incondita *ed. Frobeniana* 1535 : turbae
erant ibi inconditae *B*.
[3] qui *⸀* : quia *B*.
[4] et si *⸀* : si *B*.
[5] accidebant *Madvig* : acciderat *B* : acciderant *⸀*.

---

[1] Cf. XXXV. xxxi. 6 ff.
[2] Cf. xx. 5 above.
[3] *Nomen* is not infrequently used in the sense of " people " :

juster cause for anger. There was in the city an _{B.C. 191} undisciplined mob of the king's soldiers, a few of whom had at first been left on guard, but afterwards more came, most of them unarmed, brought there in their flight after the defeat, nor did they have enough of either strength or courage to resist a siege; and so when agents were sent ahead by Philip, who showed them that the hope of pardon was attainable, they replied that the gates were open to the king. At his first entrance some of the leading men left the city; Eurylochus [1] committed suicide. The soldiers of Antiochus—for such was the agreement—were conducted by a Macedonian escort, that no one might injure them, through Macedonia and Thrace to Lysimachia. There were also a few ships at Demetrias under the command of Isidorus; [2] they too with the prefect were sent home. After that he recovered Dolopia and Aperantia and certain cities of Perrhaebia.

XXXIV. While Philip was thus engaged, Titus Quinctius, after recovering Zacynthos from the Achaean council, crossed to Naupactus, which for two months now—and it was near destruction by this time—had been undergoing the siege, and if it were captured by force the whole name [3] of the Aetolians there seemed destined to come to annihilation. But though he was justly angry at the Aetolians because he remembered that they alone had cavilled at his glory when he was liberating Greece, and that they had not been moved by his influence when he warned them in advance that that would happen which did actually occur, and tried to deter them from their

cf., e.g., III. viii. 10 and the similar usage in the phrase *nomen Latinum.*

A.U.C.
563

4 eos deterreret, tamen sui maxime operis esse credens
nullam gentem liberatae ab se Graeciae funditus
everti, obambulare muris, ut facile nosceretur ab
5 Aetolis, coepit. Confestim a primis stationibus
cognitus est, vulgatumque per omnes ordines,
Quinctium esse. Itaque concursu facto undique
in muros manus pro se quisque tendentes consonante
clamore nominatim Quinctium orare ut opem ferret
6 ac servaret. Et tum quidem, quamquam moveretur
his vocibus, manu tamen abnuit[1] quicquam opis in se
esse[2]; ceterum postquam ad consulem venit,
7 " utrum fefellit " inquit " te, M'. Acili, quid agatur
an, cum satis pervideas, nihil id magnopere ad
8 summam rem pertinere censes ? " Erexerat expectatione consulem; et " quin expromis " inquit
" quid rei sit ? " Tum Quinctius " ecquid vides te
devicto Antiocho in duabus urbibus[3] oppugnandis
tempus terere, cum iam prope annus circumactus sit
9 imperii tui, Philippum autem, qui non aciem, non
signa hostium vidit, non solum urbes sed tot iam
gentes, Athamaniam Perrhaebiam Aperantiam Dolopiam, sibi adiunxisse, et victoriae tuae praemium te
militesque tuos nondum duas urbes, Philippum tot
10 gentes Graeciae habere[4]? Atqui non tantum interest

[1] abnuit ⟨ς⟩ : annuit B. [2] esse ⟨ς⟩ : esset B.
[3] in duabus urbibus ⟨ς⟩ : . . . ab urbibus B.
[4] uerba et . . . habere, post crescere in B⟨ς⟩ collocata, trans-
posuit Madvig.

[1] This incident raises the question of the relation between
Quinctius and Acilius (see also the note to i. 8 above). The
actions of Quinctius at this time are hardly normal activities
of a military subordinate, although they might be covered
by the powers granted him by the senate (XXXV. xxiii. 5).
One infers that Livy, and probably the Romans generally,
did not understand the situation. Acilius had just witnessed

mad purpose, yet, believing it to be his task to see B.C. 191
that no people of the Greece which had received its
freedom from him should be utterly destroyed, he
began to walk around the walls, so that he was
easily seen by the Aetolians. Immediately he was
recognized by the advanced sentinels and the word
went through all the ranks that Quinctius was there.
So there was a general rush from all quarters to the
walls, each stretching out his hands to him and with
uniform cries calling upon Quinctius by name to
come to their rescue and save them. And for the
moment, at least, although he was affected by these
words, he showed by a gesture that there was no
power in him to help them; but when he came to
the consul [1] he said, "Has it perhaps escaped you,
Manius Acilius, what you are doing, or, since you
see it clearly, do you not think that it has a great
deal to do with our ultimate policy?" He had
worked the consul up to a high pitch of wonder,
and he asked, "Why not explain what you mean?"
Then Quinctius replied: "Do you not see that you,
after defeating Antiochus, are wasting time by
besieging two cities, although now the year of your
command is almost ended, but that Philip, who had
not set eyes on the battle-line or the standards of
the enemy, has already joined to himself, not cities
alone, but so many nations—Athamania, Perrhaebia,
Aperantia, Dolopia—and that as rewards for your
victory you possess as yet not even two cities, while
Philip has so many peoples of Greece? Yet it is not

a dramatic demonstration of the influence of Quinctius with
the Greeks, and there is nothing strange about his compliance
with his suggestion, even though Quinctius had no authority
over the consul.

LIVY

nostra Aetolorum opes ac vires minui, quantum non
supra modum Philippum crescere."

XXXV. Adsentiebatur his consul; sed pudor, si
irrito incepto abscederet obsidione, occurrebat.
2 Tota inde Quinctio res permissa est. Is rursus ad
eam partem muri qua paulo ante vociferati Aetoli
fuerant rediit. Ibi cum impensius orarent ut misere-
retur gentis Aetolorum, exire aliquos ad se iussit.
3 Phaeneas ipse principesque alii extemplo egressi
sunt. Quibus provolutis ad pedes " fortuna " inquit
" vestra facit ut et irae meae et orationi temperem.
4 Evenerunt quae praedixi eventura, et ne hoc quidem
reliqui vobis est ut indignis accidisse ea videantur;
ego tamen sorte quadam nutriendae Graeciae datus
5 ne ingratis quidem benefacere absistam. Mittite
oratores ad consulem, qui indutias tanti[1] temporis
petant, ut mittere legatos Romam possitis, per
quod senatui de vobis permittatis; ego apud con-
6 sulem deprecator defensorque vobis adero." Ita,
ut censuerat Quinctius, fecerunt, nec aspernatus est
consul legationem; indutiisque in diem certam datis,
qua legatio renuntiari ab Roma posset, soluta obsidio
est et exercitus in Phocidem missus.
7 Consul cum T. Quinctio ad Achaicum concilium
Aegium traiecit. Ibi de Eleis et de exulibus Lacedaemoniorum restituendis actum est[2]; neutra
perfecta res, quia suae gratiae reservari exulum

---

[1] tanti 𝒔 : tantum B.
[2] est Weissenborn : et B.

B.C. 191

so much to our interest that the power and strength of the Aetolians should be diminished as that Philip should not grow beyond measure."

XXXV. The consul agreed with this, but shame, if he should withdraw before finishing what he had begun, came over him. The whole decision was then referred to Quinctius. He went back again to the section of the walls where the Aetolians had harangued him a little while before. When with greater fervour they begged him to have compassion on the Aetolian people, he ordered some of them to come out to him. Phaeneas himself and other chiefs at once came out. As they threw themselves at his feet, he said, "Your plight makes me restrain both my wrath and my language. Those things have happened which I told you in the beginning would happen, and not even this is left to you, that they may seem to have happened to the undeserving; yet I, appointed by some destiny for the cherishing of Greece, shall not cease to do good even to ungrateful men. Send ambassadors to the consul to ask for a truce for such a space of time that you may send delegates to Rome through whom you may put your case before the senate; I shall be with the consul to support and defend your cause." So they did as Quinctius had suggested, nor did the consul reject the embassy; granting them a truce for a definite period, in which the embassy could report back from Rome, he raised the siege and sent the army back to Phocis.

The consul with Titus Quinctius crossed to Aegium to the Achaean council. There the debate concerned the Eleans and the restoration of the Spartan exiles; neither question was settled, because the Achaeans wished the case of the exiles left as a means

257

causam [1] Achaei, Elei per se ipsi quam per Romanos
8 maluerunt Achaico contribui concilio. Epirotarum
legati ad consulem venerunt, quos non sincera fide
in amicitia fuisse satis constabat; militem tamen
nullum Antiocho dederant; pecunia iuvisse eum
insimulabantur; legatos ad regem ne ipsi quidem
9 misisse infitiabantur. Iis petentibus ut in amicitia
pristina esse liceret, respondit consul se, utrum
hostium an pacatorum eos numero haberet, nondum
10 scire; senatum eius rei iudicem fore; integram se
causam eorum Romam reicere; indutias ad id dierum
11 nonaginta dare. Epirotae Romam missi senatum
adierunt. Iis magis quae non fecissent hostilia
referentibus quam purgantibus ea de quibus argue-
bantur, responsum datum est, quo veniam impetrasse,
12 non causam probasse videri possent. Et Philippi
regis legati sub idem tempus in senatum introducti,
gratulantes de victoria. Iis petentibus ut sibi
sacrificare in Capitolio donumque ex auro liceret
ponere in aede Iovis optimi maximi, permissum ab
13 senatu. Centum pondo coronam auream posuerunt.
Non responsum solum benigne regis legatis est sed [2]
filius quoque Philippi Demetrius, qui obses Romae
14 erat, ad patrem reducendus legatis datus est. Bellum

[1] exulum causam *Madvig*: *om. B.*
[2] sed ς : et *B.*

---

[1] Cf. v. 3–8 above.
[2] This was a mark of special honour, since foreigners had
no share in Roman ritual.
[3] Cf. XXXIII. xxx. 10; XXXV. xxxi. 5 and the note.

B.C. 191

of gaining favour for themselves; while the Eleans preferred that they be united with the Achaean League on their own initiative rather than under pressure from the Romans. Ambassadors from the Epirotes came to the consul; it was clear that they had not observed the treaty of alliance with true fidelity; yet they had sent no troops to Antiochus; they were accused of having aided him with money; they did not even themselves deny that they had sent ambassadors to him.[1] When they asked that they be permitted to remain in their old status of friendship, the consul replied that he did not yet know whether to reckon them among enemies or among defeated foes; the senate would be the judge of that; he was referring the whole question of their status to Rome; for that purpose he granted them a truce for ninety days. The Epirotes sent to Rome and appealed to the senate. When they enumerated hostile acts which they had not performed rather than cleared themselves of the charges made against them, a reply was given them from which they could seem to have obtained forgiveness, not to have established their case. Ambassadors from King Philip also were at this time presented to the senate with congratulations on the victory. Their request that they be allowed to sacrifice on the Capitoline and to deposit a gift of gold in the temple of Jupiter Optimus Maximus was granted by the senate.[2] A golden crown of one hundred pounds' weight was placed there. Not only was a gracious response given to the ambassadors of the king, but also Demetrius, the son of Philip, who was a hostage at Rome,[3] was handed over to the ambassadors to be restored to his father. The war which was waged

LIVY

quod cum Antiocho rege in Graecia gestum est a
M'. Acilio consule hunc finem habuit.

XXXVI. Alter consul P. Cornelius Scipio, Galliam
provinciam sortitus, priusquam ad bellum quod cum
Bois gerendum erat proficisceretur, postulavit ab senatu ut pecunia sibi decerneretur ad ludos quos
praetor in Hispania inter ipsum discrimen pugnae
2 vovisset. Novum atque iniquum postulare est visus;
censuerunt ergo, quos ludos inconsulto senatu [1] ex
sua unius sententia vovisset, eos vel de manubiis, si
quam pecuniam ad id reservasset, vel sua ipse
impensa faceret. Eos ludos per dies decem P.
3 Cornelius fecit. Per idem fere tempus aedes Matris
Magnae Idaeae dedicata est quam deam is P.
Cornelius advectam ex Asia P. Cornelio Scipione, cui
postea Africano fuit cognomen, P. Licinio consulibus
4 in Palatium a mari detulerat. Locaverant aedem
faciendam ex senatus consulto M. Livius C. Claudius
censores M. Cornelio P.[2] Sempronio consulibus;
tredecim annis postquam locata erat,[3] dedicavit eam

---

[1] inconsulto senatu ς : sine consultu senatus B.
[2] P. *Sigonius* : t. Bς.
[3] locata erat ς : locauerat B.

---

[1] Cf. XXXV. i. 8.
[2] No commander could foresee an emergency of this magnitude in time to secure the senate's authority, and the senate
seems unreasonable. There was no good way of checking up
on commanders to see whether they had turned in all the booty
(cf., however, XXXVII. lvii. 12–14), and it was probably
customary for generals to hold out parts of it. Scipio seems
to have been careless enough or honest enough not to reserve
any booty for this purpose. This episode, together with the
following, reveals, however, friction between the senate and
the Scipios.
[3] Cf. XXIX. xiv. 1. There are numerous references to the

with King Antiochus in Greece by Manius Acilius B.C. 191
the consul came thus to an end.

XXXVI. The other consul, Publius Cornelius
Scipio, who had been allotted the province of Gaul,
before he departed to the war which was to be
waged with the Boii, demanded of the senate that
money be voted to him for the games which as
praetor in Spain he had vowed at a critical moment
in the battle.[1] His request seemed unprecedented
and unreasonable; they voted, therefore, that whatever games he had vowed on his own sole initiative,
with no authorization from the senate, he should
celebrate either out of the spoils, if he had reserved
any for that purpose, or out of his own pocket.[2]
The games were celebrated through ten days by
Publius Cornelius. About the same time a temple was
dedicated to the Great Idaean Mother, a goddess whom
this same Publius Cornelius, when she came from
Asia in the consulship of Publius Cornelius Scipio,
who later received the surname of Africanus, and
Publius Licinius, had escorted to the Palatine from
the harbour.[3] The contract for the construction of
the temple, under a decree of the senate, was let
by the censors Marcus Livius and Gaius Claudius
in the consulship of Marcus Cornelius and Publius
Sempronius;[4] thirteen years after the contract was let,

selection of Scipio Nasica as the *vir optimus* to receive the
goddess (*e.g.* XXXV. x. 9). The choice of Brutus rather than
Nasica as the dedicator of the temple may be an additional
rebuke to him. See, however, the *Periocha*.

[4] The chronology is incorrect. Africanus and Licinius
were consuls in 205 B.C. (XXVIII. xxxviii. 12) and Cethegus
and Tuditanus in 204 B.C. (XXIX. xi. 10), when the divinity
was brought to Rome. Livius and Claudius were censors in
this year (XXIX. xxxvii. 1). See also sect. 6 below.

LIVY

M. Iunius Brutus, ludique ob dedicationem eius
5 facti, quos primos scenicos fuisse Antias Valerius est
auctor, Megalesia appellatos.   Item Iuventatis aedem
in circo maximo C. Licinius Lucullus duumvir dedi-
6 cavit.   Voverat eam sexdecim [1] annis ante M. Livius
consul quo die Hasdrubalem exercitumque eius
cecidit; idem censor eam faciendam locavit M.
7 Cornelio P. Sempronio consulibus.   Huius quoque
dedicandae causa ludi facti, et eo [2] omnia cum
maiore religione facta, quod novum cum Antiocho
instabat bellum.

XXXVII. Principio eius anni, quo haec iam profecto ad bellum M'. Acilio, manente adhuc Romae P.
2 Cornelio consule agebantur, boves duos domitos in
Carinis per scalas pervenisse in tegulas aedificii pro-
ditum memoriae est.   Eos vivos comburi cineremque
3 eorum deici in Tiberim haruspices iusserunt.   Tarra-
cinae et Amiterni nuntiatum est aliquotiens lapidibus
pluvisse, Minturnis aedem Iovis et tabernas circa forum de caelo tactas esse, Volturni in ostio fluminis
4 duas naves fulmine [3] ictas conflagrasse.   Eorum
prodigiorum causa libros Sibyllinos ex senatus consulto decemviri cum adissent, renuntiaverunt ieiu-
nium instituendum Cereri [4] esse, et id quinto quoque
5 anno servandum; et ut novemdiale sacrum fieret et

---

[1] sexdecim ς : .VI. B.
[2] eo ed. Frobeniana 1535 : om. B.
[3] fulmine ς : flumine B.
[4] cereri ς : cereris B.

---

[1] It is futile to try to determine just what Antias meant.
Cf. XXXIV. liv. 3 for a similar statement.
[2] The temple was vowed at the battle of the Metaurus in
207 B.C., but Livy has not mentioned before either the vow
or the contract.

Marcus Junius Brutus dedicated the temple, and games were given by reason of the dedication, which Valerius Antias says were the first to be held with dramatic performances, and called the *Megalesia*.[1] Also a temple of Juventas in the Circus Maximus was dedicated by Gaius Licinius Lucullus the duumvir. It had been vowed sixteen years before by Marcus Livius the consul in the battle in which he destroyed Hasdrubal and his army; as censor he also let the contract for its construction in the consulship of Marcus Cornelius and Publius Sempronius.[2] By reason of this dedication also games were held, and with more intense religious feeling because the new war with Antiochus was imminent.[3]

XXXVII. In the beginning of the year in which these things happened, Manius Acilius having already set out to the war and Publius Cornelius the consul being still in Rome, it is recorded that two domesticated cattle in the Carinae climbed up a stairway to the roof of a house. The *haruspices* ordered that they be burned alive and the ashes thrown into the Tiber. At Terracina and Amiternum it was reported that there were several showers of stones, at Minurnae the temple of Jupiter and the shops around the forum were struck by lightning, at Volturnum in the mouth of the river two ships were struck by lightning and burned. On account of these portents the decemvirs were directed by a decree of the senate to consult the Sibylline Books, and they reported that a fast in honour of Ceres should be held and this repeated every fifth year; also that a nine-day festival should be celebrated and a period of prayer for one day; that those who offered the

---

[3] These events then belong to the early spring of 191 B.C.

LIVY

unum diem supplicatio esset; coronati supplicarent;
et consul P. Cornelius, quibus diis quibusque
6 hostiis edidissent decemviri, sacrificaret. Placatis
diis nunc votis rite solvendis nunc prodigiis expiandis,
in provinciam proficiscitur consul, atque inde Cn.[1]
Domitium proconsulem dimisso exercitu Romam
decedere iussit; ipse in agrum Boiorum legiones
induxit.[2]

XXXVIII. Sub idem fere tempus Ligures lege
sacrata coacto exercitu nocte improviso castra Q. Mi-
2 nucii proconsulis aggressi sunt. Minucius usque ad
lucem intra vallum militem instructum tenuit intentus, ne qua transcenderet hostis munimenta.
3 Prima luce duabus simul portis eruptionem fecit.
Nec primo impetu, quod speraverat, Ligures pulsi
sunt; duas amplius horas dubium certamen susti-
4 nuere; postremo, cum alia atque alia[3] agmina
erumperent, et integri fessis succederent ad pugnam,
tandem Ligures, inter cetera etiam vigiliis confecti,
terga dederunt. Caesa supra quattuor milia[4]
hostium; ex Romanis sociisque minus trecenti
5 perierunt. Duobus fere post mensibus P. Cornelius
consul cum Boiorum exercitu signis collatis egregie
6 pugnavit. Duodetriginta milia hostium occisa Antias
Valerius scribit, capta tria milia[5] et quadringentos,

[1] cn. ς: c. B.
[2] induxit ς: duxit B.
[3] alia ς: om. B.
[4] quattuor milia ς: .IIII. B: quattuor milia nonaginta M.
[5] tria milia ς: .III. B.

---

[1] This was in accordance with Greek ritual.
[2] This interpretation is somewhat unnatural but is necessary
to secure consistency with i. 9 above.

prayers should wear garlands;[1] and that the consul Publius Cornelius, in honour of whatever gods and with whatever victims the decemvirs should announce, should offer sacrifice. The gods were appeased now by the due performance of vows, now by the rites of atonement for the prodigies, and the consul departed to his province, ordering the proconsul Gnaeus Domitius to send his army back to Rome and leave the province;[2] he himself led the legions into the country of the Boii.

XXXVIII. About the same time the Ligures, mustering an army under a formula of devotion,[3] by night suddenly attacked the camp of Quintus Minucius the proconsul. Minucius kept his troops in formation within the rampart right up to daybreak, being anxious to prevent any crossing of the fortifications by the enemy. At daybreak he made a sally through two gates at once. But the first attack did not, as he had hoped, drive away the Ligures; for two hours longer they made the issue uncertain; finally, when column after column came forth and fresh men were relieving the exhausted in the battle, the Ligures at length, worn out by loss of sleep along with everything else, turned to flight. More than four thousand of the enemy were killed; of the Romans and allies less than three hundred were lost. About two months later Publius Cornelius the consul fought in pitched battle with the army of the Boii with notable results. Valerius Antias writes that thirty-eight thousand of the enemy were slain, three thousand four hundred captured,

[3] Violation of a *lex sacrata* was punished by devotion of the offender to the gods of the lower world. In such a case as this it would bind the troops by a vow of victory or death.

signa militaria centum viginti quattuor, equos mille
ducentos triginta, carpenta ducenta quadraginta
septem; ex victoribus mille quadringentos octoginta
7 quattuor cecidisse. Ubi ut in numero scriptori
parum fidei sit, quia in augendo eo non alius intem-
perantior est, magnam tamen victoriam fuisse ap-
paret, quod et castra capta sunt et Boi post eam
pugnam extemplo dediderunt sese, et quod supplicatio eius victoriae causa decreta ab senatu victimae-
que maiores caesae.

XXXIX. Per eosdem dies M. Fulvius Nobilior ex
ulteriore Hispania ovans urbem est ingressus.
2 Argenti transtulit duodecim milia pondo, bigati
argenti centum triginta, auri centum viginti septem
pondo.
3 P. Cornelius consul obsidibus a Boiorum gente
acceptis agri parte fere dimidia eos multavit, quo si
vellet, populus Romanus colonias mittere posset.
4 Inde Romam ut ad triumphum haud dubium dece-
dens exercitum dimisit, et adesse Romae ad diem
5 triumphi iussit; ipse postero die quam venit senatu
in aedem Bellonae vocato cum de rebus ab se gestis
disseruisset, postulavit ut sibi triumphanti liceret
6 urbem invehi. P. Sempronius Blaesus tribunus
plebis non negandum Scipioni, sed differendum
honorem triumphi censebat : bella Ligurum Gallicis
semper iuncta fuisse; eas inter se gentes mutua ex
7 propinquo ferre auxilia. Si P. Scipio devictis [1] acie

¹ devictis *edd. vett.* : deductis *Bꝰ*.

---

¹ Their submission was then not the usual formal surrender
as an admission of defeat in one battle.
² This ovation was also reported in xxi. 10–11 above.

with one hundred twenty-four military standards,
one thousand two hundred thirty horses, two hundred
forty-seven carts; of the victors the losses were
one thousand four hundred eighty-four. Although
even in this case little confidence can be placed in
this writer in a question of numbers, because no
other is more unrestrained than he in exaggeration,
yet it is clear that it was a great victory, first, because the camp was captured, second, because
the Boii surrendered immediately after the battle,[1]
third, because a thanksgiving was proclaimed and
full-grown victims slain.

XXXIX. About the same time Marcus Fulvius
Nobilior from Farther Spain entered the City in
ovation. He brought with him twelve thousand
pounds of silver, one hundred and thirty thousand
silver coins stamped with the two-horse chariot, one
hundred and twenty-seven pounds of gold.[2]

Publius Cornelius the consul accepted hostages
from the nation of the Boii and deprived them of
about one-half their land, to which, if it chose,
the Roman people could send colonies. Then,
departing to Rome to the certain expectation of a
triumph, he disbanded his army and ordered them
to be in Rome on the day of the triumph; on the
day after his arrival he himself convened the senate
in the temple of Bellona, and when he had discoursed
about his achievements he demanded that he be
permitted to ride into the City in triumph. Publius
Sempronius Blaesus, tribune of the people, declared
that the honour of a triumph should not be refused
to Scipio, but should be postponed: Ligurian wars
were always connected with Gallic; these neighbouring tribes exchanged assistance. If Publius

A.U.C.
563

Bois aut ipse cum victore exercitu in agrum Ligurum transisset, aut partem copiarum Q. Minucio misisset, qui iam tertium ibi annum dubio detineretur bello,
8 debellari cum Liguribus potuisse; nunc ad triumphum frequentandum deductos esse milites, qui egregiam navare operam rei publicae potuissent, possent etiam, si senatus, quod festinatione triumphi praetermissum esset, id restituere differendo triumpho vellet.
9 Iuberent consulem cum legionibus redire in provinciam, dare operam, ut Ligures subigantur. Nisi illi cogantur in ius iudiciumque populi Romani, ne Boios quidem quieturos; aut pacem aut bellum utrobique
10 habenda. Devictis Liguribus, paucos post menses proconsulem P. Cornelium multorum exemplo, qui in magistratu non triumphaverunt, triumphaturum esse.

XL. Ad ea consul neque se Ligures provinciam sortitum esse ait, neque cum Liguribus bellum
2 gessisse, neque triumphum de iis postulare; Q. Minucium confidere brevi subactis iis meritum[1] triumphum postulaturum atque impetraturum esse;
3 se de Gallis Bois postulare triumphum, quos acie vicerit, castris exuerit, quorum gentem biduo post pugnam totam acceperit in deditionem, a quibus
4 obsides abduxerit, pacis futurae pignus. Verum enimvero illud multo maius esse, quod tantum

---

[1] meritum *ed. Frobeniana* 1535: meritis (*an* mertas?) *B*: merito ς.

---

[1] A magistrate who left his province, even for such a purpose, would expose himself to severe criticism, if nothing more: cf. XXXVII. xlvii. 6. The argument of Blaesus is then somewhat captious.

[2] Scipio had taken a good deal for granted when he sent his army back to Rome and left his province before he was relieved. This, however, is not the ground of the tribune's objections.

Scipio, after defeating the Boii in battle, had either crossed himself with his victorious army into the country of the Ligures [1] or sent part of his troops to Quintus Minucius, who was for the third year now detained by a war of uncertain prospects, the war with the Ligures could have been finished; now the soldiers had been withdrawn to crowd the triumph, who could have rendered conspicuous service to the state, and who could do so even now if the senate wished, by deferring the triumph, to restore the condition which had been lost in the anxiety for a triumph. Let them order the consul with his legions to return to his province, to direct his attention to the subjugation of the Ligures. Unless they were brought under the sovereignty and supremacy of the Roman people, not even the Boii would remain quiet; they must have either peace or war with both. After conquering the Ligures, a few months later, Publius Cornelius the proconsul would triumph, after the example of many who had not triumphed while still in office.[2]

XL. To this the consul replied that the Ligures had not been allotted to him as his province, that he had not waged war with the Ligures, that he was not asking for a triumph over them; he felt sure that in a short time Quintus Minucius, having conquered them, would ask and receive a well-earned triumph; he was asking for a triumph over the Gallic Boii, whom he had defeated in battle, whom he had stripped of their camp, whose entire population he had, two days after the battle, received in surrender, from whom he had taken hostages as a guarantee of future peace. But this, as a matter of fact, was of far greater importance—that he had

LIVY

numerum Gallorum occiderit in acie, quot cum[1]
milibus certe Boiorum nemo ante se imperator
5 pugnaverit. Plus partem dimidiam ex quinquaginta
milibus hominum caesam, multa milia capta; senes
6 puerosque Bois superesse. Itaque id quemquam
mirari posse, cur victor exercitus, cum hostem in
provincia neminem reliquisset, Romam venerit ad
7 celebrandum consulis triumphum? Quorum militum
si et in alia provincia opera uti senatus velit, utro
tandem modo promptiores ad aliud periculum
novumque laborem ituros credat, si persoluta eis sine
detractatione prioris periculi laborisque merces sit,
an si spem pro re ferentes[2] dimittant, iam semel in
8 prima spe deceptos? Nam quod ad se attineat, sibi
gloriae in omnem vitam illo die satis quaesitum esse,
quo se virum optimum iudicatum ad accipiendam
9 matrem Idaeam misisset senatus. Hoc titulo, etsi
nec consulatus nec[3] triumphus addatur, satis honestam
honoratamque P. Scipionis Nasicae imaginem fore.
10 Universus senatus non ipse modo ad decernendum
triumphum consensit, sed etiam tribunum plebis
auctoritate sua compulit ad remittendam inter-
11 cessionem. P. Cornelius consul triumphavit de Bois.
In eo triumpho Gallicis carpentis arma signaque et
spolia omnis generis travexit et vasa aenea Gallica

---

[1] quot cum ϛ: quot cum tot B.
[2] ferentes ed. Frobeniana 1535: ferentibus Bϛ.
[3] etsi nec consulatus nec ϛ : et sine consulatu ne B.

---

[1] If the text is sound, it means that more Gauls had fallen
in this battle than the Boi had ever been able to put in the
field in previous engagements.
[2] Cf. xxxviii. 6 above.
[3] Cf. xxxvi. 3 above and the note.

slain a greater number of thousands of Gauls in battle
than any commander before him had ever fought
with, at least so far as the Boii were concerned.[1]
More than half of their fifty thousand men were
killed,[2] many thousands captured; old men and boys
only were now left to the Boii. Could anyone then
wonder why a victorious army, since it left no enemy
in the province, should come to Rome to celebrate
the triumph of the consul? If the senate wished
to use the assistance of these soldiers in another
province also, in which way, pray, would it believe
them to be more ready to meet another danger
and new toil, if without any objection the reward
had been paid them for their previous danger and
toil, or if they sent them away with hope in place
of reality, when they had once been deceived as to
their original expectation? So far as he personally
was concerned, he had won sufficient glory for
his whole life on that day when the senate had
judged him the best man and sent him to receive
the Idaean Mother.[3] From that one inscription,
even if no consulship or triumph were added, the
imago [4] of Publius Scipio Nasica would have enough
of honour and regard. The entire senate of its
own accord not only agreed to vote the triumph
but by its influence compelled the tribune to withdraw his veto. Publius Cornelius while consul
triumphed over the Boii. In that triumph he transported in Gallic carts arms and standards and spoils
of every description and Gallic vases of bronze, and

---

[4] A Roman house had a special room set aside for the *imagines*
or masks of distinguished ancestors. To each was attached
a tablet (*titulus*) listing the offices each man had held and the
other honours he had won.

A.U.C.
563

12 et cum captivis nobilibus equorum quoque captorum
gregem traduxit. Aureos torques transtulit mille
quadringentos septuaginta unum, ad hoc auri pondo
ducenta quadraginta septem, argenti infecti factique
in Gallicis vasis, non infabre suo more factis, duo milia
trecenta quadraginta pondo, bigatorum nummorum
13 ducenta triginta quattuor. Militibus qui currum
secuti sunt centenos vicenos quinos asses divisit,
14 duplex centurioni, triplex equiti. Postero die
contione advocata de rebus ab se gestis et de iniuria
tribuni bello alieno se illigantis, ut suae victoriae
fructu se fraudaret, cum disseruisset, milites ex-
auctoratos dimisit.

XLI. Dum haec in Italia geruntur, Antiochus
Ephesi securus admodum de bello Romano erat tamquam non transituris in Asiam Romanis; quam secu-
ritatem ei magna pars amicorum aut per errorem aut
2 adsentando faciebat. Hannibal unus, cuius eo tempore vel maxima [1] apud regem auctoritas erat, magis
mirari se aiebat, quod non iam in Asia essent Romani,
3 quam venturos dubitare [2]; propius esse ex Graecia in
Asiam quam ex Italia in Graeciam traicere, et multo
maiorem causam Antiochum quam Aetolos esse;
neque enim mari minus quam terra pollere Romana
4 arma. Iam pridem classem circa Maleam esse;
audire sese nuper novas naves novumque impera-

---

[1] vel maxima ς : ut maxima B.
[2] dubitare ed. Frobeniana 1535 : dubitabat Bς.

---

[1] This is said to be the first Gallic triumph in which no
copper coins were displayed : cf. XXXIII. xxxvii. 11.
[2] The narrative continues from xxi. 1 above. Antiochus
seems to have paid little attention to the Aetolian appeal in

along with prisoners of high rank a herd of captured B.C. 191 horses. He carried also golden necklaces to the number of one thousand four hundred and seventy-one, and besides he had two hundred and forty-seven pounds of gold, of silver, unwrought and wrought in Gallic vases, not unskilfully, in their manner, two thousand three hundred and forty pounds, of coins stamped with the two-horse chariot, two hundred and thirty-four thousand.[1] To the soldiers who followed his car he gave one hundred and twenty-five *asses* to each infantryman, twice that sum to each centurion and thrice to each cavalryman. The next day he called an assembly, and when he had spoken of his achievements and of the injury done by the tribune who tried to entangle him in another's war, in order to cheat him of the fruits of his victory, he absolved his soldiers of their oaths and discharged them.

XLI. While this was going on in Italy, Antiochus [2] at Ephesus was quite free from concern as to the Roman war, on the ground that the Romans would not cross to Asia; and this sense of security was given to him by most of his friends either through error or in flattery. Hannibal alone, whose influence with the king was at that time perhaps at its greatest, said that he was more surprised that the Romans were not already in Asia than doubtful that they would come; it was a shorter crossing from Greece to Asia than from Italy to Greece, and Antiochus was a far more powerful motive than the Aetolians; nor were Roman arms less powerful on sea than land. For a long time their fleet had been around Malea; he had recently heard that a new fleet and a

chap. xxvi; perhaps he had heard of their subsequent fortunes.

LIVY

5 torem rei gerendae causa ex Italia venisse; itaque
desineret Antiochus pacem sibi ipse spe vana facere.
In Asia et de ipsa Asia brevi terra marique dimicandum ei[1] cum Romanis esse, et aut imperium
adimendum orbem terrarum adfectantibus, aut ipsi
6 regnum amittendum. Unus vera et providere et
fideliter praedicere visus. Itaque ipse rex navibus
quae paratae instructaeque erant Chersonesum
petit, ut ea loca, si forte terra venirent Romani,
7 praesidiis firmaret; ceteram classem Polyxenidam
parare et deducere iussit; speculatorias naves ad
omnia exploranda circa insulas dimisit.

XLII. C. Livius praefectus Romanae classis, cum
quinquaginta navibus tectis profectus ab Roma Nea-
polim, quo ab sociis eius orae convenire iusserat
2 apertas naves quae ex foedere debebantur, Siciliam
inde petit fretoque Messanam praetervectus, cum
sex Punicas naves ad auxilium missas accepisset et ab
Reginis Locrisque et eiusdem iuris sociis debitas exe-
gisset naves, lustrata classe ad Lacinium, altum petit.
3 Corcyram, quam primam Graeciae civitatium adiit,
cum venisset, percunctatus de statu belli—necdum
enim omnia in Graecia perpacata erant—et ubi
4 classis Romana esset, postquam audivit circa Thermopylarum saltum in statione consulem ac regem
esse, classem Piraei stare, maturandum ratus omnium rerum causa, pergit protinus navigare Pelo-

[1] ei ς : et B.

---

[1] This must be Livius (xlii. 1 below), whose appointment
to the fleet was noted at ii. 6 above.
[2] By a sacrifice to propitiate hostile powers.
[3] The island also called Cephallania; also a city of the
same name on that island.

new commander to carry on the war had come from B.C. 191
Italy;[1] Antiochus, then, should cease to seek peace
for himself—a vain hope. In Asia and for Asia
itself there would soon be war on land and sea between
him and the Romans, and either the Romans, seeking dominion over the world, would lose it or he himself would lose his kingdom. He alone seemed
both to foresee the truth and to declare it loyally.
So the king himself, with the ships that were ready and
equipped, set out for the Chersonesus to strengthen
those regions with garrisons if perchance the Romans
should come by land; the rest of the fleet he ordered
Polyxenidas to refit and launch; scouting cruisers
he sent among the islands to reconnoitre everywhere.

XLII. Gaius Livius, commander of the Roman
fleet, sailed with fifty decked vessels from Rome to
Naples, where he had ordered the allies along the
coast to assemble the undecked ships which they
owed under the treaty, then headed for Sicily and,
passing Messina through the strait, picked up six
Carthaginian ships sent to aid him, received from
the people of Rhegium and Locri and the other
allies of the same status the ships which he had
demanded of them, and having purified[2] the fleet at
Lacinium struck out into the deep. When he had
arrived at Corcyra, the first city in Greece which
he reached, he inquired as to the military situation—
for everything was not yet quiet in Greece—and
as to where the Roman fleet was, and when he
heard that the consul and the king were watching
one another near the pass of Thermopylae and that
the fleet was at Piraeus, he thought that he should
make haste for every reason, and straightway proceeded to sail around the Peloponnesus. Same[3]

275

5 ponnesum. Samen [1] Zacynthumque, quia partis
Aetolorum maluerant esse, protinus depopulatus
Maleam petit, et [2] prospera navigatione usus paucis
6 diebus Piraeum ad veterem classem pervenit. Ad
Scyllaeum Eumenes rex cum tribus navibus occurrit,
cum Aeginae diu incertus consilii fuisset, utrum ad
tuendum rediret regnum—audiebat enim Antiochum Ephesi navales terrestresque parare copias—
an nusquam abscederet ab Romanis, ex quorum
7 fortuna sua penderet. A Piraeo A. Atilius traditis
successori quinque et viginti navibus tectis Romam
8 est profectus. Livius una et octoginta constratis [3]
navibus, multis praeterea minoribus, quae aut
apertae rostratae aut sine rostris speculatoria erant,
Delum traiecit.

XLIII. Eo fere tempore consul Acilius Naupactum oppugnabat. Livium Deli per aliquot
dies [4]—et est [5] ventosissima regio inter Cycladas
fretis alias maioribus, alias minoribus divisas—
2 adversi venti tenuerunt. Polyxenidas certior per
dispositas speculatorias naves factus Deli stare Ro-
3 manam classem, nuntios ad regem misit. Qui
omissis quae in Hellesponto agebat cum rostratis
navibus, quantum accelerare poterat, Ephesum redit
et consilium extemplo habuit, faciendumne periculum
4 navalis certaminis foret. Polyxenidas negabat cessandum et utique prius confligendum quam classis
Eumenis et Rhodiae naves coniungerentur Romanis ;

[1] Samen *Sigonius* : tamen *B*ϛ : samum *M*.
[2] et *ed. Frobeniana* 1535 : om. *B*.
[3] constratis *Duker* : prostratis *B* : rostratis ϛ.
[4] Deli per aliquot dies *ed. Frobeniana* 1535 : deliberanti
quod dies *B* : deliberantem aliquot dies ϛ.
[5] et est ϛ : est *B*.

and Zacynthos,[1] because they preferred to join the B.C. 191
Aetolian party, he at once plundered and then
made for Malea, and enjoying a successful voyage
after a few days he joined the old fleet at Piraeus.
At Scyllaeum King Eumenes with three ships met
him, after having long waited at Aegina, uncertain
what to do, whether to go home to defend his own
kingdom—for he kept hearing that Antiochus was at
Ephesus equipping his fleets and armies—or never to
separate from the Romans, on whom his own fortunes
depended. From Piraeus Aulus Atilius turned over
to his successor twenty-five decked ships and returned to Rome. Livius with eighty-one decked
ships and many smaller craft in addition, which were
either open ships with beaks or scouting-vessels
without beaks, crossed to Delos.

XLIII. At about this time the consul Acilius was
besieging Naupactus. Livius was detained at Delos
for several days by adverse winds, and indeed the
region around the Cyclades, which are separated from
one another, some by wider straits, some by narrower,
is exceedingly windy. Polyxenidas, being informed
by the vessels which had been sent to reconnoitre
that the Roman fleet was delayed at Delos, sent
messengers to the king. He, dropping everything
he was doing at the Hellespont, returned with his
beaked ships with all possible speed to Ephesus and
at once held a council as to whether they should
make trial of a naval battle. Polyxenidas maintained that they should not delay, but should fight
before the fleet of Eumenes and the Rhodian ships
should join the Romans; thus they would be

[1] This happened before the negotiations reported in chap.
xxxi above.

LIVY

5 ita numero non [1] ferme impares futuros se,[2] ceteris
omnibus superiores, et celeritate navium et varietate
6 auxiliorum. Nam Romanas naves cum [3] ipsas inscite
factas immobiles esse, tum etiam, ut quae in terram
7 hostium veniant, oneratas commeatu venire; suas
autem, ut pacata omnia circa se relinquentes, nihil
praeter militem atque arma habituras. Multum
etiam adiuturam notitiam maris terrarumque et
ventorum, quae omnia ignaros turbatura hostes
8 essent. Movit omnes auctor consilii, qui et re consilium exsecuturus erat. Biduum in apparatu morati
tertio die centum navibus, quarum septuaginta
tectae, ceterae apertae, minoris omnes formae erant,
9 profecti Phocaeam petierunt. Inde, cum audisset
appropinquare iam Romanam classem, rex, quia non
interfuturus navali certamini erat, Magnesiam, quae
ad Sipylum est, concessit ad terrestres copias com-
10 parandas; classis ad Cissuntem portum Erythrae-
orum, tamquam ibi aptius expectatura hostem, con-
11 tendit. Romani, ubi primum aquilones—ii [4] namque
per aliquot dies tenuerant—ceciderunt,[5] ab Delo
Phanas,[6] portum Chiorum in Aegaeum mare versum,
petunt; inde ad urbem circumegere naves, com-
12 meatuque sumpto Phocaeam traiciunt. Eumenes
Elaeam ad suam classem profectus, paucis post inde
diebus cum quattuor et viginti navibus tectis, apertis
pluribus paulo Phocaeam ad Romanos parantes
13 instruentesque [7] se ad navale certamen rediit. Inde

---

[1] non *ed. Frobeniana* 1535 : *om. B.*
[2] se *ed. Frobeniana* 1535 : ipse *B* : ipsum 𝔖.
[3] cum 𝔖 : *om. B.*
[4] ii *ed. Frobeniana* 1535 : hi *B* : duo 𝔖.
[5] tenuerant ceciderunt 𝔖 : ceciderant tenuerant *B*.
[6] ab Delo Phanas 𝔖 : ad bellophonas *B*.

practically equal in numbers, superior in everything B.C. 191 else, both in the speed of the ships and in the varied character of their auxiliaries. For the Roman ships were not only unskilfully constructed and hard to move, but were also laden down with supplies, since they were coming to a hostile country; but their own ships, since they were leaving everything around them peaceful, would carry nothing except soldiers and arms. Their acquaintance with the sea, the lands and the winds would also help greatly, and all these would make trouble for an enemy unfamiliar with them. The author of this advice, who would also put the plan into effect, had weight with all. Delaying two days in preparation, they set sail on the third day with a hundred ships, all of smaller size, seventy being decked, the rest open, and came to Phocaea. When he had heard that a Roman fleet was approaching, the king, since he did not intend to be present at the naval battle, returned from there to Magnesia, which is near Sipylus, to assemble his land forces; the fleet made haste to Cissus, the harbour of the Erythraei, as if it were more convenient to meet the enemy there. As soon as the north winds subsided—they had been blowing for several days— the Romans stood out from Delos toward Phanae, a harbour of the Chians facing the Aegean sea; there they brought the fleet around to the city and after taking on provisions crossed to Phocaea. Eumenes went to his fleet at Elaea and a few days later returned to Phocaea with twenty-four decked ships and a somewhat larger number of open vessels, finding the Romans making themselves ready and fit for a naval battle. Thence they set out with one

---

7 parantis instruentisque ς : paratis instructisque B.

LIVY

centum quinque[1] tectis navibus, apertis ferme
quinquaginta profecti, primo aquilonibus transversis
cum urgerentur in terram, cogebantur tenui agmine
prope in ordinem singulae naves ire; deinde, ut
lenita paulum vis venti est, ad Corycum portum, qui
super Cissuntem est, conati sunt traicere.

XLIV. Polyxenidas, ut appropinquare hostes adlatum est, occasione pugnandi laetus sinistrum[2] ipse
cornu in altum[3] extendit, dextrum cornu praefectos
navium ad terram explicare iubet, et aequa fronte ad
2 pugnam procedebat. Quod ubi vidit Romanus, vela
contrahit malosque inclinat et simul armamenta
3 componens opperitur insequentes naves. Iam ferme
triginta in fronte erant, quibus ut aequaret laevum
cornu, dolonibus erectis altum petere intendit, iussis
qui sequebantur adversus dextrum cornu prope
4 terram proras derigere. Eumenes agmen cogebat;
ceterum, ut demendis armamentis tumultuari
primum coeptum est, et ipse, quanta maxime celeritate potest, concitat naves. Iam omnibus in con-
5 spectu erant. Duae Punicae naves antecedebant
Romanam classem, quibus obviae tres fuerunt regiae
6 naves; et, ut in numero impari, duae regiae unam
circumsistunt, et primum ab utroque latere remos
detergunt,[4] deinde transcendunt armati et deiectis
7 caesisque propugnatoribus navem capiunt; una,
quae[5] pari Marte concurrerat, postquam captam
alteram navem vidit, priusquam ab tribus simul
8 circumveniretur, retro ad classem refugit. Livius

---

[1] centum quinque *Perizonius* : centum quinquaginta ς :
.CL. *B.*
[2] sinistrum ς : sinistro *B.*
[3] in altum ς : impetum *B.*
[4] detergunt *ed. Frobeniana* 1535: defringunt *B*ς.

hundred and five decked ships and about fifty open B.C. 191
vessels, and when at first they were driven towards
the shore by north winds blowing across their course,
the ships were compelled to proceed in a thin column,
almost in single file; then when the violence of the
wind moderated a little they tried to cross to the
harbour of Corycus, which is above Cissus.

XLIV. Polyxenidas, when the news was brought
that the enemy was coming, rejoicing at the opportunity of fighting, himself drew the left wing out
into the open sea, ordered the ship-captains to extend
the right flank towards the land, and advanced to the
fight in a regular line. When the Roman saw this
he took in sail, lowered his masts and at the same
time stowing his tackle he awaited the oncoming
ships. There were now about thirty of his ships in
front, and in order to bring his left wing into line with
them, hoisting his top-sails he tried to get out into
deep water, ordering the following ships, opposing
the enemy's right wing, to steer towards the shore.
Eumenes was in the rear, but as soon as he saw the
confusion caused by clearing for action he too urged
his ships forward at their utmost speed. Now they
were in sight of all. Two Carthaginian ships were
ahead of the Roman fleet, and three ships of the king
encountered them; and, their numbers being unequal,
two of the king's ships attacked one, and first they
sheared off the oars on both sides, then armed men
boarded it, and throwing overboard and killing the
defenders, took the ship; the one which was fighting
in equal combat, when it saw that the other ship was
taken, fled to the fleet before it should be surrounded
by three. Livius, inflamed with passion, made for

---

⁵ quae *edd. vett.*: cum *B.*

indignatione accensus praetoria nave in hostes tendit.
Adversus quam[1] eadem spe duae quae Punicam unam
navem circumvenerant cum inferrentur, demittere
remos in aquam ab utroque latere remiges stabiliendae
navis causa iussit, et in advenientes hostium naves
9 ferreas manus inicere et, ubi pugnam pedestri
similem fecissent, meminisse Romanae virtutis nec
pro viris ducere regia mancipia. Haud paulo facilius
quam ante duae unam, tunc una duas naves expug-
10 navit cepitque. Et iam classes quoque undique[2]
concurrerant, et passim permixtis navibus pugna-
11 batur. Eumenes, qui extremus commisso certamine
advenerat, ut animadvertit laevum cornu hostium
ab Livio turbatum, dextrum ipse ubi aequa pugna
erat invadit.

XLV. Neque ita multo post primum ab laevo
cornu fuga coepit.[3] Polyxenidas enim ut virtute
militum haud dubie se superari vidit, sublatis dolonibus effuse fugere intendit; mox idem et qui prope
terram cum Eumene contraxerant certamen fecerunt.
2 Romani et Eumenes, quoad sufficere remiges potuerunt et in spe erant extremi agminis vexandi,
3 satis pertinaciter secuti sunt. Postquam celeritate
navium, utpote levium, suas commeatu onustas eludi
frustra tendentes viderunt, tandem abstiterunt tredecim captis navibus cum milite ac remige, decem
4 demersis. Romanae classis una Punica navis, in
primo certamine ab duabus circumventa, periit.

---

[1] quam *ed. Veneta* 1495 : quem *Bϛ.*
[2] quoque undique *ed. Frobeniana* 1535 : undique quoque
B : undique *ϛ.*
[3] fuga coepit *edd. vett.* : fugam fecit *Bϛ.*

the enemy with the flagship. When the two which had just surrounded the Carthaginian ship came up, hoping to repeat their tactics, he ordered the rowers on both sides to trail their oars in the water to steady the ship and the men to throw iron grappling-hooks upon the approaching hostile ships, and when they had made the engagement like one on land, he bade them remember Roman valour and not to consider the king's slaves as men. With greater ease than the two had captured one before, the one ship at this time defeated and captured two. And now the fleets had clashed everywhere and with the ships intermingled the battle was raging on every side. Eumenes, who had arrived late, when the battle had already begun, seeing that the left wing of the enemy had been thrown into confusion by Livius, himself attacked their right, where the battle was evenly matched.

XLV. And not long after the flight began on the left flank. For when Polyxenidas saw that without question he was inferior in the courage of his soldiers, raising his top-sails he began a hurried flight; presently even those who had joined battle with Eumenes near the shore did the same. The Romans and Eumenes, so long as the rowers could hold out and there was any hope of harassing the rear, pursued with stubbornness enough. But when, after vain efforts, they saw that the enemy's ships, which were sailing light, were by their swiftness escaping their own, which were laden with supplies, they at length ceased, having captured thirteen ships along with their marines and rowers, and sunk ten. Of the Roman fleet, the one Carthaginian ship which, at the beginning of the battle, had been surrounded by two, was lost.

LIVY

Polyxenidas non prius quam in portu Ephesi fugae
5 finem fecit. Romani eo die, unde egressa regia
classis erat, manserunt; postero die hostem persequi
intenderunt. Medio fere in cursu obviae fuere iis
quinque et viginti[1] tectae Rhodiae naves cum Pausis-
6 trato praefecto classis. His adiunctis Ephesum
hostem persecuti ante ostium portus acie instructa
steterunt. Postquam confessionem victis satis ex-
presserunt, Rhodii et Eumenes domos dimissi;
7 Romani Chium petentes, Phoenicuntem primum
portum Erythraeae terrae praetervecti, nocte ancoris
iactis, postero die in insulam ad ipsam urbem traiecerunt. Ubi paucos dies remige maxime reficiendo
8 morati Phocaeam tramittunt. Ibi relictis ad praesidium urbis quattuor quinqueremibus ad Canas
classis venit; et, cum iam hiems appeteret, fossa
valloque circumdatis naves subductae.
9 Exitu anni comitia Romae habita, quibus creati
sunt consules L. Cornelius Scipio et C. Laelius—
Africanum intuentibus cunctis—ad finiendum cum
Antiocho bellum. Postero die praetores creati M.
Tuccius L. Aurunculeius Cn. Fulvius L. Aemilius
P. Iunius C. Atinius Labeo.

[1] iis quinque et viginti ϛ : his quique et XXX B.

Polyxenidas did not stop his flight until he reached B.C. 191
the harbour of Ephesus. The Romans on that day
remained at the place from which the king's fleet
had come; the next day they set out to pursue the
enemy. About half-way on the journey twenty-
five decked Rhodian ships under Pausistratus,
commander of the fleet, met them. Thus reinforced,
they followed the enemy to Ephesus and stood
drawn up in line of battle before the entrance to
the harbour. Now that they had wrung a confes-
sion of inferiority from the defeated, the Rhodians
and Eumenes were sent home; the Romans on
their way to Chios first sailed past Phoenicus, the
port of the Erythraean land, and at nightfall dropped
anchor; the next day they crossed to the island and
to the city itself. There they delayed a few days
resting their rowers, and then crossed to Phocaea.
Leaving four quinqueremes there as a garrison for
the city, the fleet came to Canae; and since winter
was now at hand, the ships were beached and surrounded with a wall and ditch.

At the end of the year the elections were held in
Rome, at which Lucius Cornelius Scipio and Gaius
Laelius—all looking towards Africanus [1]—were
chosen consuls to end the war with Antiochus. The
next day the praetors were elected, Marcus Tuccius,
Lucius Aurunculeius, Gnaeus Fulvius, Lucius
Aemilius, Publius Junius, Gaius Atinius Labeo.

---

[1] Lucius Scipio was the brother and Laelius the closest
friend of Scipio Africanus.

LIBRI XXXVI PERIOCHA

Acilius Glabrio consul Antiochum ad Thermopylas
Philippo rege adiuvante victum Graecia expulit idemque
Aetolos subegit. P. Cornelius Scipio Nasica consul aedem
Matris Deum quam ipse in Palatium intulerat, vir optimus
a senatu iudicatus, dedicavit. Idemque [1] Boios Gallos
victos in deditionem accepti, de his triumphavit. Prae-
terea navalia certamina prospera adversus praefectos
Antiochi regis referuntur.

[1] idemque *Rossbach* : itemque *codd.*

SUMMARY OF BOOK XXXVI

ACILIUS GLABRIO the consul, with the aid of King
Philip, defeated Antiochus at Thermopylae and drove
him from Greece, and also subdued the Aetolians. Publius
Cornelius Scipio Nasica the consul dedicated the temple
of the Mother of the Gods, whom he himself had established
on the Palatine, after being adjudged the best man by the
senate. He also received the surrender of the Gallic Boii
after their defeat, and triumphed over them. Besides,
naval victories over the officers of Antiochus are recorded.

BOOK XXXVII

LIBER XXXVII

I. L. Cornelio Scipione C. Laelio consulibus
nulla prius secundum religiones acta in senatu res
est quam de Aetolis. Et legati eorum institerunt,
quia brevem indutiarum diem habebant, et ab T.
Quinctio, qui tum Romam ex Graecia redierat,
2 adiuti sunt. Aetoli, ut quibus plus in misericordia
senatus quam in causa spei esset, suppliciter egerunt,
3 veteribus benefactis nova pensantes maleficia. Ceterum et praesentes interrogationibus undique
senatorum, confessionem magis noxae quam responsa
exprimentium,[1] fatigati sunt, et excedere curia iussi
4 magnum certamen praebuerunt. Plus ira quam
misericordia in causa eorum valebat, quia non ut
hostibus[2] sed tamquam indomitae et insociabili
5 genti suscensebant. Per aliquot dies cum certatum
esset, postremo neque dari neque negari pacem
placuit; duae condiciones iis latae sunt: vel senatui
liberum arbitrium[3] de se permitterent, vel mille
talentum darent eosdemque[4] amicos atque inimicos
6 haberent. Exprimere cupientibus, quarum rerum

---

[1] exprimentium 5: experimentum *B*.
[2] hostibus 5: hostes *B*.
[3] arbitrium 5: om. *B*.
[4] eosdemque *ed. Parisina* 1518 : eosque *B*5.

---

[1] The latter would technically make them *socii*, though in
a relation of dependency; this was one of the conditions
imposed in 189 B.C. (XXXVIII. viii. 10).

BOOK XXXVII

I. Lucius Cornelius Scipio and Gaius Laelius B.C. 190 entered upon the consulship, and after the religious observances were carried out, no question in the senate had priority over that concerning the Aetolians. And their ambassadors were urging a decision, since only a brief time of truce was allowed them, and they were seconded by Titus Quinctius, who had now returned to Rome from Greece. The Aetolians, like men who reposed more hope in the mercy of the senate than in their own case, pleaded like suppliants, balancing former services against recent misdeeds. But not only while still present were they pursued by senatorial questionings from all sides, forcing from them confessions of guilt rather than replies, but when they were ordered to leave the senate-house they gave occasion to a violent conflict. Anger had greater weight in their case than the spirit of mercy, since the senators were incensed at them not as enemies but as an untamable and anti-social people. When the contest had continued for many days, it was finally decided that peace should be neither granted nor refused; two choices were placed before them; either they should entrust themselves to the free discretion of the senate, or they should pay one thousand talents and consider the same peoples as friends and enemies.[1] When they tried to elicit a definite statement as to

LIVY

in se arbitrium senatui permitterent, nihil certi responsum est. Ita infecta pace dimissi urbe eodem die, Italia intra quindecim dies excedere iussi.

7 Tum de consulum provinciis coeptum agi est. Ambo Graeciam cupiebant. Multum Laelius in senatu poterat. Is, cum senatus aut sortiri aut comparare inter se [1] provincias consules iussisset, elegantius facturos dixit,[2] si iudicio patrum quam si

8 sorti eam rem permisissent. Scipio responso ad hoc dato cogitaturum, quid sibi faciendum esset, cum fratre uno locutus iussusque ab eo permittere audacter senatui, renuntiat collegae facturum se, quod is

9 censeret. Cum res aut nova aut vetustate exemplorum memoriae iam exoletae relata expectatione certaminis senatum erexisset, P. Scipio Africanus dixit, si L. Scipioni fratri suo provinciam Graeciam [3]

10 decrevissent, se ei legatum [4] iturum. Haec vox magno adsensu audita sustulit certamen; experiri libebat utrum plus regi Antiocho in Hannibale victo an in victore Africano consuli legionibusque Romanis auxilii foret; ac prope omnes Scipioni Graeciam, Laelio Italiam decreverunt.

[1] inter se ς : om. B.
[2] dixit ς : iussit B.
[3] graeciam ς : om. B.
[4] ei legatum Duker : legatum Bς.

---

[1] In XXXVI. xxii. 8 ff. the Aetolians discovered that Roman and Greek interpretations of diplomatic phraseology differed, and wanted to know what *liberum arbitrium* could mean. The acceptance of the first proposal in its extreme form might amount to a complete surrender.

[2] This put Africanus in a difficult position, with his brother and his friend rivals for the same appointment.

the extent to which the senate would exercise its B.C. 190 discretion [1] over them, no positive reply was given. So without any settlement they were ordered to leave the City that same day and Italy within fifteen days.

Then the question of the consular provinces began to be discussed. Both consuls wanted Greece.[2] Laelius was very influential in the senate. Laelius, when the senate had directed the consuls either to cast lots or to determine the matter of the provinces between themselves, said that they would act more fittingly if they entrusted this decision to the wisdom of the Fathers instead of to the lot. Scipio, having replied to this that he would consider what he ought to do, conferred with his brother alone, and being instructed by him to leave the matter to the senate with confidence, answered his colleague that he would do as he suggested. When this proposal, either novel or revived on the basis of ancient precedents long escaped from memory, had excited the senate with the expectation of a sharp contest, Publius Scipio Africanus said that if they should decree Greece as a province to his brother Lucius Scipio, he would go as his lieutenant.[3] These words, listened to with full approbation, ended the contest; they wanted to ascertain whether King Antiochus would find more powerful assistance in the defeated Hannibal or the Roman consul and legions in his conqueror Africanus: and almost unanimously they decreed Greece to Scipio, Italy to Laelius.

[3] Africanus probably thought that he could serve with better grace as *legatus* under his brother than under the friend who had been his own *legatus* in Africa. Other versions are found in Cicero (*Philippic* XI. 17; *Murena* 32) and elsewhere.

LIVY

II. Praetores inde provincias sortiti sunt, L.
Aurunculeius urbanam, Cn. Fulvius peregrinam,[1]
L. Aemilius Regillus classem, P. Iunius Brutus
Tuscos, M. Tuccius[2] Apuliam et Bruttios, C. Atinius
2 Siciliam. Consuli deinde, cui Graecia provincia
decreta erat, ad eum exercitum, quem a M'. Acilio—
duae autem legiones erant—accepturus esset, in
supplementum addita peditum civium Romanorum[3]
3 tria milia, equites centum, et socium Latini nominis
quinque milia, equites ducenti; et adiectum ut, cum
in provinciam venisset, si e re publica videretur esse,
exercitum in Asiam traiceret. Alteri consuli totus
4 novus exercitus decretus, duae legiones Romanae et
socium Latini nominis quindecim milia peditum,
5 equites sexcenti. Exercitum ex Liguribus Q. Minucius[4]—iam enim confectam provinciam scripserat et
Ligurum omne nomen in deditionem venisse[5]—
traducere in Boios et P. Cornelio proconsuli tradere
iussus ex agro, quo victos[6] bello multaverat, Boios
6 deducenti.[7] Duae urbanae legiones, quae[8] priore
anno conscriptae erant, M. Tuccio praetori datae et
socium ac Latini nominis peditum quindecim milia

---

[1] Cn. Fulvius peregrinam *ed. Frobeniana* 1535 : m. fuluius
peregrinam *B* : *om.* ς.
[2] Tuccius *ed. Frobeniana* 1535 : bruttius *B*ς : tutius *M*.
[3] Romanorum ς : *om. B*.
[4] Q. Minucius *edd. vett.* : q̄ *B* : p. minucius ς.
[5] uenisse ς : uenisset *B*.
[6] uictos ς : uictus *B*.
[7] deducenti *H. J. Müller* : deducendae *B*ς.
[8] quae ς : *om. B*.

---

[1] This statement is inconsistent with that in XXXVI.
xiv. 1.
[2] Cf. XXXVI. xxxix. 3.

II. The praetors then drew for their provinces; B.C. 190
Lucius Aurunculeius receiving the civil jurisdiction,
Gnaeus Fulvius that between citizens and aliens,
Lucius Aemilius Regillus the fleet, Publius Junius
Brutus the Etruscans, Marcus Tuccius Apulia and the
Brutti, Gaius Atinius Sicily. Then for the consul
to whom the province of Greece had been decreed,
in addition to the army which he would take over
from Manius Acilius—this now consisted of two
legions [1]—there were authorized as reinforcements
three thousand infantry of Roman citizens and one
hundred cavalry, and of the allies of the Latin confederacy five thousand infantry and two hundred
cavalry; it was also appended to this that when he
arrived in the province, if the public interest seemed
to demand it, he should lead the army over into
Asia. To the other consul an entirely new army
was assigned, two Roman legions and of the allies
of the Latin confederacy fifteen thousand infantry
and six hundred cavalry. Quintus Minucius was
directed to transfer his army from the Ligures—
for he had now written that the province had been
completely reduced and that all the people of the
Ligures had surrendered—to the territory of the Boii
and hand it over to Publius Scipio the proconsul,
who was removing the Boii from the land of which
he had deprived them after their defeat in the war.[2]
The two reserve legions [3] which had been enlisted
the year before were assigned to Marcus Tuccius,
along with fifteen thousand infantry and six hundred
cavalry of the allies of the Latin confederacy, to

[3] This statement is inconsistent with that in XXXVI. i. 9;
like that in sect. 2 above, it is probably derived from a different
annalistic source.

LIVY

et equites sexcenti ad Apuliam Bruttiosque obtinen-
7 dos. A. Cornelio superioris anni praetori, qui Bruttios cum exercitu obtinuerat, imperatum, si ita
consuli videretur, ut legiones in Aetoliam traiectas
8 M'. Acilio traderet, si is manere ibi vellet; si Acilius
redire Romam mallet, ut A. Cornelius cum eo
exercitu in Aetolia remaneret. C. Atinium Labeo-
nem provinciam Siciliam exercitumque a M. Aemilio [1]
accipere placuit et in supplementum scribere ex ipsa
provincia, si vellet, peditum duo milia et centum
9 equites. P. Iunius Brutus in Tuscos exercitum
novum, legionem unam Romanam et decem milia
socium ac Latini nominis scribere et quadringentos
10 equites; L. Aemilius, cui maritima provincia erat,
viginti naves longas et socios navales a M. Iunio
praetore superioris anni accipere iussus et scribere
ipse mille navales socios, duo milia peditum; cum iis
navibus militibusque in Asiam proficisci et classem a
11 C. Livio accipere. Duas Hispanias Sardiniamque
obtinentibus prorogatum in annum imperium est et
12 idem exercitus decreti. Siciliae Sardiniaeque binae
aeque ac proximo anno [2] decumae frumenti imperatae; Siculum omne frumentum in Aetoliam ad
exercitum portari iussum, ex Sardinia pars Romam
pars in Aetoliam, eodem quo Siculum.

III. Priusquam consules in provincias proficiscerentur, prodigia per pontifices procurari placuit.

---

[1] a M. Aemilio *ed. Aldina*: ab 1. aemilio *Bϛ*.
[2] aeque ac proximo anno *Madvig*: eo anno *Bϛ*: eaeque
proximae *M*.

---

[1] Cf. XXXVI. ii. 2.
[2] Livy says nothing about Valerius (XXXVI. ii. 11), who
had shared the responsibility for Sicily.

hold Apulia and the Brutti. Aulus Cornelius,[1] B.C. 190 praetor of the preceding year, who had held the Brutti with an army, was ordered to transport the legions to Aetolia, if such was the pleasure of the consul, and turn them over to Manius Acilius, if he wished to remain there; if Acilius preferred to return to Rome, Aulus Cornelius with this army should remain in Aetolia. Gaius Atinius Labeo, it was decided, should receive the province of Sicily and the army from Marcus Aemilius [2] the praetor and as reinforcements should enrol from the province itself two thousand infantry and one hundred cavalry. Publius Junius Brutus was instructed to enlist a new army to serve against the Etruscans, one Roman legion and ten thousand infantry and four hundred cavalry of the allies of the Latin confederacy; Lucius Aemilius, to whom the maritime province had been allotted, was ordered to receive twenty warships and the naval allies from Marcus Junius, praetor of the previous year, to enrol himself a thousand naval allies and two thousand marines, to proceed with these ships and troops to Asia and to take over the fleet from Gaius Livius. For the governors of the two Spains and Sardinia the *imperium* was prolonged for a year and the same armies assigned. Two tithes of grain, just as in the preceding year,[3] were levied upon Sicily and Sardinia; they ordered all the Sicilian grain to be transported to Aetolia, part of the Sardinian to Rome and part to Aetolia, the same destination as the Sicilian.

III. Before the consuls set out to their provinces it was decreed that expiation should be made for the prodigies by direction of the pontiffs. At Rome

[3] Cf. XXXVI. ii. 12–13.

LIVY

2 Romae Iunonis Lucinae templum de caelo tactum
erat ita ut fastigium valvaeque deformarentur;
Puteolis pluribus locis murus et porta fulmine icta
3 et duo homines exanimati; Nursiae sereno satis
constabat nimbum ortum; ibi quoque duos liberos
homines exanimatos; terra apud se pluvisse Tuscu-
lani nuntiabant, et Reatini mulam in agro suo
4 peperisse. Ea procurata, Latinaeque instauratae,
quod Laurentibus pars carnis [1] quae dari debet data
5 non fuerat. Supplicatio quoque earum religionum
causa fuit quibus diis decemviri ex libris ut fieret
6 ediderunt. Decem ingenui, decem virgines, patrimi
omnes matrimique, ad id sacrificium adhibiti, et decemviri nocte lactentibus rem divinam fecerunt.
7 P. Cornelius Scipio Africanus, priusquam proficisceretur, fornicem in Capitolio adversus viam qua in Capi-
tolium escenditur, cum signis septem auratis et
equis duobus et marmorea duo labra ante fornicem
posuit.
8   Per eosdem [2] dies principes Aetolorum tres et
quadraginta, inter quos Damocritus et frater eius
erant, ab duabus cohortibus missis a M'. Acilio
Romam deducti et in Lautumias coniecti sunt.
Cohortes inde ad exercitum redire L. Cornelius
9 consul iussit. Legati ab Ptolomaeo et Cleopatra
regibus Aegypti gratulantes, quod M'. Acilius consul
Antiochum regem Graecia expulisset, venerunt

---

[1] pars carnis *Madvig* : carinis *B*.   [2] eosdem ϛ : eos *B*.

---

[1] Cf. XXXII. i. 9 and the note for a similar occurrence.
[2] The present is used probably because the right still existed
in Livy's time.
[3] Cf. XXXII. xxvi. 17.
[4] The sister of the king, here Cleopatra, by Egyptian custom
and law, shared in the administration : hence *reges*.

the temple of Juno Lucina was struck by lightning B.C.190
so that the roof and the doors were damaged; at
Puteoli the wall and gates in several places were
struck by lightning and two men were killed; at
Nursia it was well established that a storm-cloud
came in sight on a clear day; there also two free
men were killed; the people of Tusculum reported
that in their neighbourhood there was a shower of
earth, and the Reatini that in their country a mule
had foaled. When expiation for all this had been
made, the Latin festival,[1] too, because the share of
the meat which is [2] due to be given to the Laurentes
was not given them, was repeated. There was also
a period of prayer by reason of these phenomena to
whatever gods the decemvirs, in accordance with the
Books, had ordered supplication to be made. Ten
noble youths and ten maidens, all children of living
fathers and mothers, were employed for this sacrifice,
and the decemvirs by night sacrificed animals not yet
weaned. Publius Cornelius Scipio Africanus, before
he left the City, constructed an arch on the Capitoline,
facing the street by which one climbs the Capitoline,
with seven statues of bronze and two equestrian
figures and two marble basins before the arch.

About the same time forty-three chiefs of the
Aetolians, among whom were Damocritus and his
brother, were brought to Rome under guard of
two cohorts sent by Manius Acilius and were thrown
into the *Lautumiae*.[3] The cohorts were then directed
by Lucius Cornelius the consul to rejoin the army.
Ambassadors from Ptolemy and Cleopatra,[4] rulers
of Egypt, came with congratulations because Manius
Acilius the consul had driven King Antiochus out
of Greece, and with recommendations that they

LIVY

A.U.C.
564

adhortantesque, ut in Asiam exercitum traicerent:
10 omnia perculsa metu non in Asia modo sed etiam
in Syria esse; reges Aegypti ad ea, quae censuisset
11 senatus, paratos fore. Gratiae regibus actae; legatis
munera dari iussa in singulos quaternum milium aeris.
IV. L. Cornelius consul peractis quae Romae
agenda erant, pro contione edixit ut milites, quos
ipse in supplementum scripsisset, quique in Bruttiis
cum A. Cornelio propraetore essent, ut hi omnes idi-
2 bus Quinctilibus Brundisium convenirent. Item tres
legatos nominavit, Sex. Digitium L. Apustium C.
Fabricium Luscinum, qui ex ora maritima undique
naves Brundisium contraherent; et omnibus iam
3 paratis paludatus [1] ab urbe est profectus. Ad
quinque milia voluntariorum, Romani sociique, qui
emerita stipendia sub imperatore P. Africano habebant, praesto fuere exeunti consuli et nomina de-
4 derunt. Per eos dies, quibus est profectus ad bellum
consul, ludis Apollinaribus, a. d. quintum [2] idus
Quinctiles caelo sereno interdiu obscurata lux est,
5 cum luna sub orbem [3] solis subisset. Et L. Aemilius

---

[1] paludatus ⟫ : paludatis B.
[2] ante diem quintum *edd. vett.* : ad quintum B⟫.
[3] orbem *Weissenborn* : urbe B : orbe B (*ex corr.*) ⟫.

---

[1] Livy uses the old name of the month, *Quinctilis,* which
was in his time called *Iulius* in honour of Caesar.
[2] Their status was that of *evocati,* reservists called to active
duty, which gave them certain special privileges.
[3] These games, celebrated in honour of Apollo, were held
annually in July.
[4] This eclipse, according to modern calculations, occurred
March 14, 190 B.C. The Roman calendar was then out of
adjustment to the extent indicated by these dates (March
14–July 11). The usual remedy was to insert an extra (intercalary) month between February and March, of such length

should transport the army into Asia : everything was B.C. 190 in a confusion of terror, they said, not only in Asia but even in Syria ; the rulers of Egypt were prepared for whatever the senate might order. Thanks were extended to the rulers ; each of the ambassadors received, in accordance with orders issued, a present of four thousand *asses*.

IV. Lucius Cornelius the consul, having finished what had to be done in Rome, issued his edict before the assembly that the soldiers whom he personally had enlisted as reinforcements and those who were among the Brutti with Aulus Cornelius the propraetor should all assemble on the Ides of July [1] at Brundisium. He named also three lieutenants, Sextus Digitius, Lucius Apustius and Gaius Fabricius Luscinus, who were to collect ships at Brundisium from all along the sea-coast ; and having now made everything ready set out from the City in uniform. About five thousand volunteers, Romans and allies, who had earned their discharges under the command of Publius Africanus, attended the consul as he was setting out and gave in their names for service with him. [2] About the time the consul departed to the war, during the *ludi Apollinares*, [3] on the fifth day before the Ides of July, in a clear sky during the day, the light was dimmed since the moon passed before the circle of the sun. [4] Lucius Aemilius

as to bring the solstitial and equinoctial periods to the proper calendar dates. The effects of such dislocations upon Livy's treatment of chronology have been frequently pointed out in the notes : cf. xxxvii. 6 below.

This particular date is rejected by Beloch (Klio XV, 1918, 391 ff. ; XXII, 1929, 464 ff.) on various grounds, among them the fact that it places the battle of Magnesia at a time inconsistent with the narrative of Polybius.

LIVY

Regillus, cui navalis provincia evenerat, eodem
tempore profectus est. L. Aurunculeio negotium
ab senatu datum est ut triginta quinqueremes,
viginti triremes faceret, quia fama erat Antiochum
post proelium navale maiorem classem aliquanto
reparare.

6 Aetoli, postquam legati ab Roma rettulerunt
nullam spem pacis esse, quamquam omnis ora maritima eorum, quae in Peloponnesum versa est, depopu-
7 lata ab Achaeis erat, periculi magis quam damni
memores, ut Romanis intercluderent iter, Coracem
occupaverunt montem; neque enim dubitabant ad
oppugnationem Naupacti eos principio veris redi-
8 turos esse. Acilio, quia id expectari sciebat, satius
visum est inopinatam[1] aggredi rem et Lamiam
9 oppugnare; nam et a Philippo prope ad excidium
adductos esse, et tunc eo ipso, quod nihil tale time-
10 rent, opprimi incautos posse. Profectus ab Elatia
primum in hostium terra circa Spercheum amnem
posuit castra; inde nocte motis signis prima luce
corona moenia est aggressus.

V. Magnus pavor ac tumultus, ut in re improvisa,
fuit. Constantius tamen, quam quis facturos crederet, in tam subito periculo, cum viri propugnarent,
feminae tela omnis generis saxaque in muros gere-
rent, iam multifariam scalis appositis urbem eo die
2 defenderunt. Acilius signo receptui dato[2] suos in

---

[1] inopinatam ς : opinatam *B*.
[2] dato ς : *om. B*.

---

[1] Cf. XXXVI. xliii–xlv.
[2] Cf. XXXVI. xxx. 4.
[3] Cf. XXXVI. xxx; xxxv.
[4] Cf. XXXVI. xxv. 8.

Regillus, to whom the naval appointment had fallen, also departed at the same time. Lucius Aurunculeius was entrusted by the senate with the task of building thirty quinqueremes and twenty triremes, since the rumour was that Antiochus after the naval battle was fitting out a very much larger fleet.[1]

The Aetolians, after their ambassadors had brought back the word from Rome that there was no hope for peace, although their whole coast which faces the Peloponnesus had been ravaged by the Achaeans, thinking more of their danger than of their losses, in order to bar the road against the Romans, seized Mount Corax;[2] for they had no doubt that they would return at the beginning of spring to besiege Naupactus.[3] Acilius, because he knew that this was their expectation, thought it better to try something unforeseen and to attack Lamia;[4] for the people had both been brought nigh to destruction by Philip and, just because at that time they feared nothing of the kind, he thought that they could be more easily taken by surprise. Setting out from Elatia he first encamped in hostile territory near the Spercheus river; thence he moved his standards by night and at daybreak attacked the walls from a girdle of entrenchments.

V. There was great panic and excitement, as is natural when something unexpected occurs. Nevertheless, with greater resolution than one would think they would display in such a sudden peril, while the men fought before the walls and the women were carrying weapons of all kinds and stones to the walls, though scaling ladders were now being brought up on all sides, they defended the city on that day. Acilius sounded the recall and led his troops back into

A.U.C.
564

castra medio ferme die reduxit; et tunc cibo et
quiete refectis corporibus, priusquam praetorium di-
mitteret, denuntiavit ut ante lucem armati paratique
essent; nisi expugnata urbe se eos in castra non
3 reducturum. Eodem tempore quo [1] pridie, pluribus
locis aggressus, cum oppidanos iam vires, iam tela
iam ante omnia animus deficeret, intra paucas horas
urbem cepit. Ibi partim divendita partim divisa
praeda, consilium habitum, quid deinde faceret
4 Nemini ad Naupactum iri placuit occupato ad Coracem ab Aetolis saltu. Ne tamen segnia aestiva
essent et Aetoli non impetratam pacem ab senatu
nihilo minus per suam cunctationem haberent,
5 oppugnare Acilius Amphissam statuit. Ab Heraclea
per Oetam exercitus eo deductus. Cum ad moenia
castra posuisset, non corona, sicut Lamiam, sed
operibus oppugnare urbem est adortus. Pluribus
simul locis aries admovebatur, et cum quaterentur
muri, nihil adversus tale machinationis genus parare
6 aut comminisci [3] oppidani conabantur; omnis spes
in armis et audacia erat; eruptionibus crebris et
stationes hostium et eos ipsos, qui circa opera et
machinas [4] erant, turbabant.[5]

VI. Multis tamen locis decussus murus erat [6] cum
adlatum est successorem Apolloniae exposito exercitu
2 per Epirum ac Thessaliam venire. Cum tredecim [7]
milibus peditum et quingentis equitibus consul

---

[1] quo ς : qui B.
[2] haberent ς : habebant B.
[3] comminisci ς : om., spat. rel. B.
[4] machinas edd. vett. : machinationes Bς.
[5] turbabant ς : turbabantur B.
[6] erat ς : om. B.   [7] tredecim Sigonius : tribus Bς.

---

[1] I.e., his council of war.

camp about noon; and then, when they had restored their bodies with food and rest, before he dismissed the council [1] he issued orders that they should be armed and ready before daybreak; unless they took the city he would not lead them back into camp. At the same time as the day before he attacked from several directions, and since the townspeople were by now lacking in strength, in weapons, and before all in courage, within a few hours he took the city. There, selling part of the plunder and dividing part among the troops, he held a council to determine what they should do next. No one urged that they move on Naupactus, the pass over Corax being held by the Aetolians. Nevertheless, that the summer might not be spent in inactivity, and that the Aetolians might not, through his delay, none the less enjoy a peace which the senate had not granted, Acilius decided to attack Amphissa. From Heraclea the army was led over Oeta. When he had made camp before the walls he did not begin to attack the city by encirclement, as at Lamia, but by siege-engines. The battering-rams were moved up in several places at once, and when the walls were shaken the townspeople did not try to prepare or devise anything against engines of this kind; all their hopes were in arms and daring; with frequent sallies they threw into confusion not only the outguards of the enemy but the men who were around the earth-works and the engines.

VI. Yet in many places the wall had been overthrown when the word was brought that the new consul had disembarked at Apollonia and was marching through Epirus and Thessaly. The consul had with him thirteen thousand infantry and five hundred

305

LIVY

veniebat. Iam in sinum Maliacum venerat;[1] et praemissis Hypatam, qui tradere urbem iuberent, postquam nihil responsum est nisi ex communi Aetolorum decreto facturos, ne teneret se oppugnatio Hypatae nondum Amphissa recepta, prae3 misso fratre Africano Amphissam ducit. Sub adventum eorum oppidani relicta urbe—iam enim magna ex parte moenibus nudata erat—in arcem, quam inexpugnabilem habent, omnes armati atque inermes concessere.

4 Consul sex milia fere passuum inde posuit castra. Eo legati Athenienses primum ad P. Scipionem praegressum agmen, sicut ante dictum est, deinde ad 5 consulem venerunt, deprecantes pro Aetolis. Clementius responsum ab Africano tulerunt, qui causam relinquendi honeste Aetolici belli quaerens Asiam et regem Antiochum spectabat, iusseratque Athenienses non Romanis solum, ut pacem bello praeferrent, sed 6 etiam Aetolis persuadere. Celeriter auctoribus Atheniensibus frequens ab Hypata legatio Aetolorum venit, et spem pacis eis sermo etiam Africani, quem priorem adierunt, auxit, commemorantis multas gentes populosque in Hispania prius, deinde in Africa in fidem suam venisse; in omnibus se maiora clementiae benignitatisque quam virtutis bellicae monu7 menta reliquisse. Perfecta[2] videbatur res, cum aditus consul idem illud responsum rettulit, quo fugati ab senatu erant. Eo tamquam novo cum icti

---

[1] in sinum Maliacum venerat *ed. Parisina* 1510 : in sinu maliaco erat *Bς*.

[2] perfecta *ς* : perfecta uirtutis *B*.

---

[1] Polybius (XXI. iv. ff.) says nothing of a visit to the consul but only of their call on Africanus.

[2] Cf. i. 5 above.

cavalry. He had already arrived at the Malian gulf; B.C. 190
and sending messengers ahead to Hypata to order the
city to surrender, when they replied that they would
do nothing except in accord with the general decision
of the Aetolians, that the siege of Hypata might not
detain him while Amphissa was as yet uncaptured,
he sent his brother Africanus in advance and led the
army to Amphissa. At their coming the citizens
abandoned the town—for it was in large part stripped
of its defences—and retired, armed and unarmed
together, to the citadel, which they held impossible
to capture.

The consul pitched camp about six miles away from
there. Thither came Athenian envoys, first to
Publius Scipio, who had preceded the main body, as
has been said before, then to the consul, inter-
ceding for the Aetolians.[1] They received a fairly
amicable response from Africanus, who was looking
for an occasion for an honourable withdrawal from
the Aetolian campaign, with his eyes on Asia and
King Antiochus, and had ordered the Athenians to
urge not only the Romans to prefer peace to war,
but also the Aetolians. Quickly, on the advice of
the Athenians, a large delegation of Aetolians came
from Hypata, and the words of Africanus, to whom
they first addressed themselves, increased their hopes
of peace, as he reminded them of the many tribes
and peoples, first in Spain, later in Africa, who had
put themselves under his protection; in all these he
had left more conspicuous monuments of his kindness
and generosity than of his military renown. The
matter seemed settled, when the consul, on being
addressed, quoted the response by which they had
been rebuffed by the senate.[2] When the Aetolians

307

Aetoli essent—nihil enim nec legatione Atheniensium nec placido Africani responso profectum videbant—referre ad suos dixerunt velle.

VII. Reditum inde Hypatam est, nec consilium
expediebatur; nam neque unde mille talentum
daretur erat, et permisso libero arbitrio ne in corpora
2 sua saeviretur, metuebant. Redire itaque eosdem
legatos ad consulem et Africanum iusserunt et
petere ut, si dare vere pacem, non tantum ostendere
frustrantes spem miserorum, vellent, aut ex summa
pecuniae demerent aut permissionem extra civium
3 corpora fieri iuberent. Nihil impetratum ut mutaret
consul; et ea quoque irrita legatio dimissa est.
4 Secuti et Athenienses sunt; et princeps legationi
eorum Echedemus fatigatos tot repulsis Aetolos et
complorantes inutili lamentatione fortunam gentis
ad spem revocavit auctor indutias sex mensium pe
5 tendi, ut legatos mittere Romam possent: dilationem
nihil ad praesentia mala, quippe quae ultima essent
adiecturam;[1] levari per multos casus tempore inter
6 posito praesentes clades posse. Auctore Echedemo
idem missi; prius P. Scipione convento, per eum

[1] adiecturam *ς* : adiectum *B*.

---

[1] The part played by Africanus is somewhat hard to understand. He had his own reputation to maintain (cf. vi. 6 above)
as had Flamininus, but he was apparently less able to control
his brother than he had perhaps expected. Scipio's greater
concern for the Asiatic war was no doubt due to ambition for
new renown for himself and his family, and probably to the
political situation in Rome. Flamininus had defeated him
badly two years before (XXXV. x), and this probably still
rankled, despite his more recent successes. A decisive victory
in Asia would strengthen greatly the position of the Scipionic
party in Rome. The result was that Scipio and Flamininus

B.C. 190

were dealt this unexpected blow—for they saw that
nothing had been accomplished either by the
embassy of the Athenians or by the generous
reply of Africanus—they said that they wished to
consult their people.

VII. They returned thence to Hypata; nor was
a decision easy to reach; for there was no source
from which a thousand talents could be paid, and
they were afraid that if " full discretion " were granted
they would suffer personal violence. They therefore
directed the same ambassadors to return to the consul
and Africanus and to ask that if they wished to
grant peace in reality, not merely to dangle it before
them, deluding the hopes of the unfortunate, they
would either diminish the amount of the indemnity
or would order that an exception regarding their
persons be made. Nothing was obtained in the way
of a change on the consul's part; and this embassy
also was dismissed without result. The Athenians
followed; and Echedemus, the leader of their
embassy, brought back hope to the Aetolians, wearied
by so many repulses and bewailing with useless
lamentations the ill-fate of their race, by suggesting
that they ask an armistice for six months that envoys
might be sent to Rome; the delay would add nothing
to their present misfortunes, since these were extreme; many things might happen in the interven-
ing time to relieve their immediate calamity. On
the proposal of Echedemus the same men were sent;
they first met Publius Scipio,[1] through whose inter-

were agreed as to the policy to be adopted towards the
Aetolians, but for different reasons: Africanus to clear the
way for the invasion of Asia, Flamininus to maintain his own
peculiar position.

A.U.C.
564

7 indutias temporis eius, quod petebant, ab consul
impetraverunt. Et soluta obsidione Amphissae M'
Acilius tradito consuli exercitu provincia decessit
et consul ab Amphissa Thessaliam repetit, ut pe
Macedoniam Thraeciamque duceret in Asiam.

8 Tum Africanus fratri: " Iter, quod insistis, L
9 Scipio, ego quoque approbo; sed totum id vertitu
in voluntate Philippi, qui si imperio nostro fidus est
et iter et commeatus et omnia quae in longo itiner
exercitus alunt iuvantque nobis suppeditabit; si i
destituit,[1] nihil per Thraeciam satis tutum habebis
10 itaque prius regis animum explorari placet. Optim
explorabitur, si nihil ex praeparato agentem opprime
11 qui mittetur." Ti. Sempronius Gracchus, longe tun
acerrimus iuvenum, ad id delectus per disposito
equos prope incredibili celeritate ab Amphissa—ind
12 enim est dimissus—die tertio Pellam pervenit. In
convivio rex erat et in multum vini processerat; e
ipsa remissio animi suspicionem dempsit novare eun
13 quicquam velle.[2] Et tum quidem comiter acceptu
hospes, postero die commeatus exercitui parato
benigne, pontes in fluminibus factos, vias, ubi [3] trans
14 itus difficiles erant, munitas vidit. Haec referen
eadem, qua ierat, celeritate Thaumacis occurrit con

---

[1] destituit ς : destituat B.
[2] quicquam uelle ς : om. B.
[3] ubi ς : om. B.

---

[1] Cf. ii. 7–8 above. Acilius had not been relieved while the
new consul was still six miles away (vi. 4 above).

[2] Scipio now had the army of Acilius plus the troops which
he had brought from Italy. Cornelius, the propraetor of
ii. 7–8 above, was in Greece to watch the Aetolians, but the
six months of truce would cover the campaigning season.

vention they obtained from the consul an armistice B.C.190
for the period which they asked. And the siege of
Amphissa being raised, Manius Acilius turned his
army over to the consul and left the province,[1] and
from Amphissa the consul went back into Thessaly,
in order to conduct the army through Macedonia
and Thrace into Asia.[2]

Then Africanus addressed his brother: " The
route which you propose to follow, Lucius Scipio,
I likewise approve; but it all hangs on the good-will
of Philip, if he is loyal to our empire and will furnish
us a safe passage and supplies and everything which
feeds and aids an army on a long march; if he fails
us, there will be no real security in going through
Thrace; therefore my first counsel is to test the
attitude of the king. It will be most successfully
tested if the man who is sent finds him doing nothing
in anticipation of such a visit." Tiberius Sempronius Gracchus,[3] by far the most energetic of the
young men of the time, was chosen for this errand
and, using relays of horses, with almost unbelievable
speed, from Amphissa—for he was sent from there—
on the third day reached Pella. The king was at a
banquet and had gone far with his drinking; this
very cheerfulness of mind relieved all anxiety that
Philip planned to make any new trouble. And at
that time the guest was graciously welcomed, and
the next day he saw supplies in abundance prepared
for the army, bridges built over the rivers, roads
constructed where travel was difficult. Taking back
this information, with the same speed as on his
journey hither, he met the consul at Thaumaci.

[3] He later married the daughter of Africanus (XXXVIII.
lvii. 6-7).

A.U.C.
564

suli. Inde certiore et maiore spe laetus exercitus
ad praeparata omnia in Macedoniam pervenit.
15 Venientes regio apparatu et accepit et prosecutus est
rex. Multa in eo et dexteritas et humanitas visa,
quae commendabilia apud Africanum erant, virum
sicut ad cetera egregium, ita a comitate, quae sine
16 luxuria esset, non aversum. Inde non per Macedoniam modo sed etiam Thraeciam prosequente et
praeparante omnia Philippo ad Hellespontum per-
ventum est.

VIII. Antiochus post navalem ad Corycum pugnam cum totam hiemem liberam in apparatus terrestres maritimosque habuisset, classi maxume reparan-
dae, ne tota maris possessione pelleretur, intentus
2 fuerat. Succurrebat superatum se, cum classis
afuisset Rhodiorum; quodsi ea quoque—nec com-
missuros Rhodios, ut iterum morarentur—certamini
adesset, magno sibi navium numero opus fore, ut
viribus et [1] magnitudine classem hostium aequaret.
3 Itaque et Hannibalem in Syriam miserat ad Phoeni-
cum accersendas naves, et Polyxenidam, quo minus
prospere res gesta erat, eo enixius et eas, quae
4 erant, reficere et alias parare naves iussit. Ipse in
Phrygia hibernavit undique auxilia accersens. Etiam
in Gallograeciam miserat; bellicosiores ea tempestate erant, Gallicos adhuc, nondum exoleta stirpe
5 gentis, servantes animos. Filium Seleucum in Aeolide reliquerat cum exercitu ad maritimas con-

---

[1] et ⌐: ut B.

---

[1] Livy seems to say that some of the original Gallic invaders
were still alive; since they had come into Asia about 278 B.C.,
he probably means that the current generation had not yet
been enervated by the easier life of Asia.

From there the army, rejoicing to find its hopes surer and greater, reached Macedonia, where everything was in readiness. As they drew near the king welcomed them and escorted them in royal state. There were seen in him many signs both of efficiency and of courtesy, which served to recommend him to Africanus, a man who, eminent as he was in every way, was not averse to courtesy, provided that it was without luxury. Thence not only through Macedonia but also through Thrace, with Philip escorting them and making everything easy for them, the journey to the Hellespont was accomplished.

VIII. Antiochus, after the naval battle off Corycus, when he had spent all the free winter period in preparations on land and sea, had devoted most energy to refitting his fleet, that he might not lose entirely his control of the sea. It came to his mind that he had been defeated when the fleet of the Rhodians was absent; but if this—and the Rhodians would not let it happen again that they should be behind-hand—should also be present at a battle, he would need a great number of ships to equal the fleet of the enemy in strength and size. So he had both despatched Hannibal to Syria to summon ships of the Phoenicians and ordered Polyxenidas, as he had been none too successful before, so to make the greater efforts in equipping the ships that remained and in assembling new ones. He himself wintered in Phrygia, summoning allies from all sides. He had sent even to Galatia; the inhabitants at that time were of a warlike disposition, still retaining their Gallic tempers, the native strain having not yet disappeared.[1] He had left his son Seleucus in Aeolis to hold in check the cities on the coast which on one

A.U.C. 564
tinendas[1] urbes, quas illinc a Pergamo Eumenes
hinc a Phocaea Erythrisque Romani sollicitabant
6 Classis Romana, sicut ante dictum est, ad Canas
hibernabat; eo media ferme hieme rex Eumenes
cum duobus[2] milibus peditum, equitibus quingentis
7 venit. Is cum magnam praedam agi posse dixisset
ex agro hostium, qui circa Thyatiram esset, hortando
perpulit Livium, ut quinque milia militum secum
mitteret. Missi ingentem praedam intra paucos dies
averterunt.

IX. Inter haec Phocaeae seditio orta quibusdam
ad Antiochum multitudinis animos avocantibus
2 Gravia hiberna navium erant, grave tributum, quod
togae quingentae imperatae erant cum quingentis
3 tunicis, gravis etiam inopia frumenti, propter quam
naves quoque et praesidium Romanum excessit
Tum vero liberata metu factio erat, quae plebem in
4 contionibus ad[3] Antiochum trahebat; senatus et
optimates in Romana societate perstandum cense
bant; defectionis auctores plus apud multitudinem
5 valuerunt. Rhodii, quo magis cessatum priore
aestate erat, eo maturius aequinoctio verno eundem
Pausistratum classis praefectum cum sex et triginta
6 navibus miserunt. Iam Livius a Canis cum triginta
navibus suis et[4] septem quadriremibus quas secum
Eumenes rex adduxerat Hellespontum petebat, ut
ad transitum exercitus, quem terra venturum opina
7 batur, praepararet, quae opus essent. In portum

[1] continendas ς: obtinendas *B*.
[2] duobus *edd. vett.*: .XX. *BM*ς.
[3] ad ς: *om. B.* [4] suis et *Madvig*: et *B*ς.

side Eumenes from Pergamum and on the other the B.C. 190
Romans from Phocaea and Erythrae were trying to
rouse. The Roman fleet, as has been said above,
was wintering at Canae; there, about the middle of
the winter, King Eumenes came with two thousand
infantry and five hundred cavalry. When he said
that a great quantity of booty could be secured from
the country of the enemy around Thyatira, he urged
and finally persuaded Livius to send five thousand
men with him. They were sent and within a few
days carried off a huge amount of plunder.

IX. Meanwhile an uprising began at Phocaea
when certain persons tried to draw away the sympathies of the crowd to Antiochus. The quartering
of the ships was a burden, the tribute was a burden,
since five hundred outer-garments with five hundred
under-garments had been demanded of them; the
shortage of grain was another burden, on account of
which the fleet too and the Roman garrison departed.
Then indeed the faction which was trying to win the
people over to Antiochus in their public meetings
was freed from fear; the senate and the nobility
thought that they should persist in the Roman
alliance; the party which urged revolt was stronger
with the mass of the people. The Rhodians, the
greater their delay the preceding summer, the
earlier now, namely, at the spring equinox, placed
the same Pausistratus in charge of the fleet and
despatched him with thirty-six ships. Already Livius
from Canae, with his own thirty ships and seven
quadriremes which King Eumenes had brought with
him, was on his way to the Hellespont, that he might
make everything ready for the crossing of the army,
which, he thought, would come by land. He first

315

quem vocant Achaeorum classem primum advertit; inde Ilium escendit, sacrificioque Minervae facto legationes finitimas ab Elaeunte et Dardano et Rhoeteo, tradentes in fidem civitates suas, benigne
8 audivit. Inde ad Hellesponti fauces navigat et decem navibus in statione contra Abydum relictis cetera classe in Europam ad Sestum oppugnandam
9 traiecit. Iam subeuntibus armatis muros fanatici Galli primum cum sollemni habitu ante portam occurrunt; iussu se matris deum famulos deae venire memorant ad precandum Romanum, ut parce-
10 ret moenibus urbique. Nemo eorum violatus est. Mox universus senatus cum magistratibus ad de-
11 dendam urbem processit. Inde Abydum traiecta classis. Ubi cum temptatis [1] per colloquia animis nihil pacati responderetur, ad oppugnationem sese expediebant.

X. Dum haec in Hellesponto geruntur, Polyxenidas regius praefectus—erat autem exul Rhodius—cum audisset profectam ab domo popularium suorum clas-
2 sem, et Pausistratum praefectum superbe quaedam et contemptim in se contionantem dixisse, praecipuo certamine animi adversus eum sumpto nihil aliud dies noctesque agitabat animo, quam ut verba magni-
3 fica eius rebus confutaret. Mittit ad eum hominem et illi notum, qui diceret et se Pausistrato patriaeque suae magno usui, si liceat, fore, et a Pausistrato se

---

[1] temptatis ς : tempestatis *B*.

---

[1] The Greeks were supposed to have anchored there during the Trojan war.
[2] The *Galli* were priests of the Magna Mater whose temple in Rome had been dedicated the year before (XXXVI. xxxvi. 3), and may have been chosen as intercessors because of that

brought the ships into what they call the harbour of
the Achaeans,[1] thence he went up to Ilium, and
after sacrificing to Minerva gave a gracious audience
to embassies from Elaeus and Dardanus and Rhoeteum offering to entrust their cities to his good faith.
Thence he sailed to the entrance to the Hellespont,
and leaving ten ships on guard off Abydus crossed
with the rest of the fleet to lay siege to Sestus.
When the soldiers were already approaching the walls,
some fanatical *Galli*[2] with their ritual dress first met
them before the gate; they said that by the order
of the Mother of the Gods they, the servants of the
goddess, were coming to implore the Romans to
spare the walls and the city. None of them was
injured. Presently the whole senate with the magistrates came to surrender the city. Then the fleet
crossed to Abydus. After trying their disposition
in conferences and receiving no pacific reply, they
prepared for a siege.

X. While this was going on in the Hellespont,
Polyxenidas the king's prefect—he was an exile
from Rhodes—hearing that the fleet of his countrymen had left home and that their commander
Pausistratus, while haranguing the assembly, had
spoken haughtily and contemptuously about him,
feeling a peculiar jealousy towards him, thought of
nothing by day or night except how he might employ
deeds to refute these high-sounding words. He
sent to him a man, who was also well-known to him,
to say that he could be of great service to Pausistratus
and the country if he were permitted, and could be

connection. They are described as *fanatici* because of the
nature of their cult. Polybius (XXXI. vi.) says that there
were only two priests in the party. The *Galli* were eunuchs.

LIVY

4 restitui in patriam posse. Cum, quonam modo ea
fieri possent, mirabundus Pausistratus percunctaretur,
fidem petenti dedit agendae communiter rei aut
5 tegendae silentio. Tum internuntius: regiam classem aut totam aut maiorem eius partem Polyxenidam
traditurum ei; pretium tanti meriti nullum aliud
6 pacisci quam reditum in patriam. Magnitudo rei
nec ut crederet nec ut aspernaretur dicta effecit.[1]
Panhormum Samiae terrae petit, ibique ad explo-
7 randam rem quae oblata erat substitit. Ultro
citroque nuntii cursare, nec fides ante Pausistrato
facta est quam coram nuntio eius Polyxenidas sua
manu scripsit se ea quae pollicitus esset facturum
8 signoque suo impressas tabellas misit. Eo vero
pignore velut auctoratum sibi proditorem ratus est:
neque enim eum qui sub rege viveret commissurum
fuisse, ut adversus semet ipsum indicia manu sua
9 testata daret. Inde ratio simulatae proditionis com-
posita. Omnium se rerum apparatum omissurum
Polyxenidas dicere; non remigem, non socios navales
10 ad classem frequentes habiturum; subducturum per
simulationem reficiendi quasdam naves, alias in pro-
pinquos portus dimissurum; paucas ante portum
Ephesi in salo habiturum, quas, si exire res cogeret,
11 obiecturus certamini foret. Quam neglegentiam
Polyxenidam in classe sua habiturum Pausistratus
audivit, eam ipse extemplo habuit, partem navium
ad commeatus accersendos Halicarnassum, partem

[1] effecit ς : efficit B.

restored by Pausistratus to his home. When Pausistratus in wonder asked how this could be done, the man asked and received a pledge to co-operate in the business or to bury it in silence. Then the go-between said this: Polyxenidas would surrender to him the royal fleet, either the whole or the greater part of it; as reward for so great a service he stipulated nothing else than restoration to his fatherland. The importance of the matter caused Pausistratus neither to believe nor to scorn the message. He sailed to Panhormus in the land of Samos and waited there to investigate the offer that had been made. Messengers travelled back and forth, nor was Pausistratus convinced until in the presence of his agent Polyxenidas with his own hand wrote that he would do what he had promised, and sealing the tablets with his own device sent them to him. By this pledge he thought that the traitor was bound to him: for a man who lived under a king would not have permitted himself to give proofs, attested by his own hand, to be used against himself. The plan of carrying out the pretended treachery was then settled. Polyxenidas said that he would give over the preparation of everything; he would not have rowers or naval allies in sufficient numbers with the fleet; he would draw up on shore certain ships under pretence of repairing them and would send others away to neighbouring ports; a few he would keep before the harbour of Ephesus in the open sea, and these, if conditions demanded it, he would expose to battle. The same carelessness which he heard that Polyxenidas would adopt in his own fleet, Pausistratus at once himself put into practice, sending part of the fleet to collect stores at Halicarnassus and part to the

LIVY

Samum ad urbem misit, ipse ad Panhormum mansit,[1]
ut paratus esset, cum signum adgrediendi a pro-
12 ditore accepisset. Polyxenidas augere simulando
errorem; subducit quasdam naves, alias velut sub-
ducturus esset, navalia reficit; remiges ex hibernis
non Ephesum accersit, sed Magnesiam occulte
cogit.

XI. Forte quidam Antiochi miles, cum Samum rei
privatae causa venisset, pro speculatore deprehensus
2 deducitur Panhormum ad praefectum. Is percunc-
tanti quid Ephesi ageretur, incertum metu an erga
3 suos haud sincera fide, omnia aperit: classem instructam paratamque in portu stare; remigium
omne Magnesiam missum;[2] perpaucas naves sub-
ductas esse et navalia detegi;[3] numquam intentius
4 rem navalem administratam esse. Haec ne pro
veris audirentur, animus errore et spe vana praeoccupatus fecit. Polyxenidas satis omnibus comparatis, nocte remige a Magnesia accersito, de-
ductisque raptim quae subductae erant navibus, cum
diem non tam apparatu absumpsisset,[4] quam quod
5 conspici proficiscentem classem nolebat, post solis
occasum profectus septuaginta navibus tectis vento
adverso ante lucem Pygela portum tenuit. Ibi cum
interdiu ob eandem causam quiesset, nocte in
6 proxima Samiae terrae traiecit. Hinc Nicandro
quodam archipirata quinque navibus tectis Palinurum
iusso petere, atque inde armatos, qua proximum

---

[1] ipse ad Panhormum mansit *aut* ipse Panhormi substitit
M. *Müller*: om. *Bς*.
[2] Magnesiam missum *Crévier*: magnesiam ad sypilum
missum *Bς*: magnesiam missum ad sipulum *M*.
[3] detegi *Weissenborn*: tegi *Bς*.
[4] absumpsisset *ς*: adsumpsisset *B*.

city of Samos, and he himself remained at Panhormus,
to be ready when he received from the traitor the
signal to attack. Polyxenidas by trickery added to
his confusion of mind; he beached some ships and
fitted up dock-yards as if he were on the point of
drawing up others; the rowers he did not summon
from winter quarters to Ephesus but collected secretly
at Magnesia.

XI. There was a certain soldier of Antiochus who
had come to Samos on private business, and was
arrested as a spy and taken to Panhormus to the
prefect. When the prefect asked what was going on
at Ephesus—it is uncertain whether it was because
of fear or from disloyalty to his own people—he
revealed everything: the fleet, arrayed and equipped,
was in the harbour; all the rowers had been sent to
Magnesia; a few ships had been beached and the
docks dismantled; never had greater energy been
devoted to naval matters. That this story was not
accepted as the truth was due to a mind preoccu-
pied with falsehood and delusive hope. Polyxenidas,
having now completed his arrangements and summoned the rowers by night from Magnesia, hastily
launched the ships which had been drawn up on the
shore, and when he had spent a day not so much in
preparation as because he did not want the departing
fleet to be seen, he set out after sunset, the wind
being favourable, with seventy decked ships and
before daylight reached the harbour of Pygela.
He rested there by day for the same reason and during
the next night crossed to the Samian country. Then
he directed Nicander, a certain pirate chief, to proceed to Palinurus with five decked ships and then to
lead the marines by the shortest road through the

A.U.C.
564

per agros iter esset, Panhormum ad tergum hostium
ducere, ipse interim classe divisa, ut ex utraque
parte fauces portus teneret, Panhormum petit.
7 Pausistratus primo ut in re necopinata turbatus
parumper, deinde vetus miles celeriter collecto
animo terra melius arceri quam mari hostes posse
ratus, armatos duobus agminibus ad promunturia,
8 quae cornibus obiectis ab alto portum [1] faciunt,
ducit, inde facile telis ancipitibus [2] hostem summo-
turus. Id inceptum eius Nicander a terra visus cum
turbasset, repente mutato consilio naves conscendere
9 omnes iubet. Tum vero ingens pariter militum
nautarumque trepidatio orta, et velut fuga in naves
fieri, cum se mari terraque simul cernerent circum-
10 ventos. Pausistratus unam viam salutis esse ratus,
si vim facere per fauces portus [3] atque erumpere in
mare apertum posset, postquam conscendisse suos
vidit, sequi ceteris iussis [4] princeps ipse concitata
11 nave remis ad ostium portus tendit. Superantem
iam fauces navem [5] eius Polyxenidas tribus quinqueremibus circumsistit. Navis rostris icta sup-
primitur; telis obruuntur propugnatores, inter quos
12 et Pausistratus impigre pugnans interficitur. Navium
reliquarum ante portum aliae, aliae [6] in portu de-
prensae, quaedam a Nicandro, dum moliuntur a
13 terra, captae; quinque tantum Rhodiae naves cum
duabus Cois [7] effugerunt terrore flammae micantis

[1] portum ς : profundum B.
[2] telis ancipitibus ed. Parisina 1513 : ex ancipitibus Bς.
[3] portus ς : om. B.
[4] iussis ς : iussit B.
[5] nauem ς : naues B.
[6] aliae aliae edd. vett. : aliae B : ex edd. et codd. alii aliud.
[7] duabus Cois ed. Frobeniana 1535 : duabus copiis Bς :
cois duabus M.

322

fields to Panhormus to take the enemy in the rear, B.C. 190
and he himself in the meantime, dividing the fleet
that he might hold the entrance to the harbour on
both sides, set out for Panhormus. Pausistratus at
first, as one in an unexpected situation, was terrified
for a while, then, being a veteran soldier, he quickly
collected his thoughts and decided that it was better
to resist the enemy on land than on sea, and led the
troops in two columns to the promontories which,
like horns projecting into the sea, form the harbour,
expecting to repel the enemy easily with weapons
falling upon them from both sides. When the sight
of Nicander, coming by land, had upset this plan,
he suddenly changed his intention and ordered
them all to go aboard the ships. Then there was
great confusion among the marines and sailors, and
a sort of flight to the ships began, when they saw
themselves surrounded by land and sea at once.
Pausistratus thought that there was one way of
safety, if he could force a way through the entrance
of the harbour and escape into the open sea, and
when he saw that all had embarked he ordered the
rest to follow him, and at the head of the column,
urging his ship forward with the oars, he made for
the entrance of the harbour. As the ship was
passing the entrance Polyxenidas with three quinqueremes surrounded it. The ship was struck by the
beaks and sunk; the defenders were overwhelmed
with missiles, and among them Pausistratus too,
fighting bravely, was killed. Some of the remaining
ships were taken outside the harbour and others
inside, and some were captured by Nicander as they
were pushing off from the beach; only five Rhodian
and two Coan ships escaped, making a way for

LIVY

via sibi inter confertas naves facta; contis enim binis
a prora prominentibus trullis ferreis multum con-
14 ceptum ignem prae se portabant. Erythraeae triremes cum haud procul a Samo Rhodiis navibus,
quibus ut essent praesidio veniebant, obviae fugientibus fuissent, in Hellespontum ad Romanos cursum
15 averterunt. Sub idem tempus Seleucus proditam
Phocaeam porta una per custodes aperta recepit;
et Cyme aliaeque [1] eiusdem orae urbes ad eum metu
defecerunt.

XII. Dum haec in Aeolide geruntur, Abydus cum
per aliquot dies obsidionem tolerasset praesidio regio
2 tutante moenia, iam omnibus fessis Philota quoque
praefecto praesidii permittente magistratus eorum
cum Livio de condicionibus tradendae urbis agebant.
Rem distinebat [2] quod, utrum armati an inermes
3 emitterentur regii, parum conveniebat. Haec agentibus cum intervenisset nuntius Rhodiorum cladis.
4 emissa [3] de manibus res est; metuens enim Livius
ne successu tantae rei inflatus Polyxenidas classem
quae ad Canas erat opprimeret, Abydi obsidione
custodiaque Hellesponti extemplo relicta naves, quae
subductae Canis erant, deduxit; et Eumenes
5 Elaeam venit. Livius omni classe, cui adiunxerat
duas triremes Mitylenaeas, Phocaeam petit. Quam
cum teneri valido regio praesidio audisset, nec
procul Seleuci castra esse, depopulatus maritimam

---

[1] aliaeque *ed. Frobeniana* 1535 : liaeque *B.*
[2] distinebat ⸋ : destinabat *B.*
[3] emissa *ed. Aldina* : omissa *B⸋.*

---

[1] Polybius (XXI. vi) describes these contrivances in greater
detail. The drums or scoops were swung from the poles and
could be tripped by suitable chains from the deck to spill
fire on ships that approached.

themselves among the crowded vessels by means of B.C. 190
the fear of darting flames; for each, with two poles
projecting from their prows, carried ahead of it a
great quantity of fire in iron drums.[1] When the
triremes of Erythrae had met, not far from Samos,
the fleeing Rhodian ships which they were coming
to assist, they turned their course toward the Hellespont and the Romans. About the same time Seleucus
recovered Phocaea, which was betrayed when one
gate was opened by the sentinels; and Cyme and
other towns of the same region revolted to him from
fear.

XII. When these events were happening in Aeolis
and Abydus had for some days withstood the siege,
a royal garrison defending the walls, and all were
now wearied, with the consent of even Philotas,
prefect of the garrison, their magistrates treated
with Livius as to the terms for surrendering the city.
The question that delayed a settlement was that
there was no agreement as to whether they should
be released armed or unarmed. As they were
discussing this the arrival of the announcement of
the disaster to the Rhodians caused the matter to
pass out of their hands; for Livius, fearing that
Polyxenidas, elated by his success in so great an
enterprise, would attack the fleet which was at
Canae, immediately abandoned the siege of Abydus
and the guarding of the Hellespont and launched
the ships which had been drawn up on the beach
at Canae; Eumenes too came to Elaea. Livius with
the entire fleet, to which were added two triremes
from Mitylene, sailed for Phocaea. When he heard
that this was held by a strong royal garrison and that
the camp of Seleucus was not far away, he ravaged

325

LIVY

6 oram, et praeda maxime hominum raptim in naves
imposita tantum moratus, dum Eumenes cum [1]
7 classe adsequeretur, Samum petere intendit. Rhodiis
primo audita clades simul pavorem simul luctum ingentem fecit; nam praeter navium militumque
iacturam, quod floris, quod roboris in iuventute
8 fuerat,[2] amiserant, multis nobilibus secutis inter
cetera auctoritatem Pausistrati, quae inter suos
merito maxima erat; deinde, quod fraude capti,
quod a cive potissimum suo forent, in iram luctus
9 vertit. Decem extemplo naves, et diebus post
paucis decem alias praefecto omnium Eudamo
miserunt, quem aliis virtutibus bellicis haudquaquam
Pausistrato parem, cautiorem, quo minus animi erat,
10 ducem futurum credebant. Romani et Eumenes rex
in Erythraeam primum classem applicuerunt. Ibi
noctem unam morati postero die Corycum [3] promun-
11 turium tenuerunt. Inde cum in proxima Samiae
vellent traicere, non expectato solis ortu, ex quo
statum caeli notare gubernatores possent, in incertam
12 tempestatem miserunt. Medio in cursu, aquilone
in septentrionem verso, exasperato fluctibus mari
iactari coeperunt.

XIII. Polyxenidas Samum petituros ratus hostes,
ut se Rhodiae classi coniungerent, ab Epheso profectus primo ad Myonnesum stetit; inde ad Macrin
quam vocant insulam traiecit, ut praetervehentis
classis si quas[4] aberrantes ex agmine naves posset

---

[1] cum *ς* : in *B*.
[2] fuerat *ς* : *om. B*.
[3] Corycum *Weissenborn* : corycum pelorum *Bς*.
[4] praetervehentis classis si quas *ed. Frobeniana* 1535:
praeteruehementis classis quas *B* : praeteruehens si quas
M : praeteruehentes quas *ς*.

the sea-coast and, quickly loading the booty, especially the men, into the ships, waiting only until
Eumenes with his fleet should overtake him, he
set sail for Samos. To the Rhodians the news of
the disaster brought at first mingled terror and
grief; for besides the destruction of ships and
marines, they had lost all the beauty and strength
of their youth, many nobles having been attracted,
among other things, by the prestige of Pausistratus, which had justly been very great among
his people; then the fact that they had been
entrapped by guile, and, more than that, by their
own fellow-citizen, turned their grief into anger.
They straightway sent ten ships and a few days later
ten more, all under the prefect Eudamus, who, they
believed, would be a leader in no respect equal to
Pausistratus in other military qualities, but the more
cautious as he was less high-spirited. The Romans
and King Eumenes sailed first to Erythraea. Then,
after a wait of one night, on the following day they
gained the promontory of Corycus. Wishing to
cross from there to the nearest parts of the land of
Samos, without waiting for sunrise, so that from it
the pilots might be able to judge the state of the
heavens, they started out into uncertain weather.
Half-way across, the north-east wind veering to the
north, the ships began to be tossed by seas roughened
by the wind.

XIII. Polyxenidas thought that the Roman fleet
would make for Samos to join the Rhodian ships,
and starting from Ephesus first stood off Myonnesus,
then crossed to the island which they call Macris,
that he might fall upon any individual ship of the
passing fleet as it got out of formation or attack the

327

A.U.C.
564

2 aut postremum agmen opportune adoriretur. Postquam sparsam tempestate classem vidit, occasionem
primo adgrediendi ratus, paulo post increbrescente
3 vento et maiores iam volvente fluctus, quia pervenire
se ad eos videbat non posse, ad Aethaliam insulam
traiecit, ut inde postero die Samum ex alto petentes
4 naves adgrederetur. Romani, pars exigua, primis
tenebris portum desertum Samiae tenuerunt, classis
cetera nocte tota in alto iactata in eundem portum
5 decurrit. Ibi ex agrestibus cognito hostium naves
ad Aethaliam stare, consilium habitum, utrum extemplo decernerent an Rhodiam expectarent classem.
6 Dilata re—ita enim placuit—Corycum unde venerant
traiecerunt. Polyxenidas quoque, cum frustra stetis-
set, Ephesum rediit. Tum Romanae naves vacuo
7 ab hostibus mari Samum traiecerunt. Eodem et
Rhodia classis post dies paucos venit. Quam ut
expectatam esse appareret, profecti extemplo sunt
Ephesum, ut aut decernerent navali certamine aut,
si detractaret hostis pugnam, quod plurimum in-
tererat ad animos civitatium, timoris confessionem
8 exprimerent. Contra fauces portus instructa in
frontem navium acie stetere. Postquam nemo
adversus ibat, classe divisa pars in salo ad ostium
portus in ancoris stetit, pars in terram milites exposuit.
9 In eos iam ingentem praedam late depopulato agro

rear of the column at a suitable opportunity. When B.C. 190
he saw that the fleet was scattered by the storm,
he first thought that he had a chance to attack, but
a little later, the wind freshening and rolling up
even greater waves, since he realized that he could
not get to them, he crossed to the island of Aethalia,
that thence on the following day he might fall upon
the ships which were trying to reach Samos from the
sea. A small part of the Romans reached at dusk a
deserted harbour in Samian territory, the rest of the
fleet, tossed all night in the open sea, ran to the same
port. There they learned from peasants that the
enemy's fleet was standing off Aethalia, and a
council was held whether they should fight at once
or wait for the Rhodian fleet. Action being postponed—for such was the decision—they crossed to
Corycus whence they had come. Polyxenidas also,
after waiting in vain, returned to Ephesus. Then
the Roman fleet, the sea being empty of the enemy,
crossed to Samos. The Rhodian fleet also arrived at
the same place a few days later, and thus, to make it
clear that this was what they were awaiting, a start
was immediately made for Ephesus, that they might
either fight a naval battle or, if the enemy declined
the engagement, which was a matter of great import
for its effect on the dispositions of the cities, they
might wrest from him an admission of cowardice.
They took their position facing the entrance to the
harbour with the fleet drawn up in order of battle.
When no one came out to meet them, the fleet
divided, and part remained at anchor in the open
sea opposite the entrance, part landed the marines
on the coast. And when they were bringing in a
vast amount of booty, having devastated the country

agentes Andronicus Macedo, qui in praesidio Ephesi
erat, iam moenibus appropinquantes eruptionem
fecit, exutosque magna parte praedae ad mare ac
10 naves redegit. Postero die insidiis medio ferme
viae positis ad eliciendum extra moenia Macedonem [1]
Romani ad urbem agmine iere; inde, cum ea ipsa
suspicio ne quis exiret deterruisset, redierunt ad
11 naves; et terra marique fugientibus certamen
hostibus Samum unde venerat classis repetit. Inde
duas sociorum ex Italia, duas Rhodias triremes cum
praefecto Epicrate Rhodio [2] ad fretum Cephallaniae
12 tuendum praetor misit. Infestum id latrocinio
Lacedaemonius Hybristas cum iuventute Cephalla-
num faciebat, clausumque iam mare commeatibus
Italicis erat.

XIV. Piraei L. Aemilio Regillo succedenti ad
2 navale imperium Epicrates occurrit; qui audita clade
Rhodiorum, cum ipse duas tantum quinqueremes haberet, Epicratem cum quattuor navibus in Asiam
secum reduxit; prosecutae etiam apertae Atheniensium naves sunt. Aegaeo mari traiecit Chium.[3]
3 Eodem Timasicrates Rhodius cum duabus quadriremibus ab Samo nocte intempesta [4] venit, deductusque ad Aemilium praesidii causa se missum ait,
quod eam oram maris infestam onerariis regiae
naves excursionibus crebris [5] ab Hellesponto atque
Abydo facerent. Traicienti Aemilio a Chio Samum

---

[1] macedonem ς : macedonum B.
[2] Rhodio Perizonius : rhodiorum Bς.
[3] Chium Duker : om. Bς.
[4] intempesta ς : intempestate B.
[5] crebris ς : om. B.

---

[1] One would expect that the task of keeping this part of
the sea open would fall upon the fleet in Italian waters.

far and wide, Andronicus the Macedonian, who was B.C. 190
in the garrison at Ephesus, made a sally as they
approached the walls, and stripping them of a large
part of their plunder drove them to the sea and the
ships. On the next day, placing an ambuscade at
about the half-way point, the Romans marched in
column towards the city to draw out the Macedonian;
then, since the very suspicion that this would be
done prevented anyone from coming out, they returned to the ships; and, the enemy avoiding battle
on land and sea, the fleet returned to Samos, whence
it had come. Then the praetor sent two triremes of
the allies from Italy and two from Rhodes, with
Epicrates the Rhodian in command, to defend the
strait of Cephallania. The Spartan Hybristas with
the young men of the Cephallanians was making this
dangerous with his piracy, and the sea was already
closed to supplies from Italy.[1]

XIV. At Piraeus Epicrates met Lucius Aemilius
Regillus, who was taking over the command on the
sea[2]; and on hearing of the defeat of the Rhodians,
since he himself had only two quinqueremes, he took
Epicrates with his four ships back to Asia with him;
open Athenian vessels also accompanied him. In the
Aegean sea they crossed to Chios. There Timasicrates the Rhodian came on a stormy night with two
quadriremes from Samos, and when brought in to
Aemilius he said that he had been sent as an escort
because this coast of the sea was made dangerous to
cargo-boats because of the frequent raids of the king's
ships from the Hellespont and Abydus. As Aemilius
was crossing from Chios to Samos, he was joined by two

[2] Cf. iv. 5 above; from ii. 10 above it would be assumed
that Aemilius would have a more powerful fleet.

A.U.C.
564

duae Rhodiae quadriremes, missae obviam ab Livio,
et rex Eumenes cum duabus quinqueremibus
4 occurrit. Samum postquam ventum est, accepta
ab Livio classe et sacrificio, ut adsolet, rite facto
Aemilius consilium advocavit. Ibi C. Livius—is
enim est primus rogatus sententiam—neminem
fidelius posse dare consilium dixit quam eum qui id
alteri suaderet quod ipse, si in eodem loco esset,
5 facturus fuerit: se in animo habuisse tota classe
Ephesum petere et onerarias ducere multa saburra
gravatas, atque eas in faucibus portus supprimere;
6 et eo minoris molimenti ea claustra esse, quod in
fluminis modum longum et angustum et vadosum
ostium portus sit. Ita adempturum se maris usum
hostibus fuisse inutilemque classem facturum.

XV. Nulli ea placere sententia. Eumenes rex
quaesivit, quid tandem? Ubi demersis navibus
frenassent claustra maris, utrum libera sua classe
abscessuri inde forent ad opem ferendam sociis
terroremque hostibus praebendum, an nihilo minus
2 tota classe portum obsessuri? Sive enim abscedant,
cui dubium esse quin hostes extracturi demersas
moles sint et minore molimento aperturi portum,
quam obstruatur?[1] Sin autem manendum ibi nihilo
3 minus sit, quid[2] attinere claudi portum? Quin
contra illos, tutissimo portu, opulentissima urbe
fruentes, omnia Asia praebente quieta aestiva acturos;
Romanos aperto in mari fluctibus tempestatibusque
obiectos, omnium inopes, in adsidua statione futuros,
4 ipsos magis adligatos impeditosque, ne quid eorum

---

[1] obstruatur *edd. vett.* : instruatur *Bς.*
[2] sit, quid *edd. vett.* : quit *B* : quid *ς.*

Rhodian quadriremes sent by Livius to meet him, and B.C. 190
by King Eumenes with two quinqueremes. When
they reached Samos Aemilius took over the fleet
from Livius and after duly performing the sacrifice
in the usual way called a council. There Gaius
Livius—for he was the first to be asked his opinion—
said that no one could give more loyal advice than
the man who, if he were in the same situation, would
have done what he advised the other to do: he had
it in mind to proceed to Ephesus with the entire
fleet, taking along numerous cargo-boats heavily
loaded with sand, and to sink them at the mouth of
the harbour; the closing of the harbour would involve
the less difficulty because the mouth of the harbour
was like a river, long, narrow, and full of shoals.
Thus they would have taken away from the enemy
the use of the sea and immobilized his fleet.

XV. This suggestion was approved by no one.
King Eumenes asked what came next? When they
had sunk the ships and closed the gate to the sea,
would they then, with the whole fleet released, go
away from there to give aid to the allies and cause
terror to the enemy or would they none the less
block the harbour with the whole fleet? For if they
go away, who doubts that the enemy will raise the
sunken hulls and open up the harbour with less
trouble than was taken to close it? But if they are to
stay none the less, what good does it do to close it?
On the contrary, the enemy, enjoying a very safe
harbour and a very prosperous city, with Asia supplying their every want, will spend a quiet summer;
but the Romans, exposed on the open sea to waves and
storms, needing everything, will be continually on
guard, themselves hampered and prevented from

quae agenda sint possint agere, quam ut hostes
5 clausos habeant.[1] Eudamus praefectus Rhodiae
classis magis eam sibi displicere sententiam ostendit
6 quam ipse quid censeret faciendum dixit. Epicrates
Rhodius omissa in praesentia Epheso mittendam
navium partem in Lyciam censuit, et Patara, caput
7 gentis, in societatem adiungenda.[2] In duas magnas
res id usui fore, et Rhodios pacatis contra insulam
suam terris totis viribus incumbere in unius belli,
8 quod adversus Antiochum sit, curam posse, et eam
classem, quae in Cilicia compararetur, intercludi,
ne Polyxenidae coniungatur. Haec maxime movit
9 sententia; placuit tamen Regillum classe tota evehi
ad portum Ephesi ad inferendum hostibus terrorem.

XVI. C. Livius cum duabus quinqueremibus Romanis et quattuor quadriremibus Rhodiis et duabus
apertis Zmyrnaeis in Lyciam est missus, Rhodum
prius iussus adire et omnia cum iis communicare
2 consilia. Civitates, quas praetervectus est, Miletus
Myndus Halicarnassus Cnidus Cous, imperata enixe
3 fecerunt. Rhodum ut ventum est, simul et ad
quam rem missus esset, iis exposuit et consuluit
eos. Approbantibus cunctis et ad eam quam
habebat classem, adsumptis tribus quadriremibus,
4 navigat Patara. Primo secundus ventus ad ipsam
urbem ferebat eos, sperabantque subito terrore
aliquid moturos; postquam circumagente se vento
fluctibus dubiis volvi coeptum est mare, pervicerunt

----

[1] habeant ς : habebant B.
[2] adiungenda J. F. Gronovius : adiungendam Bς.

being able to do anything they want to do except B.C. 190 keeping the enemy blockaded. Eudamus, the commander of the Rhodian fleet, showed that he disliked the proposal rather than announced any plan of his own. Epicrates the Rhodian thought that they should leave Ephesus for the present and send part of the fleet to Lycia and win Patara, the chief city of the country, to their alliance. This would be useful in two important respects: first, that the Rhodians, with the lands opposite their island tranquil, could devote all their energies to the one war that was being waged against Antiochus; second, that the fleet which was being assembled in Cilicia could be prevented from joining Polyxenidas. This suggestion carried the greatest weight; nevertheless, it was decided that Regillus should move with the whole fleet to the harbour of Ephesus in order to strike terror into the enemy.

XVI. Gaius Livius with two Roman quinqueremes and four Rhodian quadriremes and two undecked ships from Zmyrna was sent to Lycia, with orders to visit Rhodes first and inform them of the whole plan. The cities which he passed, Miletus, Myndus, Halicarnassus, Cnidus, Cos, willingly executed his orders. When he came to Rhodes, at the same time he both explained for what purpose he was sent and asked their advice. With the approval of all and the addition of three quadriremes to the fleet which he had, he sailed to Patara. At first a favourable breeze bore them towards the city itself, and they hoped that they would accomplish something by causing a sudden panic; after the wind changed and the sea began to be tossed about with waves rolling this way and that, they did indeed win to the land by the use of

LIVY

5 quidem remis, ut tenerent terram; sed neque
circa urbem tuta statio erat, nec ante ostium portus
in salo stare poterant aspero mari[1] et nocte immi-
6 nente. Praetervecti moenia portum Phoenicunta,
minus duum milium spatio inde distantem, petiere,
7 navibus a maritima vi tutum; sed altae[2] insuper
imminebant rupes, quas celeriter oppidani adsumptis
regiis[3] militibus, quos in praesidio habebant, ceperunt.
8 Adversus quos Livius, quamquam erant iniqua ac
difficilia ad exitus loca, Issaeos auxiliares et Zmyrnae-
9 orum expeditos iuvenes misit. Hi, dum missilibus
primo et adversus paucos levibus excursionibus[4]
lacessebatur magis quam conserebatur pugna, sus-
10 tinuerunt certamen; postquam plures ex urbe
adfluebant, et iam omnis multitudo effundebatur,
timor incessit Livium[5] ne et auxiliares circumveniren-
11 tur et navibus etiam ab terra periculum esset. Ita
non milites solum sed etiam navales socios, remigum
turbam, quibus quisque poterat telis, armatos in
12 proelium eduxit. Tum quoque anceps pugna fuit,
neque[6] milites solum aliquot, sed L. Apustius tumultuario proelio cecidit; postremo tamen fusi
fugatique sunt Lycii atque in urbem compulsi, et
Romani cum haud incruenta victoria ad naves re-
13 dierunt. Inde in Telmessicum profecti sinum, qui
latere uno Cariam altero Lyciam contingit, omisso

[1] peruicerunt . . . mari ς : om. B.
[2] altae ς : aliae B.
[3] regiis ς : regis B.
[4] levibus excursionibus ed. Frobeniana 1535 : leuibus Bς:
leuibus et excursionibus M.
[5] liuium ς : om. B.

336

their oars despite the wind; but they could neither _{B.C. 190} find safe anchorage near the city nor stand off shore before the entrance to the harbour in deep water since the sea was rough and night was coming on. Passing the walls they made for the port of Phoenicus, less than two miles distant from there, which was sheltered for the ships from the violence of the sea; but high cliffs towering above it threatened it, and these the citizens, joining the troops of the king whom they had as a garrison, quickly seized. Against them Livius, although the country was uneven and difficult to traverse, sent the auxiliaries from Issa and the light-armed young men from Zmyrna. These, as long as there was a harassing attack with missiles, at the beginning, with small raids against parties of a few men rather than a regular engagement, sustained the contest; when larger numbers were rushing out of the city and now the whole population was pouring forth, fear struck Livius lest the auxiliaries should be surrounded and even the ships endangered from the shore. So he led out to the fight not only the marines but also the naval allies and even the throng of rowers, using whatever weapons each could find. Then also there was a battle of uncertain issue, and not only were some soldiers lost, but Lucius Apustius fell in this desultory fighting; finally, however, the Lycians were routed and put to flight and driven into the city, and the Romans, having won a victory not without bloodshed, returned to their ships. Then he set out for the gulf of Telmessus, which touches Caria on one side and Lycia on the

---

⁹ neque *ed. Frobeniana* 1535 : non quod *siue* non quid *B* : non quod *et* non quidem ⸍.

LIVY

consilio Patara amplius temptandi[1] Rhodii domum
14 dimissi sunt, Livius praetervectus Asiam in Graeciam
transmisit, ut conventis Scipionibus, qui tum circa
Thessaliam erant, in Italiam traiceret.

XVII. Aemilius postquam omissas in Lycia res
et Livium profectum in Italiam[2] cognovit, cum ipse
ab Epheso tempestate repulsus irrito incepto Samum
2 revertisset, turpe ratus temptata frustra Patara esse,
proficisci eo[3] tota classe et summa vi adgredi urbem
3 statuit.   Miletum et ceteram oram sociorum praetervecti in Bargylietico sinu escensionem[4] ad Iasum fecerunt.   Urbem regium tenebat praesidium ; agrum
4 circa Romani hostiliter depopulati sunt.   Missis
deinde, qui per colloquia principum et magistratuum
temptarent animos, postquam nihil in potestate sua
responderunt esse, ad urbem oppugnandam ducit.
5 Erant Iasensium exules cum Romanis ; ii[5] frequentes
Rhodios orare institerunt ne urbem et vicinam sibi et
cognatam innoxiam perire sinerent ; sibi exilii
nullam aliam causam esse quam fidem erga Ro-
6 manos ; eadem vi regiorum,[6] qua ipsi pulsi sint,[7]
teneri eos qui in urbe maneant ; omnium Iasensium

[1] omisso consilio Patara amp. temp. *Weissenborn*, XXXIII.
xx. 10 *conferens* : pataram amp. temp. *B* : omisso patara
amp. temp. ꝟ: omissa conatu *et* omissa spe amp. temp. *alii*.
[2] in italiam ꝟ : *om. B.*
[3] eo ꝟ : *om. B.*
[4] escensionem *edd. vett.* : descensionem *B*ꝟ.
[5] ii *ed. Frobeniana* 1535 : ibi *M* : *om. B*ꝟ.
[6] regiorum ꝟ : religionum *B.*
[7] sint *ed. Frobeniana* 1535 : sunt *B*ꝟ.

---

[1] Livius should have reported to Aemilius before he left,
but chose to disregard military etiquette. The nature of
his business with the consul is not disclosed. The last sentence

other, and giving up any design of further action B.C. 190 against Patara, the Rhodians were sent home and Livius, skirting Asia, crossed to Greece, in order that after conferring with the Scipios, who were then around Thessaly, he might cross to Italy.

XVII. When Aemilius learned that the campaign in Lycia had been abandoned and that Livius had departed for Italy,[1] since he himself had been driven back from Ephesus by a storm and had returned to Samos without accomplishing anything, thinking that it was disgraceful that Patara had been fruitlessly attacked, he determined to proceed thither with his entire fleet and attack the city with all his resources. Sailing past Miletus and the rest of the coast held by the allies, in the gulf of Bargyliae they marched up inland to Iasus. A garrison belonging to the king held the city; the Romans, in the manner of enemies, devastated the surrounding fields. Then he sent agents to test the sentiments of the magistrates and important citizens by conferences, and when they replied that it was not at all in their power to decide, he led his troops to attack the city. There were exiles from Iasus among the Romans; and they in great numbers began to appeal to the Rhodians not to allow an innocent city, both neighbouring and related to them, to be destroyed; their own sole cause for exile was their fidelity to the Romans; the same might of the royal garrison, by which they themselves had been driven out, constrained those who remained in the city; there was

of the preceding chapter shows that Livy thought of these events as contemporaneous with those related in chaps. vi.–vii. above, but he is probably wrong in his estimate of the time consumed.

LIVY

unam mentem esse, ut servitutem regiam effugerent.
7 Rhodii moti precibus Eumene etiam rege adsumpto
simul suas necessitudines commemorando, simul
obsessae regio praesidio urbis casum miserando
8 pervicerunt, ut oppugnatione abstineretur. Profecti inde pacatis ceteris cum oram Asiae legerent,
Loryma—portus adversus Rhodum est—pervene-
9 runt. Ibi in principiis sermo primo inter tribunos
militum secretus oritur, deinde ad aures ipsius
Aemilii pervenit, abduci classem ab Epheso, ab suo
bello, ut ab tergo liber relictus hostis in tot pro-
pinquas sociorum urbes omnia impune conari posset.
10 Movere ea Aemilium; vocatosque Rhodios cum
percontatus esset, num[1] Pataris universa classis
in portu stare posset, cum respondissent non posse,[2]
causam nactus omittendae rei Samum naves reduxit.

XVIII. Per idem tempus Seleucus Antiochi filius,
cum per omne hibernorum tempus exercitum in
Aeolide continuisset partim sociis ferendo opem,
2 partim quos in societatem perlicere non poterat
depopulandis, transire in[3] fines regni Eumenis,
dum is[4] procul ab domo cum Romanis et Rhodiis
3 Lyciae maritima oppugnaret, statuit. Ad Elaeam
primo infestis signis accessit; deinde omissa oppugnatione urbis agros hostiliter depopulatus ad caput

---

[1] num *Weissenborn*: utrum nam, *fortasse recte* Bς.
[2] non posse ς: *om.* B.
[3] in ς: *om.* B.
[4] is ς: *om.* B.

---

[1] The Roman naval operations of this period seem peculiarly
aimless, and to lack even the virtue of being good training
exercises. The case of Livius shows that they had some
intelligence regarding the movements of the consul, yet

one single purpose among all the Iasenses, to escape from their enslavement to the king. The Rhodians, moved by their prayers, and receiving also the support of King Eumenes, both by speaking of their own relationship and at the same time by lamenting the hard plight of a city dominated by a royal garrison, prevailed upon the praetor to abandon the siege. Leaving there, with everything else pacified, as they skirted the coast of Asia they came to Loryma—this is a harbour opposite Rhodes. There some secret talk first began among the military tribunes in their quarters and finally reached the ears of Aemilius himself—that the fleet was drawn away from Ephesus and from their own war that the enemy, left free in the rear, might with complete impunity make any venture against so many near-by cities of the allies. This gossip worried Aemilius; when he summoned the Rhodians and asked them whether the whole fleet could be sheltered in the harbour at Patara and they had replied in the negative, he found this pretext for abandoning the expedition and took the ships back to Samos.[1]

XVIII. About the same time Seleucus, the son of Antiochus, after holding the army in Aeolis for the whole period of the winter, partly assisting his allies, partly plundering those whom he could not win over to his alliance, decided to invade the territory of Eumenes while he was far from home, engaged with the Romans and Rhodians in the naval operations off Lycia. He first approached Elaea with his army formed for battle; then, abandoning the attack on the city, he devastated the fields in hostile fashion,

Aemilius shows no disposition to co-operate in any really effective fashion.

LIVY

arcemque regni Pergamum ducit oppugnandam.
4 Attalus primo stationibus ante urbem positis et
excursionibus levisque [1] armaturae magis lacessebat
5 quam sustinebat hostem; postremo cum per levia
certamina expertus nulla parte virium se parem esse
intra moenia se recepisset, obsideri urbs coepta est.
6 Eodem ferme tempore [2] et Antiochus ab Apamea
profectus Sardibus primum, deinde haud procul
Seleuci castris ad caput Caici amnis stativa habuit
cum magno exercitu mixto variis ex gentibus.
7 Plurimum terroris in [3] Gallorum mercede conductis
quattuor milibus erat.[4] Hos paucis . . . admixtis [5]
ad pervastandum passim Pergamenum agrum milites
8 misit.[6] Quae postquam Samum nuntiata sunt, primo
Eumenes avocatus domestico bello cum classe Elaeam
petit; inde, cum praesto fuissent equites peditumque
expediti, praesidio eorum tutus, priusquam hostes
sentirent aut moverentur, Pergamum contendit.
9 Ibi rursus [7] levia per excursiones proelia fieri coepta
Eumene summae rei discrimen haud dubie detractante.[8] Paucos post dies Romana Rhodiaque classis
ut regi opem ferrent, Elaeam ab Samo venerunt.
10 Quos ubi exposuisse copias Elaeae et tot classes in
unum convenisse portum Antiocho adlatum est, et
sub [9] idem tempus audivit consulem cum exercitu

---

[1] leuisque ⴽ : et leuis B.
[2] ferme tempore edd. vett. : tempore ferme Bⴽ.
[3] in ed. Frobeniana 1535 : om. B.
[4] erat ⴽ : om. B.
[5] paucis . . . admixtis Weissenborn : paucis Dahis admixtis
H. J. Müller, xxxviii. 3, infra, conferens : paucis admixtos Bⴽ.
[6] misit ⴽ : emisit B.
[7] ibi rursus ⴽ : ubi B.
[8] detractante ⴽ : retractante B.
[9] et sub ⴽ : sub B.

and marched off to lay siege to Pergamum, the chief B.C. 190 city and citadel of the kingdom. Attalus [1] at first, stationing outposts before the city and organizing raids of the cavalry and light infantry, harassed rather than resisted the enemy; finally, when, after learning from such skirmishing that he was equal in no aspect of his strength, he had retired within the walls, the siege of the city began. About the same time Antiochus also set out from Apamea and established a base first at Sardis, then at the mouth of the Caïcus river, with a great army composed of men of various nationalities. The greatest source of terror consisted of four thousand Gauls who served for pay. These troops, with a few others intermixed,[2] he sent to lay waste the territory of Pergamum in every direction. When the news of this reached Samos, Eumenes, called away by the war at home, first went to Elaea with his fleet; then, since cavalry and light infantry were at hand, protected by their guard, before the enemy discovered it or made any move, he hastened to Pergamum. Then again small battles began to take place, growing out of raids, Eumenes without doubt avoiding a decisive engagement. A few days later the Roman and Rhodian fleets came to Elaea from Samos to assist the king. When it was reported to Antiochus that they had landed their troops at Elaea and that so many fleets had assembled in one harbour, and when about the same time he had learned that the consul with his army was already in Macedonia and

---

[1] Attalus was the brother of Eumenes (XXXV. xxiii. 10).
[2] Something has dropped out of the text. Various suggestions have been made as to what should be read, among them *Dahis*. I have been more non-committal.

LIVY

iam in Macedonia esse pararique, quae ad transitum
Hellesponti opus essent, tempus venisse ratus.
11 priusquam terra marique simul urgeretur, agendi
de pace [1] tumulum quendam adversus Elaeam castris
12 cepit; ibi peditum omnibus copiis [2] relictis cum
equitatu—erant autem sex milia equitum—in campos
sub ipsa Elaeae moenia descendit misso caduceatore
ad Aemilium, velle se de pace agere.

XIX. Aemilius Eumene a Pergamo accito adhibitis
et Rhodiis consilium habuit. Rhodii haud aspernari
pacem; Eumenes nec honestum dicere esse eo
tempore de pace agi, nec exitum rei imponi posse :
2 "qui enim " inquit " aut honeste, inclusi moenibus [3]
et obsessi, velut leges pacis accipiemus? Aut cui
rata ista pax erit, quam sine consule, non ex auctoritate senatus, non iussu populi Romani pepigerimus?
3 Quaero enim pace per te facta rediturusne extemplo
in Italiam sis, classem exercitumque deducturus,
an expectaturus, quid de ea re consuli placeat, quid
4 senatus censeat aut populus iubeat? Restat ergo ut
maneas in Asia, et rursus in hiberna copiae reductae
omisso bello exhauriant commeatibus praebendis
5 socios, deinde,[4] si ita visum iis sit, penes quos potestas

---

[1] agendi de pace *ed. Moguntina* : agendi de pace esse *Bς*.
[2] copiis *ς* : *om. B.*
[3] moenibus *ς* : *om. B.*
[4] deinde *ς* : *om. B.*

---

[1] Polybius (XXI. x.) gives a more detailed account.
[2] While Aemilius had the *imperium*, that of Scipio was
superior to his, and it is not certain that Aemilius had any
authority on land, since he had been assigned the *maritima
provincia* (ii. 10 above). There would surely have been a
dispute had Aemilius concluded a peace treaty under such
conditions, before the arrival of the consul, and in any case

was making ready what was necessary for the passage B.C. 190 of the Hellespont, he decided that the time had come, before he should be beset on land and sea at once, to treat for peace, and he occupied with his camp a hill facing Elaea; there, leaving all his infantry forces in camp, with the cavalry, numbering six thousand, he went down into the open country under the very walls of Elaea and sent a herald to Aemilius to say that he wished to discuss the question of peace.[1]

XIX. Aemilius summoned Eumenes from Pergamum and the Rhodians and held a council. The Rhodians did not disdain peace; Eumenes maintained that it was neither honourable to discuss the question of peace at that time nor possible to reach a conclusion to the discussion: "For how," he said, 'shall we honourably, shut up and besieged within our walls, accept what may be called terms of peace? Again, in whose eyes will this be a valid peace, which we shall conclude without a consul, with no authority of the senate, without the order of the Roman people? Now I ask, if peace is made by *you*, will you return immediately to Rome and withdraw your fleet and army, or wait to see what the consul's pleasure is regarding it, what the senate decrees, or what the people orders?[2] And so the result is that you stay in Asia and that your forces, led back once more to their winter stations, abandoning the war, exhaust your allies with furnishing supplies, and then, if it seems proper to those with whom the authority lies, start

the ratification of senate and assembly was necessary. The position of Eumenes is sound in Roman constitutional practice, as well as consistent with his own dignity. He did not wish Antiochus to use the siege of Pergamum as something with which to bargain.

A.U.C.
564

fuerit, instauremus novum de integro bellum, quod possumus, si ex hoc impetu rerum nihil prolatando remittitur, ante hiemem diis volentibus perfecisse."

6 Haec sententia vicit, responsumque Antiocho est ante consulis adventum de pace agi non posse.

7 Antiochus pace nequiquam temptata, evastatis Elaeensium primum, deinde Pergamenorum agris, relicto ibi Seleuco filio, Adramytteum hostiliter itinere facto petit agrum opulentum, quem vocant Thebes

8 campum, carmine Homeri nobilitatum; neque alio ullo loco Asiae maior regiis[1] militibus parta est praeda. Eodem Adramytteum, ut urbi praesidio essent, navibus circumvecti Aemilius et Eumenes venerunt.

XX. Per eosdem forte dies Elaeam ex Achaia mille pedites cum centum equitibus, Diophane omnibus iis copiis praeposito, accesserunt, quos egressos navibus obviam missi ab Attalo nocte

2 Pergamum deduxerunt. Veterani omnes et periti belli erant, et ipse dux Philopoemenis, summi tum omnium Graecorum imperatoris, discipulus. Qui biduum simul ad quietem hominum equorumque et ad visendas hostium stationes, quibus locis temporibusque accederent reciperentque sese, sumpserunt.

3 Ad radices fere collis in quo posita urbs est regii succedebant; ita libera ab tergo populatio erat. Nullo ab urbe, ne in stationes quidem qui[2] procul

4 iacularetur, excurrente, postquam semel, compulsi metu, se moenibus incluserunt, contemptus eorum

---

¹ regiis ⟨ : om. B.   ² qui edd. vett. : om. Bⲥ.

---

[1] The city, but not the plain, of Thebe is mentioned by Homer (Il. I. 366, etc.).

[2] Cf. XXXVI. xxxi. 6.   [3] Cf. XXXV. xxv. 7, etc.

wholly afresh a new war, although this war, if there B.C. 190
is no slackening, through delay, of the impetus we now
have, we can have finished, with the aid of the gods,
before winter." This argument prevailed, and the
answer was given to Antiochus that until the arrival
of the consul the question of peace could not be
discussed. Antiochus, having tried in vain for peace,
devastated first the lands of the Elaeans, then of
the Pergamenians, and leaving there his son Seleucus,
marching as though through a hostile country to
Adramytteum, sought the rich land which they call
the plain of Thebe, celebrated in the poem of Homer,[1]
and in no place in Asia was richer booty won by the
king's troops. Likewise to Adramytteum came
Aemilius and Eumenes, brought thither by the fleet.

XX. About this time there arrived at Elaea from
Achaea one thousand infantry and one hundred
cavalry, all under the command of Diophanes,[2]
and when they debarked guides, sent by Attalus to
meet them, escorted them by night to Pergamum.
They were all veterans and skilled in war, and their
leader too was a pupil of Philopoemen,[3] at that time
the foremost general of all the Greeks. They took
two days for the double purpose of resting men and
horses and reconnoitring the enemy's dispositions and
learning at what times and places they advanced and
retired. The king's troops would come up to about
the base of the hill on which the town stood; thus
the rear area was open for foraging. When no one
came out of the city, not even to throw a javelin
from a distance against the outposts, after the people
had once, under the impulse of fear, shut themselves
up within the walls, a feeling of contempt for them
and hence carelessness arose among the forces of

et inde neglegentia apud regios oritur. Non stratos,
5 non infrenatos magna pars habebant equos; paucis
ad arma et ordines relictis dilapsi ceteri sparserant
se toto passim campo, pars [1] in iuvenales lusus lasci-
viamque versi, pars vescentes sub umbra, quidam
6 somno etiam strati. Haec Diophanes ex alta urbe
Pergamo contemplatus arma suos capere et ad
portam praesto esse iubet; ipse Attalum adit et
in animo sibi esse dixit hostium stationem temptare.
7 Aegre id permittente Attalo, quippe qui centum
equitibus adversus sescentos, mille peditibus cum
quattuor milibus pugnaturum cerneret, porta egressus
haud procul statione hostium, occasionem opperiens,
8 consedit. Et qui Pergami erant amentiam magis
quam audaciam credere esse, et hostes paulisper [2]
in eos versi, ut nihil moveri viderunt, nec ipsi quicquam
ex solita neglegentia, insuper etiam eludentes
9 paucitatem, mutarunt. Diophanes quietos [3] aliquamdiu suos, velut ad spectaculum modo eductos,
10 continuit; postquam dilapsos ab ordinibus hostes
vidit, peditibus quantum accelerare possent sequi
iussis, ipse princeps inter equites cum turma sua,
quam potuit effusissimis habenis, clamore ab omni
simul pedite atque equite sublato stationem hostium
11 improviso invadit. Non homines solum sed equi
etiam territi, cum vincula abrupissent, trepidationem
12 et tumultum inter suos fecerunt. Pauci stabant

---

[1] pars ς : om. B.   [2] paulisper ς : om. B.
[3] quietos ς : quietus B.

the king. A large part of them had no saddles or
bridles for their horses; a few being left with the
arms and at their posts, the rest were scattered and
dispersed here and there over the whole plain, some
engaged in youthful play and pastime, some picnick-
ing in shady spots, some even lying asleep. Diophanes, watching this from the high-lying city of
Pergamum, ordered his men to take their arms and
be ready at the gates; he himself went to Attalus
and told him that it was his purpose to make an
attempt on an outpost of the enemy. When Attalus
allowed it reluctantly, seeing that there were one
hundred cavalry against six hundred, one thousand
infantry against four thousand, Diophanes marched
out of the gate and took his place not far from
the outpost of the enemy, watching his chance.
Both the people in Pergamum believed this to be
folly rather than fearlessness, and the enemy,
having watched them for a while and seen no
signs of activity, themselves made no change in
their customary carelessness, especially since they
were scornful of their small numbers. Diophanes
kept his men quiet for a while, as if they had been
led out merely to watch a show; when he saw
that the enemy had broken ranks, ordering the
infantry to follow as fast as they could, he
himself, at the head of the cavalry with his own
troop, the horses being given the loosest possible
rein, and a shout raised at the same moment by
every footman and trooper, attacked the outpost
of the enemy without warning. Not the men alone
but even the horses were terrified, and when
they broke their halters they caused consternation
and confusion among their own men. A few horses

impavidi equi; eos ipsos non sternere, non infrenare aut escendere facile poterant multo maiorem quam pro numero equitum terrorem Achaeis inferentibus. 13 Pedites vero [1] ordinati et praeparati sparsos per neglegentiam et semisomnos prope adorti sunt. 14 Caedes passim fugaque per campos facta est. Diophanes secutus effusos, quoad tutum fuit, magno decore genti Achaeorum parto—spectaverant enim e moenibus Pergami non viri modo sed feminae etiam—in praesidium urbis redit.

XXI. Postero die regiae magis compositae et ordinatae stationes quingentis passibus longius ab urbe posuerunt castra, et Achaei eodem ferme tem- 2 pore atque in eundem locum processerunt. Per multas horas intenti utrimque velut iam futurum impetum expectavere; [2] postquam haud procul occasu [3] solis redeundi [4] in castra tempus erat, regii signis collatis abire agmine ad iter magis quam 3 ad pugnam composito coepere. Quievit Diophanes dum in conspectu erant; deinde eodem [5] quo pridie impetu in postremum agmen incurrit, tantumque rursus pavoris ac tumultus incussit ut, cum terga caederentur, nemo pugnandi causa restiterit; trepidantesque et vix ordinem agminis servantes in castra 4 compulsi sunt. Haec Achaeorum audacia Seleucum ex agro Pergameno movere castra coegit.

Antiochus postquam Romanos ad tuendum Adramytteum venisse [6] audivit, ea quidem urbe

---

[1] pedites uero ς : uero pedites B.
[2] expectauere ς : expectare B.
[3] occasu ς : occasus B.
[4] redeundi ς : redeunt B.
[5] eodem ς : eo B.
[6] uenisse ς : om. B.

stood fearlessly; even these they could not easily
saddle or bridle or mount, the Achaeans causing far
more terror than was warranted by the number of
troopers. But the infantry, in formation and ready,
attacked men who were scattered around in disorder and nigh half asleep. There was slaughter
and flight everywhere through the plains. Diophanes
pursued the fugitives as far as it was safe, having won
great glory for the Achaean people—for both men
and women were watching from the walls of Pergamum—and returned to the garrisoning of the city.

XXI. The next day the king's outguards with
better order and discipline established themselves
five hundred paces farther from the city, and the
Achaeans came out about the same time and to the
same place. For many hours both parties waited
on the alert as if an attack were about to come;
after the time, not far from sunset, of returning to
camp had arrived, the royal troops, grouped around
their standards,[1] began to depart in a formation
adapted to marching rather than fighting. Diophanes remained quiet as long as they were in sight;
then, with the same impetuosity as the day before,
he fell violently upon the rear and caused again so
much panic and dismay that although they were
being cut down from behind no one stood fast to
fight; trembling and with difficulty keeping their
march-formation they were driven back into camp.
This bold conduct of the Achaeans forced Seleucus
to move his camp from the country of Pergamum.

When Antiochus heard that the Romans had come
to defend Adramytteum, he left that city, at any

---

[1] This meaning of the phrase is unusual but seems to be
required here.

A.U.C.
564

abstinuit; depopulatus agros Peraeam inde, coloniam
5 Mitylenaeorum, expugnavit. Cotton et Corylenus et
Aphrodisias et Prinne primo impetu captae sunt.
6 Inde per Thyatiram Sardis rediit. Seleucus in ora
maritima permanens aliis terrori erat, aliis praesidio.
Classis Romana cum Eumene Rhodiisque Mitylenen
primo, inde retro unde profecta erat Elaeam redit.
7 Inde Phocaeam petentes ad insulam quam Bacchium
vocant—imminet urbi Phocaeensium—appulerunt et,
quibus ante abstinuerant templis signisque—egregie
autem exornata insula erat—cum hostiliter diri-
8 puissent, ad ipsam urbem transmiserunt. Eam
divisis inter se partibus cum oppugnarent et videretur
sine operibus, armis scalisque capi posse, missum
ab Antiocho praesidium trium milium armatorum
9 cum intrasset urbem, extemplo oppugnatione omissa
classis ad insulam se recepit nihil aliud quam depopulato circa urbem hostium agro.

XXII. Inde placuit Eumenen domum dimitti
et [1] praeparare consuli atque exercitui, quae ad
transitum Hellesponti opus essent, Romanam Rhodi-
amque classem redire Samum atque ibi in statione
esse, ne Polyxenidas ab Epheso moveret. Rex
2 Elaeam, Romani ac Rhodii Samum redierunt. Ibi
M. Aemilius frater praetoris decessit.

Rhodii celebratis exsequiis adversus classem, quam
fama erat ex Syria venire, tredecim suis navibus

---

[1] et ς : om. B.

---

[1] I.e., the subordinate commanders received orders to
undertake specific missions in the attack : cf. XXV. xxx. 6.

rate, alone; but after laying waste their lands he B.C. 190
took by storm Peraea, a colony of the Mitylenaeans.
Cotto and Corylenus and Aphrodisias and Prinne fell
at the first assault. Thence he returned to Sardis
by way of Thyatira. Seleucus, remaining on the sea-
coast, was a source of fear to some and of assistance
to others. The Roman fleet with Eumenes and the
Rhodians went first to Mitylene and then returned
to Elaea whence it had come. Then, on their way
to Phocaea, they put in at the island which they call
Bacchium—it overlooks the city of the Phocaeans—
and when they had plundered like enemies the
temples and shrines which they had not previously
laid hands on—the island was beautifully adorned—
they crossed to the city itself. Dividing the tasks[1]
among themselves, they attacked it, and it seemed
possible to take it without siege-works, by assault
and escalade, but a garrison of three thousand
armed soldiers, sent by Antiochus, entered the city,
and at once the attack was abandoned and the fleet
returned to the island, without doing anything other
than devastating the farms of the enemy around the
town.

XXII. It was then determined that Eumenes
should return home and make ready for the consul
and the army whatever was necessary for the crossing of the Hellespont, and that the Roman and
Rhodian fleets should return to Samos and there
remain on guard lest Polyxenidas should move from
Ephesus. The king returned to Elaea, the Romans
and Rhodians to Samos. There Marcus Aemilius,
the brother of the praetor, died.

The Rhodians, when his funeral was over, with
thirteen of their own ships and one Coan quin-

353

et una Coa quinqueremi, altera Cnidia Rhodum, ut
3 ibi in statione essent, profecti sunt. Biduo ante
quam Eudamus cum classe ab Samo veniret, tredecim
ab Rhodo naves cum Pamphilida praefecto adversus
eandem Syriacam classem missae adsumptis quattuor[1]
navibus, quae Cariae praesidio erant, oppugnantibus
regiis Daedala et quaedam alia Peraeae castella
obsidione exemerunt. Eudamum confestim exire
4 placuit. Additae huic quoque sunt ad eam classem,
5 quam habebat, sex[2] apertae naves. Profectus cum
quantum accelerare poterat maturasset, ad portum
quem Megisten vocant praegressos consequitur.
Inde uno agmine Phaselidem cum venissent, optimum
visum est ibi hostem opperiri.

XXIII. In confinio Lyciae et Pamphyliae Phaselis
est; prominet penitus in altum conspiciturque
prima terrarum Rhodum a Cilicia petentibus et
procul navium praebet prospectum. Eo maxime,
ut in obvio classi hostium essent, electus locus est;
2 ceterum, quod non providerunt, et loco gravi et
tempore anni—medium enim aestatis erat—ad hoc
insolito odore ingruere morbi vulgo, maxime in
3 remiges, coeperunt. Cuius pestilentiae metu profecti cum praeterveherentur Pamphylium sinum, ad
Eurymedontem amnem appulsa classe audiunt ab
4 Aspendiis ad Sidam hostes esse. Tardius navi-

---

[1] quattuor ς : om. B.
[2] sex ς : tres BM.

---

[1] Cf. viii. 3 above.

quereme and another from Cnidus, set out for Rhodes, B.C. 190
so as to be on guard there against a fleet which
was reported to be coming from Syria.[1] Two days
before Eudamus with his fleet arrived from Samos,
thirteen ships from Rhodes, with Pamphilidas in
command, had been sent against the same Syrian
fleet and, picking up four ships which were guarding
Caria, they relieved the blockade of Daedala and
several other fortresses of Peraea which were besieged by the king's troops. It was decided that
Eudamus should leave at once. Six undecked vessels
were given to him in addition to the fleet which he
had. When he had departed and made all possible
haste, he overtook the ships which had gone on
ahead at the harbour which they call Megiste.
After proceeding to Phaselis in one column, it
seemed best to await the enemy there.

XXIII. Phaselis is on the border of Lycia and
Pamphylia; it projects far into the deep, and is the
first land sighted by travellers who are going to
Rhodes from Cilicia and it allows ships to be
sighted from afar. For that reason especially
the place was chosen, so that they might be
ready to meet the hostile fleet; but, and this they
had not foreseen, on account both of the un-
healthy country and of the time of year—for it
was midsummer—besides, from the unaccustomed
odour, diseases began to spread generally, especially among the rowers. In fear of this epi-
demic, they went on, and when they were sailing
past the gulf of Pamphylia, putting in at the
mouth of the river Eurymedon, they learned from
the people of Aspendus that the enemy was off
Sida. The king's navy had sailed rather slowly by

LIVY

gaverant regii adverso tempore etesiarum, quod velut
statum favoniis ventis est. Rhodiorum duae et
triginta quadriremes et quattuor triremes fuere;
5 regia classis septem et triginta maioris formae
navium erat; [1] in quibus tres hepteres, quattuor
hexeres habebat. Praeter has decem triremes
erant. Et hi adesse hostes ex specula quadam
6 cognoverunt. Utraque classis postero die luce
prima, tamquam eo die pugnatura, e portu movit;
et postquam superavere Rhodii promunturium quod
ab Sida prominet in altum, extemplo et conspecti
7 ab hostibus sunt et ipsi eos viderunt. Ab regiis [2]
sinistro cornu, quod ab alto obiectum erat, Hannibal,
dextro Apollonius, purpuratorum unus, praeerat,
8 et iam in frontem derectas [3] habebant naves. Rhodii
longo agmine veniebant; prima praetoria navis
Eudami erat; cogebat agmen [4] Chariclitus; Pamphi-
9 lidas mediae classi praeerat. Eudamus postquam
hostium aciem instructam et paratam ad concurren-
dum vidit, et ipse in altum evehitur et deinceps quae
sequebantur servantes [5] ordinem in frontem derigere
10 iubet. Ea res primo [6] tumultum praebuit; nam
nec sic in altum [7] evectus erat ut [8] ordo omnium
navium ad terram explicari posset, et festinans ipse

[1] formae nauium erat ⲋ: ferme nauium erant B.
[2] regiis J. F. Gronovius: regis BM: regio ⲋ.
[3] derectas ⲋ: decretas B.   [4] agmen ⲋ: om. B.
[5] seruantes ⲋ: serentis B.   [6] primo ⲋ: primum B.
[7] nec sic in altum ed. Frobeniana 1535: nec in alto B:
eudamus in altum Mⲋ.
[8] ut ⲋ: om. B.

---

[1] The use of statum here is peculiar. Usually employed to
denote the appointment of days for festivals and similar
occasions, it here suggests that this season was reserved (by
Nature) for the etesian winds.

reason of the unfavourable season of the etesian B.C. 190
gales, which is, as it were, allotted to[1] winds from
the north-west. There were thirty-two[2] Rhodian
quadriremes and four triremes; the royal fleet consisted of thirty-seven ships of larger size; among
them they had three of seven banks of oars and four
of six. Besides these there were ten triremes. And
they saw from a certain watch-tower that the enemy
was close at hand. At daybreak next day both
fleets moved out of port as if to fight that day; and
after the Rhodians had passed the promontory which
juts out from Sida into the sea, they were seen by the
enemy and sighted them as well. On the side of the
king's fleet, on the left flank, which extended into
open water, Hannibal was in command; on the right,
Apollonius, one of the nobles; and already they had
the ships formed in a straight line. The Rhodians
were approaching in a long column; first was the
flagship of Eudamus; Chariclitus brought up the
rear; Pamphilidas was in command of the centre of
the fleet. When Eudamus saw the enemy arrayed
and ready to engage, he too sailed out into deep
water and directed the following ships, keeping their
relative positions to one another, to form in a straight
line. This order at first produced confusion; for he
had not gone far enough out to sea to permit the
array of all the ships to form in line toward the shore,[3]

---

[2] This number cannot be made to agree with those given
in xxii. 2–4 above.

[3] The manoeuvre described is that of forming line to the
left. The flagship moved at a right oblique but failed to gain
enough distance to the right to make room for the rear ships.
Eudamus may have misjudged the distance or have been in too
great haste; the sixth ship also moved off at too acute an angle
to the original direction and increased the crowding on the left.

praepropere cum quinque solis navibus Hannibali
occurrit; ceteri quia in frontem derigere iussi erant,
11 non sequebantur. Extremo agmini loci nihil ad
terram relicti erat; trepidantibusque iis inter se
iam in dextro cornu adversus Hannibalem pugnabatur.

XXIV. Sed momento temporis et navium virtus
et usus maritimae rei terrorem omnem Rhodiis
2 dempsit. Nam et in altum celeriter evectae naves
locum post se quaeque venienti ad terram dedere,
et si qua concurrerat rostro cum hostium nave, aut
proram lacerabat, aut remos detergebat, aut libero
inter ordines discursu praetervecta in puppim impe-
3 tum dabat. Maxime exterruit hepteris regia a
multo minore Rhodia nave uno ictu demersa; itaque
iam[1] haud dubie dextrum cornu hostium in fugam
4 inclinabat.[2] Eudamum in alto multitudine navium
maxime Hannibal, ceteris omnibus longe prae-
stantem, urgebat, et circumvenisset, ni signo sublato
ex praetoria nave, quo dispersam classem in unum
colligi mos erat, omnes quae in dextro cornu vicerant
5 naves ad opem ferendam suis concurrissent. Tum
et Hannibal quaeque circa eum naves erant capessunt fugam; nec insequi Rhodii ex magna parte

---

[1] iam ς : om. B.
[2] inclinabat ς : declinabat B.

---

[1] The congestion described in the preceding note automatically corrected itself, the ships naturally turning to the
right where the battle was on. The ships that broke through
the hostile line gave still more space for manoeuvre.

[2] These were the standard forms of naval attack. The
Romans, although they had no native instinct for naval warfare, introduced some familiar and effective variations on these
tactics.

[3] This statement must not be taken too literally: cf. sect.
9 below.

and in his excessive haste, with only five ships, B.C. 190 he encountered Hannibal; the rest, because they had been ordered to form in line, did not follow. There was no room left on the land side for the tail of the column; while they were entangled with one another the battle with Hannibal was already begun on the right flank.

XXIV. But in an instant of time both the excellence of their ships and their experience in naval warfare took away all fear from the Rhodians. For the ships, sailing quickly out into deep water, each gave the one in rear a place on the land side,[1] and, moreover, if a ship clashed head on with a ship of the enemy, it either crushed its prow or broke off its oars or, passing through the open intervals between the files, it attacked the stern.[2] The greatest fear was caused when a seven-banked ship of the king was sunk [3] with one blow by a much smaller Rhodian vessel; so now without question the right wing of the enemy was turned to flight. Eudamus, in the open, although he was superior in everything else, was hard pressed by Hannibal, particularly on account of the greater number of his ships, and Hannibal would have surrounded him had not the flagship of his fleet displayed the signal by which, as the custom is, a scattered fleet is collected into one place, and all the ships which had been victorious on the right [4] flank had hurried off to bear aid to their comrades. Then Hannibal also and the ships which followed him began to retire; nor could the Rhodians pursue,

---

[4] Livy appears here to change his point of view. The "right wing" of sect. 3 is that of the king's fleet, while the "right flank" here is that of the Rhodians. One or the other, however, may be a simple error on the part of Livy or a scribe.

aegris et ob id celerius fessis remigibus potuerunt.

6 Cum in alto ubi substiterant cibo reficerent vires,[1]
contemplatus Eudamus hostes claudas mutilatasque
naves apertis navibus remulco trahentes, viginti
paulo amplius integras abscedentes, e turri praetoriae
navis silentio facto " exsurgite " inquit " et egregium

7 spectaculum capessite oculis." Consurrexere omnes
contemplatique trepidationem fugamque hostium
prope[2] una voce omnes ut sequerentur exclamaverunt.

8 Ipsius Eudami multis ictibus vulnerata navis erat;
Pamphilidam et Chariclitum insequi quoad putarent

9 tutum iussit. Aliquamdiu secuti sunt; postquam
terrae appropinquabat Hannibal, veriti ne include-
rentur vento in hostium ora, ad Eudamum revecti
hepterem captam, quae primo concursu icta erat,

10 aegre Phaselidem pertraxerunt. Inde Rhodum non
tam victoria laeti, quam alius alium accusantes, quod
cum potuisset, non omnis submersa aut capta classis

11 hostium foret, redierunt. Hannibal, ictus[3] uno
proelio adverso, ne tum quidem praetervehi Lyciam
audebat, cum coniungi veteri regiae classi quam

12 primum cuperet; et ne id ei facere liberum esset,
Rhodii Chariclitum cum viginti navibus rostratis

13 ad Patara et Megisten portum miserunt. Eudamum
cum septem navibus maximis ex ea classe, cui praefuerat, Samum redire ad Romanos iusserunt, ut,
quantum consilio, quantum auctoritate valeret,
compelleret Romanos ad Patara expugnanda.

---

[1] reficerent uires ⵌ : reficerentur *BM*.
[2] prope ⵌ : ac prope *BM*.
[3] ictus ⵌ : uictus *BM*.

B.C. 190

since many of their rowers were sick and for that reason more quickly exhausted. While they were restoring their strength with food in the open water, Eudamus watched the enemy towing their lame and crippled ships with hawsers from open vessels, and hardly more than twenty moving off undamaged, and from the bridge of the flagship he called for silence and exclaimed, " Stand up and look upon a glorious sight." Every man stood up, and seeing the confusion and panic of the enemy, they cried almost with one voice " Let us pursue." The ship of Eudamus himself had been damaged by many blows ; but he ordered Pamphilidas and Chariclitus to follow as far as they deemed it safe. They pursued for some distance ; but when Hannibal was close to land, fearing that they might be detained by the wind near a hostile coast, they returned to Eudamus, and with difficulty towed to Phaselis the captured seven-banked ship which had been struck at the first onset. Thence they returned to Rhodes, not so much rejoicing in their victory as blaming one another because, when it had been possible, the entire fleet of the enemy had not been sunk or captured. Hannibal, discouraged by this one defeat, did not even then dare to pass Lycia, anxious though he was to join the old fleet of the king as soon as possible ; and, that this course might not be open to him, the Rhodians sent Chariclitus with twenty beaked ships to Patara and the harbour of Megiste. Eudamus, with the seven largest ships of the fleet which he had commanded, they ordered to rejoin the Romans at Samos, in order that with whatever wisdom and whatever influence he had, he might urge the Romans to the capture of Patara.

LIVY

XXV. Magnam Romanis laetitiam prius victoriae
2 nuntius, deinde adventus attulit Rhodiorum; et
apparebat, si Rhodiis ea cura dempta fuisset, vacuos
eos tuta eius regionis maria praestaturos. Sed
profectio Antiochi ab Sardibus simul metus [1] ne
opprimerentur maritimae urbes, abscedere custodia
3 Ioniae atque Aeolidis prohibuerunt; Pamphilidam
cum quattuor navibus tectis ad eam classem quae
4 circa Patara erat miserunt. Antiochus non civitatium modo quae circa se erant contrahebat praesidia,
sed ad Prusiam Bithyniae regem legatos miserat
litterasque, quibus transitum in Asiam Romanorum
5 increpabat: venire eos ad omnia regna tollenda, ut
nullum usquam in orbe [2] terrarum nisi Romanum
6 imperium esset; Philippum, Nabim expugnatos; se
tertium peti; ut quisque proximus ab oppresso sit,
per omnes velut continens incendium pervasurum;
7 ab se gradum in Bithyniam fore, quando Eumenes
8 in voluntariam servitutem concessisset. His motum
Prusiam litterae Scipionis consulis, sed magis fratris
eius Africani, ab suspicione tali averterunt, qui
praeter consuetudinem perpetuam populi Romani
augendi omni honore regum sociorum maiestatem,
domesticis ipse exemplis Prusiam ad promerendam
9 amicitiam suam compulit: regulos se acceptos in

---

[1] simul metus *Heraeus* : om. *B5̄*.
[2] in orbe *Madvig* : orbis *B5̄*.

---

[1] The "responsibility" apparently concerns Patara, which
was strategically situated, both to threaten Rhodes and to
bar the way to reinforcements coming to Antiochus from
Syria by sea or land (cf. xv. 7-8 above). More pressing tasks,

XXV. Great joy was brought to the Romans first B.C. 190
by the news of the victory and then by the coming of
the Rhodians, and it was evident that if the Rhodians
had been relieved of their present responsibility [1]
their hands would be free and they would guarantee
the safety of the seas in that quarter. But it was
the departure of Antiochus from Sardis, and at the
same time the fear that the coast cities would be
crushed, which prevented them from leaving the
guarding of Ionia and Aeolis; the Rhodians sent
Pamphilidas with four decked ships to the fleet which
was off Patara. Antiochus was not only collecting
reinforcements from the states which surrounded
him, but had sent ambassadors and letters to Prusias,
king of Bithynia, in which he complained of the
crossing of the Romans into Asia: they were coming
to destroy all kingdoms, so that in the whole world
there might be no empire save that of Rome; Philip,
Nabis, had been defeated; he himself was the third
to be attacked; as each came next after the last
destroyed, the fire, catching, so to speak, one after
another in succession, would be everywhere; from
himself their next step would be into Bithynia, since
Eumenes had already given himself into voluntary
slavery. Prusias, troubled by this message, was
diverted from such suspicions by the letter of Scipio
the consul, and more by the words of his brother
Africanus, who, by citing the enduring tradition
among the Roman people of increasing with every
sign of honour the dignity of allied kings, and also,
by giving examples from his personal experience,
induced Prusias to merit his friendship: tribal chief-

however, prevent the Romans from repeating, on a larger
scale, their previous unsuccessful expeditions against Patara.

LIVY

fidem in Hispania reges [1] reliquisse; Masinissam non
in patrio modo locasse regno, sed in Syphacis, a quo
10 ante expulsus fuisset, regnum imposuisse; et esse
eum non Africae modo regum longe opulentissimum,
sed toto in orbe terrarum cuivis regum vel maiestate
11 vel viribus parem. Philippum et Nabim, hostes et
bello superatos ab T. Quinctio, tamen in regno
12 relictos. Philippo quidem anno priore etiam stipendium remissum et filium obsidem redditum; et
quasdam civitates extra Macedoniam patientibus
Romanis imperatoribus recepisse eum. In eadem
dignitate et Nabim futurum fuisse, nisi eum suus
primum furor, deinde fraus Aetolorum absumpsisset.
13 Maxime confirmatus est animus regis, postquam ad
eum C. Livius, qui praetor ante classi [2] praefuerat,
14 legatus ab Roma venit et edocuit quanto et spes
victoriae certior Romanis quam Antiocho et amicitia
sanctior firmiorque apud Romanos futura esset.

XXVI. Antiochus postquam a spe societatis Pru-
siae decidit, Ephesum ab Sardibus est profectus ad
classem quae per aliquot menses instructa ac parata
2 fuerat visendam, magis quia terrestribus copiis
exercitum Romanum et duos Scipiones imperatores
videbat sustineri non posse, quam quod res navalis
ipsa per se aut temptata sibi umquam feliciter aut
3 tunc magnae et certae fiduciae esset. Erat tamen
momentum in praesentia spei, quod et magnam

---

[1] in Hispania reges *ed. Frobeniana* 1535: hispaniae regem
B: hispaniae reges ς.   [2] classi ς: classis *B*: *om. M.*

---

[1] Polybius (XXI. xi) redistributes and rearranges the
arguments of both sides, attributing to Prusias himself the
fear mentioned in sect. 5, naming some of the *reguli* of sect.
9 and adding one in Illyria. There are small differences in
the account of Nabis, but essentially the two chapters are the
same in substance.

tains, taken under his protection in Spain, he had B.C. 190
left kings; Masinissa he had not only established on
his ancestral throne but had placed on that of
Syphax, by whom he had been driven out before;
and he was both by far the richest of the kings of
Africa and equal, whether in majesty or in power, to
any king whatsoever in the whole world. Philip
and Nabis, enemies, defeated, too, in war by Titus
Quinctius, had yet been left in their kingdoms.
Philip the year before, in fact, had had his tribute
cancelled and his hostage-son restored, and had
recovered certain cities outside of Macedonia with
the consent of the Roman generals. Nabis too would
have been in the same position of honour had not his
own madness and then the treachery of the Aetolians
destroyed him. The favourable inclination of the
king was especially strengthened after Gaius Livius,
the commissioner, who as praetor earlier had commanded the fleet, came from Rome and showed
him how much surer were the Roman prospects of
victory than those of Antiochus and how friendship
with the Romans would be more respected and
dependable.[1]

XXVI. When Antiochus lost his hope of an alliance
with Prusias, he went to Ephesus from Sardis to
inspect the fleet which for some months had been
equipped and ready, more because he saw that with
his land forces he could not withstand the Roman
army and its generals, the two Scipios, than because
he had ever tried actual combat by sea with much
success or had at this time any great and assured
confidence. There was, however, a reason for hope
at the moment, in that he had heard, first, that the
larger part of the Rhodian fleet was in the vicinity

A.U.C.
564

partem Rhodiae classis circa Patara esse et Eumenen
regem cum omnibus navibus suis consuli obviam in
4 Hellespontum profectum audierat; aliquid etiam
inflabat animos classis Rhodia ad Samum per occa-
5 sionem fraude praeparatam absumpta. His fretus,
Polyxenida cum classe ad temptandam omni modo
certaminis fortunam misso, ipse copias ad Notium
ducit. Id oppidum Colophonium, mari imminens,
abest a vetere Colophone duo ferme milia passuum.
6 Et ipsam urbem suae potestatis esse volebat, adeo
propinquam Epheso,[1] ut nihil terra marive ageret,
quod non subiectum oculis Colophoniorum ac per
7 eos notum extemplo Romanis esset, et hos[2] audita
obsidione non dubitabat ad opem sociae urbi ferendam
classem ab Samo moturos; eam occasionem Poly-
8 xenidae ad rem gerendam fore. Igitur operibus
oppugnare urbem aggressus, ad mare partibus
duabus pariter munitionibus deductis, utrimque
vineas et aggerem muro iniunxit et testudinibus
9 arietes admovit. Quibus territi malis Colophonii
oratores Samum ad L. Aemilium, fidem praetoris
10 populique Romani implorantes, miserunt. Aemilium
et Sami segnis diu mora offendebat, nihil minus
opinantem quam Polyxenidam, bis nequiquam ab se
11 provocatum, potestatem pugnae facturum esse, et
turpe existimabat Eumenis classem adiuvare consulem ad traiciendas in Asiam legiones, se Colophonis
obsessae auxilio, incertam finem habituro, alligari.
12 Eudamus Rhodius, qui et tenuerat eum Sami cupien-

---

[1] Epheso ς: om. B.   [2] et hos *Madvig*: quos Bς.

---

[1] The *testudo* is ordinarily a temporary device, formed by
the overlapping shields of an attacking column in close formation; here it is a portable roof to cover a battering-ram and
its crew.

of Patara and, second, that King Eumenes with all B.C. 190
his ships had gone to meet the consul at the Hellespont; an additional stimulant to his spirits was the
destruction of the Rhodian fleet at Samos under
conditions attained by trickery. Relying on these
circumstances, he sent Polyxenidas with the fleet to
try fortune in any sort of engagement and himself
led his troops to Notium. This is a town of Colophon,
overlooking the sea, distant from old Colophon about
two miles. And he wished to have the town itself
in his hands, being so close to Ephesus that he could
do nothing on land or sea which was not observed
by the Colophonians, and through them was not
immediately known to the Romans, and he had no
doubt that when they heard of its siege they would •
move the fleet from Samos to bear aid to an allied
city; this would be the opportunity for Polyxenidas
to bring about an engagement. Therefore he began
to lay siege to the city, constructing a line of fortifications down to the sea on each side alike, and in both
ran mantlets and an outwork up to the wall and moved
battering-rams under shelter.[1] Terrified by these
misfortunes, the Colophonians sent to Lucius Aemilius
the praetor at Samos representatives to beg for the
protection of the praetor and the Roman people.
Aemilius, idle at Samos, was chafing under the long
delay, thinking of nothing less than that Polyxenidas,
twice challenged by him in vain, would offer the
opportunity for battle, and he thought it a dis-
grace that the fleet of Eumenes should assist the
consul in transporting the legions into Asia while he
was entangled in aiding the beleaguered Colophon,
an operation of indefinite duration. Eudamus the
Rhodian, who also had detained him at Samos,

LIVY

tem proficisci in Hellespontum, cunctique instare
13 et dicere: quanto satius esse vel socios obsidione
eximere vel victam iam semel classem iterum vincere
et totam maris possessionem hosti[1] eripere, quam
desertis sociis, tradita Antiocho Asia terra marique
in Hellespontum, ubi satis esset Eumenis classis, ab
sua parte belli discedere.

XXVII. Profecti ab Samo ad petendos commeatus
consumptis iam omnibus Chium parabant traicere;
id erat horreum Romanis, eoque omnes ex Italia
2 missae onerariae derigebant cursum. Circumvecti
ab urbe ad aversa insulae—obiecta aquiloni ad Chium
et Erythras sunt—cum pararent traicere, litteris
certior fit praetor frumenti vim magnam Chium ex
Italia venisse, vinum portantes naves tempestatibus
3 retentas esse; simul adlatum est Teios regiae classi
commeatus benigne praebuisse, quinque milia vasorum vini esse pollicitos. Teum ex medio cursu
classem repente avertit, aut volentibus iis usurus[2]
commeatu parato hostibus, aut ipsos pro hostibus
4 habiturus. Cum derexissent ad terram proras,
quindecim ferme eis naves circa Myonnesum appparu-
erunt, quas primo[3] ex classe regia praetor esse ratus
institit[4] sequi; apparuit deinde piraticos celoces et
5 lembos esse. Chiorum maritimam oram depopulati

[1] hosti *ed. Frobeniana* 1535: *om. Bꞅ.*
[2] iis usurus ꞅ : his usurum *B.*
[3] primo ꞅ : prime *B.*
[4] institit ꞅ : instituit *B.*

---

[1] Again we see the perplexities which lack of communications and of satisfactory liaison between army and navy
caused Aemilius. He probably had no instructions from the
consul as to the co-operation he expected or from the senate
as to his general policy. The multiplicity of possible lines

although he wished to leave for the Hellespont, and B.C. 190
all the others, kept urging him and saying: how much
better it would be either to relieve the allies from
siege or again to defeat the navy already once
defeated and to wrest completely from the enemy
his mastery of the sea than, abandoning the allies
and surrendering to Antiochus the land and sea of
Asia, to go off to the Hellespont, where the fleet of
Eumenes was sufficient, and run away from his own
share in the war.[1]

XXVII. Leaving Samos to seek provisions, everything being now consumed, they were preparing to
cross to Chios; this was the granary of the Romans,
and thither all the cargo-boats from Italy directed
their course. Sailing from the city to the other side
of the island—the side facing Chios and Erythrae is
exposed to the north wind—as they were preparing
to cross, the praetor was informed by letter that a
great quantity of grain had come from Italy, but the
ships carrying wine had been delayed by storms;
at the same time it was reported that the Teans had
generously offered stores to the king's fleet and had
promised five thousand casks of wine. When half-
way across he suddenly turned the fleet towards Teos,
intending either to use, with their consent, the provisions prepared for the enemy, or to treat the Teans
as foes. When they had turned their prows towards
the land, about fifteen ships came into sight rounding
Myonnesus, which at first the praetor, thinking they
were from the king's fleet, started to pursue; then
it was seen that they were swift and light pirate-
vessels. They had plundered the sea-coast of the

of action resulted in his adopting none of them and in exposing
him to pressure from his allies.

A.U.C.
564

cum omnis generis praeda revertentes postquam
videre ex alto classem, in fugam verterunt. Et
celeritate superabant levioribus et ad id fabrefactis
6 navigiis, et propiores terrae erant; itaque priusquam appropinquaret classis, Myonnesum perfugerunt, unde se e portu ratus abstracturum naves,
7 ignarus loci sequebatur praetor. Myonnesus promunturium inter Teum Samumque est. Ipse collis
est in modum metae in acutum cacumen a fundo
satis lato fastigatus [1]; a continenti artae semitae
aditum habet,[2] a mari exesae fluctibus rupes claudunt,
ita ut quibusdam locis superpendentia saxa plus in
altum, quam quae in statione sunt naves, promineant.[3]
8 Circa ea appropinquare non ausae naves, ne sub
ictu [4] superstantium rupibus piratarum essent, diem
9 trivere. Tandem sub noctem vano incepto cum
abstitissent, Teum postero die accessere, et in portu
qui ab tergo urbis est—Geraesticum ipsi appellant—
navibus constitutis praetor ad depopulandum circa
urbem agrum emisit milites.

XXVIII. Teii, cum in oculis populatio esset,
oratores cum infulis et velamentis ad Romanum
2 miserunt. Quibus purgantibus civitatem omnis facti
dictique hostilis adversus Romanos, et iuvisse eos
commeatu [5] classem hostium arguit, et quantum vini
Polyxenidae promisissent; quae si eadem Romanae

---

[1] fastigatus *ed. Romana* 1472 : castigatus *B* : fatigatus ς.
[2] habet ς : habent *B*.
[3] promineant ς : *om. B.*
[4] sub ictu ς : subiecto *B.*
[5] commeatu ς : omni commeatu *B.*

Chians and were returning with all sorts of booty B.C. 190
when they saw the fleet from the open sea and turned
to flight. They were both superior in speed, their
ships being lighter and designed with that in view,
and nearer the shore; so before the fleet approached
them they escaped to Myonnesus, and the praetor
followed, thinking that he would lure the ships out
of port, as he was ignorant of the place. Myonnesus
is a promontory between Teos and Samos. It is a
hill shaped like a cone terminating in a sharp point
from a fairly extensive base [1]; from the mainland it
has an approach by a steep path, on the side of the
sea cliffs worn by the waves close it in, so that in some
places the overhanging rocks rise to a greater height
than do the ships which lie at anchor. In this
vicinity, not daring to approach lest they come
within range of the pirates posted on the cliffs, they
wasted a day. When at length at nightfall they
abandoned their fruitless undertaking, they came the
next day to Teos, and stationing the ships in the
harbour which is behind the town—the islanders
call it Geraesticus—the praetor sent out troops to
ravage the land around the city.

XXVIII. The Teans, when the plundering was
going on before their eyes, sent envoys with fillets and
badges of suppliants to the Romans. When they tried
to clear the state of any deed or word unfriendly to
the Romans, he both charged them with aiding the
fleet of the enemy with provisions and reminded them
how much wine they had promised Polyxenidas; if they
would give the Romans the same amount, he would

[1] The *meta* in the technical sense was a cone-shaped marker,
used in the circus to indicate how many laps of a race had been
finished.

LIVY

classi darent, revocaturum se a populatione militem;
3 si minus, pro hostibus eos habiturum. Hoc tam triste
responsum cum rettulissent legati, vocatur in contionem a magistratibus populus, ut quid agerent con-
4 sultarent. Eo forte die Polyxenidas cum regia
classe a Colophone profectus postquam movisse a
Samo Romanos audivit et ad Myonnesum piratas
persecutos Teiorum agrum depopulari, naves in
5 Geraestico portu stare, ipse adversus Myonnesum
in insula—Macrin nautici vocant—ancoras portu
6 occulto iecit. Inde ex propinquo explorans quid
hostes agerent, primo in magna spe fuit, quem ad
modum Rhodiam classem ad Samum circumsessis ad
exitum faucibus portus [1] expugnasset, sic et Romanam expugnaturum. Nec est dissimilis natura loci:
7 promunturiis coeuntibus inter se ita clauditur portus,
8 ut vix duae simul inde naves possint exire. Inde
nocte occupare fauces Polyxenidas in animo habebat,
et denis navibus ad promunturia stantibus, quae ab
utroque cornu in latera exeuntium navium pugnarent,
ex cetera classe, sicut ad Panhormum fecerat, armatis
in littora expositis terra marique simul hostes oppri-
9 mere. Quod non vanum ei consilium fuisset ni, cum
Teii facturos se imperata promisissent, ad accipiendos
commeatus aptius visum esset Romanis in eum
portum, qui ante urbem est, classem transire.
10 Dicitur et Eudamus Rhodius vitium alterius portus
ostendisse, cum forte duae naves in arto ostio impli-
11 citos remos fregissent; et inter alia id quoque movit

---

[1] portus *ς* : *om. B.*

recall his men from plundering; if not, he would B.C. 190
treat them as enemies. When the envoys had taken
back this threatening answer, the people was summoned to an assembly by the magistrates to consult
as to what they should do. On that day, as it
happened, Polyxenidas with the royal fleet left
Colophon, and when he heard that the Romans had
moved from Samos, had pursued the pirates to
Myonnesus, and were devastating the fields of the
Teans, while the ships lay in the harbour of Geraes-
tus, he himself dropped anchor opposite Myonnesus
in a concealed harbour of an island—the sailors
call it Macris. Thence, reconnoitring at close range
to see what the enemy was doing, he at first was very
hopeful that as he had defeated the Rhodians at
Samos by blockading the passage out of the harbour,
so he would capture the Roman fleet. The nature of
the place is not unlike: the headlands coming
together close the harbour so that with difficulty
two ships at a time can pass through. Polyxenidas
then conceived the design of occupying the exit by
night, and with ten ships standing off each promontory, which could attack from both flanks the sides
of the ships as they came out, and of landing armed
men from the rest of the fleet, as he had done at
Panhormus, to attack the enemy by land and sea at
once. This plan would not have failed had not the
Romans, when the Teans had promised to do as
they had been ordered, thought it more convenient
to move the fleet around to the port which lies in front
of the city, to receive the supplies. Also Eudamus
the Rhodian is said to have called attention to a fault
of the other harbour, when by chance two ships had
broken their oars, entangled in the narrow entrance;

A.U.C.
564

praetorem, ut traduceret classem, quod ab terra periculum erat, haud procul inde Antiocho stativa habente.

XXIX. Traducta classe ad urbem ignaris omnibus egressi milites nautaeque sunt ad commeatus et 2 vinum maxime dividendum in naves, cum medio forte diei agrestis quidam ad praetorem adductus nuntiat alterum iam diem classem stare ad insulam Macrin, et paulo ante visas quasdam moveri tamquam ad 3 profectionem naves. Re subita perculsus praetor tubicines canere iubet, ut si qui per agros palati essent redirent; tribunos in urbem mittit ad cogendos 4 milites nautasque in naves. Haud secus quam in repentino incendio aut capta urbe trepidatur, aliis in urbem currentibus ad suos revocandos, aliis ex urbe naves cursu repetentibus, incertisque [1] clamoribus, quibus ipsis tubae obstreperent, turbatis imperiis 5 tandem concursum ad naves est. [2] Vix suas quisque noscere aut adire prae tumultu poterat; trepidatumque cum periculo et in mari et in terra foret, ni partibus divisis Aemilius cum praetoria nave primus e portu in altum evectus, excipiens insequentes, suo 6 quamque ordine in frontem instruxisset, Eudamus Rhodiaque classis substitissent ad [3] terram, ut et sine trepidatione conscenderent et ut quaeque parata 7 esset exiret navis. Ita et explicuere ordinem primae in conspectu praetoris, et coactum agmen

---

[1] incertisque 𝔰 : incertis B.
[2] est 𝔰 : et B.   [3] ad 𝔰 : in B.

---

[1] Cf. xxi. 8 above.

and among other things the praetor was induced to B.C. 190
transfer the fleet by the fact that there was danger
from the land, since Antiochus had his base at no
great distance away.

XXIX. The fleet having moved over to the city without the knowledge of anyone, the marines and sailors
landed to divide the provisions, and especially the
wine, among the ships, when about midday a peasant
was brought before the praetor and said that for two
days now a fleet had anchored off the island of Macris
and a little while before had been seen in motion as
if getting ready for departure. The praetor, dismayed by this sudden crisis, ordered the trumpets
sounded for the return of the men who were straggling
through the fields and sent the tribunes to the town
to muster the marines and sailors on ship-board. Just
as in a sudden fire or at the capture of a city there was
panic, some running to the city to summon their
comrades, others hurrying at full speed from the
town to the ships, with confused shouts and these
almost drowned out by the trumpets, at length,
despite conflicting orders they were assembled at the
ships. Scarcely could any man know or go aboard
his own vessel in the excitement; and there would
have been a dangerous panic, both on sea and on
land, if, distributing the tasks,[1] Aemilius with the flagship had not led the way out of the harbour into open
water, drawing after him those that followed, and had
arranged them in line, each in his own place, and
Eudamus and the Rhodian fleet had not remained near
the shore, so that both the embarkation was without
confusion and each ship set forth as it was ready.
So the ships in front opened up their line under
the eyes of the praetor, and the Rhodians formed the

A.U.C.
564

ab Rhodiis est, instructaque acies, velut cernerent
regios, in altum processit. Inter Myonnesum et
Corycum promunturium erant, cum hostem con-
8 spexere. Et regia classis, binis in ordinem navibus
longo agmine veniens, et ipsa aciem adversam
explicuit laevo tantum evecta[1] cornu, ut amplecti
et circuire dextrum cornu Romanorum posset.
9 Quod ubi Eudamus qui cogebat agmen vidit, non
posse aequare ordinem Romanos et tantum non
iam circuiri ab dextro cornu, concitat naves—et
erant Rhodiae longe omnium celerrimae tota classe—
aequatoque cornu praetoriae navi, in qua Polyxenidas
erat, suam obiecit.

XXX. Iam totis classibus simul[2] ab omni parte
pugna conserta erat. Ab Romanis octoginta naves
pugnabant, ex quibus Rhodiae duae et viginti erant;
2 hostium classis undenonaginta navium fuit; maximae
formae naves tres hexeres habebat, duas hepteres.
Robore navium et virtute militum Romani longe
praestabant,[3] Rhodiae naves agilitate et arte guber-
3 natorum et scientia remigum; maximo tamen
terrori hostibus fuere quae ignes prae se portabant,
et quod unum iis[4] ad Panhormum circumventis[5]
saluti fuerat, id tum maximum momentum ad
4 victoriam fuit. Nam metu ignis adversi regiae naves,
ne prorae[6] concurrerent, cum declinassent, neque
ipsae ferire rostro hostem poterant, et obliquas se

---

[1] euecta ς : euecto B.
[2] classibus simul ed. Frobeniana 1535 : simul classibus
Bς.
[3] praestabant Madvig : rodios praestabant Bς.
[4] unum iis ς : unus is B.
[5] circumuentis ς : circumuectis B.
[6] prorae Crévier : prope B : prora M.

rear of the column, and the line thus formed, as if B.C. 190 they saw the royal fleet, moved out into deep water. They were between Myonnesus and the promontory of Corycus when they sighted the enemy. And the king's fleet, advancing in a long column with two ships abreast, likewise formed in line facing the enemy, with its left flank so far extended that it could enfold and surround the right wing of the Romans. When Eudamus, who brought up the rear, perceived that the Romans could not extend their front to equal it and could not prevent their being encircled on the right of the line, he speeded up his ships—and the Rhodians were by far the fastest of all in the whole fleet—and making the flanks equally long he drove his own ship at the flagship, in which was Polyxenidas.

XXX. Now the engagement began through the entire fleets in every place at once. On the Roman side eighty ships were fighting, of which twenty-two were Rhodian; the fleet of the enemy consisted of eighty-nine vessels; of ships of the largest size they had three with six banks of oars and two with seven. In strength of ships and courage of soldiers the Romans were far the best, the Rhodian ships in quickness of movement and skill of pilots and dexterity of rowers; yet the greatest terror was caused the enemy by those which carried fire before their prows,[1] and that which was their sole source of safety at Panhormus when they were surrounded was at this time the greatest factor in their victory. For when, from fear of the flames in front of them, the royal ships had swerved to avoid the collision of their prows, they were unable to strike the enemy with their beaks,

---

[1] Cf. xi. 13 above and the note.

LIVY

A.U.C.
564

5 ipsae ad ictus praebebant, et si qua concurrerat,
obruebatur infuso igni, magisque ad incendium quam
6 ad proelium trepidabant. Plurimum tamen, quae
solet, militum virtus in bello valuit. Mediam
namque aciem hostium Romani cum rupissent,
circumvecti ab tergo pugnantibus adversus Rhodios
regiis sese obiecere; momentoque temporis et media
acies Antiocho et laevo cornu circumventae [1] naves
7 mergebantur. Dextera pars integra sociorum magis
clade quam suo periculo terrebantur; ceterum,
postquam alias circumventas, praetoriam navem
Polyxenidae relictis sociis vela dantem videre,
sublatis raptim dolonibus—et erat secundus petentibus Ephesum ventus—capessunt fugam quadraginta
duabus navibus in ea pugna amissis, quarum decem
8 tres captae in potestatem hostium venerunt, ceterae
9 incensae aut demersae. Romanorum duae naves
fractae sunt, vulneratae aliquot; Rhodia una capta
memorabili casu. Nam cum rostro percussisset
Sidoniam navem, ancora,[2] ictu ipso excussa e nave
sua, unco dente, velut ferrea manu iniecta, adligavit
10 alterius proram; inde tumultu iniecto cum divellere
se ab hoste cupientes inhiberent Rhodii, tractum
ancorale et implicitum remis latus alterum detersit;
debilitatam ea ipsa quae icta cohaeserat navis cepit.

---

[1] circumuentae ⟨⟩ : circumuectae B.
[2] ancora ed. Frobeniana 1535 : in ancora B⟨⟩.

---

[1] Appian (*Syr.* 27) gives somewhat different figures : the
Roman fleet consisted of 83 ships, of which 25 were Rhodian.
The enemy lost only 29 ships (in XL. lii. 6 Livy still insists
on 42). Even if we accept the account of Appian the Roman
losses were exceedingly small.

and while turning they exposed themselves broadside B.C. 190
to blows, and if one did clash it was covered by flames
pouring upon it, and they were more afraid of the fire
than of the battle. Nevertheless, as usual, the valour
of the soldiers had the greatest effect in the battle.
For when the Romans had broken the centre of the
hostile line, they swung around and took in the rear
the royal ships which were engaged with the
Rhodians; and in an instant of time both in the centre
and on the left flank the ships of Antiochus were surrounded and sunk. The uninjured right wing was
terrified more by the destruction of their comrades
than by their own peril; but after they saw the
others surrounded and the flagship of Polyxenidas
abandoning the allies and setting sail, they quickly
raised their top-sails—and the wind was favourable
for ships bound for Ephesus—and took to flight, with
a loss of forty-two ships in this fight, of which
thirteen were captured and fell into the hands of the
enemy and the rest were burned or sunk. Two
Roman ships were damaged severely, several somewhat injured [1]; one Rhodian ship was captured by
a curious accident. When it had struck a Sidonian
vessel with its beak, its anchor,[2] dislodged from its
own ship by the very shock, caught the prow of the
other ship with its fluke, falling like an iron hand;
then, in the ensuing excitement, since the Rhodians
backed water trying to disengage themselves from the
enemy, the anchor-cable, fouling the blades, swept
one side clean of oars; the crippled ship was then
captured by the very vessel which it had struck and

---

[2] The anchor was hung suspended abaft of the prow;
it might easily then have fallen as Livy says and served as a
grappling-iron.

A.U.C.
564

Hoc maxime modo ad Myonnesum navali proelio pugnatum est.

XXXI. Quo territus Antiochus, quia possessione maris pulsus longinqua tueri diffidebat se posse, praesidium ab Lysimachia, ne opprimeretur ibi ab Romanis, deduci pravo [1] ut res ipsa postea docuit,

2 consilio iussit. Non enim tueri solum Lysimachiam a primo impetu Romanorum facile erat, sed obsidionem etiam tota hieme tolerare et obsidentes quoque ad ultimam inopiam adducere extrahendo tempus et interim spem pacis per occasionem temp-

3 tare. Nec Lysimachiam tantum hostibus tradidit post adversam navalem pugnam, sed etiam Colophonis obsidione abscessit et Sardis recepit se;

4 atque inde in Cappadociam ad Ariarathen, qui auxilia [2] accerserent, et quocumque alio poterat, ad copias contrahendas, in unum iam consilium, ut acie dimicaret, intentus misit.

5 Regillus Aemilius post victoriam navalem profectus Ephesum, derectis ante portum navibus, cum confessionem ultimam concessi maris hosti expressisset, Chium, quo ante navale proelium cursum ab

6 Samo intenderat, navigat. Ibi naves in proelio quassatas cum refecisset, L. Aemilium Scaurum cum triginta navibus Hellespontum ad exercitum traiciendum misit, Rhodios parte praedae et spoliis

7 navalibus decoratos domum redire iubet. Rhodii

---

[1] prauo ς : *om. B.*
[2] auxilia ς : *om. B.*

---

[1] Lysimachia was strongly situated on the European side of the Hellespont and its abandonment removed the last obstacle in Scipio's way to Asia. Appian (*Syr.* 28) is equally severe with Antiochus and more specific.

grappled. In this manner, in the main, the sea-
fight off Myonnesus was conducted.

XXXI. Antiochus was alarmed at this because,
having lost his dominion of the sea, he doubted whether
he could defend his distant possessions, and ordered
his garrison withdrawn from Lysimachia,[1] lest it be
destroyed there by the Romans—a foolish decision,
as the actual outcome showed later. For it was not
only easy to defend Lysimachia from the first assault
of the Romans, but even to maintain a siege for an
entire winter and to reduce the besiegers even to the
extremity of want by dragging out the time and
meanwhile to try every chance to realize hopes of a
peaceful settlement. Not only did he surrender
Lysimachia to the enemy after the defeat on the sea,
but he abandoned the siege of Colophon and withdrew
to Sardis; and thence he sent agents to Ariarathes[2]
in Cappadocia to ask for auxiliaries, and he devoted
himself entirely, in every possible way, to collecting
troops, having now but one purpose—to settle the
question on the battle-field.

Aemilius Regillus after the naval victory proceeded
to Ephesus, and arraying his ships in front of the
harbour, when he had forced from the enemy the
final admission that he had yielded control of the sea,
he sailed to Chios, whither he had been bound before
the naval battle. When he had repaired there the
damaged ships, he sent Lucius Aemilius Scaurus with
thirty ships to the Hellespont to ferry the army
across, and the Rhodians, honoured with part of the
booty and naval trophies,[3] he ordered to return home;

[2] He was the son-in-law of Antiochus (Appian, *Syr.* 5).
[3] Usually captured figureheads and beaks, such as those
which gave their name to the Rostra in the Roman Forum.

LIVY

impigre praevertere ad traiciendas copias consulis ;
atque eo quoque functi officio, tum demum Rhodum
rediere. Classis Romana ab Chio Phocaeam traiecit.
8 In sinu maris intimo posita haec urbs est, oblonga
forma; duum milium et quingentorum passuum [1]
spatium murus amplectitur, coit deinde ex utraque
parte in artiorem velut cuneum; Lamptera ipsi
9 appellant. Mille et ducentos passus ibi latitudo
patet; inde lingua in altum mille passuum excurrens
medium fere sinum velut nota distinguit; ubi [2]
cohaeret faucibus angustis, duos in utramque
10 regionem versos portus tutissimos habet. Qui in
meridiem vergit, Naustathmon ab re appellant, quia
ingentem vim navium capit; alter prope ipsum
Lamptera est.

XXXII. Hos portus tutissimos cum occupasset
Romana classis, priusquam aut scalis [3] aut operibus
moenia aggrederetur, mittendos censuit praetor, qui
principum magistratuumque animos temptaret.
Postquam obstinatos vidit, duobus simul locis oppug-
2 nare est adortus. Altera pars infrequens aedificiis
erat; templa deum aliquantum tenebant loci; ea
prius ariete admoto quatere muros turresque coepit ;
3 dein cum eo multitudo occurreret ad defendendum,
4 altera quoque parte admotus aries; et iam utrimque
sternebantur muri. Ad quorum casum cum impetum Romani milites per ipsam stragem ruinarum
5 facerent, alii scalis etiam ascensum in muros temptarent, adeo obstinate restitere [4] oppidani ut facile

---

[1] passuum ⸑ : passus *B*.
[2] ubi *ed. Frobeniana* 1535 : urbs *B*⸑.
[3] aut scalis ⸑ : *om. B*.
[4] restitere ⸑ : resistere *B*.

the Rhodians in their zeal chose first to transport the B.C. 190
consul's army; and having finished this additional
task, then at length they returned to Rhodes. The
Roman fleet from Chios crossed to Phocaea. This
city is situated at the extremity of a bay of the sea
and is oblong in shape; it is surrounded by a wall
of twenty-five hundred paces in length and it grows
narrower at each end like a wedge; the people themselves call it Lampter.[1] There the width is twelve
hundred paces; thence a tongue, like a dividing line,
runs a mile into the sea, almost through the centre of
the bay; where it joins the narrow entrance-way it
produces two very safe harbours facing in opposite
directions. The one which faces south they call
Naustathmus, because it shelters a great number of
ships; the other is near Lampter itself.

XXXII. When these exceedingly safe harbours
had been occupied by the Roman fleet, before he
attacked the walls by either escalade or siege, the
praetor thought he should send agents to test the
attitude of the leading citizens and magistrates.
When he found them intractable he began to attack
in two places at once. One part was not thickly
built up; temples of the gods occupied much space;
here first he moved a battering-ram and began to
shake the walls and towers; then, when the multitude rushed to its defence, a ram was moved up
on the other side also; and now the walls were
being overthrown on both sides. As they fell in,
when the Roman soldiers were making their assault
right over the heaps of ruins and still others were
trying to climb the walls with ladders, the townspeople resisted so stubbornly that it was easily

[1] Literally, the lighthouse.

LIVY

appareret plus in armis et virtute quam in moenibus
6 auxilii esse. Coactus ergo periculo militum praetor
receptui cani iussit, ne obiceret incautos furentibus
7 desperatione ac rabie. Dirempto proelio, ne tum
quidem ad quietem versi, sed undique omnes ad
munienda et obmolienda quae ruinis strata erant
8 concurrerunt. Huic operi intentis supervenit Q.
Antonius a praetore missus, qui castigata pertinacia
eorum maiorem curam Romanis quam illis ostenderet
9 esse, ne in perniciem urbis pugnaretur ; si absistere
furore vellent, potestatem iis dari eadem condicione,
qua prius C. Livii in fidem venissent, se tradendi.
10 Haec cum audissent, quinque dierum spatio ad
deliberandum sumpto, temptata interim spe auxilii
ab Antiocho, postquam legati missi ad regem nihil [1]
in eo praesidii esse retulerant, tum portas aperuerunt,
11 pacti ne quid hostile paterentur. Cum signa in
urbem inferrentur et pronuntiasset praetor parci se
deditis velle, clamor undique est sublatus, indignum
facinus esse, Phocaeenses, numquam fidos socios,
12 semper infestos hostes, impune eludere. Ab hac
voce velut signo a praetore dato ad diripiendam
urbem passim discurrunt. Aemilius primo resistere
et revocare dicendo captas, non deditas diripi urbes
et in iis tamen imperatoris, non militum arbitrium

---

[1] ad regem nihil *edd. vett.* : ab rege *B* : ab rege nihil ⟨r⟩.

---

[1] Livy does not state them.
[2] Cf. ix. 1–5 above.

apparent that they placed more reliance on arms and B.C. 190 courage than in walls. Compelled, therefore, by the danger to his soldiers, the praetor ordered the recall sounded, lest he expose reckless men to those who were raging with despair and fury. When the fighting stopped, not even then did they turn to rest, but rushed in every direction to build and repair what had been laid in ruins. While engaged in this work, Quintus Antonius, sent by the praetor, approached them and, reproving their obstinacy, pointed out that it was more to the interest of the Romans than themselves that the fighting should not continue until the city was destroyed; if they wished to refrain from their madness, the opportunity was open to them of surrendering on the same terms as were granted when they submitted to Gaius Livius before.[1] When they heard this they took a space of five days to deliberate, meanwhile searching for some hope of aid from Antiochus; but after the ambassadors sent to the king had reported that there was no protection in him, then they opened the gates, bargaining that they should not be treated as enemies. When the standards entered the city and the praetor had proclaimed that he wished to spare the surrendered, there was a shout raised on all sides that it was a shameful thing that the Phocaeans, never faithful allies,[2] always dangerous foes, should get off scot-free. With such shouts, as if they had received a signal from the praetor, they rushed off in every direction to plunder the city. Aemilius at first opposed and tried to recall them, saying that captured, not surrendered, cities were plundered and that even so in these cases the decision rested with the commander, not the soldiers. After wrath and

LIVY

13 esse. Postquam ira et avaritia imperio potentiora
erant, praeconibus per urbem missis liberos omnes
in forum ad se convenire iubet, ne violarentur;
et in omnibus quae ipsius potestatis fuerunt fides
14 constitit praetoris: urbem agrosque et suas leges iis
restituit; et, quia hiems iam appetebat, Phocaeae
portus ad hibernandum classi delegit.

XXXIII. Per idem fere tempus consuli, trans-
gresso Aeniorum Maronitarumque fines, nuntiatur
victam regiam classem ad Myonnesum relictamque a
2 praesidio Lysimachiam esse. Id multo quam de navali
victoria laetius fuit, utique postquam eo venerunt,
refertaque urbs omnium rerum commeatibus velut
in adventum exercitus praeparatis eos excepit,[1] ubi
inopiam ultimam laboremque in obsidenda urbe
3 proposuerant sibi. Paucos dies stativa habuere,
impedimenta aegrique ut consequerentur, qui passim
per omnia Thraciae castella, fessi morbis ac longi-
4 tudine viae, relicti erant. Receptis omnibus ingressi
rursus iter per Chersonesum Hellespontum per-
veniunt. Ubi omnibus cura regis Eumenis ad
traiciendum praeparatis velut in pacata littora nullo
prohibente, aliis alio[2] delatis navibus, sine tumultu
5 traiecere. Ea vero res Romanis auxit animos,
concessum sibi transitum cernentibus[3] in Asiam,

---

[1] excepit ς : excit B.
[2] aliis alio ed. Mediolaniensis 1505 : alii alio B : alio aut
ab alio ς.
[3] transitum cernentibus edd. vett. : transire cernentibus
tum Bς.

---

[1] This resumes the narrative of Scipio's march through
Thrace. Part of the condensed account in vii. 16 above is
thus repeated.

greed proved stronger than authority, he sent heralds B.C. 190 through the city ordering all freemen to assemble in the forum in his presence, if they would escape harm; and in everything which was under his control the word of the praetor held good; the city, the farm-lands and their laws were restored to them; and, since winter was approaching, he chose the harbours of Phocaea as the winter station for the fleet.

XXXIII. About the same time the consul,[1] having crossed the territories of the Aenians and Maronians, received the news of the defeat of the royal fleet off Myonnesus and the abandonment of Lysimachia by its garrison. This gave him much greater joy than the naval victory, especially after they arrived there, and the city, filled with supplies of all kinds stored up as if for the arrival of the army, received them, where they had pictured to themselves the prospect of extreme want and hardship in besieging the city. For a few days they remained there, in order that the baggage might catch up, and the sick who, throughout all the forts of Thrace, exhausted by illness and the length of the march had been left behind. When all had rejoined they again took up the march through Chersonesus and came to the Hellespont. There all preparation for crossing had been made through the energy of King Eumenes,[2] and they crossed to shores in, as it were, a state of peace, with no one opposing them, without confusion, different ships seeking different ports. This circum-stance increased the ardour of the Romans, seeing that the crossing into Asia had been conceded to them, which they had believed would be the occasion

[2] Livy neglects to mention the services rendered by Scaurus and the Rhodians.

LIVY

quam rem magni certaminis futuram crediderant.
6 Stativa deinde ad Hellespontum aliquamdiu habuerunt, quia dies forte, quibus ancilia moventur, religiosi
7 ad iter inciderant. Idem dies P. Scipionem propiore
etiam religione, quia salius erat,[1] diiunxerant [2] ab
exercitu; causaque et is ipse morae erat, dum
consequeretur.

XXXIV. Per eos forte dies legatus ab Antiocho
in castra venerat Byzantius Heraclides, de pace
2 adferens mandata; quam impetrabilem fore magnam
ei spem attulit mora et cunctatio Romanorum, quos,
simul Asiam attigissent, effuso agmine ad castra regia
3 ituros crediderat. Statuit tamen non prius consulem adire quam P. Scipionem, et ita mandatum
ab [3] rege erat. In eo maximam spem habebat,
praeterquam quod et magnitudo animi et satietas
4 gloriae placabilem eum maxime faciebat, notumque
erat gentibus, qui victor ille in Hispania, qui deinde
in Africa fuisset, etiam quod filius eius captus in
5 potestate regis erat. Is ubi et quando et quo casu
captus sit, sicut pleraque alia, parum inter auctores
constat. Alii principio belli, a Chalcide Oreum

[1] erat ς : om. B.
[2] diiunxerant J. F. Gronovius : deuinxerant B : disiunxe-
rant M : deiunxerat (-ant) ς.
[3] mandatum ab ς : mandatus a B.

---

[1] The *ancilia* were a set of twelve shields, one of which had
fallen from heaven in the time of Numa. Since the safety
of Rome depended upon it, Numa had eleven duplicates made,
so that no one knew which was the original. Their care was
entrusted to a college of priests called the *Salii*. Every March
(this again indicates serious dislocation of the calendar)
the shields were carried around the city (*ancilia movere*), and
these days were *religiosi*, or days on which only necessary
duties were performed (Festus, p. 278). It is uncertain how

of a great battle. Then for a considerable time B.C. 190
they remained stationary in camp on the Hellespont,
because it happened that the days on which the
ancilia [1] were moved were sacred and had fallen in
the period of the journey. These same days had
detached Publius Scipio from the army, their religious
character concerning him even more because he was
a Salian priest [2]; he too caused a delay until he
overtook the army.

XXXIV. During these days, by chance, an ambassador from Antiochus had come to the camp,
Heraclides of Byzantium, bringing instructions about
peace; real hope that this was attainable was created
in him by the delay and procrastination of the
Roman army, which, he had believed, as soon as they
reached Asia would make at full speed for the camp
of the king. He decided to approach first not the
consul but Publius Scipio, and so he had been
instructed by the king. In him he placed his greatest
hopes, for in addition to the fact that both the
greatness of his soul and his having had his fill of
glory rendered him especially approachable, it was
known to all men what kind of conqueror he had been
in Spain and later in Africa, his son also was a
prisoner in the hands of the king. Where and when
and by what chance he had been captured, like many
other things, is by no means unanimously explained
by the sources. Some say that at the beginning of
the war, when he was travelling from Chalcis to

scrupulously an army on campaign observed them, but in this
case it appears that Scipio grasped this convenient opportunity
for their observance; see the following note.

[2] Africanus apparently took his duties seriously even during
a war.

LIVY

petentem, circumventum ab regiis navibus tradunt;
6 alii, postquam transitum in Asiam est, cum turma
Fregellana missum exploratum ad regia castra, effuso
obviam equitatu cum reciperet sese, in eo tumultu
delapsum ex equo [1] cum duobus equitibus oppressum,
7 ita ad regem deductum esse. Illud satis [2] constat,
si pax cum populo Romano [3] maneret hospitiumque
privatim regi cum [4] Scipionibus esset, neque liberalius
neque benignius haberi colique adolescentem quam
8 cultus est potuisse. Ob haec cum adventum P.
Scipionis legatus expectasset, ubi is venit, consulem
adit petitque ut mandata audiret.

XXXV. Advocato frequenti consilio legati verba
2 sunt audita. Is, multis ante legationibus ultro
citroque nequiquam de pace missis, eam ipsam
fiduciam impetrandi sibi esse dixit, quod priores
legati nihil impetrassent: Zmyrnam enim et Lampsacum
et Alexandriam Troadem et Lysimachiam in
3 Europa iactatas in illis disceptationibus esse; quarum
Lysimachia iam cessisse regem, ne quid habere eum
in Europa dicerent; eas quae in Asia sint civitates
tradere paratum esse, et si quas alias Romani, quod
suarum partium fuerint, vindicare ab imperio regio
4 velint; impensae quoque in bellum factae partem
dimidiam regem praestaturum populo Romano.

---

[1] in eo tumultu delapsum ex equo *Kreyssig*: delapsum
equo *B*: in eo delapsum tumultu ex equo *M*: in eo tumultu ς.
[2] illud satis ς: *om. B.*
[3] populo romano ς: praetore *B.*
[4] regi cum ς: regium *B.*

---

[1] The first three cities here mentioned have frequently been
spoken of by Livy: cf. *e.g.* XXXV. xlii. 2; Lysimachia has
not figured in the debates and Polybius (XXI. xiii) omits it
from his account of this incident.

Oreus, he was surrounded by the king's ships, others B.C. 190
that after they had crossed to Asia he had been sent
with a troop from Fregellae to reconnoitre in the
direction of the king's camp, and that when the
cavalry rushed out to meet them and he had retreated,
in the confusion he had fallen from his horse and had
been captured with two troopers and so conducted
to the king. What is well established is that if peace
had continued with the Roman people and if personal
relations of mutual hospitality had existed between
the king and the Scipios, the young man could not
have been treated and entertained with greater
kindliness and generosity than he had received.
For these reasons, when the ambassador had waited
for the arrival of Publius Scipio, at his coming he
called upon the consul and begged him to hear his
instructions.

XXXV. A full council was called and the speech
of the envoy was heard. He said that, after many
earlier embassies about peace had been sent backwards and forwards in vain, his own very confidence
was due to the fact that the previous ambassadors had
succeeded in nothing : for Zmyrna and Lampsacus
and Alexandria Troas and Lysimachia [1] in Europe
had been objects of contention in those discussions ;
of these, the king had already withdrawn from
Lysimachia, that they might not say that he had
possessions in Europe ; the cities in Asia he was
ready to surrender, and any other cities which the
Romans, because they belonged to their party,
wished to separate from the king's realm ; of the
money too which had been spent on the war, the
king would guarantee to the Roman people the
payment of one-half. These were the terms of

5 Hae condiciones erant pacis; reliqua oratio fuit ut memores rerum humanarum et suae fortunae moderarentur et alienam ne urgerent. Finirent Europa imperium, id quoque immensum esse;
6 et parari singula acquirendo facilius potuisse quam
7 universa teneri posse; quod si Asiae quoque partem aliquam abstrahere velint, dummodo non dubiis regionibus finiant, vinci suam temperantiam Romana cupiditate pacis et concordiae causa regem passurum. Ea, quae legato magna ad pacem impetrandam
8 videbantur, parva Romanis visa: nam et impensam quae in bellum facta esset, omnem praestare regem
9 aequum censebant, cuius culpa bellum excitatum esset, et non Ionia modo atque Aeolide deduci debere
10 regia praesidia, sed [1] sicut Graecia omnis liberata esset, ita quae in Asia sint omnes liberari urbes; id aliter fieri non posse, quam ut cis Taurum montem possessione Asiae Antiochus cedat.

XXXVI. Legatus postquam [2] nihil aequi in consilio impetrare se censebat, privatim—sic enim imperatum erat—P. Scipionis temptare animum est
2 conatus. Omnium primum filium ei sine pretio redditurum regem dixit; deinde ignarus et animi Scipionis et moris Romani, auri pondus ingens pollicitus, et nomine tantum regio [3] excepto societatem omnis regni, si per eum pacem impetrasset.
3 Ad ea Scipio: " Quod Romanos omnes, quod me ad

---

[1] sed ϛ: si B.
[2] legatus postquam ϛ: postquam legatus B.
[3] regio ϛ: regio et B.

---

[1] Polybius omits this comparison of Asia and Greece.

peace; the rest of his speech was that mindful of B.C. 190 human destiny, they should deal temperately with their own fortune and not hardly with that of others. Let them limit their empire to Europe, that even this was very large; that it was possible to conquer and gain it part by part more easily than to hold the whole; but if they wished to take some part of Asia too, provided they limited it by easily recognizable natural features, the king would permit his own self-restraint to be overcome by Roman greed for the sake of peace and harmony. What seemed to the ambassador great incentives for concluding peace seemed unimportant to the Romans: as to the money that had been spent on the war, they deemed it only fair that the king should assume payment of it all, since it was by his fault that the war had been fomented, and that the king's garrisons should be withdrawn not only from Ionia and Aeolis, but, just as all Greece had been liberated, so all the cities which were in Asia should be set free[1]; this could not be accomplished otherwise than by the retirement of Antiochus from the occupation of Asia on this side of the Taurus mountains.

XXXVI. Since the ambassador realized that he could obtain no fairness in the council, he tried privately—for such were his orders—to win over Publius Scipio. First of all, he said that the king would restore to him his son without a ransom; then, ignorant of both the spirit of Scipio and the Roman tradition, he promised him a great sum of money and, with the single exception of the title of king, partnership in the entire kingdom if, through his aid, he succeeded in obtaining peace. To this Scipio replied: "That you do not know the Romans

LIVY

quem missus es ignoras, minus miror, cum te fortu-
4 nam eius a quo venis ignorare cernam. Lysimachia
tenenda erat, ne Chersonesum intraremus, aut ad
Hellespontum obsistendum, ne in Asiam traiceremus,
si pacem tamquam ab sollicitis de belli eventu
5 petituri eratis; concesso vero in Asiam transitu et
non solum frenis, sed etiam iugo accepto quae disceptatio ex aequo, cum imperium patiendum sit,
6 relicta est? Ego ex munificentia regia maximum
donum filium habebo; aliis, deos precor, ne umquam
7 fortuna egeat mea; animus certe non egebit. Pro
tanto in me munere gratum me in se esse sentiet, si
privatam gratiam pro privato beneficio desiderabit;
publice,[1] nec habebo [2] quicquam ab illo nec dabo.
8 Quod in praesentia dare possim, fidele consilium
est. Abi, nuntia [3] meis verbis, bello absistat, pacis
9 condicionem nullam recuset." Nihil ea moverunt
regem, tutam fore belli aleam ratum, quando perinde
ac victo iam [4] sibi leges dicerentur. Omissa igitur
in praesentia mentione pacis totam curam in belli
apparatum intendit.

XXXVII. Consul omnibus praeparatis ad propo-
sita exsequenda cum ex stativis movisset, Dardanum

---

[1] desiderabit; publice *ed. Frobeniana* 1535: desiderabit
publici *B* : desiderabit sed publice *M* : desiderat sed publice
(publici) ς.
[2] habebo ς: habeo *B*.
[3] est. abi nuntia ς: *om., spat. rel. B.*
[4] uicto iam ς: uictoriam *B*.

---

[1] Livy has been at some pains to portray in this speech the
incorruptible Roman, who will, while he accepts, allow not
even the greatest private obligation to influence his public
conduct. The rest of this narrative, save for this interpretation, is found in Polybius (XXI. xv).
[2] Antiochus had now nothing to lose by fighting, since the

as a race, that you do not know me, to whom you B.C. 190
have been sent, I am less surprised to find since I
see that you do not know the situation of the man
from whom you come. Lysimachia should have
been held, to prevent our entering the Chersonesus,
or resistance should have been offered at the Hellespont, to prevent our crossing into Asia, if you intended
to ask peace from foes who were anxious about the
outcome of the war; but when we were given
passage into Asia and when not only our reins
but also our yoke was accepted, what debate is
left on the basis of equity, when you are obliged
to put up with our sovereignty? Of the generous
offers of the king, I accept the greatest, my son;
as to the rest, I pray the gods that my estate
will never need them; my soul, at any rate, will not
need them. In return for so great a gift to me, he
will find me grateful to him if he desires private
gratitude in return for a private kindness; in my
public capacity I shall take nothing from him and
give him nothing. What I can give him at this
moment is my sincere advice. Go, advise him in
my words that he abandon the war and refuse no
terms of peace." [1] His words had no effect upon
the king, who thought that the gamble of war would
be a safe one, since even now terms were declared
to him as if he already had been defeated. Mention
of peace was forgotten for the moment, and all his
energy was devoted to preparation for war.[2]

XXXVII. When everything was ready for the
execution of his designs and when he had moved
from his base, the consul first advanced to Dardanus

terms of peace were already as severe as they were ever likely
to be.

LIVY

primum, deinde Rhoeteum utraque civitate obviam
2 effusa [1] venit. Inde Ilium processit, castrisque in
campo qui est subiectus [2] moenibus positis in urbem
3 arcemque cum escendisset, sacrificavit Minervae
praesidi arcis et Iliensibus in omni rerum verborum-
que honore ab se oriundos Romanos praeferentibus
et Romanis laetis origine sua. Inde profecti [3]
4 sextis castris ad caput Caici amnis pervenerunt. Eo
et [4] Eumenes rex, primo conatus ab Hellesponto
reducere classem in hiberna Elaeam, adversis deinde
ventis cum aliquot [5] diebus superare Lecton promunturium non potuisset, in terram egressus, ne deesset
principiis rerum, qua proximum fuit, in castra
5 Romana cum [6] parva manu contendit. Ex castris
Pergamum remissus ad commeatus expediendos,
tradito frumento quibus iusserat consul, in eadem
stativa rediit. Inde plurium dierum praeparatis
cibariis consilium erat ire ad hostem priusquam
hiems opprimeret.
6 Regia castra circa Thyatiram erant. Ubi cum
audisset Antiochus P. Scipionem aegrum Elaeam
delatum, legatos qui filium ad eum reducerent misit.

[1] utraque ciuitate obuiam effusa ς : utramque ciuitatem
obuiam effusam B.
[2] subiectus ς : obiectus B.
[3] profecti ς : profectis B : profectus B (ex corr.).
[4] eo et ed. Frobeniana 1535 : eo et omnes Bς.
[5] aliquot ed. Aldina : aliquot deinde Bς.
[6] cum ς : om. B.

---

[1] The tradition of the Roman descent from the Trojans was
already familiar in the second century B.C.: cf. XXIX.
xii. 14.
[2] The maladjustment of the Roman calendar makes the
chronology of the campaign difficult, and efforts to find a
solution must be regarded as unsuccessful. It suffices here

and then to Rhoeteum, and both peoples thronged B.C. 190
to meet him. Then he went on to Ilium, and encamp-
ing on the level ground which lies below the walls,
he went up to the city and the citadel and offered
sacrifice to Minerva, the guardian of the citadel; the
people of Ilium, on their part, with every mark of
honour in deed or word proclaiming the Romans as descendants, and the Romans rejoicing in their descent.[1]
Departing thence, on the sixth day of marching they
came to the mouth of the Caïcus river. Thither too
came King Eumenes, having first tried to conduct
his fleet back from the Hellespont to Elaea to winter,
but then when on account of opposing winds he could
not for several days round the promontory of Lecton,
he disembarked at the nearest point, so as not to miss
the preliminaries of the campaign, and hastened to the
Roman camp with a small force. From his camp he
was sent back to Pergamum to obtain supplies, and
when he had delivered the grain to the consul as he was
directed, he returned to the same station. From
there the plan was, after previously preparing several
days' rations, to march against the enemy before
winter should prevent.[2]

The king's camp was near Thyatira. When
Antiochus learned there that Publius Scipio was sick
and had been taken to Elaea, he sent ambassadors to
return his son to him. The gift was not only grateful

to assemble the evidence of Livy: (1) the eclipse of March
14, dated by Livy July 11 (iv. 4 and the note); (2) the preparations for wintering made by Aemilius (xxxii. 14) and by
Eumenes (sect. 4 above); (3) the prospective approach of
winter (xxxix. 2); (4) the observance, probably belated,
of the festival of the *ancilia* (xxxiii. 6). Beloch (p. 387, quoting
Diest through Kromayer) says that the rainy season in this
region begins in November.

LIVY

7 Non animo solum patrio gratum munus, sed corpori
8 quoque salubre gaudium fuit; satiatusque tandem
complexu filii " renuntiate " inquit " gratias regi me
agere, referre aliam gratiam nunc non posse quam
ut suadeam, ne ante in aciem descendat quam in
9 castra me redisse audierit." Quamquam sexaginta
milia peditum, plus duodecim milia equitum animos
interdum ad spem certaminis faciebant, motus
tamen Antiochus tanti auctoritate viri, in quo ad
incertos belli eventus omnis fortunae posuerat
subsidia, recepit se[1] et transgressus Phrygium
amnem circa[2] Magnesiam quae ad Sipylum est
10 posuit castra; et ne, si[3] extrahere tempus vellet,
munimenta Romani temptarent, fossam sex cubita
11 altam, duodecim latam cum duxisset, extra duplex
vallum fossae circumdedit, interiore labro murum
cum turribus crebris obiecit, unde facile arceri
transitu fossae hostis posset.

XXXVIII. Consul circa Thyatiram esse regem
ratus, continuis itineribus quinto die ad Hyrcanum
2 campum descendit. Inde cum profectum audisset,
secutus vestigia citra[4] Phrygium amnem, quattuor
3 milia ab hoste posuit castra. Eo mille ferme equites
—maxima pars Gallograeci erant, et Dahae quidam
aliarumque gentium sagittarii equites intermixti—
tumultuose amni traiecto in stationes impetum
4 fecerunt. Primo turbaverunt incompositos; dein,

---

[1] recepit se ς : recepit B.
[2] circa ς : circaque B.
[3] ne si ed. Frobeniana 1535 : ne B : nisi M : ne dum ς.
[4] citra ς : circa B.

---

[1] Livy's description is vague and the fortifications unusual
in design if I have interpreted correctly. I understand
fossae with *labro*.

to a father's heart, but the joy was healing also to his B.C. 190
body; and at length sated with embracing his son, he
said, "Take the message to the king that I tender
my thanks to him, but at present I can show my
gratitude in no other way than to counsel him not
to come forth in line of battle until he hears that I
have returned to camp." Although sixty thousand
infantry and more than twelve thousand cavalry
sometimes inspired his mind with hope as to the
battle, yet Antiochus, moved by the authority
of so great a man (in whom, having regard to the
uncertain issues of war, he had placed his every hope
of assistance), retired, crossed the river Phrygius and
established his camp in the vicinity of Magnesia,
which is near Sipylus; and, inasmuch as he wished
to delay matters, that the Romans might not attempt
his fortifications, when he had constructed a ditch
six cubits deep and twelve cubits wide, on the outside
he threw a double wall around the trench, on the
inner lip of which he raised a wall with numerous
towers, whence the enemy could easily be prevented
from crossing the ditch.[1]

XXXVIII. The consul, thinking that the king was
near Thyatira, marching continuously, came down
on the fifth day into the Hyrcanian plain. When he
found that the king had gone, following his trail
along the river Phrygius, he encamped four miles
from the enemy. There about a thousand cavalry
—they were mostly Galatians with some Dahae and
mounted archers [2] of other tribes mixed with them
—crossing the river in a confused mass, made an
attack on the outguards. At first this threw them
into confusion, since they were not in formation;

[2] Cf. XXXV. xlviii. 3–5.

399

cum longius certamen fieret et[1] Romanorum ex
propinquis castris facili[2] subsidio cresceret numerus,
regii fessi iam et plures non sustinentes recipere se
conati circa ripam amnis, priusquam flumen in-
grederentur, ab instantibus tergo aliquot interfecti
5 sunt. Biduum[3] deinde silentium fuit neutris trans-
gredientibus amnem; tertio post die Romani simul
omnes transgressi sunt et duo milia fere et quin-
6 gentos passus ab hoste posuerunt castra. Metanti-
bus et muniendo occupatis tria milia delecta equitum
peditumque regiorum magno terrore ac tumultu
7 advenere; aliquanto pauciores in statione erant;
hi tamen per se, nullo a[4] munimento castrorum milite
avocato, et primo aequum proelium sustinuerunt,
et crescente certamine pepulerunt hostes centum ex
8 iis occisis, centum ferme captis. Per quadriduum
insequens instructae utrimque acies pro vallo stetere;
quinto die Romani processere in medium campi;
9 Antiochus nihil promovit signa, ita ut extremi
minus mille pedes a vallo abessent.

XXXIX. Consul postquam detractari certamen
vidit, postero die in consilium advocavit, quid sibi
faciendum esset, si Antiochus pugnandi copiam non
2 faceret? Instare hiemem; aut sub pellibus haben-
dos milites fore,[5] aut, si concedere in hiberna vellet,
3 differendum esse in aestatem bellum. Nullum

---

[1] et *Duker*: *om.* B⌐.
[2] propinquis castris facili *ed. Frobeniana* 1535: propinquo
castris facile B⌐.
[3] biduum ⌐: *om.* B.
[4] a *edd. vett.*: *om.* B⌐.
[5] fore ⌐: *om.* B.

then, as the battle continued for a longer time and B.C. 190
the number of the Romans increased, it being easy
to reinforce them from the adjacent camp, the king's
troops were wearied and, unable to withstand the
larger numbers, tried to retire along the banks of the
river, and before they crossed the stream many were
killed by the Romans, who pressed on from the rear.
For the next two days everything was quiet, neither
side crossing the river; on the third day after, the
Romans all crossed the river at the same time and
made camp about twenty-five hundred paces from
the enemy. As they were laying out the camp and
engaged in fortifying it, about three thousand picked
infantry and cavalry from the king's army came up,
causing great fear and confusion; the number on
outpost was considerably smaller; they nevertheless
by themselves, without calling away any troops from
the fortifying of the camp, both at first kept the
contest even and later, as the battle grew more
fierce, beat off the enemy, killing a hundred of them
and capturing about a hundred. For the next four
days both battle-lines were drawn up and stood
before the ramparts; on the fifth day the Romans
advanced to the middle of the space; Antiochus did
not advance his standards, but stood so that his rear
troops were less than a thousand paces from the wall.

XXXIX. After the consul perceived that the
enemy declined to fight, he called a council the next
day, to consider what they should do if Antiochus
would not give them an opportunity for a battle.
Winter, he said, was at hand; either they would
have to keep the troops in tents or, if it was decided
to withdraw to winter quarters, the war would have
to be postponed to the summer. No enemy was

LIVY

umquam hostem Romani aeque contempserunt.
Conclamatum undique est duceret extemplo et
4 uteretur ardore militum qui tamquam non pugnandum cum tot milibus hostium, sed par numerus
pecorum trucidandus esset, per fossas, per vallum
castra invadere parati erant, si in proelium hostis
5 non exiret. Cn. Domitius ad explorandum iter, et
qua parte adiri hostium vallum posset, missus, postquam omnia certa rettulit, postero die propius
admoveri castra placuit; tertio signa in medium
6 campi prolata et instrui acies coepta est. Nec
Antiochus ultra tergiversandum ratus, ne et suorum
animos minueret detractando certamen et hostium
spem augeret, et ipse copias eduxit, tantum progressus
a castris ut dimicaturum appareret.
7 Romana acies unius prope formae fuit et hominum
et armorum genere. Duae legiones Romanae, duae
socium ac Latini nominis erant; quina milia et quad-
8 ringenos [1] singulae habebant. Romani mediam
aciem, cornua Latini tenuerunt; hastatorum prima
signa dein principum erant, triarii postremos claude-
9 bant. Extra hanc velut iustam aciem a parte

---

[1] quadringenos *ed. Frobeniana* 1535 : quadrigenos *Bς*.

---

[1] The Latin organizations were usually called *alae* (XXXI.
xxi. 7 and the note), and this word may have dropped out here.
It is equally possible that Polybius did not distinguish them
in this case.

[2] The usual strength was 5,000 (XXVI. xxviii. 7) or 5,200
men (XL. xxxi. 2), but was sometimes as high as 6,200
(XXIX. xxiv. 14).

[3] This is the typical battle formation of the legion, the three
lines corresponding roughly to the modern front-line, support
and reserve. Each unit of *hastati*, who formed also the
skirmish-line, occupied enough frontage to permit the

B.C. 190

ever held in such contempt by the Romans. The
cry from all sides was that he should immediately lead
them out and take advantage of the enthusiasm of
the soldiers, who, as if their task was, not to fight
with so many thousands of the enemy, but to slaughter
the same number of cattle, were ready to attack
the camp over ditch, over wall, if the enemy would
not come out to fight. Gnaeus Domitius was sent
to reconnoitre the route of approach and where
they could come up to the enemy's rampart, and
when he brought back complete and definite information, it was decided that on the following day they
would move the camp nearer; on the third day the
standards were advanced to the centre of the space
and the battle-line began to form. Nor did Antiochus think that he should remain longer on the
defensive, lest he both diminish the courage of his
own men by declining battle and increase the hopes
of the enemy, and he too led out his forces, advancing
so far from the camp that it was clear that he meant
to engage.

The Roman battle-line is generally about uniform
in its arrangement, both as to number and as to their
equipment. There were two Roman legions and
two [1] of allies of the Latin confederacy; each consisted of five thousand four hundred men.[2] The
Romans held the centre, the Latins the flanks; the
advanced units were the *hastati*, then came the
principes; the *triarii* held the rear.[3] Outside this,
which may be called the regular battle-line, on the

---

principes to pass through them as reinforcements and replacements; the *triarii* were held out until the decisive blow was
to be struck or a counter-attack organized.

LIVY

dextra consul Achaeorum caetratis immixtos auxiliares Eumenis, tria milia ferme peditum, aequata
fronte instruxit; ultra eos equitum minus tria milia
opposuit, ex quibus Eumenis octingenti, reliquus
10 omnis Romanus equitatus erat; extremos Tralles et
Cretenses—quingentorum utrique numerum exple-
11 bant—statuit. Laevum cornu non egere videbatur
obiectis [1] talibus auxiliis, quia flumen ab ea parte
ripaeque deruptae claudebant; quattuor tamen inde
12 turmae equitum oppositae. Haec summa copiarum
erat Romanis, et duo milia mixtorum Macedonum
Thracumque, qui voluntate secuti erant; hi praesidio
13 castris relicti sunt. Sedecim elephantos post triarios
in subsidio [2] locaverunt; nam praeterquam quod
multitudinem regiorum elephantorum—erant autem
quattuor et quinquaginta—sustinere non videbantur
posse, ne pari quidem numero Indicis Africi resistunt,
sive quia magnitudine—longe enim illi praestant—
sive robore animorum vincuntur.[3]

XL. Regia acies varia magis multis gentibus,
dissimilitudine armorum auxiliorumque erat. Decem
et sex milia peditum more Macedonum armati
2 fuere, qui phalangitae appellabantur. Haec media
acies fuit, in fronte in decem partes divisa; partes
eas interpositis binis elephantis distinguebat; a
fronte introrsus in [4] duos et triginta ordines armatorum
3 acies patebat. Hoc et roboris in regiis copiis erat,

---

[1] non egere videbatur obiectis *M. Müller* : non uerebatur
obiectis *B* : non uidebatur egere *M.*

[2] in subsidio ς : om. *B.*

[3] uincuntur ς : uincentur *B.*   [4] in ς : inter *BM.*

right flank and in line with the legions, the consul placed the auxiliaries of Eumenes mixed with the Achaean "targeteers," being about three thousand infantry; outside them he stationed less than three thousand cavalry, eight hundred of whom belonged to Eumenes, all the rest being Roman [1] cavalry; on the extreme flank he placed the Tralli and Cretans, each contingent amounting to about five hundred men. The left flank did not seem to need such auxiliaries placed there, since the river and its steep banks gave protection on that side; nevertheless, he stationed there four troops of cavalry. This was the whole of the Roman force, with two thousand Macedonians and Thracians who had followed as volunteers; they were left as a guard for the camp. They placed sixteen elephants in reserve behind the *triarii*, for, in addition to the fact that they seemed unable to face the greater number of the king's elephants—there were fifty-four of them—African elephants cannot resist even an equal number of Indian, whether because the latter are superior in size—for in fact they are far larger—or in fighting spirit.

XL. The king's battle-line was more varied, made up of many races and auxiliary forces differently armed. There were sixteen thousand infantry armed in the Macedonian fashion, who are called *phalangitae*.[2] They formed the centre of the line, and their frontage was divided into ten sections; these sections were separated by intervals in which two elephants each were placed; from the front the formation extended thirty-two ranks in depth. This was the main strength of the king's army, and

---

[1] This seems to include the Latin cavalry.

[2] Cf. XXXVI. xviii. 2.

LIVY

et perinde cum alia specie tum eminentibus tantum [1]
inter armatos elephantis magnum terrorem praebe-
4 bat. Ingentes ipsi erant; addebant speciem fronta-
lia et cristae et tergo impositae turres turribusque
superstantes praeter rectorem quaterni armati.
5 Ad latus dextrum phalangitarum mille et quingentos
Gallograecorum pedites opposuit. His tria milia
equitum [2] loricatorum—cataphractos ipsi appellant—
adiunxit. Addita his ala mille ferme equitum;
6 agema eam [3] vocabant; Medi erant, lecti viri, et
eiusdem regionis mixti multarum gentium equites.
Continens his grex sedecim elephantorum est op-
7 positus in subsidiis. Ab eadem parte, paulum
producto cornu, regia cohors erat [4]; argyraspides a
8 genere armorum appellabantur; Dahae deinde,
equites sagittarii,[5] mille et ducenti; tum levis
armatura, trium milium, pari ferme numero, pars
Cretenses, pars Tralles; duo milia et quingenti Mysi
9 sagittarii his adiuncti erant. Extremum cornu
claudebant quattuor milia, mixti [6] Cyrtii funditores
10 et Elymaei sagittarii. Ab laevo cornu phalangitis
adiuncti erant Gallograeci pedites mille et quingenti
et [7] similiter his armati duo milia Cappadocum—
11 ab Ariarathe missi erant regi [8]; inde auxiliares
mixti omnium generum, duo milia septingenti, et
tria milia cataphractorum equitum et mille alii equites,

---

[1] tantum ς : om. B.
[2] equitum Sigonius : peditum Bς.
[3] agema eam ed. Frobeniana 1535 : haegemean B : ageam
eam M : haec gemeam ς.
[4] erat ς : om. B.
[5] sagittarii ed. Frobeniana 1535 : sagittariorum Bς.
[6] mixti ς : misti M : om. B.
[7] et ed. Frobeniana 1535 : om. Bς.
[8] regi ς : regii B.

it caused great terror, not only from its general
appearance, but by reason of the elephants, standing
out especially conspicuously among the soldiers.
They were of great size; head-armour and crests
and towers placed upon their backs, and, in addition
to the driver, four soldiers riding in each tower, added
to their impressiveness. On the right of the *phalangitae* he stationed fifteen hundred Galatian
infantry. To these he added three thousand
armoured cavalry—they call them *cataphracti*.[1] In
addition to these there was a squadron of about
a thousand cavalry; they called it the *agema*;[2]
they were Medes, picked men, and cavalry from
many races in the same region mingled with them.
Adjoining them a herd of sixteen elephants was
posted in reserve. On this side, the flank being
advanced a little, was the royal bodyguard; they
were called *argyraspides*[3] from the character of their
equipment; then the Dahae, mounted archers, to the
number of twelve hundred; then the light infantry,
three thousand in number, about equally divided
between Cretans and Tralli; to them two thousand
five hundred Mysian archers were added. The
extremity of this flank consisted of four thousand
mixed Cyrtians, slingers, and Elymaeans, archers. On
the left flank, next the *phalangitae*, were posted fifteen
hundred Galatian infantry and two thousand Cappa-
docians similarly armed—they had been sent to the
king by Ariarathes; then twenty-seven hundred
auxiliaries mixed from all races, and three thousand
armoured cavalry and one thousand other cavalry,

---

[1] Cf. XXXV. xlviii. 3.

[2] In XLII. lviii. 9 (cf. note), the *agema* seems to be distinguished from the *equitum sacra, alia,* lii. 4.

[3] They carried silver shields.

LIVY

regia ala levioribus tegumentis suis equorumque,
alio haud dissimili habitu; Syri plerique erant
12 Phrygibus et Lydis immixti. Ante hunc equitatum
falcatae quadrigae et cameli quos appellant dromadas.
His insidebant Arabes sagittarii, gladios tenues
habentes longos quaterna cubita, ut ex tanta alti-
13 tudine contingere hostem possent. Inde alia multitudo, par ei, quae in dextro cornu erat [1]: primi
Tarentini, deinde Gallograecorum equitum duo
milia et quingenti, inde Neocretes mille et eodem
armatu Cares et Cilices mille et quingenti et totidem
14 Tralles et quattuor milia caetratorum: Pisidae erant
et Pamphylii et Lycii; tum Cyrtiorum et Elymaeo-
rum paria in dextro cornu locatis auxilia, et sedecim
elephanti modico intervallo distantes.

XLI. Rex ipse in dextro cornu erat [2]; Seleucum
filium et Antipatrum fratris filium in laevo praeposuit [3]; media acies tribus permissa, Minnioni et
Zeuxidi et Philippo, magistro elephantorum.
2 Nebula matutina, crescente die levata in nubes,
caliginem dedit; umor inde ab austro velut pluvia [4]
3 perfudit omnia; quae nihil admodum Romanis,
eadem perincommoda regiis erant; nam et ob-
scuritas lucis in acie modica Romanis non adimebat

---

[1] erat ς : erant B.
[2] cornu erat ς : om. B.
[3] praeposuit ς : proposuit B.
[4] pluvia H. J. Müller, sed non omnino placet : om. Bς.

---

[1] Livy has not accounted for the 60,000 infantry and more
than 12,000 cavalry of xxxvii. 9 above (about 43,700 infantry
and 12,000 cavalry). But Antiochus held out a strong guard
for the camp, and Livy does not give the strength of all the
contingents. Appian (Syr. 32) differs from Livy in several
respects.

the royal squadron, with lighter armour for them- B.C. 190
selves and their horses, but otherwise with equipment not unlike the rest; they were mostly Syrians
mingled with Phrygians and Lydians. In front of
this cavalry were scythe-bearing chariots and camels
of the breed called dromedaries. These were ridden
by Arab archers carrying slender swords four cubits
long, that they might be able to reach the enemy
from so great a height. Then came another great
crowd, corresponding to that on the right flank:
first the Tarentini, then twenty-five hundred Galatian
cavalry, next a thousand Neocretans and fifteen
hundred Carians and Cilicians similarly equipped, and
the same number of Tralli and four thousand " targeteers ": these were Pisidians and Pamphylians
and Lycians; then auxiliaries of the Cyrtians and
Elymaeans equal to those stationed on the right
flank, and sixteen elephants a short distance away.[1]

XLI. The king himself was on the right flank;
he placed his son Seleucus and Antipater the son of
his brother on the left; the centre of the line was
entrusted to three commanders, Minnio and Zeuxis
and Philippus, the master of the elephants.[2]

A morning mist, lightening into clouds as the day
advanced, caused a fog; the moisture from this, like
a rain brought on by the west wind, covered everything; these conditions brought absolutely no dis-
comfort to the Romans, but at the same time they
were very inconvenient for the king's army; for the
faintness of the light, in a line of moderate frontage,

---

[2] There is no mention of Hannibal, but in XXXVIII.
lviii. 10 Nasica speaks as if he had been present. It would
be ironical if the battle which was to test the prowess of the
two great generals were fought when both were absent.

in omnes partes conspectum, et umor toto fere gravi
4 armatu nihil gladios aut pila hebetabat; regii tam
lata acie ne ex medio quidem cornua sua conspicere [1]
poterant, nedum extremi inter se conspicerentur,
et umor arcus fundasque et iaculorum amenta
5 emollierat. Falcatae quoque quadrigae, quibus se
perturbaturum hostium aciem Antiochus crediderat,
6 in suos terrorem verterunt. Armatae autem in
hunc maxime modum erant : cuspides circa temonem
ab iugo decem cubita exstantes velut cornua habebant,
7 quibus, quidquid obvium daretur transfigerent, et in
extremis iugis binae circa eminebant falces, altera [2]
aequata iugo, altera inferior in terram devexa, illa
ut quidquid ab latere obiceretur abscideret, haec ut
prolapsos subeuntesque contingeret; item ab axibus
rotarum utrimque binae eodem modo diversae
8 deligabantur falces. Sic armatas quadrigas, quia,
si [3] in extremo aut in medio locatae forent, per
suos agendae erant, in prima acie, ut ante dictum est,
9 locaverat rex. Quod ubi Eumenes vidit, haud
ignarus quam anceps esset pugnae [4] et auxilii genus,[5]
si quis pavorem magis equis iniceret, quam iusta
adoriretur pugna, Cretenses sagittarios funditoresque
et iaculatores cum aliquot turmis [6] equitum non

---

[1] conspicere *ς* : circumspicere *B.*
[2] altera *ς* : om. *B.*
[3] quia si *ed. Frobeniana* 1535 : quasi *Bς.*
[4] q.a.e.p. *Fügner* : p.q.a.e. *B.*
[5] genus *ς* : gens *B.*
[6] cum aliquot turmis *Crévier* : om. *Bς.*

---

[1] These thongs were wrapped around the shafts of javelins
to impart to them a rotary motion, thereby giving longer
range and more accurate aim.
[2] The lack of intelligibility of this account is the best
indication that Livy had never seen such a chariot. Other

did not deprive the Romans of a view in all directions, B.C. 190
and the moisture, in a force almost entirely composed of heavy infantry, did not at all dull the swords
and spears; the king's troops, with their line so
widely extended, could not see the flanks even from
the centre, much less one flank from the other, and
the moisture had softened the bowstrings and slings
and the thongs [1] of the javelins. The scythe-
bearing chariots also, by which Antiochus had
expected to cause panic in the hostile line, turned
their terror upon their own men. They were in
general equipped in the following fashion: they had
points along the pole, projecting like horns ten cubits
from the yoke, with which to pierce whatever
they encountered, and on the ends of the yokes there
were two scythes standing out in two directions, one
in line with the yoke, the other pointed downward
towards the ground, the former to cut up whatever
was near it on the sides, the latter to wound men
who had fallen and came under the chariot; also
from the hubs of the wheels on both sides two
other scythes, pointing in different directions, were
similarly fastened. [2] The chariots so equipped,
because, if they were stationed on the flanks or in
the centre, they would of necessity have been driven
through their own ranks, had been posted by the
king, as has been said, in the front rank. When
Eumenes saw this, being not unaware how uncertain
was this sort of fighting and this kind of auxiliary,
if one could frighten the horses rather than meet
them in regular battle, he ordered the Cretan archers
with the slingers and dart-throwers, with some

descriptions differ in various particulars: cf. Xenophon *Anab.*
I. viii. 10; Curtius IV. ix. 5; Vegetius III. xxiv. etc.

LIVY

confertos, sed quam maxime possent dispersos ex-
currere iubet et ex omnibus simul partibus tela
10 ingerere. Haec velut procella partim vulneribus
missilium undique coniectorum partim clamoribus
dissonis ita consternavit equos ut repente velut
11 effrenati passim incerto cursu ferrentur; quorum
impetus et levis armatura et expediti funditores et
velox Cretensis momento declinabant; et eques
insequendo tumultum ac pavorem equis camelisque,
et ipsis simul consternatis, augebat clamore et ab
12 alia circumstantium turba multiplici adiecto. Ita
medio inter duas acies campo exiguntur quadrigae;
amotoque inani ludibrio, tum demum ad iustum
proelium signo utrimque dato concursum est.

XLII. Ceterum vana illa res verae mox cladis
causa fuit. Auxilia enim subsidiaria, quae proxima
locata erant, pavore et consternatione quadrigarum
territa et ipsa in fugam versa nudarunt omnia usque
2 ad cataphractos equites. Ad quos cum dissipatis
subsidiis pervenisset equitatus Romanus, ne primum
quidem impetum sustinuerunt; pars eorum [1] fusi
sunt, alii propter gravitatem tegumentorum armorum-
3 que oppressi sunt.[2] Totum deinde laevum cornu inclinavit, et turbatis auxiliaribus, qui [3] inter equitem
et [4] quos appellant phalangitas erant, usque ad
4 mediam aciem terror [5] pervenit. Ibi simul per-

---

[1] i.s.p.e. *Madvig*: i.p.e.s. *Bς*.
[2] oppressi sunt ς: pressi sunt *B*.
[3] qui ς: quia *B*.   [4] et *ed. Frobeniana* 1535: *om. B*.
[5] aciem terror ς: *om. B*.

---

[1] The "bystanders" here are the infantry which was not
yet engaged but which took this vocal part in this phase of the
battle. Thucydides (VII. lxx.–lxxi.) had described the shout-
ing of soldiers and civilians on shore during the naval battle

troops of cavalry, not in mass-formation but as widely B.C. 190
separated as possible, to rush out and shower weapons
upon them from all sides at once. This storm, as it
were, partly by the wounds dealt by weapons hurled
from all directions, partly by the discordant shouts,
so frightened the horses that, as if they were set
free from the reins, they rushed in every direction,
not knowing where they were going; their charges
were easily avoided by the light infantry and the
lightly-equipped slingers and the swift-footed
Cretans; and the cavalry pursuing increased the
confusion and fright of the horses and camels, these
too being overcome with terror, while added to it all
were the manifold cries of the throng of bystanders.[1]
So the chariots were driven away from the space
between the two lines and, this idle show being ended,
then at length the signal was given on both sides and
the clash of regular battle began.

XLII. That trivial thing, however, was presently the
cause of real calamity. For the supporting auxiliaries
which had been stationed next them, dismayed by the
panic and fright of the chariots, also turned to flight
and exposed the whole line as far as the armoured
cavalry. And they, when the Roman cavalry
reached them, their supports being scattered, did not
sustain even the first shock; part of them fled;
others were held back on account of the weight of
their armour and weapons. The whole left flank
then wavered, and when the auxiliaries were broken,
who were between the cavalry and those who were
called the *phalangitae*, the panic spread as far as the
centre. There, as soon as the ranks were thrown

at Syracuse, and the inclusion of such details became a
regular feature of the technique of historical composition.

LIVY

turbati ordines et impeditus intercursu suorum usus
praelongarum hastarum—sarisas Macedones vocant
—intulere signa Romanae legiones et pila in pertur-
5 batos coniecere. Ne interpositi quidem elephanti
militem Romanum deterrebant, adsuetum iam ab
Africis bellis et vitare impetum beluae et ex trans-
verso aut pilis incessere aut, si propius subire posset,
6 gladio nervos incidere. Iam media acies fere
omnis a fronte prostrata erat, et subsidia circumita
ab tergo caedebantur, cum in parte alia fugam
suorum et prope iam ad ipsa castra clamorem paven-
7 tium accepere. Namque Antiochus a dextro cornu,
cum ibi fiducia fluminis nulla subsidia cerneret
praeter quattuor turmas equitum, et eas dum applicant
se suis ripam nudantes, impetum in eam partem cum
8 auxiliis et cataphracto equitatu fecit; nec a fronte
tantum instabat, sed circumito a flumine cornu iam
ab latere urgebat, donec fugati equites primum, dein
proximi peditum effuso cursu ad castra compulsi
sunt.

XLIII. Praeerat castris M. Aemilius tribunus
militum, M. Lepidi filius, qui post paucos annos
2 pontifex maximus factus est. Is [1] qua fugam cernebat suorum, cum praesidio omni [2] occurrit et stare
primo, deinde redire in pugnam iubebat pavorem et
3 turpem fugam increpans; minae exinde erant, in

---

[1] is *edd. vett.* : *om. B꜡.*
[2] omni *edd. vett.* : omnium *B꜡.*

---

[1] Cf. XXVII. xxxix. 8.
[2] The expression is careless, but the context demands
that this statement refer to the Romans, who were being driven
back on their own left although victorious everywhere else.
[3] In 180 B.C. (XL. xlii. 12).

into disorder and the use of the very long spears
—the Macedonians call them *sarisae*—was prevented
by their own friends rushing among them, the
Roman legions advanced and hurled their javelins
into the disorganized mass. Not even the elephants
posted in the intervals deterred the Roman soldiers,
accustomed already by the wars in Africa both to
avoid the charges of the beasts and either to assail
them with spears from the side or, if they could
approach closer, to hamstring them with their swords.[1]
By now almost the entire centre was being beaten
back from the front and the auxiliaries flanking them
were being cut down in the rear, while on another
side the Romans[2] heard the rout of their comrades
and the shouts of the panic-stricken now almost at
the camp itself. For Antiochus, on his right flank,
since he saw that there were no auxiliaries there
except four troops of cavalry, because of the Romans'
confidence in the river, and that these, while they were
maintaining contact with their neighbours, were
leaving the bank unguarded, made an attack upon
them with the auxiliaries and the armoured cavalry;
nor did he charge from the front alone, but encircling
them from the river was already pressing on from
the flank, until first the cavalry fled and then the
infantry who were nearest were driven headlong
towards the camp.

XLIII. The camp was under the command of
Marcus Aemilius, tribune of the soldiers, the son of
that Marcus Lepidus who a few years later became
pontifex maximus.[3] When he saw the flight of his
men, he met them with his entire guard and ordered
them first to halt and then to return to the battle,
taunting them with fear and disgraceful flight; then

A.U.C.
564

perniciem suam caecos ruere ni dicto parerent;
postremo dat suis signum, ut primos[1] fugientium
caedant, turbam insequentium ferro et vulneribus
4 in hostem redigant. Hic maior timor minorem vicit;
ancipiti coacti metu primo constiterunt; deinde et
ipsi rediere in pugnam, et Aemilius cum suo praesidio
—erant autem[2] duo milia virorum fortium—effuse
5 sequenti regi acriter obstitit, et Attalus, Eumenis
frater, ab dextro cornu, quo laevum hostium primo
impetu fugatum fuerat, ut ab[3] sinistro fugam suorum
et tumultum circa castra vidit, in tempore cum
6 ducentis equitibus advenit. Antiochus postquam et
eos, quorum terga modo viderat, repetentes pugnam
et aliam et a castris et ex acie adfluentem turbam
7 conspexit, in fugam vertit equum. Ita utroque
cornu victores Romani per acervos corporum, quos
in media maxime acie cumulaverant, ubi et robur
fortissimorum virorum et arma gravitate fugam
8 impedierant, pergunt ad castra diripienda. Equites
primi omnium Eumenis, deinde et alius equitatus
toto passim campo sequuntur hostem et postremos,
9 ut quosque adepti sunt, caedunt. Ceterum fugientibus maior pestis, intermixtis quadrigis elephantisque
et camelis, erat sua[4] ipsorum[5] turba, cum solutis
ordinibus velut caeci super alios alii ruerent et

---

[1] primos ⲋ : primo B.
[2] autem ⲋ : om. B.
[3] ut ab ed. Frobeniana 1535 : ab Bⲋ.
[4] sua Heusinger : et sua Bⲋ.
[5] ipsorum ⲋ : ipsius B.

B.C. 190

he uttered threats that they were rushing blindly to
their own deaths if they did not obey his orders;
finally, he gave the signal to his own men to kill the
first of the fugitives and with steel and wounds to
drive against the enemy the mass of those that
followed. This greater fear prevailed over the lesser;
driven by terror in front and rear they first halted;
then they too returned to the fight, and Aemilius
with his own guard—they were two thousand gallant
men—boldly withstood the onrushing king, and
Attalus, the brother of Eumenes, from the right
flank, where the enemy's left had been routed at the
first attack, when he saw the flight of the troops on
the left and the mellay around the camp, himself
came in the nick of time with two hundred cavalry.
When Antiochus saw the troops at whose backs he
had just been looking returning to the fight, and
another body coming from the camp and another
from the battle-line, he turned his horse to flight. So
on both wings the victorious Romans, over piles of
corpses which they had heaped up, especially in the
centre, where the strength of the bravest troops [1]
and the weight of their arms had delayed the flight of
the enemy, proceeded to plunder the camp. The
cavalry of Eumenes first of all, then the rest of the
cavalry, pursued the enemy over the whole plain,
killing the hindmost as they overtook them. But a
greater peril to the fugitives, the chariots and
elephants and camels being mingled with them, was
the disordered mob of their own men, since their
ranks once broken, as if blind they rushed one over

---

[1] Appian several times mentions the gallant stand of the
phalangitae; when the time for flight came their weapons
impeded them.

LIVY

10 incursu [1] beluarum obtererentur. In castris quoque
ingens et maior prope quam in acie caedes est edita;
nam et primorum fuga in castra maxime inclinavit,[2]
et huius fiducia multitudinis, qui [3] in praesidio erant,
11 pertinacius pro vallo pugnarunt. Retenti in portis
valloque, quae se impetu ipso capturos crediderant,
Romani, postquam tandem perruperunt, ab ira
graviorem ediderunt caedem.

XLIV. Ad quinquaginta milia peditum caesa eo
die dicuntur, equitum tria milia; mille et quadringenti capti et quindecim cum rectoribus elephanti.
2 Romanorum aliquot vulnerati sunt; ceciderunt non
plus trecenti pedites, quattuor et viginti equites et
de Eumenis exercitu quinque et viginti.
3 Et illo quidem die victores direptis hostium castris
cum magna praeda in sua reverterunt; postero die
spoliabant caesorum corpora et captivos contrahe-
4 bant. Legati ab Thyatira et Magnesia ab Sipylo ad
5 dedendas urbes venerunt. Antiochus cum paucis
fugiens, in ipso itinere pluribus congregantibus se,
modica manu armatorum media ferme nocte Sardis
6 concessit. Inde, cum audisset Seleucum filium et
quosdam amicorum Apameam progressos, et ipse
quarta vigilia cum coniuge ac filia petit Apameam.
7 Xenoni tradita custodia urbis, Timone Lydiae praeposito; quibus spretis consensu oppidanorum et

----

[1] ruerent et incursu *ed. Frobeniana* 1535 : ruerunt incursu
B : ruerent incursu *et* ruerent et cursu *et* ruentes incursu ς.
[2] inclinauit ς : declinauit *B*.
[3] qui ς : quae *B*.

----

[1] Sardis.

the other or were trampled down by the charging B.C. 190
beasts. In the camp also there was great slaughter,
greater, almost, than on the battle-field; for the first
body of fugitives had chiefly made for the camp and,
gaining confidence from this increase in numbers,
the garrison fought with greater stubbornness from
the rampart. The Romans, finding themselves held
up at the gates and by the wall, which they had
expected to carry at the first onset, when they
finally broke through, in their passion caused greater
destruction.

XLIV. About fifty thousand infantry are said to
have been slain on that day and three thousand
cavalry; fourteen hundred were captured and
fifteen elephants with their drivers. Of the Romans,
many were wounded; there were killed not more
than three hundred infantry and twenty-four
cavalry, and from the army of Eumenes twenty-five.

And on that day, indeed, the victors, having
plundered the camp of the enemy, returned to their
own laden with booty; on the next day they de-
spoiled the bodies of the slain and gathered up the
prisoners. Ambassadors from Thyatira and Magnesia
near Sipylus came to surrender their cities. Antiochus, fleeing with a few companions and collecting
more along the way, with a moderate-sized body of
soldiers reached Sardis about midnight. Thence,
when he heard that his son Seleucus and some of his
friends had gone to Apamea, he too, about the
fourth watch, with his wife and daughter sought
Apamea. The guardianship of the city [1] was handed
over to Xeno, and Timo was placed in charge of
Lydia; but no regard was paid to them and, with
the consent of the citizens and the soldiers who

militum, qui in arce erant, legati ad consulem missi sunt.

XLV. Sub idem fere tempus et ab Trallibus et a Magnesia quae super Maeandrum est, et ab Epheso 2 ad dedendas urbes venerunt. Reliquerat Ephesum Polyxenidas audita pugna, et classi usque ad Patara Lyciae pervectus, metu stationis Rhodiarum navium,[1] quae ad Megisten erant, in terram egressus cum 3 paucis itinere pedestri Syriam petit. Asiae civitates in fidem consulis dicionemque populi Romani sese tradebant. Sardibus iam consul erat; eo et P. Scipio ab Elaea, cum primum pati laborem viae potuit, venit.

4 Sub idem fere tempus caduceator ab Antiocho per P. Scipionem a consule petit impetravitque, ut 5 oratores mittere liceret regi. Paucos post dies Zeuxis, qui praefectus Lydiae fuerat,[2] et Antipater, 6 fratris filius, venerunt. Prius Eumene convento, quem propter vetera certamina aversum[3] maxime a pace credebant esse, et placatiore eo et sua et regis spe invento, tum P. Scipionem et per eum consulem 7 adierunt; praebitoque iis petentibus frequenti consilio ad mandata edenda, " non tam quid ipsi dicamus habemus " inquit Zeuxis " quam ut a vobis quaeramus, Romani, quo piaculo expiare errorem regis, pacem veniamque impetrare a victoribus 8 possimus. Maximo semper animo victis regibus

---

[1] nauium ς : om. B. 　　[2] fuerat ς : erat B.
[3] auersum ς ; uersum B,

were in the citadel, ambassadors were sent to the
consul.

XLV. About the same time ambassadors came
also from Tralles and from Magnesia which is on
the Meander river and from Ephesus to surrender
their cities. Polyxenidas had left Ephesus when he
heard of the battle, and having sailed with the fleet
as far as Patara in Lycia, in fear of the guard of
Rhodian ships which were at Megiste, he disembarked
with a few men and made his way by land to Syria.
The cities of Asia entrusted themselves to the good
faith of the consul and the dominion of the Roman
people. The consul was now at Sardis; thither too
came Publius Scipio from Elaea, as soon as he could
stand the hardships of the journey.

About the same time a herald from Antiochus,
through the mediation of Publius Scipio, asked and
obtained from the consul permission for the king to
send ambassadors. A few days later Zeuxis, who
had been governor of Lycia, and Antipater, the son
of his brother, arrived. First meeting Eumenes,
who, they thought, on account of their ancient
quarrels, would be particularly opposed to peace,
and finding him more favourably disposed towards
peace than either they or the king had expected,
they next interviewed Publius Scipio and through
him the consul; and at their request they were
received by a full council at which to announce their
errand, and Zeuxis spoke thus: "We do not ourselves have anything to say so much as we ask of
you, Romans, by what atonement we can expiate
the error of the king and obtain peace and pardon
from the conquerors. In your extreme generosity
you have always pardoned defeated kings and

populisque ignovistis ; quanto id maiore et placatiore animo [1] decet vos facere in hac victoria, quae vos
9 dominos orbis terrarum fecit ? Positis iam adversus omnes mortales certaminibus haud secus quam deos consulere et parcere vos generi humano oportet."
10 Iam antequam legati venirent, decretum erat quid [2]
11 responderetur. Respondere Africanum placuit. Is in hunc modum locutus fertur : "Romani ex iis, quae in deum immortalium potestate erant, ea
12 habemus, quae dii dederunt ; animos, qui nostrae mentis sunt, eosdem in omni fortuna gessimus gerimusque, neque eos secundae res extulerunt nec adversae minuerunt. Eius rei, ut alios omittam, Hannibalem vestrum vobis testem darem, nisi vos ipsos
13 dare possem. Postquam traiecimus Hellespontum, priusquam castra regia, priusquam aciem videremus, cum communis Mars et incertus belli eventus esset, de pace vobis agentibus quas pares paribus ferebamus condiciones, easdem nunc victores victis ferimus :
14 Europa abstinete ; Asia omni, quae cis Taurum montem est, decedite. Pro impensis deinde in bellum factis quindecim milia talentum Euboicorum dabitis, quingenta praesentia, duo milia et quingenta, cum senatus populusque Romanus pacem comprobaverint ; milia deinde [3] talentum per duodecim
15 annos. Eumeni quoque reddi quadringenta [4] talenta et quod frumenti reliquum ex eo quod patri debitum

---

[1] animo ⟨⟩ : om. B.
[2] quid ⟨⟩ : quod B.
[3] milia deinde Gruter : deinde B⟨⟩.
[4] quadrigenta ⟨⟩ : .XL. B.

---

[1] The Euboean talent was a universal standard of value, frequently employed in international transactions (XXXVIII.

peoples; with how much greater magnanimity and with inclinations how much more peaceful should you act in this victory which has made you masters of the world? Laying aside now quarrels with all mortals, you, like the gods, should consider and spare the human race." Even before the ambassadors arrived it had been decided what to reply. It was agreed that Africanus should answer. He is reported to have spoken to this effect: " Out of such things as were under the control of the immortal gods, we Romans have those things which the gods have given us; but our souls, which are subject to the will of our minds, we have kept and still keep unchanged in every kind of fortune, and neither has prosperity puffed them up nor has adversity depressed them. As proof of this, to omit all else, I should cite to you your Hannibal as witness if I could not cite yourselves. After we crossed the Hellespont, before we set eyes on the king's camp or beheld his battle-line, when Mars was approachable to both sides and the outcome of the war undetermined, when you raised the question of terms of peace, we offered conditions, as equals to equals, and these same conditions we now propose as victors to vanquished: keep your hands off Europe; withdraw from all Asia on this side of the Taurus mountains. Then, for the expenses incurred in the war, you will pay fifteen thousand Euboean talents,[1] five hundred now, twenty-five hundred when the senate and the Roman people shall have ratified this treaty, then one thousand talents annually for twelve years. To Eumenes too it is our pleasure that four hundred talents be paid and the balance of the grain

xxxviii. 13; Polybius I. lxii; XV. xviii. etc.). Its value was the same as that of the Attic talent.

LIVY

16 est placet. Haec cum pepigerimus, facturos vos
ut pro certo habeamus, erit quidem aliquod pignus,
si obsides viginti nostro arbitratu dabitis; sed
numquam satis liquebit nobis ibi pacem esse populo
Romano, ubi Hannibal erit; eum ante omnia depos-
17 cimus. Thoantem quoque Aetolum, concitorem
Aetolici belli, qui et illorum fiducia vos et vestra illos
in nos armavit, dedetis et cum eo Mnasilochum
Acarnana et Chalcidenses Philonem et Eubulidam.
18 In deteriore sua fortuna pacem faciet rex, quia serius
facit quam facere potuit. Si nunc moratus fuerit,
sciat regum maiestatem difficilius ab summo fastigio
ad medium detrahi quam a mediis ad ima praecipitari.''
19 Cum iis mandatis ab rege missi erant legati ut omnem
pacis condicionem[1] acciperent; itaque Romam
mitti legatos placuit. Consul in hiberna exercitum
Magnesiam ad Maeandrum et Tralles Ephesumque
20 divisit. Ephesum ad consulem paucos post dies
obsides ab rege adducti sunt, et legati, qui Romam
21 irent, venerunt. Eumenes quoque eodem tempore

---

[1] condicionem ς : om. B.

---

[1] Nothing has been said of Hannibal since the defeat of the
fleet by the Rhodians (xxiv. 11 above), but Nepos (*Hannibal* 9)
says that he fled to Crete, and Livy (XXXIX. li. 1) and
Polybius (XXIII. xiii) report him in Bithynia after Magnesia.
Possibly his departure from the kingdom of Antiochus should
be placed before the battle rather than after it. For various
reasons the genuineness of this item in Scipio's speech seems
open to question, although Polybius (XXI. xvii) also has it.
The Romans seem not to have taken the demand for Hannibal
and the others mentioned in the next sentence very seriously:
no such clause was included in the negotiations at the
Hellespont (xxxv above), although Scipio asserts that their
demands were unchanged (the clauses in this chapter which

which is due his father. When we have made this B.C. 190
agreement, in order that we may hold it as certain that
you will carry it out, there will be some guarantee if
you give us twenty hostages of our selection; but
never will it be quite clear to us that the Roman people
is at peace in any place where Hannibal shall be; him
we demand before all else.[1] Thoas the Aetolian,
too, provoker of the Aetolian war, who by your confidence in them armed you and by their confidence
in you armed them against us, you will surrender,
and with him Mnasilochus the Acarnanian[2] and
Philo and Eubulidas of Chalcis.[3] It wi.l be in a
worse plight that the king will make peace because
he makes it later than he could have done. If he
delays now, let him know that the majesty of kings
falls with greater difficulty from the topmost point
to the middle than it is hurled from the middle to the
lowest point." The ambassadors from the king had
been sent with instructions authorizing them to
accept any proffer of peace; and so it was decided
that ambassadors should be sent to Rome. The
consul divided his army to winter at Magnesia on
the Meander and at Tralles and at Ephesus. A
few days later the hostages were delivered by the
king to the consul at Ephesus and the envoys who
were to go to Rome arrived. Eumenes also set out

differ are rather interpretations than modifications); provision
was made for amendments to the treaty with respect to these
persons (XXXVIII. xxxviii. 8); the vindictiveness of Scipio's
language is disproportionate to the actual damage done by
Hannibal in this war and inconsistent with the character of
Scipio as it is revealed in his other relations with Hannibal.

[2] Cf. XXXVI. xii. 4.

[3] Not mentioned before by Livy, but cf. Polybius XXI.
xvii.

LIVY

profectus est Romam, quo legati regis. Secutae
eos sunt legationes omnium Asiae populorum.

XLVI. Dum haec in Asia geruntur, duo fere sub
idem tempus cum triumphi spe proconsules [1] de
provinciis Romam redierunt, Q. Minucius ex Liguribus,
2 M'. Acilius ex Aetolia. Auditis utriusque rebus
gestis Minucio negatus triumphus, Acilio magno
consensu decretus; isque triumphans de rege
3 Antiocho et Aetolis urbem est invectus. Praelata
in eo triumpho sunt signa militaria ducenta triginta
et argenti infecti tria milia pondo, signati tetrachmum Atticum centum decem tria milia, cistophori
ducenta undequinquaginta, vasa argentea caelata
4 multa magnique ponderis; tulit et suppellectilem
regiam argenteam ac vestem magnificam, coronas
aureas, dona sociarum civitatium, quadraginta quinque, spolia omnis generis. Captivos nobiles, Aetolos
5 et regios duces, sex et triginta duxit. Damocritus,
Aetolorum dux, paucos ante dies, dum e carcere noctu
effugisset, in ripa Tiberis consecutis custodibus,
priusquam comprehenderetur, gladio se transfixit.
6 Milites tantum qui sequerentur currum defuerunt;
alioqui magnificus et spectaculo et fama rerum
triumphus fuit.

7 Huius triumphi minuit laetitiam nuntius ex Hispania tristis, adversa pugna in Bastetanis ductu L.[2]

---

[1] triumphi spe proconsules *ed. Frobeniana* 1535 : triumphi
spe *B* : *ex ceteris, alii aliud.*
[2] L. ⸖ : *om. B.*

---

[1] The *cistophorus* was a coin worth three *denarii* and stamped
with the image of the chest used in the mysteries.
[2] Acilius was later accused of appropriating part of the
booty to his own use (lvii. 12–13 below).

for Rome at the same time as the ambassadors of the B.C. 190
king. They were followed by embassies of all the
peoples of Asia.

XLVI. While this was going on in Asia, two proconsuls at about the same time came from their
provinces to Rome with hopes of triumphs; Quintus
Minucius from the Ligures, Manius Acilius from
Aetolia. When the achievements of the two had
been heard, Minucius was refused a triumph, Acilius
was granted one with general approval; and he rode
into the City in triumph over King Antiochus and
the Aetolians. There were carried in this triumph
two hundred thirty military standards, three thousand
pounds of silver bullion, one hundred thirteen thousand minted Attic four-drachma pieces, *cistophori* [1]
to the number of two hundred and forty-nine thousand, embossed silver vessels in large numbers and
of great weight; he displayed also a set of silver
furniture belonging to the king and a splendid
garment, forty-five golden crowns, the gifts of allied
cities, and spoils of all kinds.[2] He led thirty-six
noble prisoners, Aetolians and commanders in the
king's army.[3] Damocritus the Aetolian chief, a few
days before, escaped from prison by night, and while
the guards were pursuing him along the banks of
the Tiber, slew himself with a sword before he was
arrested. Only soldiers to follow the car were
lacking; otherwise the triumph was splendid both
as a spectacle and for the exploits it commemorated.

The pleasure of this triumph was diminished by a
sad message from Spain, that in a defeat at the hands
of the Lusitani in the country of the Bastetani near

[3] In iii. 8 above there were forty-three such prisoners.
Probably still others had died or escaped.

427

Aemilii proconsulis apud oppidum Lyconem cum
Lusitanis sex milia de Romano exercitu cecidisse,
8 ceteros paventes intra vallum compulsos aegre
castra defendisse et in modum fugientium magnis
9 itineribus in agrum pacatum reductos. Haec ex
Hispania nuntiata. Ex Gallia legatos Placentinorum
et Cremonensium L. Aurunculeius praetor in senatum
10 introduxit. Iis querentibus inopiam colonorum, aliis
belli casibus aliis [1] morbo absumptis, quosdam taedio
accolarum Gallorum reliquisse colonias, decrevit
senatus uti C. Laelius consul, si ei videretur, sex
milia familiarum conscriberet [2] quae in eas colonias
dividerentur, et ut L. Aurunculeius praetor triumviros
11 crearet ad eos colonos deducendos. Creati M.
Atilius Serranus L. Valerius P. F. Flaccus L. Valerius
C. F. Tappo.

XLVII. Haud ita multo post, cum iam consularium
comitiorum appeteret tempus, C. Laelius consul ex
2 Gallia Romam redit. Is non solum ex facto absente
se senatus consulto in supplementum Cremonae et
Placentiae colonos scripsit, sed ut novae coloniae duae
in agrum qui Boiorum fuisset [3] deducerentur, et
rettulit et auctore eo patres censuerunt. [4]

3 Eodem tempore litterae L. Aemilii praetoris adlatae de navali pugna ad Myonnesum facta, et L.

---

[1] aliis b.c. aliis 𝔰 : alii b.c. alii *B*.
[2] conscriberet 𝔰 : *om. B*.
[3] fuisset 𝔰 : fuissent *B*.
[4] censuerunt 𝔰 : censuerant *B*.

428

the town of Lyco, six thousand of the Roman army B.C. 190
under the command of Lucius Aemilius the proconsul had fallen and the rest had been driven in
panic inside the rampart, had defended the camp
with difficulty and had been led back like fugitives
with forced marches into pacified territory. This
was the news from Spain. From Gaul, ambassadors
from the people of Placentia and Cremona were
introduced to the senate by Lucius Aurunculeius the
praetor. When they complained of the shortage of
colonists, some having been taken off by the fortunes
of war, and some by disease, while others had left
the colonies from reluctance to live with their Gallic
neighbours, the senate decreed that Gaius Laelius
the consul, if it should seem wise to him, should
enrol six thousand families to be divided between
these colonies and that Lucius Aurunculeius the
praetor should create a board of three to conduct
these colonists to their homes. The board created
consisted of Marcus Atilius Serranus, Lucius Valerius
Flaccus, the son of Publius, and Lucius Valerius
Tappo, the son of Lucius.

XLVII. Not very long afterwards, since the time
for the consular election was at hand, Gaius Laelius
the consul returned from Gaul to Rome. He not only
enrolled, in accordance with the decree of the senate
passed in his absence, colonists as reinforcements for
Cremona and Placentia, but he also moved that two
new colonies should be established in the country
which had belonged to the Boii, and on his proposal
the Fathers so voted.

At the same time a despatch from Lucius Aemilius
the praetor arrived, announcing the naval battle
fought off Myonnesus and the fact that Lucius

LIVY

Scipionem consulem in Asiam exercitum traiecisse.
4 Victoriae navalis ergo in diem unum supplicatio decreta
est, in alterum diem, quod exercitus Romanus tum
primum in Asia posuisset castra, ut ea res prospera
5 et laeta eveniret. Vicenis¹ maioribus hostiis in
singulas supplicationes sacrificare consul est iussus.
6 Inde consularia comitia magna contentione habita.
M. Aemilius Lepidus petebat adversa omnium fama,
quod provinciam Siciliam petendi causa non consulto
7 senatu ut sibi id facere liceret, reliquisset.² Petebant cum eo M. Fulvius Nobilior Cn. Manlius Volso³
M. Valerius Messalla. Fulvius consul unus creatur,
cum ceteri centurias non explessent, isque postero
die Cn. Manlium Lepido deiecto—nam Messalla
8 iacuit—collegam dixit.⁴ Praetores exinde facti duo
Q. Fabii, Labeo et Pictor—Pictor flamen⁵ Quirinalis
eo anno inauguratus fuerat—M. Sempronius Tuditanus
Sp. Postumius Albinus L. Plautius Hypsaeus⁶ L.
Baebius Dives.

¹ uicenis ⌠ : uicinis *B.*
² reliquisset ⌠ : requisisset *B.*
³ Volso *ed. Mediolaniensis* 1480 ; *cf. infra,* xlviii. 1 : *om. B⌠.*
⁴ dixit ⌠ : duxit *B.*
⁵ Pictor flamen *Weissenborn* : flamen *B⌠.*
⁶ L. Plautius Hypsaeus ⌠ : *om. B.*

---

¹ An election required the votes of a majority of the centuries for each candidate, and Fulvius alone had a majority,
the other votes being split in such a way that no one else had
a sufficient number.

Livy's account of the subsequent procedure is badly confused, and evidence with which to revise it is lacking. The
first question is the date of the election of Fulvius. He could
have presided at the election of his colleague only if he had
himself been chosen on the last day of the preceding official
year. The colloquialisms *deiecto* and *iacuit* and the technical
phrase *collegam dixit* indicate that a second election was

430

Scipio the consul had transferred his army to Asia. B.C. 190
By reason of the naval victory a period of prayer for
one day was proclaimed and a second day was added
because a Roman army had then for the first time
encamped in Asia, in order that this event might turn
out prosperously and successfully. The consul was
directed to sacrifice twenty full-grown victims on
each day of the period of supplication.

Then the consular elections were held with active
rivalry. Marcus Aemilius Lepidus was a candidate
amid universal disapproval because he had left his
province of Sicily to conduct his campaign without a
vote of the senate authorizing him to do so. The
candidates with him were Marcus Fulvius Nobilior,
Gnaeus Manlius Volso, and Marcus Valerius Messalla.
Fulvius was the only consul elected, since the others
did not win the necessary number of centuries,[1]
and he on the following day announced the choice
of Gnaeus Manlius as his colleague, Lepidus being
defeated—for Messalla had no chance.[2] Then the
praetors were chosen; two named Quintus Fabius,
Labeo and Pictor—Pictor had been installed as
priest of Quirinus that year, Marcus Sempronius
Tuditanus, Spurius Postumius Albinus, Lucius
Plautius Hypsaeus, Lucius Baebius Dives.

held and that Fulvius did not co-opt his colleague, and the
last indicates that Fulvius presided at that election. On the
other hand, the consuls and praetors were apparently inaugurated together as usual, and in that case Fulvius could
not have been elected on the last day of one year and Manlius
on the first day of the next. Livy has probably erroneously
reconstructed the event from contradictory and ambiguous
sources.

[2] Livy's use of *iacuit* is an echo of the political slang of his
own day.

LIVY

XLVIII. M. Fulvio Nobiliore et Cn. Manlio Vol-
sone consulibus Valerius Antias auctor est rumorem
celebrem Romae fuisse et paene pro certo habitum,
2 recipiendi Scipionis adulescentis causa consulem L.
Scipionem et cum eo P. Africanum in colloquium
3 evocatos regis et ipsos comprehensos esse, et ducibus
captis confestim ad castra Romana exercitum ductum,
eaque expugnata et deletas omnes copias Romanorum
4 esse.   Ob haec Aetolos sustulisse animos et abnuisse
imperata facere, principesque eorum in Macedoniam
et in Dardanos et in Thraeciam ad conducenda mer-
5 cede auxilia profectos.   Haec qui nuntiarent Romam,
A. Terentium Varronem et M. Claudium Lepidum
ab A. Cornelio propraetore ex Aetolia missos esse.
6 Subtexit deinde fabulae huic legatos Aetolos in
senatu [1] inter cetera hoc quoque interrogatos esse,
unde audissent imperatores Romanos in Asia captos
ab Antiocho rege et exercitum deletum [2] esse;
7 Aetolos respondisse ab suis legatis se, qui cum consule
fuerint, certiores factos.   Rumoris huius quia neminem alium auctorem habeo, neque adfirmata res mea
opinione sit nec pro vana praetermissa.

XLIX. Aetoli legati in senatum introducti, cum
et causa eos sua et fortuna hortaretur, ut confitendo
seu [3] culpae seu errori veniam supplices peterent,
2 orsi a beneficiis in populum Romanum et prope

---

[1] senatu *ed. Frobeniana* 1531 : senatum *Bς*.
[2] deletum *ς* : delectu *B*.
[3] seu *ς* : se *B*.

---

[1] The meaning of this sentence is obscure.   The assumption
that it is a criticism of the historiography of Antias is contradicted by the first clause, and Livy, of course, was aware
that the story was untrue.

432

XLVIII. In the consulship of Marcus Fulvius _{B.C. 189} Nobilior and Gnaeus Manlius Volso, Valerius Antias records that a rumour was generally circulated in Rome and taken as almost certain that, for the purpose of recovering the young Scipio, the consul Lucius Scipio and with him Publius Africanus had been invited to a conference with the king and had been arrested, and that after the capture of their generals the army had been led against the Roman camp, that this had been captured and all the Roman forces destroyed; that for this reason the Aetolians had taken heart and refused to obey orders and their chiefs had gone to Macedonia and the Dardanians and to Thrace to secure auxiliaries for hire and that Aulus Terentius and Marcus Claudius Lepidus had been sent to bring this report by Aulus Cornelius the propraetor in Aetolia. It added a further item to the story that the Aetolian ambassadors among other things were also asked in the senate, from what sources they had learned that the Roman commanders in Asia had been taken prisoners by King Antiochus and the army wiped out; that the Aetolians replied that they had been informed by their ambassadors who had been with the consul. Because I have no other authority for this story the rumour, in my judgment, should not have been given credence nor yet dismissed as without foundation.[1]

XLIX. The Aetolian ambassadors, when introduced to the senate, although both their own interests and their situation urged them by confessing their fault or their mistake, whichever one chooses to call it, to supplicate for pardon, began by reciting their services to the Roman people, and almost belliger-

LIVY

exprobrantes virtutem suam in Philippi bello et
3 offenderunt aures insolentia sermonis et eo, vetera
et oblitterata repetendo, rem adduxerunt ut haud
paulo plurium maleficiorum gentis quam beneficiorum
memoria subiret animos patrum, et quibus miseri-
4 cordia opus erat, iram et odium irritarent. Interro-
gati ab uno senatore, permitterentne [1] arbitrium de
se populo Romano, deinde ab altero, habiturine [2]
eosdem quos populus Romanus socios et hostes [3]
essent, nihil ad ea respondentes egredi templo iussi
5 sunt. Conclamatum deinde prope ab universo senatu
est totos adhuc Antiochi Aetolos esse et ex unica ea
spe pendere animos eorum; itaque bellum cum
haud dubiis hostibus gerendum perdomandosque
6 feroces animos esse. Illa etiam res accendit quod
eo ipso tempore quo pacem ab Romanis petebant,
Dolopiae atque Athamaniae bellum inferebant.
7 Senatus consultum in M'. Acilii sententiam, qui
Antiochum Aetolosque devicerat, factum est ut
Aetoli eo die iuberentur proficisci ab urbe et intra
8 quintumdecimumdiemItalia excedere. A. Terentius
Varro ad custodiendum iter eorum missus, denuntiatumque,[4] si qua deinde legatio ex Aetolis, nisi permissu imperatoris, qui eam provinciam obtineret,
et cum legato Romano venisset Romam, pro hostibus
omnes futuros. Ita dimissi Aetoli.

[1] permitterentne ς : permitterent B.
[2] habiturine ς : habiturosne B.
[3] hostis ς : hostus B.
[4] denuntiatumque ς : nuntiatumque B.

---

[1] These are the alternatives of i. 5 above.

ently lauded their own valour in the war with Philip B.C. 189
and offended men's ears by their insolent language
and, by recalling old and forgotten incidents, brought
things to such a pass, that the memory of the misdeeds of that people, far more numerous than their
services, filled the minds of the Fathers, and that
men whose need was for mercy roused only anger
and hatred. On being questioned by one senator
whether they would leave the decision regarding
themselves to the Roman people, and then by
another whether they would agree to have the same
friends and enemies as the Roman people,[1] and
making no reply to the questions, they were
ordered to leave the temple. The shout went up
from almost the entire senate that the Aetolians
still belonged entirely to Antiochus and that their
thoughts turned on this one hope; and so the war
should go on with them, as beyond doubt enemies,
and their haughty spirits should be well broken.
This circumstance too inflamed their minds, that
at the very time when they were asking peace of
the Romans they were invading Dolopia and Athamania. A decree of the senate was passed on
the motion of Manius Acilius, the man who had
conquered Antiochus and the Aetolians, that the
Aetolians should be ordered to leave the City that
day and Italy within fifteen days. Aulus Terentius
Varro was delegated to safeguard their journey,
and formal notice was served that if any embassy
thereafter from the Aetolians came to Rome except
with the consent of the commander who held that
province and accompanied by a Roman commissioner,
they would treat all its members as enemies. In
this fashion the Aetolians were dismissed.

435

LIVY

L. De provinciis deinde consules rettulerunt; sor-
2 tiri eos Aetoliam et Asiam placuit; qui Asiam sortitus
3 esset, ei exercitus quem L. Scipio haberet est
decretus et in eum supplementum quattuor milia
peditum Romanorum, ducenti equites, et sociorum
ac Latini nominis octo milia peditum, quadringenti
equites; his copiis ut bellum cum Antiocho gereret.
4 Alteri consuli exercitus qui erat in Aetolia est
decretus, et ut in supplementum scriberet permissum
civium sociorumque eundem numerum,[1] quem collega.
5 Naves quoque idem consul, quae priore anno paratae
erant, ornare iussus ac ducere secum; nec cum
Aetolis solum bellum gerere, sed etiam in Cephal-
6 laniam insulam traicere. Mandatum eidem ut, si
per commodum rei publicae facere posset, ut ad
7 comitia Romam veniret; nam, praeterquam quod
magistratus annui subrogandi essent, censores quoque
placere creari. Si qua res eum teneret, senatum
certiorem faceret[2] se ad comitiorum tempus occurrere
8 non posse. Aetolia M. Fulvio, Asia Cn. Manlio
sorte evenit. Praetores deinde sortiti sunt, Sp.
Postumius Albinus urbanam et inter peregrinos,
M. Sempronius Tuditanus Siciliam, Q. Fabius Pictor,
flamen Quirinalis, Sardiniam, Q. Fabius Labeo
classem, L. Plautius Hypsaeus Hispaniam citeriorem,
9 L. Baebius Dives Hispaniam ulteriorem. Siciliae
legio una et classis, quae in ea provincia erat, decreta,

---

[1] eundem numerum 5̄ : om. B.
[2] faceret 5̄ : facere B.

---

[1] Cf. iv. 5 above.   [2] Cf. XXXVI. xxxi. 10 and the note.

L. Then the question of the provinces was brought B.C. 189
up by the consuls; it was decided that they should
draw lots for Aetolia and Asia; the one to whom
Asia was allotted should be assigned the army which
Lucius Scipio had, and as reinforcement for it four
thousand Roman infantry and two hundred cavalry,
and of the allies of the Latin confederacy eight
thousand infantry and four hundred cavalry; with
these forces he was to conduct the war against
Antiochus. To the other consul the army which
was in Aetolia was decreed, and he was authorized
to enlist as reinforcements the same number of
citizens and allies as his colleague. The same consul, moreover, was directed to fit out and take with
him the ships which had been built the year before; [1]
and not to wage war with the Aetolians alone, but
also to cross to the island of Cephallania. [2] The
same consul was instructed, if he could do so advan-
tageously to the state, to come to Rome for the
elections; for, apart from the fact that the new
annual magistrates were to be chosen, it was their
pleasure to elect censors also. If anything detained
him, he should inform the senate that he could not
be present at the time of the elections. Aetolia
fell to Marcus Fulvius, Asia to Gnaeus Manlius, as
a result of the drawing. The praetors then drew
lots, and Spurius Postumius Albinus received the
civil jurisdiction and that between citizens and
aliens, Marcus Sempronius Tuditanus Sicily, Quintus
Fabius Pictor, the priest of Quirinus, Sardinia,
Quintus Fabius Labeo the fleet, Lucius Plautius
Hypsaeus Nearer Spain, Lucius Baebius Dives
Farther Spain. For Sicily one legion and the fleet
which was in the province were decreed; and the

LIVY

et ut duas decumas frumenti novus praetor [1] imperaret Siculis; earum alteram in Asiam, alteram in
10 Aetoliam mitteret. Idem [2] ab Sardis exigi atque ad
eosdem exercitus id frumentum, ad quos Siculum,
11 deportari iussum. L. Baebio supplementum in Hispaniam datum mille Romani pedites, equites quinquaginta, et sex milia peditum Latini nominis,
12 ducenti equites; Plautio Hypsaeo in Hispaniam
citeriorem mille Romani dati sunt pedites, duo milia
socium Latini nominis et ducenti equites; cum his
supplementis ut singulas legiones duae Hispaniae
13 haberent. Prioris anni magistratibus, C. Laelio
cum suo exercitu prorogatum in annum [3] imperium
est; prorogatum et P. Iunio propraetori in Etruria
cum eo exercitu, qui in provincia esset, et M.
Tuccio propraetori in Bruttiis et Apulia.

LI. Priusquam in provincias praetores irent certamen inter P. Licinium pontificem maximum fuit et
Q. Fabium Pictorem [4] flaminem Quirinalem, quale
patrum memoria inter L. Metellum et Postumium
2 Albinum fuerat. Consulem illum cum C. Lutatio
collega in Siciliam ad classem proficiscentem ad sacra
3 retinuerat Metellus, pontifex maximus; praetorem
hunc, ne in Sardiniam proficisceretur,[5] P. Licinius
tenuit. Et in senatu et ad populum magnis con-
4 tentionibus certatum, et imperia inhibita ultro
citroque, et pignera capta, et multae dictae, et
tribuni appellati, et provocatum ad populum est.

---

[1] praetor ς: p.r. B.   [2] idem ς: idem idem B.
[3] in annum ς: om. B.   [4] Pictorem ς: praetorem B.
      [5] proficisceretur ς: proficiscetur B.

---

[1] Probably a phrase concerning Roman cavalry has been
lost.

new praetor was ordered to levy two tithes of grain on
the Sicilians; one of them he should send to Asia, the
other to Aetolia. The same was also ordered to be
exacted from the Sardinians and the corn shipped to
the same armies as that from Sicily. To Lucius
Baebius as replacements for service in Spain were
given one thousand Roman infantry and fifty cavalry
and six thousand infantry and two hundred cavalry
of the Latin confederacy; to Plautius Hypsaeus for
Nearer Spain were assigned one thousand Roman
infantry [1] and of the allies of the Latin confederacy
two thousand infantry and two hundred cavalry;
with these additions the two Spains would have one
legion each. As for the magistrates of the year
before, prorogation of the *imperium* for one year was
ordered for Gaius Laelius with his army; the same
was done for Publius Junius, propraetor in Etruria,
with the army which was in the province, and for
Marcus Tuccius, propraetor among the Brutti and in
Apulia.

LI. Before the praetors went to their provinces
there was a dispute between Publius Licinius the
pontifex maximus and Quintus Fabius Pictor the
priest of Quirinus, such as within the memory of our
fathers arose between Lucius Metellus and Postumius
Albinus. When that consul was setting out with
his colleague Gaius Lutatius to Sicily and the fleet,
Metellus the pontifex maximus had detained him
for the religious ceremonies; this praetor was prevented from going to Sardinia by Publius Licinius.
Both in the senate and before the assembly the
quarrel was carried on with great vigour, and orders
were issued on both sides and guarantees taken and
fines imposed and tribunes applied to and appeals

A.U.C. 565

5 Religio ad[1] postremum vicit; ut dicto audiens esset[2] flamen pontifici iussus; et multa iussu populi ei 6 remissa. Ira provinciae ereptae praetorem magistratu abdicare se conantem patres auctoritate sua deterruerunt et[3] ut ius inter peregrinos diceret[4] 7 decreverunt. Dilectibus deinde intra paucos dies —neque enim multi milites legendi erant—perfectis consules praetoresque in provincias proficiscuntur.

8 Fama dein de rebus in Asia gestis temere vulgata sine auctore, et post dies paucos nuntii certi litteraeque 9 imperatoris Romam adlatae, quae non tantum gaudium ab recenti metu attulerunt—desierant enim victum in Aetolia regem[5] metuere—quam a vetere[6] fama, quod ineuntibus id bellum gravis hostis et suis viribus, et quod Hannibalem rectorem 10 militiae haberet, visus fuerat. Nihil tamen aut de consule mittendo in Asiam mutandum aut minuendas eius copias censuerunt metu, ne cum Gallis foret bellandum.

LII. Haud multo post M. Aurelius Cotta legatus

[1] ad ς: *om. B.* [2] esset ς: essent *B.*
[3] et ς: sed *B.* [4] diceret ς: dicere *B.*
[5] regem *aut* Antiochum *Madvig*: *om. Bς.*
[6] a vetere *Rubens*: auerterunt *Bς.*

[1] Livy's account of this affair is more vivid than accurate. The phrase *ultro citroque* probably belongs to all the verbs that follow, which describe various aspects of procedure under the *ius civile*; *pignera capta* refers to the giving of bonds for appearance in court, while the other items are regular legal consequences. The praetor exercises jurisdiction by virtue of his *imperium,* the pontifex by virtue of his right to supervise and if necessary to coerce priests of lower rank. In case of a judgment the right of appeal to the assembly (*provocatio*) existed.

presented to the assembly.[1] The religious argu-   B.C. 189
ment finally prevailed; the priest was ordered [2] to
obey the pontifex, and by command of the people
the fine was remitted to him. When, in anger at
being deprived of his province,[3] he tried to resign
his office, the Fathers by their influence prevented
him and decreed that he should exercise jurisdiction
between citizens and aliens. The levies being then
completed within a few days—for not many soldiers
were to be enrolled—the consuls and praetors
departed to their provinces.

Then there was a rumour idly circulated with no
definite authority about events in Asia, and a few
days later trustworthy messengers and the despatches
of the consul reached Rome, which did not so much
bring joy after recent fear—for they had ceased to
fear the king after his defeat in Aetolia—as on
account of his former reputation, since, when they
entered upon the war he seemed a dangerous adver-
sary, partly because of his own resources and partly
because he had Hannibal as his director of operations. Nevertheless, they decreed that there should
be neither any change in the plan to send the consul
to Asia nor any diminution in his forces, for fear
that he would be compelled to fight with the Gauls.[4]

LII. Not much later Marcus Aurelius Cotta,

[2] This order came presumably from the assembly when the
appeals were laid before it. The remission of the fine is
clearly its work.

[3] A provincial command required absence from Rome and
was thus incompatible with religious duties. Since resigna-
tion was not provided for in the constitutional system, the
senate found employment in Rome for Fabius by re-establish-
ing the two judicial *provinciae*.

[4] Livy means the Galatians, who had sent troops to aid
Antiochus (xv. 5, etc. above).

441

A.U.C.
565

L. Scipionis cum Antiochi regis legatis et Eumenes
2 rex Rhodiique Romam venerunt. Cotta in senatu
primum, deinde in contione[1] iussu patrum quae acta
in Asia essent exposuit. Supplicatio inde in triduum
decreta est, et quadraginta maiores hostiae immolari
3 iussae. Tum omnium primum Eumeni senatus datus
est. Is cum breviter et egisset gratias patribus quod
obsidione se ac fratrem exemissent regnumque ab
iniuriis Antiochi vindicassent, et gratulatus esset,
4 quod terra marique res prospere gessissent, quodque
regem Antiochum fusum fugatumque et exutum
castris prius Europa, post et[2] Asia, quae cis Taurum
5 montem est, expulissent, sua deinde merita malle
eos ex imperatoribus suis legatisque quam se com-
6 memorante cognoscere[3] dixit. Haec approbantibus
cunctis iubentibusque dicere ipsum, omissa in id
verecundia, quid sibi ab senatu populoque Romano
tribui aequum censeret; propensius cumulatiusque,
si quo possit, prout eius merita sint, senatum fac-
7 turum, ad ea rex, si ab aliis sibi praemiorum optio
deferretur, libenter, data modo facultate consulendi
senatum Romanum, consilio amplissimi ordinis usurum fuisse, ne quid aut immoderate[4] cupisse aut
8 petisse parum modeste videri posset; verum enimvero
cum ipsi daturi sint, multo magis munificentiam eorum

---

[1] contione ⟨ς⟩ : contentione *B*.
[2] post et ⟨ς⟩ : et *B* : postea *M*.
[3] cognoscere *ed. Frobeniana* 1535 : cognosci *B*⟨ς⟩.
[4] immoderate ⟨ς⟩ : immoderata *B*.

representing Lucius Scipio, came with the ambassadors of King Antiochus, and King Eumenes and
the Rhodians arrived in Rome. Cotta first in the
senate and then before the assembly by order of
the senate described what had occurred in Asia.
A period of thanksgiving was then proclaimed for
three days and forty full-grown victims were ordered
sacrificed. Then first of all Eumenes was granted
an audience by the senate. When he had briefly
thanked the Fathers because they had rescued
him and his brother from siege and saved his kingdom from the violence of Antiochus, and then congratulated them because success had attended their
efforts on land and sea and because they had driven
King Antiochus, defeated, routed and stripped of his
camp, first out of Europe and then out of Asia on
this side of the Taurus mountains, he said next that
he preferred that they should hear of his own services
from their own commanders and legates than from his
relation of them. All applauded this, and bade
him lay aside his modesty in this respect and say himself what he thought should properly be given him by
the senate and the Roman people: the senate, they
said, would act with greater readiness and greater
generosity, if it were possible, in accordance with his
merits; to this the king replied that if a choice of
rewards were offered him by others, he would have
been glad, if only the privilege of consulting the
Roman senate were granted him, to enjoy the advice
of that most distinguished body, that he might not
seem either to have conceived immoderate ambitions
or to have stated them with too little restraint; but
in fact, since they themselves were planning to
give something to him, so much the more should

LIVY

in se fratresque suos ipsorum arbitrii debere esse.
9 Nihil hac oratione eius patres conscripti deterriti
sunt quo minus dicere ipsum iuberent, et, cum
aliquamdiu hinc indulgentia hinc modestia inter
permittentes in vicem non magis mutua quam inex-
plicabili facilitate certatum esset, Eumenes ex
10 templo excessit. Senatus in eadem perstare sententia, ut absurdum esse diceret ignorare regem,
quid sperans aut petens venerit; quae accommodata
regno suo sint, ipsum optime scire; Asiam longe
melius quam senatum nosse; revocandum igitur et
cogendum quae vellet quaeque sentiret expromere.

LIII. Reductus a praetore in templum rex et
dicere iussus "perseverassem" inquit "tacere,
patres conscripti, nisi Rhodiorum legationem mox
vocaturos vos scirem, et illis auditis mihi necessitatem
2 fore dicendi. Quae quidem eo difficilior oratio erit,
quod ea postulata eorum futura sunt, ut non solum
nihil, quod contra me sit, sed ne[1] quod ad ipsos
3 quidem proprie pertineat, petere videantur. Agent
enim causam civitatium Graecarum, et liberari eas
dicent debere. Quo impetrato, cui dubium est quin
et a nobis aversuri sint non eas modo civitates quae
liberabuntur, sed etiam veteres stipendiarias nostras,

---

[1] sed ne ⌐ : et ne B.

---

[1] This point is a trifle embarrassing, since Rome had denied
to Antiochus the right to recover cities that had once been
free : cf. XXXV. xvi. 10–11. Rome now begins to see some
of the pitfalls which confront her in the east.

444

their generosity to him and his brothers be controlled by their own judgment. The Fathers were
not deterred by these words from urging him to
speak, and when the argument had continued for
some time between generosity on one side and
modesty on the other, between men who were leaving
the decision to one another with a suavity not more
equal in both than difficult to modify, Eumenes left
the temple. The senate remained unaltered in the
same determination, to the point of saying that it
seemed unreasonable that the king should not know
with what hopes and aspirations he had come; he
himself knew best what was suitable for his kingdom; he was far better acquainted with Asia than
the senate; he should therefore be recalled and
compelled to say what he wished and what were his
opinions.

LIII. The king was therefore brought back into
the temple by the praetor, and, being ordered to
speak, began thus: "I should have continued, conscript Fathers, in my silence, did I not know that
you would presently summon the embassy of the
Rhodians and that after they were heard it would
be necessary for me to speak. This discussion,
indeed, will be the more difficult because these
demands of theirs will be such that they will not
only seem to ask nothing which is against my interests, but not even seem to ask for what is particularly
their concern. For they will plead the cause of the
Greek cities, and will say that they should be set
free. If this is granted, who doubts that they will
deprive us not merely of the states that are to be
liberated but of our ancient tributaries [1] as well, while
they themselves will have nominally, indeed, allies,

445

LIVY

4 ipsi [1] autem tanto obligatos beneficio verbo socios, re
vera subiectos imperio et obnoxios habituri sint?
5 Et, si dis placet, cum has tantas opes affectabunt,
dissimulabunt ulla parte id ad se pertinere; vos
modo id decere et conveniens esse ante factis dicent.
6 Haec vos ne decipiat oratio providendum vobis erit,
neve non solum inaequaliter alios nimium deprimatis
ex sociis vestris, alios praeter modum extollatis, sed
etiam ne, qui adversus vos arma tulerint, in meliore
7 statu sint quam socii et [2] amici vestri. Quod ad me
attinet, in aliis rebus cessisse intra finem iuris mei
cuilibet videri malim quam nimis pertinaciter in
obtinendo eo tetendisse; [3] in certamine autem amicitiae vestrae, benevolentiae erga vos, honoris, qui
ab vobis habebitur, minime aequo animo vinci
possum. Hanc ego maximam hereditatem a patre
accepi, qui primus omnium Asiam Graeciamque
8 incolentium in amicitiam venit vestram eamque
perpetua et constanti fide ad extremum vitae finem
9 perduxit; nec animum dumtaxat vobis fidelem ac
bonum praestitit, sed omnibus interfuit bellis, quae
in Graecia gessistis, terrestribus navalibus, omni
genere commeatuum, ita ut nemo sociorum vestrorum
10 ulla parte aequari posset, vos adiuvit; postremo, cum
Boeotos ad societatem vestram hortaretur, in ipsa
contione intermortuus haud multo post exspiravit.
11 Huius ego vestigia ingressus voluntati [4] quidem et

---

[1] ipsi *ed. Frobeniana* 1535 : sibi *Bϛ*.
[2] et *ed. Aldina* : aut *Bϛ*.
[3] eo tetendisse *ϛ* : eos tendisse *B*.
[4] voluntati *ed. Frobeniana* 1531 : uolunte *B* : uoluntate *ϛ*.

---

[1] Cf. XXVI. xxiv. 9; this was in 211 B.C.
[2] Literally, fainting; cf. XXXIII. ii. 2; for his obituary cf.
XXXIII. xxi. 1–5.

bound to them by so great a service, but in reality
subject to their dominion and dependent upon it?
And—heaven help us!—while they have their eyes
fixed on such power, they will pretend that this is
no concern of theirs; they will say only that this
is suitable conduct for you and consistent with
what you have done in the past. That you shall
not be entrapped by such reasoning must be your
own care, and not only that you shall not unduly
hold down some of your allies inequitably and raise
up others beyond proper limits, but also that those
who have borne arms against you shall not be in
better case than your allies and friends. So far as
I am concerned, I should prefer to seem, in other
respects, to have yielded something to anyone,
though it was within the limits of my rights, than
to have struggled too stubbornly to maintain it;
but in a contest of friendship towards you, of good-
will towards you, of respect which is due you, I
cannot willingly be overcome. This is the greatest
inheritance I have received from my father, who
first [1] of all the inhabitants of Asia and Greece
entered into your friendship and who maintained it
with constant and true faith to the very end of his
life; nor did he merely assume a pose of being your
loyal and well-disposed friend, but he took part in
all your wars which you waged in Greece, and he
aided you with military and naval forces and all
manner of supplies, so that none of your allies can
be ranked on an equality with him in any respect;
last of all, while he was urging the Boeotians to
join your alliance, collapsing [2] in the very midst of
his speech, he breathed his last only a little while
afterwards. I, following in his footsteps, have not

447

LIVY

studio in colendis vobis adicere—etenim inex-
12 superabilia haec erant—nihil potui; rebus ipsis
meritisque et impensis officiorum ut superare possem,[1]
fortuna tempora Antiochus et bellum in Asia gestum
13 praebuerunt materiam. Rex Asiae et partis Europae
Antiochus filiam suam in matrimonium mihi dabat;
restituebat extemplo civitates quae defecerant a
nobis; spem magnam in posterum amplificandi regni
faciebat, si secum bellum adversus vos gessissem.
14 Non gloriabor eo, quod nihil in vos deliquerim; illa
potius, quae vetustissima domus nostrae[2] vobiscum
15 amicitia digna sunt, referam. Pedestribus navalibusque copiis, ut nemo sociorum vestrorum me
aequiperare posset, imperatores vestros adiuvi;
commeatus terra marique suppeditavi; navalibus
proeliis, quae multis locis facta sunt, omnibus adfui;
16 nec labori meo nec periculo usquam peperci. Quod
miserrimum est in bello, obsidionem passus sum,
Pergami inclusus cum discrimine ultimo simul vitae
17 regnique. Liberatus deinde obsidione, cum alia
parte Antiochus alia Seleucus circa arcem regni mei
castra haberent, relictis meis rebus tota classe ad
Hellespontum L. Scipioni consuli vestro occurri, ut
18 eum in traiciendo exercitu adiuvarem. Posteaquam
in Asiam exercitus vester est transgressus, numquam
a consule abscessi; nemo miles Romanus magis
adsiduus in castris fuit vestris quam ego fratresque
mei; nulla expeditio, nullum equestre proelium sine

---

[1] ut superare possem ς : om. B.
[2] nostrae ς : uestrae B.

been able to add anything to his good-will, indeed, B.C. 189
and his zeal in honouring you—for these are not to
be surpassed; that I was able to outdo him in actual
accomplishments and services and expenditure of
effort for you, fate, the times, Antiochus, and the
war waged in Asia have furnished opportunity.
Antiochus, king of Asia and part of Europe, wished
to give me his daughter in marriage; he offered to
restore at once the cities which had revolted from
us; he held out great prospects of future enlarge-
ment of my kingdom, if I should join him in war
upon you.[1] I shall not make a boast of the fact
that I have done you no wrong; I shall rather relate
what is worthy of the very ancient friendship between
our house and you. With my army and navy, on
such a scale that no one of your allies could equal
it, I aided your commanders; I supplied them with
provisions on land and sea; I took part in all the
naval battles which were fought in many places;
I never spared either my toil or my peril. The
most wretched fate in war, siege, I suffered, shut up
in Pergamum, to the extreme peril at once of life
and throne. Then, freed from siege, when Antiochus
on one side, Seleucus on the other, had their camps
around the citadel of my kingdom, I let my own
affairs go and with my whole fleet met Lucius
Scipio at the Hellespont to aid him in transporting
his army across. After your army arrived in Asia,
I never left the consul; no Roman soldier was more
constantly in your camp than I and my brothers;
no raid, no cavalry engagement, took place without

---

[1] Polybius (XXII. iii) has Antiochus offer Eumenes his
daughter and a share in his kingdom. Appian (*Syr.* 5) says
that he declined the marriage.

LIVY

19 me factum est; in acie ibi steti, eam partem sum [1]
tutatus in qua me consul esse voluit. Non sum hoc
dicturus, patres conscripti: quis hoc bello meritis
20 erga vos mecum comparari potest? Ego nulli
omnium neque populorum neque regum, quos in
magno honore habetis, non ausim me comparare.
21 Masinissa hostis vobis ante quam socius fuit, nec
incolumi regno cum auxiliis suis, sed extorris, expulsus, amissis omnibus copiis, cum turma equitum in
22 castra confugit vestra; tamen eum, quia [2] in Africa
adversus Syphacem et Carthaginienses fideliter atque
impigre vobiscum stetit, non in patrium solum regnum restituistis, sed adiecta opulentissima parte
Syphacis regni praepotentem inter Africae reges
23 fecistis. Quo tandem igitur nos praemio atque
honore digni apud vos sumus, qui numquam hostes,
24 semper socii fuimus? Pater, ego, fratres mei non in
Asia tantum, sed etiam procul ab domo in Peloponneso in Boeotia in Aetolia, Philippi Antiochi
Aetolico bello, terra marique pro vobis arma tulimus.
25 'Quid ergo postulas?' dicat aliquis. Ego, patres
conscripti, quoniam dicere utique volentibus vobis
parendum est, si vos ea mente ultra Tauri iuga
emostis Antiochum, ut ipsi teneretis eas terras,
nullos accolas nec finitimos habere quam vos malo,
26 nec ulla re alia tutius stabiliusque regnum meum
27 futurum spero; sed si vobis decedere inde atque
deducere exercitus in animo est, neminem digniorem

---

[1] sum 𝔰 : *om. B.*   [2] quia 𝔰 : qui *B.*

me; I stood in the battle-line and defended that B.C. 189
sector in which the consul wished me to be. I
shall not, conscript Fathers, ask: Who can be
compared with me in his services in this war? I
should not venture to compare myself with anyone,
either people or king, whom you hold in great
honour. Masinissa was your enemy before he was
your ally, nor was it while his kingdom was uninjured
and he could bring his own troops to your help, but
when he was an exile, banished, with all his resources
gone, that he fled with one troop of cavalry to your
camp; nevertheless, because he stood loyally and
steadfastly with you in Africa against Syphax and
the Carthaginians, you not only restored him to his
paternal kingdom but, bestowing upon him the
richest part of the realm of Syphax, you made him
pre-eminent among the kings of Africa. Of what
reward and honour, pray, are we then worthy in
your sight, who have never been your enemies,
always your allies? My father, myself, my brothers,
not in Asia alone, but far from home, in the Peloponnesus, in Boeotia, in Aetolia, in the wars with Philip,
with Antiochus, with the Aetolians, on land and sea,
have borne arms in your cause. But someone may
say, ' What then do you ask? ' As to that, conscript
Fathers, (since I must in any case obey your wish
that I should speak) if you expelled Antiochus beyond the heights of Taurus with the intention of
yourselves holding those lands, there are no neighbours or settlers whom I prefer to you, nor do I
expect that my kingdom will be safer or more
enduring under any other circumstances; but if it
is your purpose to retire and withdraw your armies
from there, I should dare to say that no one of

LIVY

esse ex sociis vestris, qui bello [1] a vobis parta possideat
28 quam me dicere ausim. At enim magnificum est
liberare civitates servas. Ita opinor, si nihil hostile
adversus vos fecerunt; sin autem Antiochi partis
fuerunt, quanto est vestra prudentia et aequitate
dignius sociis bene meritis quam hostibus vos
consulere ? "

LIV. Grata oratio regis patribus fuit, et facile
apparebat munifice omnia et propenso animo facturos.
2 Interposita Zmyrnaeorum brevis legatio est, quia non
aderat [2] quidam Rhodiorum. Collaudatis egregie
Zmyrnaeis, quod omnia ultima pati quam se regi
3 tradere maluissent, introducti Rhodii sunt. Quorum
princeps legationis expositis initiis amicitiae cum
populo Romano meritisque [3] Rhodiorum Philippi
4 prius, deinde Antiochi bello " nihil " inquit " nobis
tota nostra actione, patres conscripti,[4] neque
difficilius neque molestius est, quam quod cum
5 Eumene nobis disceptatio est, cum quo uno maxime
regum et privatim singulis et, quod magis nos movet,
6 publicum civitati nostrae hospitium est. Ceterum

---

[1] bello ϛ : in bello *B*.   [2] aderat *Ruperti* : aderant *B*ϛ.
[3] meritisque ϛ : meritis *B*.   [4] patres conscripti ϛ : *om. B.*

---

[1] This speech is in essence the same as that in Polybius
(XXII. ii.–iv. incl.), but somewhat more effectively expressed.
The problems confronting Roman statesmanship now assume
more definite outline. Rome must choose between offending
Eumenes or the Rhodians or both and abandoning the policy
enunciated by Flamininus, unless some universally satisfactory
compromise can be found. The liberation of the Ionian cities
was frequently mentioned in the earlier negotiations with
Antiochus, though later it was replaced by a demand that he
cease to interfere in European affairs. Compare the speech
of Sulpicius (XXXV. xvi.) with that of Africanus (xlv. above).
[2] Polybius (XXII. v.) gives a generally similar account,
but with a less definite statement of the action taken.

your allies is more worthy than I to hold what you B.C. 189
have won in war. But there will be protests because
it is a fine thing to liberate enslaved cities. Such is
my opinion, if they have committed no hostile acts
against you; but if they were of Antiochus' party,
how much more worthy of your wisdom and justice
is it to have regard for well-deserving allies than for
enemies?" [1]

LIV. The speech of the king pleased the Fathers,
and it was quite evident that they would deal with
the whole matter generously and in a sympathetic
spirit. A brief audience was then accorded the
delegation from the Zmyrnaeans, since one of the
Rhodians had not yet arrived. The Zmyrnaeans were
conspicuously lauded because they had preferred
to endure all extremities rather than submit to the
king,[2] and the Rhodians were introduced. The chief
of their embassy, after setting forth the origins of
their friendship with the Roman people and the
services of the Rhodians, first in the war with Philip
and later in the war with Antiochus, continued thus:
"Nothing in all our pleading, conscript Fathers, is
so difficult for us or so painful as the fact that our
difference of opinion is with Eumenes, with whom
alone of kings and in preference to all others, both
individuals of our community privately and, what
moves us more, our state publicly, is in relations of
hospitality.[3] But it is not our personal feelings,

[3] *Hospitium* was a relationship entered into usually by
individuals with one another, but sometimes by individuals
with communities or communities with communities, in which
each party owed the other certain services. The relation once
formed was hereditary and was under divine protection.
Since each owed the other support in any endeavour, it required courage on the part of the Rhodians to oppose Eumenes.

A.U.C.
565

non animi nostri, patres conscripti, nos, sed rerum
natura, quae potentissima est, disiungit, ut nos liberi
etiam aliorum libertatis causam agamus, reges serva
omnia et subiecta imperio suo esse velint. Utcumque
7 tamen res sese habet, magis verecundia nostra adversus regem nobis obstat quam ipsa disceptatio aut
nobis impedita est aut vobis perplexam delibera-
8 tionem praebitura videtur. Nam si aliter socio atque
amico regi et bene merito hoc ipso in bello, de cuius
praemiis agitur, honos haberi nullus posset, nisi
liberas civitates in servitutem traderetis ei, esset
9 deliberatio anceps ne aut regem amicum inhonoratum
dimitteretis, aut decederetis instituto vestro gloriamque Philippi bello partam nunc servitute tot
10 civitatium deformaretis; sed ab hac necessitate aut
gratiae in amicum minuendae aut gloriae vestrae
egregie vos fortuna vindicat. Est enim deum
benignitate non gloriosa magis quam dives victoria
vestra, quae vos facile isto velut aere alieno exsolvat.
11 Nam et Lycaonia et Phrygia utraque et Pisidia
omnis et Chersonesus, quaeque circumiacent Europae,
12 in vestra sunt potestate, quarum una quaelibet regi
adiecta multiplicare regnum Eumenis potest, omnes
vero datae maximis eum regibus aequare. Licet
13 ergo vobis et praemiis belli ditare socios et non
decedere instituto vestro et meminisse, quem titulum
praetenderitis prius adversus Philippum, nunc
adversus [1] Antiochum belli, quid feceritis Philippo

---

[1] aduersus ⌐: om. B.

---

[1] The region around ancient Troy and a district farther
inland were both called Phrygia.

conscript Fathers, which part us, but the nature of
things, which is all-powerful, so that we who are
free are pleading the cause of liberty for others as
well, while kings wish everything to be enslaved
and subject to their will. Yet, however that may
be, the fact is rather that it is our respect for the
king which stands in our way than that the question
itself is either involved for us or likely, as it seems,
to cause you any hesitancy in deciding. For if in
no other way could honour be paid an allied and
friendly king and one who had rendered good
service in this very war, about whose compensation
there was debate, than by your giving free cities
into servitude to him, the discussion would be of
doubtful issue, lest you either send away a friendly
king without his meed of honour or depart from your
tradition and stain the glory won in the war with
Philip by now enslaving so many cities; but from
this necessity of either diminishing your recompense
to a friend or detracting from your own fame,
fortune offers you a splendid escape. For by the
bounty of heaven, your victory brings not more glory
than riches, and it may easily discharge what you may
call your debt. For Lycaonia and both Phrygias [1]
and all Pisidia and the Chersonesus, all of which
adjoin Europe, are in your power, and any of these,
bestowed upon the king, can greatly enlarge the
kingdom of Eumenes, and the gift of them all can
make him equal to the greatest of kings. It is
possible for you both to enrich your allies with
prizes of war and not to depart from your tradition
and to remember what banner you displayed before
you earlier in the war against Philip and now in
the war against Antiochus—what you have done after

14 victo, quid nunc a vobis, non magis quia fecistis,
quam quia id vos facere decet, desideretur atque
expectetur. Alia enim aliis et honesta et probabilis

15 est causa armorum; illi agrum, hi vicos, hi oppida,
hi portus oramque aliquam maris ut possideant; vos
nec cupistis haec antequam haberetis, nec nunc,
cum orbis terrarum in dicione vestra sit, cupere

16 potestis. Pro dignitate et gloria apud omne humanum
genus, quod vestrum nomen imperiumque iuxta ac
deos immortales iam pridem intuetur, pugnastis.
Quae parare et quaerere arduum fuit, nescio an tueri

17 difficilius sit. Gentis vetustissimae nobilissimaeque
vel fama rerum gestarum vel omni commendatione
humanitatis doctrinarumque tuendam ab servitio
regio libertatem [1] suscepistis; hoc patrocinium
receptae in fidem et clientelam vestram universae

18 gentis perpetuum vos praestare decet. Non, quae
in solo [2] antiquo sunt, Graecae magis urbes sunt
quam coloniae earum, illinc [3] quondam profectae in
Asiam; nec terra mutata mutavit genus aut mores.

19 Certare pio certamine cuiuslibet bonae artis ac
virtutis ausi sumus [4] cum parentibus quaeque civitas

20 et conditoribus suis. Adistis Graeciae, adistis [5]
Asiae urbes plerique; nisi quod longius a vobis

---

[1] libertatem ⸝ : ad libertatem B.
[2] solo Crévier : solo modo B⸝.
[3] illinc ⸝ : om., spat. rel. B.
[4] sumus ⸝ : simus B.
[5] adistis ⸝ : ad istas B.

---

[1] I have chosen to express rather the obligation of the patron
to the client, as the Romans understood it, than the relation
of the client to the patron.

[2] The Rhodians claimed to be of Dorian descent but are
speaking here of the Greek colonies generally.

defeating Philip and what to-day, not more because B.C. 189
you did so formerly than because it becomes you
to do so, is desired and expected at your hands.
One nation has one and another nation has another
just and reasonable cause for taking up arms; those
that they may possess lands, these cities, these
towns, these harbours and some strip of coast; you
have neither desired these things before you had
them, nor now, when the world is in your hands,
can you desire them. For the sake of standing and
fame in the eyes of the whole world, which for long
now has regarded your name and empire as next
after those of the immortal gods, you have waged
your wars. What it was difficult to get and acquire, it
may be perhaps still more difficult to keep. You have
undertaken to defend against slavery to a king the
liberty of a most ancient people, most famed either
from the renown of its achievements or from universal
praise of its culture and learning; this champion-
ship of a whole people taken under your protection
and guardianship [1] it befits you to guarantee for ever.
The cities which are on the ancient soil are not more
Greek than their colonies, which once set out from
there for Asia; nor does a change of habitation
change race or manners. We [2] have dared to vie
in reverent rivalry in every noble art and virtue
with our fathers, every city too with its founders.
Many of you have visited the cities of Greece, have
visited the cities of Asia [3]; except that we are

---

[3] Such a statement would certainly have been true in the
time of Livy but less certainly in the time of Antiochus. Since
it is not in Polybius, it may be regarded, along with the whole
of the eulogy of Greek culture, as part of Livy's rhetorical
embroidery.

LIVY

21 absumus, nulla vincimur alia re. Massilienses, quos,
si natura insita velut ingenio terrae vinci posset,[1]
iam pridem efferassent tot indomitae circumfusae
gentes, in eo honore, in ea merito dignitate audimus [2]
apud vos esse, ac si medium umbilicum Graeciae
22 incolerent. Non enim sonum modo linguae vesti-
tumque et habitum, sed ante omnia mores et leges et
ingenium sincerum integrumque a [3] contagione
23 accolarum servarunt. Terminus est nunc imperii
vestri mons Taurus; quidquid intra eum cardinem
est, nihil longinquum vobis debet videri; quo arma
vestra pervenerunt, eodem ius hinc profectum per-
24 veniat. Barbari, quibus pro legibus semper domi-
norum imperia fuerunt, quo gaudent, reges [4]
habeant; Graeci suam fortunam, vestros animos
25 gerunt.[5] Domesticis quondam viribus etiam imperium amplectebantur; nunc imperium, ubi est, ibi
ut sit perpetuum, optant; libertatem vestris tueri
26 armis satis habent, quoniam suis non possunt. At
enim quaedam civitates cum Antiocho senserunt.
Et aliae prius cum Philippo, et cum Pyrrho Tarentini;
ne alios populos enumerem, Carthago libera cum suis
27 legibus est. Huic vestro exemplo quantum debeatis,
videte, patres conscripti; inducetis in animum negare
Eumenis cupiditati, quod iustissimae irae vestrae
28 negastis. Rhodii et in hoc [6] et in omnibus bellis
quae in illa ora gessistis, quam [7] forti fidelique vos

---

[1] posset ς : posset et B.
[2] audimus ς : audiuimus B.
[3] a ς : om. B.
[4] reges ς : regis B.
[5] gerunt ς : om. B.
[6] et in hoc edd. vett.: om. Bς.
[7] quam ς : om. B.

farther distant from you, we are inferior in no
respect. The people of Massilia, whom, if inborn
nature could be conquered, so to speak, by the
temper of a land, so many untamed tribes around
them would long ago have barbarized, we hear are
held in the same respect and deservedly paid the
same honour by you as if they dwelt in the very
navel of Greece. For they have kept not only the
sound of their speech along with their dress and their
outward appearance, but, before all, their manners
and laws and character pure and free from the corruption of their neighbours. The Taurus mountains
are now the limit of your empire; nothing, whatever lies within this boundary, should seem remote
to you; where your army had made its way, thither
too let your law advance and make its way. Let
barbarians, to whom the mandates of their lords have
ever served as laws, since in that they take delight,
have kings; Greeks have their own fortunes, but
souls like yours. Once they even possessed empire,
as a result of their own might; now they hope that
empire may abide for ever where it now resides;
they hold it sufficient to maintain liberty through
your arms since they cannot through their own.
But, someone may say, some cities sided with
Antiochus. True, and others formerly with Philip
and the Tarentines with Pyrrhus; not to mention
other peoples, Carthage is free and enjoys its own
laws. See, conscript Fathers, how much you owe
to your own precedent; you will persuade yourselves to refuse to the ambition of Eumenes what
you have refused to your own wrath, just as it may
be. Both in this and in all wars which you waged
in our region, we Rhodians leave it to you to judge

LIVY

opera adiuverimus, vestro iudicio relinquimus. Nunc in pace consilium id adferimus, quod si comprobaritis, magnificentius vos victoria usos esse quam vicisse omnes existimaturi sint." Apta magnitudini Romanae oratio visa est.

LV. Post Rhodios Antiochi legati vocati sunt. Ii vulgato petentium veniam more errorem fassi 2 regis obtestati sunt patres conscriptos ut suae potius clementiae quam regis culpae, qui satis superque poenarum dedisset,[1] memores consulerent; postremo pacem datam a L. Scipione imperatore, quibus 3 legibus dedisset, confirmarent auctoritate sua. Et senatus eam pacem servandam censuit,[2] et paucos post dies populus iussit. Foedus in Capitolio cum Antipatro principe legationis et eodem fratris filio regis Antiochi est ictum.

4 Auditae deinde et aliae legationes ex Asia sunt. Quibus omnibus datum responsum decem legatos more maiorum senatum missurum ad res Asiae

---

[1] dedisset ϛ : dedissent B.
[2] censuit ϛ : om. B.

---

[1] The somewhat cool reception accorded the Rhodian argument, in contrast with that given Eumenes, prompts one to examine both its rhetorical quality and its sources. The version of it in Polybius (XXII. v–vi) is less rhetorical and puts greater emphasis upon the facts and the political aspects of the argument. His final comment, quite unlike that of Livy, is that it was " temperate and fair " (μετρίως καὶ καλῶς). The speech in Livy seems skilfully constructed, with its shrewd emphasis upon the original policy of the Romans (cf. the note to liii. 28 above), its artful playing upon Roman sympathies in the eulogy of Greek culture and the clever suppression of Rhodian ambitions, in sharp contrast with the method of Eumenes. We note too that while Eumenes took into account the possibility that the Romans would remain permanently

with what courageous and constant aid we have B.C. 189
assisted you. Now in peace we offer you this counsel,
and if you approve it all men will think that you
have used your victory more gloriously than you
have won it." This speech seemed well adapted
to the high position of Rome.[1]

LV. After the Rhodians the ambassadors of
Antiochus were summoned. In the usual fashion
of envoys begging for mercy, they confessed the
wrongdoing of the king and implored the conscript
Fathers, in arriving at a decision, to pay regard
to their own clemency rather than to the error of
the king, who had paid a sufficient and more
than sufficient penalty; finally, they requested that
they would ratify by their authority the peace
proposed by Lucius Scipio the commander, on the
terms which he had stated. And the senate voted
that this treaty of peace should be ratified, and a
few days later the assembly so ordered. The treaty
was struck on the Capitoline with Antipater the
chief of the embassy and likewise the son of the
brother of King Antiochus.

Then other embassies also from Asia were heard.[2]
To all these the same reply was given, that the
senate, in the fashion of their forefathers, would send
ten commissioners to adjudge cases arising in Asia

in Asia, the Rhodians take it for granted that this will not be
the case.

[2] In addition to the major parties interested in the settlement, Antiochus, Eumenes and the Rhodians, there were
apparently many other cities and states which neither Polybius nor Livy finds it necessary to mention by name, but
whose claims had to be considered. One can easily imagine
that the senate would feel somewhat bewildered, since war
and victory had previously been simple problems in their
experience.

LIVY

5 disceptandas componendasque; summam tamen
hanc fore,[1] ut cis Taurum montem, quae intra[2]
regni Antiochi fines fuissent, Eumeni attribuerentur
praeter Lyciam Cariamque usque ad Maeandrum
6 amnem; ea ut civitatis Rhodiorum essent; ceterae
civitates Asiae quae Attali stipendiariae fuissent
eaedem[3] vectigal Eumeni penderent; quae vectigales Antiochi fuissent, eae liberae atque immunes
7 essent. Decem legatos hos decreverunt: Q. Minucium Rufum L. Furium Purpurionem Q. Minucium
Thermum Ap. Claudium Neronem Cn. Cornelium
Merulam M. Iunium Brutum L. Aurunculeium
L. Aemilium Paulum P. Cornelium Lentulum P.
Aelium Tuberonem.

LVI. His, quae praesentis disceptationis essent,
libera mandata; de summa rerum senatus consti-
2 tuit. Lycaoniam omnem et Phrygiam utramque
et Mysiam, quam Prusia rex ademerat, restituit regi
et Milyas[4] et Lydiam Ioniamque[5] extra ea oppida
quae libera fuissent quo die cum rege Antiocho

---

[1] fore ς : om. B.
[2] montem quae intra ς : montemque B.
[3] eaedem ς : eadem B.
[4] quam Prusia rex ademerat, restituit regi et Milyas et
M. Müller XXXVIII. xxxix. 15 ff. conferens: regias siluas
et BMς.
[5] Lydiam Ioniamque Crévier : lydiae ioniaeque BMς.

---

[1] The terms of the final settlement, conforming in general
to the principle here stated, are given in XXXVIII. xxxviii.
It is obvious that an effort has been made to satisfy both
Eumenes and the Rhodians.

[2] The first three of these had been consuls. If the otherwise unknown Cn. Cornelius Merula is a mistake for Cn.
Corn. Merenda, all the others had been praetors. In contrast
to the habit of including former commanders in commissions
sent to Greece, the Scipios and Acilius are—rather pointedly

and to settle differences; yet the general principle B.C. 189 followed would be this, that on this side of the Taurus mountains the districts which had been within the boundaries of the kingdom of Antiochus should be assigned to Eumenes with the exception of Lycia and Caria as far as the Meander river; that these should be given to the Rhodian state; that the other cities of Asia which had paid tribute to Attalus should also be tributaries to Eumenes; that those which had been vassals of Antiochus should be independent and free from tribute.[1] They chose these ten commissioners: Quintus Minucius Rufus, Lucius Furius Purpurio, Quintus Minucius Thermus, Appius Claudius Nero, Gnaeus Cornelius Merula, Marcus Junius Brutus, Lucius Aurunculeius, Lucius Aemilius Paulus, Publius Cornelius Lentulus, Publius Aelius Tubero.[2]

LVI. In matters pertaining to any discussion to be conducted on the spot, they were given a free hand; as to the chief issue involved, the senate made the decision. All Lycaonia and both Phrygias and Mysia, which King Prusias had taken from him, were restored to the king, as well as the Milyae [3] and Lydia and Ionia with the exception of those cities which had been free on the day when the battle with King Antiochus had been fought, and,

perhaps—omitted, as is Flamininus. The return of Paulus from Spain has not been mentioned before, and his name may have been added later as a concession to the Scipionic party. The commission is then undistinguished for either reputation or demonstrated capacity, though I hesitate to say that this was deliberate.

[3] Livy uses the name of the people for the name of the district. The reading here adopted has been restored from XXXVIII. xxxix. 16.

A.U.C.
565

3 pugnatum est, et nominatim Magnesiam ad Sipylum,
et Cariam, quae Hydrela appellatur, agrumque
Hydrelitanum ad Phrygiam vergentem, et castella
4 vicosque ad Maeandrum amnem et oppida, nisi
quae libera ante bellum fuissent, Telmessum item
nominatim et castra Telmessium, praeter agrum,
qui Ptolemaei Telmessii fuisset. Haec omnia quae
5 supra sunt scripta regi Eumeni iussa dari. Rhodiis
Lycia data extra eundem Telmessum et castra
Telmessium [1] et agrum, qui Ptolemaei Telmessii
fuisset; hic et ab Eumene et Rhodiis exceptus.[2]
6 Ea quoque iis pars Cariae data quae propior Rhodum
insulam trans Maeandrum amnem est, oppida, vici,
castella, agri, qui ad Pisidiam vergunt, nisi quae
eorum oppida in libertate fuissent pridie, quam cum
Antiocho rege in Asia pugnatum est.

7 Pro his cum gratias egissent Rhodii, de Solis
urbe, quae in Cilicia [3] est, egerunt: Argis et illos,
sicut sese, oriundos esse; ab ea germanitate frater-
nam sibi cum iis caritatem esse; petere hoc extra-
ordinarium munus ut eam civitatem ex servitute
8 regia eximerent. Vocati sunt legati regis Antiochi
actumque cum iis est nec [4] quicquam impetratum

---

[1] praeter . . . Telmessium ς : om. B.
[2] hic . . . exceptus Ruperti : haec . . . excepta Bς.
[3] Cilicia ς : lycia B.
[4] iis est nec ς : his est ne B.

---

[1] The eastern part of Caria north of the Meander river.
[2] He was probably in some way related to the Ptolemies
of Egypt, and the special treatment given this district may
be due to the fact that it was regarded as their property.
[3] These dispositions imply some minute geographical
knowledge of Asia Minor, and one wonders how the Romans

by name, Magnesia near Sipylus and Caria which B.C. 189
they call Hydrela [1] and the territory of Hydrela
which faces Phrygia, and the forts and villages
along the Meander river and the towns, except
those which had been free before the war; Telmessus also and the camp of the Telmessii, except the
land which had belonged to Ptolemy of Telmessus.[2]
All these places which have been written down above
were given to King Eumenes. The Rhodians were
given Lycia except the same Telmessus and the camp
of the Telmessii and the land which had belonged to
Ptolemy of Telmessus; this district was made an
exception in the case of both Eumenes and the
Rhodians. Also that part of Caria which is nearer
to the island of Rhodes across the Meander river
was given to them, and the towns, villages, forts
and lands which face Pisidia except those of the
towns which had been free the day before the battle
had been fought with King Antiochus in Asia.[3]

When the Rhodians had expressed their thanks for
all this, they thus spoke regarding the city of Soli,
which is in Cilicia: they also, like themselves, were
sprung from Argos; by reason of this kinship there
was a fraternal affection between them; they asked
this exceptional favour, that they might rescue this
city from slavery to the king. The ambassadors of
King Antiochus were summoned, and the question
was taken up with them but was not settled,

acquired it. The presumable sources, in the absence of large-
scale and accurate maps, were the ambassadors from the
Asiatic states and possibly Cotta. The distinction of towns
free on the day of and the day before the battle is hard to
explain, but is obviously some kind of compromise, possibly
suggested by the Rhodians.

LIVY

testante foedera [1] Antipatro, adversus quae ab
Rhodiis non Solos, sed Ciliciam peti et iuga Tauri
9 transcendi. Revocatis in senatum Rhodiis, cum
quanto opere tenderet [2] legatus regius exposuissent,
adiecerunt si utique eam rem ad civitatis suae
dignitatem pertinere censerent Rhodii, senatum
omni modo expugnaturum pertinaciam legatorum.
10 Tum vero impensius quam ante Rhodii gratias
egerunt, cessurosque sese potius arrogantiae Anti-
patri quam causam turbandae pacis [3] praebituros
dixerunt. Ita nihil de Solis mutatum est.

LVII. Per eos dies quibus haec gesta sunt, legati
Massiliensium nuntiarunt L. Baebium praetorem in
provinciam Hispaniam proficiscentem ab Liguribus
2 circumventum, magna parte comitum caesa vulnera-
tum ipsum cum paucis sine lictoribus Massiliam
3 perfugisse et intra triduum exspirasse. Senatus ea
re audita decrevit uti P. Iunius Brutus, qui propraetor in Etruria esset, provincia exercituque
traditis [4] uni, cui videretur ex legatis, ipse in ulteriorem Hispaniam proficisceretur, eaque ei provincia
4 esset. Hoc senatus consultum litteraeque a Sp.
Postumio praetore in Etruriam missae sunt, pro-

---

[1] foedera ς : foedere B.
[2] tenderet ς : tenderent B.
[3] turbandae pacis ς : turbandas paucis B.
[4] traditis ς : tradito B.

---

[1] The phraseology of the treaty had reference to the western
end of the Taurus range, where it approaches the sea in Cilicia.
Soli was beyond this point, and any assumption by the Romans
of the right to dispose of the city would be a violation of the
treaty even before it was concluded.

[2] Justice seems to have been entirely on the side of Antiochus
in this instance.

Antipater citing the treaty [1] in opposition to what the Rhodians had said, to the effect that not Soli but Cilicia was their object, and that they were crossing the ridges of Taurus. The Rhodians were recalled to the senate, and when they had explained how forcibly the king's ambassador had argued, they went on to say that if the Rhodians believed that this matter absolutely concerned their national honour, the senate would in every way overcome the resistance of the ambassadors. Then indeed the Rhodians thanked them more lavishly than before, and said that they would rather yield to the stubbornness of Antipater than offer any reason for disturbing the settlement. So no change was made with respect to Soli. [2]

LVII. During the period in which this took place, ambassadors from the Massilienses reported that Lucius Baebius the praetor, who was on his way to Spain, had been surrounded by the Ligures, that a large part of his retinue had been killed and himself wounded, that he with a few attendants but no lictors had taken refuge at Massilia and had died within three days. [3] The senate, on receiving this news, voted that Publius Junius Brutus, who was propraetor in Etruria, should turn over his province and army to whichever of his lieutenants he saw fit, that he himself should set out for Farther Spain and that this should be his province. This decree of the senate and these despatches were forwarded by the praetor Spurius Postumius to Etruria, and

---

[3] The pacification of Liguria (xlvi. 1 above) was apparently not complete after all, and the senate was wise in refusing Minucius a triumph. Easy triumphs over Liguria were notorious in the time of Cicero (*Brutus* 255).

LIVY

fectusque in Hispaniam est P. Iunius propraetor.
5 In qua provincia prius aliquanto quam successor
veniret,[1] L. Aemilius Paulus, qui postea regem
Persea magna gloria vicit, cum priore anno haud
prospere rem gessisset,[2] tumultuario exercitu collecto
6 signis collatis cum Lusitanis pugnavit. Fusi fugatique hostes; caesa decem octo milia armatorum;
duo milia trecenti capti et castra expugnata. Huius
victoriae fama tranquilliores in Hispania res fecit.[3]
7   Eodem anno ante diem tertium Kal. Ianuarias
Bononiam Latinam coloniam ex senatus consulto L.
Valerius Flaccus M. Atilius Serranus L. Valerius [4]
8 Tappo triumviri deduxerunt. Tria milia hominum
sunt deducta; equitibus septuagena [5] iugera, ceteris
colonis quinquagena sunt data. Ager captus de
Gallis Bois fuerat,[6] Galli Tuscos expulerant.
9   Eodem anno censuram multi et clari viri petierunt. Quae res, tamquam in se parum magni certaminis causam haberet, aliam contentionem multo [7]
10 maiorem excitavit. Petebant T. Quinctius Flamininus P. Cornelius Cn. F. Scipio L. Valerius Flaccus

----

¹ ueniret ⟨ : uenit et *B*.
² gessisset ⟨ : gessisset et *B*.
³ hispania res fecit ⟨ : hispaniam recepit *B*.
⁴ F.M.A.S.L.V. ⟨ : *om. B*.
⁵ septuagena ⟨ : septuaginta *B*.
⁶ fuerat ⟨ : fuerant *B*.
⁷ multo ⟨ : *om. B*.

----

¹ Cf. XLIV. xl. ff.
² Cf. xlvi. 7 above.
³ In xlvi. 10–11 this board was created to establish the new
colonists in Placentia and Cremona, and in xlvii. 2 provision

Publius Junius the propraetor departed for Spain. B.C. 189 In this province, shortly before his successor arrived, Lucius Aemilius Paulus, who afterwards won great glory by the defeat of King Perseus,[1] after fighting unsuccessfully [2] the previous year, collected an emergency army and engaged in pitched battle with the Lusitani. The enemy was routed and put to flight; eighteen thousand armed men were killed; two thousand three hundred were taken prisoners and the camp was captured. The fame of this victory made things quieter in Spain.

In the same year, on the third day before the Kalends of January, a Latin colony was established at Bononia by authorization of the senate, by Lucius Valerius Flaccus, Marcus Atilius Serranus and Lucius Valerius Tappo, the board of three appointed for the purpose.[3] Three thousand men were placed there; the cavalrymen received seventy *iugera* each, the rest of the colonists fifty each.[4] The land had been taken from the Gallic Boii; the Boii had expelled the Etruscans.

In the same year many distinguished men sought the censorship. As if it contained within itself too little cause for rivalry, it gave rise to a far greater controversy.[5] The candidates were Titus Quinctius Flamininus, Publius Cornelius Scipio, the son of Gnaeus, Lucius Valerius Flaccus, Marcus Porcius

was made for two colonies rather than one in this region. Nothing was said there about the composition of the board, and Livy has either confused accounts or tacitly enlarged the jurisdiction of the board.

[4] The allotments are unusually large, and the normal ratio of 2 : 1 is not maintained.

[5] The censorship was in itself a great prize, but at this time it was also the occasion for the prosecution of Glabrio.

LIVY

M. Porcius Cato M. Claudius Marcellus[1] M'. Acilius
Glabrio, qui Antiochum ad Thermopylas Aetolosque
11 devicerat. In hunc maxime, quod multa congiaria
distribuerat,[2] quibus magnam partem hominum
12 obligarat, favor populi se inclinabat. Id cum aegre
paterentur tot nobiles, novum sibi hominem tantum
praeferri, P. Sempronius Gracchus et C. Sempronius
Rutilus, tribuni plebis,[3] ei diem dixerunt, quod
pecuniae regiae praedaeque aliquantum captae in
Antiochi castris neque in triumpho tulisset, neque
13 in aerarium rettulisset. Varia testimonia legatorum
tribunorumque militum erant. M. Cato ante alios
testis conspiciebatur; cuius auctoritatem perpetuo
14 tenore vitae partam toga candida elevabat. Is
testis, quae vasa aurea atque argentea castris captis
inter aliam praedam regiam vidisset, ea se in tri-
15 umpho negabat vidisse. Postremo in huius maxime
invidiam desistere se petitione Glabrio dixit quando,
quod taciti indignarentur nobiles homines, id aeque
novus competitor intestabili periurio incesseret.

LVIII. Centum milium multa irrogata erat; bis

---

[1] Marcellus *ed. Frobeniana* 1535 : gellius *Bς.*
[2] congiaria distribuerat *Wesenberg* : congiaria habuerat
B : concilia (consilia) habuerat ς.
[3] tribuni plebis *edd. vett.* : *om. Bς.*

---

[1] A *novus homo* was one whose ancestors had never held any
of the major magistracies. The feeling of the aristocracy
was probably less bitter in the second century than it was in
Livy's time, but it existed then, and the fact that the chief
witness, Cato, was another new man did not ease the tension.
Speeches of Cato against Glabrio were known to the Romans.
[2] In XXXVI. xxxvi. 2 the senate seems to take it for granted
that not all the booty would be turned in to the treasury
(see the note). It would seem then that the accusation in this
case was based on political rather than moral grounds and that it
was arranged to keep Acilius out of the race for the censorship.

Cato, Marcus Claudius Marcellus, Manius Acilius B.C. 189
Glabrio, who had defeated Antiochus and the Aetolians
at Thermopylae. Towards him particularly, because
he had distributed many largesses, by which he had
placed a large part of the voters under obligation,
the support of the people inclined. When so many
nobles were angered that a new man [1] should be so
far preferred to them, Publius Sempronius Gracchus
and Gaius Sempronius Rutilus, tribunes of the
people, laid an accusation against him, that some of
the king's money and much of the booty taken in the
camp of Antiochus had neither been displayed by him
in the triumph nor turned in to the treasury.[2] Conflicting evidence was given by his lieutenants and
military tribunes. Marcus Cato was conspicuous as
a witness before the rest; but the honour gained in
the whole course of his life was diminished by his
candidate's dress.[3] In his testimony he said that
vessels of gold and silver which he had seen in the
captured camp along with the rest of the royal
booty he had not seen in the triumph. Finally,
in order chiefly to make Cato unpopular, Glabrio
said that he would drop his candidacy, since, while
the nobles kept silent, though indignant, it was
attacked with detestable[4] perjury by one who was
as much a new man as himself.

LVIII. The fine proposed was one hundred thou-

[3] A *candidatus* was so called because he appeared during
a campaign wearing a *toga candida*. Cato's testimony was
partially discredited because the conviction of Acilius would
improve Cato's own chances of election.

[4] The full force of *intestabilis* is difficult to convey, since it
refers to conduct or character which disqualify the individual
from serving as a witness or making a will, that is, from performing the normal functions of a citizen.

LIVY

de ea certatum est; tertio, cum de petitione desti-
tisset reus, nec populus de multa suffragium ferre
2 voluit, et tribuni eo negotio destiterunt. Censores
T. Quinctius Flamininus M. Claudius Marcellus
creati.

3 Per eos dies L. Aemilio Regillo, qui classe praefectum Antiochi regis devicerat, extra urbem in
aede Apollinis cum senatus datus esset, auditis rebus
gestis eius, quantis cum classibus hostium dimicasset,
quot[1] inde naves demersisset aut cepisset, magno
consensu patrum triumphus navalis est decretus.
4 Triumphavit Kal. Februariis. In eo triumpho undequinquaginta coronae aureae translatae sunt, pecunia
nequaquam pro[2] specie regii triumphi, tetrachma
Attica triginta quattuor milia ducenta, cistophori
5 centum triginta duo milia trecenti. Supplicationes
deinde fuerunt ex senatus consulto, quod L. Aemilius
in Hispania[3] prospere rem publicam gessisset.

6 Haud ita multo post L. Scipio ad urbem venit;
qui ne cognomini fratris cederet, Asiaticum se appel-
7 lari voluit. Et in senatu et in contione de rebus ab
se gestis disseruit. Erant qui fama id maius bellum
quam difficultate rei fuisse interpretarentur: uno
memorabili proelio debellatum, gloriamque eius

---

[1] quot ς : quod B.
[2] pro J. F. Gronovius : tanta pro Bς.
[3] in Hispania edd. vett. : in graecia B : in graecia hispania
(aut in hispania) ς.

---

[1] Roman procedure required three separate sessions of the
court, at the third of which the verdict was rendered. If one
party failed to appear at this session, the case was automatically
forfeited to the other side and no verdict was, as a rule, given.
[2] These speeches seem to be the customary arguments in
favour of the grant of a triumph. Since a general with the

sand *asses*; the case was twice argued [1]; the third
time, since the defendant had ceased to be a candidate and the people was unwilling to cast a ballot regarding the fine, the tribunes too dropped the case. Titus Quinctius Flamininus and Marcus Claudius Marcellus were chosen censors.

About this time Lucius Aemilius Regillus, who with his fleet had conquered the prefect of King Antiochus, having been granted an audience by the senate in the temple of Apollo outside the City, when they had heard his achievements, with how great fleets of the enemy he had fought and how many of their ships he had sunk or captured, with the complete approval of the Fathers was granted a naval triumph. He triumphed on the Kalends of February. In that triumph forty-nine golden crowns were displayed, money in no wise comparable to the magnificence of the triumph, to wit, thirty-four thousand two hundred Attic four-drachma pieces and one hundred thirty-two thousand three hundred *cistophori*. Then there were supplications decreed by the senate because Lucius Aemilius had administered affairs successfully in Spain.

Not long thereafter Lucius Scipio came to the City; and, that he might not be inferior to his brother in the matter of names, he requested that he be saluted as *Asiaticus*. Both in the senate and before the assembly [2] he made speeches about his accomplishments. There were some who tried to make out that that war had been magnified by rumour beyond its actual difficulty: that it had been brought to a conclusion by a single noteworthy battle, and

imperium could not cross the *pomerium*, it is uncertain what assembly Livy means.

A.U.C.
565

8 victoriae praefloratam ad Thermopylas esse. Ceterum vere [1] aestimanti Aetolicum magis ad Thermopylas bellum quam regium fuit; quota enim parte [2] virium suarum ibi dimicavit Antiochus? In Asia totius Asiae steterunt vires ab ultimis Orientis finibus [3] omnium gentium contractis auxiliis.

LIX. Merito ergo et diis immortalibus quantus maximus poterat habitus est honos, quod ingentem victoriam facilem etiam fecissent, et [4] imperatori 2 triumphus est decretus. Triumphavit mense intercalario pridie Kal. Martias. Qui triumphus spectaculo oculorum maior quam Africani fratris eius fuit, recordatione rerum et aestimatione periculi certaminisque non magis comparandus quam si imperatorem imperatori aut Antiochum ducem Hannibali 3 conferres. Tulit in triumpho signa militaria ducenta viginti quattuor, oppidorum simulacra centum triginta quattuor, eburneos dentes mille ducentos triginta unum, aureas coronas ducentas triginta 4 quattuor, argenti pondo centum triginta septem milia quadringenta viginti, tetrachmum Atticorum ducenta viginti quattuor [5] milia, cistophori trecenta

---

[1] uere ⟨ : *om. B.*
[2] quota enim parte ⟨ : quod enim partae *B.*
[3] ultimis Orientis finibus *Weissenborn* : ultimis orientis *B* : ultimi (*aut* ultimis orientis) ⟨.
[4] et *ed. Frobeniana* 1535 : *om. B⟨.*
[5] uiginti quattuor ⟨ : quattuordecim *B.*

---

[1] It is difficult to form an intelligent opinion from Livy as to this question. From Livy's narrative it seems as if the Aetolians had done little in this battle and too little in the war to warrant a triumph over them. On the other hand, it is true that the king had only a small fraction of his forces

that the glory of that victory had been robbed B.C. 189 of distinction beforehand at Thermopylae. But to one who judges aright the battle at Thermopylae was with the Aetolians rather than the king; for with what part of his own forces had the king fought there?[1] In Asia the strength of all Asia from the farthest parts of the east and of all nations stood as his assembled army.

LIX. Justly, therefore, was both all possible honour paid to the immortal gods because they had made this notable victory even easy, and a triumph awarded to the general. He triumphed during the intercalary[2] month on the day before the Kalends of March. This triumph was more dazzling to the eyes than that of his brother Africanus, but in the recollection of what had transpired and in the judgment of the danger and struggle no more to be compared with it than if you were to put side by side general with general or Antiochus with Hannibal as a commander. He carried in the triumph two hundred and twenty-four military standards, representations of towns to the number of one hundred and thirty-four, of ivory tusks one thousand two hundred and thirty-one, two hundred and thirty-four golden crowns, one hundred and thirty-seven thousand four hundred and twenty pounds of silver, two hundred and twenty-four thousand Attic fourdrachma pieces, three hundred and twenty-one thousand seven hundred *cistophori*, one hundred and

---

there. But this discredits Thermopylae rather than Magnesia as a decisive engagement.

[2] When the civil and the natural year were too far apart, an additional (intercalary) month was inserted between February and March. The length of this extra month varied.

LIVY

viginti unum milia septuaginta, nummos aureos
Philippeos centum quadraginta milia, vasorum argen-
5 teorum—omnia caelata erant—mille pondo et quadringenta viginti tria, aureorum pondo viginti
tria. Et duces regii, praefecti, purpurati duo et
6 triginta ante currum ducti. Militibus quini viceni
denarii dati, duplex centurioni, triplex equiti. Et
stipendium militare et frumentum duplex post
triumphum datum; proelio in Asia facto duplex
dederat. Triumphavit anno fere post quam consulatu abiit.[1]

LX. Eodem fere tempore et Cn. Manlius consul
in Asiam et Q. Fabius Labeo praetor ad classem
2 venit. Ceterum consuli non deerat cum Gallis belli
materia. Mare pacatum erat devicto Antiocho,
cogitantique Fabio, cui rei potissimum insisteret, ne
otiosam provinciam habuisse videri posset, optimum
3 visum est in Cretam insulam traicere. Cydoniatae
bellum adversus Gortynios Gnosiosque gerebant, et
captivorum Romanorum atque Italici generis magnus
numerus in servitute esse per totam insulam [2] dice-
4 batur. Classe ab Epheso profectus cum primum
Cretae litus attigit, nuntios circa civitates misit ut
armis absisterent captivosque in suis quaeque urbibus
agrisque conquisitos reducerent, et legatos mitterent
ad se, cum quibus de rebus ad Cretenses pariter
5 Romanosque pertinentibus ageret. Nihil magnopere

---

[1] abiit ⲋ : abit B.
[2] insulam ⲋ : italiam B.

---

[1] These gold coins, of a probable value of twenty drachmae,
were first minted by Philip I, and retained his name.
[2] This is said to be the first triumph at which the donative
to the troops had been in silver; copper was the usual medium.

forty thousand gold coins of Philip,[1] one thousand _{B.C. 189} four hundred and twenty-three pounds of silver vases —all were embossed—and one thousand and twenty-three pounds of vases of gold. Also thirty-two royal generals, prefects and nobles, were led before his car. To the soldiers twenty-five *denarii* each [2] were given, twice that amount to each centurion, thrice to each trooper. And double the pay and rations of a soldier were given them after the triumph; after the battle was fought in Asia he had given them the double allowance.[3] He triumphed about a year after he had retired from the consulship.

LX. About the same time both the consul Gnaeus Manlius arrived in Asia and the praetor Quintus Fabius Labeo came to the fleet. Now a cause for war upon the Galatians was not lacking to the consul. The sea was peaceful after the defeat of Antiochus, and as Fabius reflected as to what occupation he should choose by preference, lest he have a year of idleness in office, it seemed best to cross to the island of Crete. The people of Cydonia were waging war on the Gortynians and Gnosians, and a great number of prisoners, both Romans and men of the Italian race, were said to be in slavery throughout the whole island. Setting out with the fleet from Ephesus, as soon as he landed on the Cretan coast, he sent messengers around to the cities to tell them that they should lay down their arms and should restore the prisoners, gathered up by each in his own city and lands, and should send ambassadors to him to treat of matters which concerned equally the Cretans and the Romans. The Cretans did not

---

[3] Soldiers received their pay annually, their rations monthly. This bonus, then, amounts to a considerable sum.

LIVY

ea Cretenses moverunt; captivos praeter Gortynios
nulli reddiderunt. Valerius Antias quattuor milia
6 captivorum, quia belli minas timuerint,[1] ex tota
insula reddita[2] scripsit; eamque causam Fabio,
cum rem nullam aliam gessisset, triumphi navalis
7 impetrandi ab senatu fuisse. A Creta Ephesum
Fabius redit; inde tribus navibus in Thraciae oram
missis ab Aeno et Maronea praesidia Antiochi deduci
iussit, ut in libertate eae civitates essent.

---

[1] timuerint *Bekker* : timuerunt *Bς*.
[2] reddita ς : redditas *B*.

pay much attention to this: none of them restored B.C. 189
the prisoners except the Gortynians. Valerius Antias
wrote that four thousand prisoners were given back
from the whole island because they feared the threat
of war; and that this was the explanation of the
fact that Fabius, although he had done nothing else,
received a naval triumph from the senate. From
Crete Fabius returned to Ephesus; thence he sent
three ships to the coast of Thrace and ordered the
garrisons of Antiochus withdrawn from Aenos and
Maronea, that these states might be at liberty.[1]

---

[1] These cities seem to have been overlooked before, possibly
because the withdrawal of Antiochus from Lysimachia was a
de facto abandonment of his territorial claims in Europe.

LIBER XXXVII PERIOCHA

L. CORNELIUS SCIPIO consul legato Scipione Africano fratre (qui se legatum fratris futurum dixerat, si ei Graecia provincia decerneretur, cum C. Laelio, qui multum in senatu poterat, ea provincia dari videretur) profectus ad bellum adversus Antiochum regem gerendum, primus omnium Romanorum ducum in Asiam [1] traiecit. Regillus adversus regiam classem Antiochi feliciter pugnavit ad Myonnesum Rhodis iuvantibus. Filius Africani captus ab Antiocho patri remissus est. Victo deinde Antiocho ab L. Cornelio Scipione adiuvante Eumene, rege Pergami, Attali filio, pax data est ea condicione ut omnibus provinciis citra Taurum montem cederet. L. Cornelius Scipio, qui cum Antiocho debellaverat, cognomine fratri exaequatus Asiaticus appellatus. Colonia deducta est Bononia. Eumenis, quo iuvante Antiochus victus erat, regnum ampliatum. Rhodis quoque qui et ipsi iuverant quaedam civitates concessae. Aemilius Regillus, qui praefectos Antiocho navali proelio devicerat, navalem triumphum deduxit. M'.[2] Acilius Glabrio de Antiocho, quem Graecia expulerat, et de Aetolis triumphavit.

---

[1] Asiam *Rossbach* : Asia *codd.*
[2] M'. *edd.* : M. *codd.*

SUMMARY OF BOOK XXXVII

Lucius Cornelius Scipio the consul, with his brother Scipio Africanus as his lieutenant (Africanus had said that he would be his brother's lieutenant if the province of Greece were assigned to him, although it seemed that that province would be given to Gaius Laelius, who was very influential in the senate), started out to conduct the war against King Antiochus, and was the first of all Roman generals to cross to Asia. Regillus fought successfully with the royal fleet of Antiochus off Myonnesus, with the aid of the Rhodians. The son of Africanus was captured by Antiochus and restored to his father. When Antiochus had been conquered by Lucius Cornelius Scipio, with the assistance of Eumenes, son of Attalus and king of Pergamum, peace was granted him under this condition, that he should withdraw from all the districts on this side of the Taurus mountains. Lucius Cornelius Scipio, who had finished the war with Antiochus, was put on a level with his brother by the surname of " Asiaticus." A colony was established at Bononia. Eumenes, by whose aid Antiochus had been defeated, had his kingdom enlarged. To the Rhodians too, who had also co-operated, certain cities were granted. Aemilius Regillus, who had defeated the prefects of Antiochus in a naval battle, celebrated a naval triumph. Manius Acilius Glabrio triumphed over Antiochus, whom he had driven out of Greece, and over the Aetolians.

INDEX OF NAMES

(The References are to Pages)

INDEX OF NAMES

INDEX OF NAMES

485

INDEX OF NAMES

486

INDEX OF NAMES

INDEX OF NAMES

489

INDEX OF NAMES

Printed in Great Britain by
Richard Clay and Company, Ltd.,
Bungay, Suffolk

THE LOEB CLASSICAL LIBRARY

VOLUMES ALREADY PUBLISHED

Latin Authors

AMMIANUS MARCELLINUS. Translated by J. C. Rolfe. 3 Vols. (Vols. I. and II. 3rd *Imp.*, Vol. III. 2nd *Imp. revised.*)

APULEIUS : THE GOLDEN ASS (METAMORPHOSES). W. Adlington (1566). Revised by S. Gaselee. (7th *Imp.*)

S. AUGUSTINE : CITY OF GOD. 7 Vols. Vol. I. G. E. McCracken.

ST. AUGUSTINE, CONFESSIONS OF. W. Watts (1631). 2 Vols. (Vol. I. 7th *Imp.*, Vol. II. 6th *Imp.*)

ST. AUGUSTINE, SELECT LETTERS. J. H. Baxter. (2nd *Imp.*)

AUSONIUS. H. G. Evelyn White. 2 Vols. (2nd *Imp.*)

BEDE. J. E. King. 2 Vols. (2nd *Imp.*)

BOETHIUS : TRACTS and DE CONSOLATIONE PHILOSOPHIAE. Rev. H. F. Stewart and E. K. Rand. (6th *Imp.*)

CAESAR : ALEXANDRIAN, AFRICAN and SPANISH WARS. A. G. Way.

CAESAR : CIVIL WARS. A. G. Peskett. (6th *Imp.*)

CAESAR : GALLIC WAR. H. J. Edwards. (10th *Imp.*)

CATO : DE RE RUSTICA ; VARRO : DE RE RUSTICA. H. B. Ash and W. D. Hooper. (3rd *Imp.*)

CATULLUS. F. W. Cornish ; TIBULLUS. J. B. Postgate ; PERVIGILIUM VENERIS. J. W. Mackail. (13th *Imp.*)

CELSUS : DE MEDICINA. W. G. Spencer. 3 Vols. (Vol. I. 3rd *Imp. revised*, Vols. II. and III. 2nd *Imp.*)

CICERO : BRUTUS, and ORATOR. G. L. Hendrickson and H. M. Hubbell. (3rd *Imp.*)

[CICERO] : AD HERENNIUM. H. Caplan.

CICERO : DE FATO ; PARADOXA STOICORUM ; DE PARTITIONE ORATORIA. H. Rackham (With De Oratore, Vol. II.) (2nd *Imp.*)

CICERO : DE FINIBUS. H. Rackham. (4th *Imp. revised.*)

CICERO : DE INVENTIONE, etc. H. M. Hubbell.

CICERO : DE NATURA DEORUM and ACADEMICA. H. Rackham. (3rd *Imp.*)

CICERO : DE OFFICIIS. Walter Miller. (7th *Imp.*)

CICERO : DE ORATORE. 2 Vols. E. W. Sutton and H. Rackham. (3rd *Imp.*)

CICERO : DE REPUBLICA and DE LEGIBUS ; SOMNIUM SCIPIONIS. Clinton W. Keyes. (4th *Imp.*)

CICERO : DE SENECTUTE, DE AMICITIA, DE DIVINATIONE. W. A. Falconer. (6th *Imp.*)

CICERO : IN CATILINAM, PRO FLACCO, PRO MURENA, PRO SULLA. Louis E. Lord. (3rd *Imp. revised.*)

CICERO: LETTERS TO ATTICUS. E. O. Winstedt. 3 Vols. (Vol. I. 7th *Imp.*, Vols. II. and III. 4th *Imp.*)
CICERO: LETTERS TO HIS FRIENDS. W. Glynn Williams. 3 Vols. (Vols. I. and II. 3rd *Imp.*, Vol. III. 2nd *Imp. revised.*)
CICERO: PHILIPPICS. W. C. A. Ker. (4th *Imp. revised.*)
CICERO: PRO ARCHIA, POST REDITUM, DE DOMO, DE HARUSPICUM RESPONSIS, PRO PLANCIO. N. H. Watts. (3rd *Imp.*)
CICERO: PRO CAECINA, PRO LEGE MANILIA, PRO CLUENTIO, PRO RABIRIO. H. Grose Hodge. (3rd *Imp.*)
CICERO: PRO CAELIO, DE PROVINCIIS CONSULARIBUS, PRO BALBO. J. H. Freese and R. Gardner.
CICERO: PRO MILONE, IN PISONEM, PRO SCAURO, PRO FONTEIO, PRO RABIRIO POSTUMO, PRO MARCELLO, PRO LIGARIO, PRO REGE DEIOTARO. N. H. Watts. (3rd *Imp.*)
CICERO: PRO QUINCTIO, PRO ROSCIO AMERINO, PRO ROSCIO COMOEDO, CONTRA RULLUM. J. H. Freese. (3rd *Imp.*)
CICERO: PRO SESTIO, IN VATINIUM. J. H. Freese and R. Gardner.
CICERO: TUSCULAN DISPUTATIONS. J. E. King. (4th *Imp.*)
CICERO: VERRINE ORATIONS. L. H. G. Greenwood. 2 Vols. (Vol. I. 3rd *Imp.*, Vol. II. 2nd *Imp.*)
CLAUDIAN. M. Platnauer. 2 Vols. (2nd *Imp.*)
COLUMELLA: DE RE RUSTICA. DE ARBORIBUS. H. B. Ash, E. S. Forster and E. Heffner. 3 Vols. (Vol. I. 2nd *Imp.*)
CURTIUS, Q.: HISTORY OF ALEXANDER. J. C. Rolfe. 2 Vols. (2nd *Imp.*)
FLORUS. E. S. Forster and CORNELIUS NEPOS. J. C. Rolfe. (2nd *Imp.*)
FRONTINUS: STRATAGEMS and AQUEDUCTS. C. E. Bennett and M. B. McElwain. (2nd *Imp.*)
FRONTO: CORRESPONDENCE. C. R. Haines. 2 Vols. (3rd *Imp.*)
GELLIUS, J. C. Rolfe. 3 Vols. (Vol. I. 3rd *Imp.*, Vols. II. and III. 2nd *Imp.*)
HORACE: ODES and EPODES. C. E. Bennett. (14th *Imp. revised.*)
HORACE: SATIRES, EPISTLES, ARS POETICA. H. R. Fairclough. (9th *Imp. revised.*)
JEROME: SELECTED LETTERS. F. A. Wright. (2nd *Imp.*)
JUVENAL and PERSIUS. G. G. Ramsay. (8th *Imp.*)
LIVY. B. O. Foster, F. G. Moore, Evan T. Sage, and A. C. Schlesinger. 14 Vols. (Vol. I. 5th *Imp.*, Vol. V. 4th *Imp.*, Vols. II.–IV., VII., IX.–XII. 3rd *Imp.*, Vols. VI., VIII., 2nd *Imp. revised.*)
LUCAN. J. D. Duff. (4th *Imp.*)
LUCRETIUS. W. H. D. Rouse. (7th *Imp. revised.*)
MARTIAL. W. C. A. Ker. 2 Vols. (Vol. I. 5th *Imp.*, Vol. II. 4th *Imp. revised.*)
MINOR LATIN POETS: from PUBLILIUS SYRUS to RUTILIUS NAMATIANUS, including GRATTIUS, CALPURNIUS SICULUS, NEMESIANUS, AVIANUS, and others with "Aetna" and the "Phoenix." J. Wight Duff and Arnold M. Duff. (3rd *Imp.*)
OVID: THE ART OF LOVE and OTHER POEMS. J. H. Mozley. (4th *Imp.*)

2

OVID : FASTI.   Sir James G. Frazer.   (*2nd Imp.*)

OVID : HEROIDES and AMORES.   Grant Showerman.   (*6th Imp.*)

OVID : METAMORPHOSES.   F. J. Miller.   2 Vols.   (Vol. I. 11*th Imp.*, Vol. II. 9*th Imp.*)

OVID : TRISTIA and EX PONTO.   A. L. Wheeler.   (*3rd Imp.*)

PERSIUS.   Cf. JUVENAL.

PETRONIUS.   M.   Heseltine,   SENECA   APOCOLOCYNTOSIS. W. H. D. Rouse.   (*9th Imp. revised.*)

PLAUTUS.   Paul Nixon.   5 Vols.   (Vol. I. 6*th Imp.*, II. 5*th Imp.*, III. 4*th Imp.*, IV. and V. 2*nd Imp.*)

PLINY : LETTERS.   Melmoth's Translation revised by W. M. L. Hutchinson.   2 Vols.   (Vol. I. 7*th Imp.*, Vol. II. 6*th Imp.*)

PLINY : NATURAL HISTORY.   H. Rackham and W. H. S. Jones. 10 Vols.   Vols. I.–V. and IX.   H. Rackham.   Vols. VI. and VII. W. H. S. Jones.   (Vols. I.–III. 3*rd Imp.*, Vol. IV. 2*nd Imp.*)

PROPERTIUS.   H. E. Butler.   (*7th Imp.*)

PRUDENTIUS.   H. J. Thomson.   2 Vols.

QUINTILIAN.   H. E. Butler.   4 Vols.   (Vols. I. and IV. 4*th Imp.*, Vols. II. and III. 3*rd Imp.*)

REMAINS OF OLD LATIN.   E. H. Warmington.   4 vols.   Vol. I. (ENNIUS AND CAECILIUS.)   Vol. II.   (LIVIUS, NAEVIUS, PACUVIUS, ACCIUS.)   Vol. III.   (LUCILIUS and LAWS OF XII TABLES.)   Vol. IV.   (*2nd Imp.*)   (ARCHAIC INSCRIPTIONS.)

SALLUST.   J. C. Rolfe.   (*4th Imp. revised.*)

SCRIPTORES HISTORIAE AUGUSTAE.   D. Magie.   3 Vols.   (Vol. I. 3*rd Imp. revised*, Vols. II. and III. 2*nd Imp.*)

SENECA : APOCOLOCYNTOSIS.   Cf. PETRONIUS.

SENECA : EPISTULAE MORALES.   R. M. Gummere.   3 Vols. (Vol. I. 4*th Imp.*, Vols. II. and III. 2*nd Imp.*)

SENECA : MORAL ESSAYS.   J. W. Basore.   3 Vols.   (Vol. II. 3*rd Imp.*, Vols. I. and III. 2*nd Imp. revised.*)

SENECA : TRAGEDIES.   F. J. Miller.   2 Vols.   (Vol. I. 4*th Imp.*, Vol. II. 3*rd Imp. revised.*)

SIDONIUS : POEMS AND LETTERS.   W. B. Anderson.   2 Vols. (Vol. I. 2*nd Imp.*)

SILIUS ITALICUS.   J. D. Duff.   2 Vols.   (Vol. I. 2*nd Imp.*, Vol. II. 3*rd Imp.*)

STATIUS.   J. H. Mozley.   2 Vols.   (*2nd Imp.*)

SUETONIUS.   J. C. Rolfe.   2 Vols.   (Vol. I. 7*th Imp.*, Vol. II. 6*th Imp. revised.*)

TACITUS : DIALOGUS.   Sir Wm. Peterson.   AGRICOLA and GERMANIA.   Maurice Hutton.   (*6th Imp.*)

TACITUS : HISTORIES AND ANNALS.   C. H. Moore and J. Jackson. 4 Vols.   (Vols. I. and II. 4*th Imp.*, Vols. III. and IV. 3*rd Imp.*)

TERENCE.   John Sargeaunt.   2 Vols.   (*7th Imp.*)

TERTULLIAN : APOLOGIA and DE SPECTACULIS.   T. R. Glover. MINUCIUS FELIX.   G. H. Rendall.   (*2nd Imp.*)

VALERIUS FLACCUS.   J. H. Mozley.   (*3rd Imp. revised.*)

VARRO : DE LINGUA LATINA.   R. G. Kent.   2 Vols.   (*2nd Imp. revised.*)

VELLEIUS PATERCULUS and RES GESTAE DIVI AUGUSTI.   F. W. Shipley.   (*2nd Imp.*)

VIRGIL. H. R. Fairclough. 2 Vols. (Vol. I. 19th *Imp.*, Vol. II. 14th *Imp. revised.*)

VITRUVIUS : DE ARCHITECTURA. F. Granger. 2 Vols. (Vol. I. 3rd *Imp.*, Vol. II. 2nd *Imp.*)

Greek Authors

ACHILLES TATIUS. S. Gaselee. (2nd *Imp.*)

AELIAN : ON THE NATURE OF ANIMALS. 3 Vols. Vol. I. A. F. Scholfield.

AENEAS TACTICUS, ASCLEPIODOTUS and ONASANDER. The Illinois Greek Club. (2nd *Imp.*)

AESCHINES. C. D. Adams. (3rd *Imp.*)

AESCHYLUS. H. Weir Smyth. 2 Vols. (Vol. I. 7th *Imp.*, Vol. II. 6th *Imp. revised.*)

ALCIPHRON, AELIAN, PHILOSTRATUS LETTERS. A. R. Benner and F. H. Fobes.

ANDOCIDES, ANTIPHON, Cf. MINOR ATTIC ORATORS.

APOLLODORUS. Sir James G. Frazer. 2 Vols. (3rd *Imp.*)

APOLLONIUS RHODIUS. R. C. Seaton. (5th *Imp.*)

THE APOSTOLIC FATHERS. Kirsopp Lake. 2 Vols. (Vol. I. 8th *Imp.*, Vol. II. 6th *Imp.*)

APPIAN : ROMAN HISTORY. Horace White. 4 Vols. (Vol. I. 4th *Imp.*, Vols. II.–IV. 3rd *Imp.*)

ARATUS. Cf. CALLIMACHUS.

ARISTOPHANES. Benjamin Bickley Rogers. 3 Vols. Verse trans. (5th *Imp.*)

ARISTOTLE : ART OF RHETORIC. J. H. Freese. (3rd *Imp.*)

ARISTOTLE : ATHENIAN CONSTITUTION, EUDEMIAN ETHICS, VICES AND VIRTUES. H. Rackham. (3rd *Imp.*)

ARISTOTLE : GENERATION OF ANIMALS. A. L. Peck. (2nd *Imp.*)

ARISTOTLE : METAPHYSICS. H. Tredennick. 2 Vols. (4th *Imp.*)

ARISTOTLE : METEOROLOGICA. H. D. P. Lee.

ARISTOTLE : MINOR WORKS. W. S. Hett. On Colours, On Things Heard, On Physiognomies, On Plants, On Marvellous Things Heard, Mechanical Problems, On Indivisible Lines, On Situations and Names of Winds, On Melissus, Xenophanes, and Gorgias. (2nd *Imp.*)

ARISTOTLE : NICOMACHEAN ETHICS. H. Rackham. (6th *Imp. revised.*)

ARISTOTLE : OECONOMICA and MAGNA MORALIA. G. C. Armstrong; (with Metaphysics, Vol. II.). (Vol. I. 4th *Imp.*, Vol. II. 3rd *Imp.*)

ARISTOTLE : ON THE HEAVENS. W. K. C. Guthrie. (3rd *Imp. revised.*)

ARISTOTLE : On Sophistical Refutations, On Coming to be and Passing Away, On the Cosmos. E. S. Forster and D. J. Furley.

ARISTOTLE : ON THE SOUL, PARVA NATURALIA, ON BREATH. W. S. Hett. (2nd *Imp. revised.*)

ARISTOTLE : ORGANON, CATEGORIES : On Interpretation, Prior Analytics. H. P. Cooke and H. Tredennick. (3rd *Imp.*)

ARISTOTLE : PARTS OF ANIMALS. A. L. Peck; MOTION AND
PROGRESSION OF ANIMALS. E. S. Forster. (*4th Imp. revised.*)
ARISTOTLE : PHYSICS. Rev. P. Wicksteed and F. M. Cornford.
2 Vols. (Vol. I. *2nd Imp.*, Vol. II. *3rd Imp.*)
ARISTOTLE : POETICS and LONGINUS. W. Hamilton Fyfe;
DEMETRIUS ON STYLE. W. Rhys Roberts. (*5th Imp. revised.*)
ARISTOTLE : POLITICS. H. Rackham. (*4th Imp. revised.*)
ARISTOTLE : PROBLEMS. W. S. Hett. 2 Vols. (*2nd Imp. revised.*)
ARISTOTLE : RHETORICA AD ALEXANDRUM (with PROBLEMS.
Vol. II.). H. Rackham.
ARRIAN : HISTORY OF ALEXANDER and INDICA. Rev. E. Iliffe
Robson. 2 Vols. (Vol. I. *3rd Imp.*, Vol. II. *2nd Imp.*)
ATHENAEUS : DEIPNOSOPHISTAE. C. B. Gulick. 7 Vols.
(Vols. I.-IV., VI., VII. *2nd Imp.*, Vol. V. *3rd Imp.*)
ST. BASIL : LETTERS. R. J. Deferrari. 4 Vols. (*2nd Imp.*)
CALLIMACHUS: FRAGMENTS. A. C. Trypanis.
CALLIMACHUS, Hymns and Epigrams, and LYCOPHRON. A. W.
Mair ; ARATUS. G. R. Mair. (*2nd. Imp.*)
CLEMENT OF ALEXANDRIA. Rev. G. W. Butterworth. (*3rd Imp.*)
COLLUTHUS. Cf. OPPIAN.
DAPHNIS AND CHLOE. Thornley's Translation revised by
J. M. Edmonds ; and PARTHENIUS. S. Gaselee. (*4th Imp.*)
DEMOSTHENES I: OLYNTHIACS, PHILIPPICS and MINOR ORA-
TIONS. I.-XVII. AND XX. J. H. Vince. (*2nd Imp.*)
DEMOSTHENES II : DE CORONA and DE FALSA LEGATIONE.
C. A. Vince and J. H. Vince. (*3rd Imp. revised.*)
DEMOSTHENES III : MEIDIAS, ANDROTION, ARISTOCRATES,
TIMOCRATES and ARISTOGEITON, I AND II. J. H. Vince.
(*2nd Imp.*)
DEMOSTHENES IV-VI : PRIVATE ORATIONS and IN NEAERAM.
A. T. Murray. (Vol. IV. *3rd Imp.*, Vols. V. and VI. *2nd Imp.*)
DEMOSTHENES VII : FUNERAL SPEECH, EROTIC ESSAY, EXORDIA
and LETTERS. N. W. and N. J. DeWitt.
DIO CASSIUS : ROMAN HISTORY. E. Cary. 9 Vols. (Vols. I.
and II. *3rd Imp.*, Vols. III.-IX. *2nd Imp.*)
DIO CHRYSOSTOM. J. W. Cohoon and H. Lamar Crosby. 5 Vols.
Vols. I.-IV. *2nd Imp.*)
DIODORUS SICULUS. 12 Vols. Vols. I.-VI. C. H. Oldfather.
Vol. VII. C. L. Sherman. Vols. IX. and X. R. M. Geer.
Vol. XI. F. Walton. (Vols. I.-IV. *2nd Imp.*)
DIOGENES LAERTIUS. R. D. Hicks. 2 Vols. (Vol. I. *4th Imp.*,
Vol. II. *3rd Imp.*)
DIONYSIUS OF HALICARNASSUS : ROMAN ANTIQUITIES. Spel-
man's translation revised by E. Cary. 7 Vols. (Vols. I.-V.
2nd Imp.)
EPICTETUS. W. A. Oldfather. 2 Vols. (Vol. I. *3rd Imp.*, II. *2nd
Imp.*)
EURIPIDES. A. S. Way. 4 Vols. (Vol. I. *7th imp.*, Vol. II. *8th
Imp.*, Vols. III. and IV. *6th Imp.*) Verse trans.
EUSEBIUS : ECCLESIASTICAL HISTORY. Kirsopp Lake and
J. E. L. Oulton. 2 Vols. (Vol. I. *3rd Imp.*, Vol. II. *5th
Imp.*)

GALEN : ON THE NATURAL FACULTIES. A. J. Brock. (4th Imp.)

THE GREEK ANTHOLOGY. W. R. Paton. 5 Vols. (Vols. I.–IV. 5th Imp., Vol. V. 3rd Imp.)

GREEK ELEGY AND IAMBUS with the ANACREONTEA. J. M. Edmonds. 2 Vols. (Vol. I. 3rd Imp., Vol. II. 2nd Imp.)

THE GREEK BUCOLIC POETS (THEOCRITUS, BION, MOSCHUS). J. M. Edmonds. (7th Imp. revised.)

GREEK MATHEMATICAL WORKS. Ivor Thomas. 2 Vols. (3rd Imp.)

HERODES. Cf. THEOPHRASTUS : CHARACTERS.

HERODOTUS. A. D. Godley. 4 Vols. (Vol. I. 4th Imp., Vols. II. and III. 5th Imp., Vol. IV. 3rd Imp.)

HESIOD AND THE HOMERIC HYMNS. H. G. Evelyn White. 7th Imp. revised and enlarged.)

HIPPOCRATES and the FRAGMENTS OF HERACLEITUS. W. H. S. Jones and E. T. Withington. 4 Vols. (Vol. I. 4th Imp., Vols. II.–IV. 3rd Imp.)

HOMER : ILIAD. A. T. Murray. 2 Vols. (7th Imp.)

HOMER : ODYSSEY. A. T. Murray. 2 Vols. (8th Imp.)

ISAEUS. E. W. Forster. (3rd Imp.)

ISOCRATES. George Norlin and LaRue Van Hook. 3 Vols. (2nd Imp.)

ST. JOHN DAMASCENE : BARLAAM AND IOASAPH. Rev. G. R. Woodward and Harold Mattingly. (3rd Imp. revised.)

JOSEPHUS. H. St. J. Thackeray and Ralph Marcus. 9 Vols. Vols. I.–VII. (Vol. V. 3rd Imp., Vols. I.–IV., VI. and VII. 2nd Imp.)

JULIAN. Wilmer Cave Wright. 3 Vols. (Vols. I. and II. 3rd Imp., Vol. III. 2nd Imp.)

LUCIAN. A. M. Harmon. 8 Vols. Vols. I.–V. (Vols. I. and II. 4th Imp., Vol. III. 3rd Imp., Vols. IV. and V. 2nd Imp.)

LYCOPHRON. Cf. CALLIMACHUS.

LYRA GRAECA. J. M. Edmonds. 3 Vols. (Vol. I. 5th Imp., Vol. II. revised and enlarged, and III. 4th Imp.)

LYSIAS. W. R. M. Lamb. (3rd Imp.)

MANETHO. W. G. Waddell : PTOLEMY : TETRABIBLOS. F. E. Robbins. (3rd Imp.)

MARCUS AURELIUS. C. R. Haines. (4th Imp. revised.)

MENANDER. F. G. Allinson. (3rd Imp. revised.)

MINOR ATTIC ORATORS (ANTIPHON, ANDOCIDES, LYCURGUS. DEMADES, DINARCHUS, HYPEREIDES). K. J. Maidment and J. O. Burrt. 2 Vols. (Vol. I. 2nd Imp.)

NONNOS : DIONYSIACA. W. H. D. Rouse. 3 Vols. (2nd Imp.)

OPPIAN, COLLUTHUS, TRYPHIODORUS. A. W. Mair. (2nd Imp.)

PAPYRI. NON-LITERARY SELECTIONS. A. S. Hunt and C. C. Edgar. 2 Vols. (2nd Imp.) LITERARY SELECTIONS. (Poetry). D. L. Page. (3rd Imp.)

PARTHENIUS. Cf. DAPHNIS AND CHLOE.

PAUSANIAS : DESCRIPTION OF GREECE. W. H. S. Jones. 5 Vols. and Companion Vol. arranged by R. E. Wycherley. (Vols. I. and III. 3rd Imp., Vols. II., IV. and V. 2nd Imp.)

PHILO. 10 Vols. Vols. I.–V.; F. H. Colson and Rev. G. H. Whitaker. Vols. VI.–IX.; F. H. Colson. (Vols. I., III., V., and VI. 3rd *Imp.*, Vol. IV. 4th *Imp.*, Vols. II., VII.–IX. 2nd *Imp.*)

PHILO: two supplementary Vols. (*Translation only.*) Ralph Marcus.

PHILOSTRATUS: THE LIFE OF APPOLLONIUS OF TYANA. F. C. Conybeare. 2 Vols. (Vol. I. 4th *Imp.*, Vol. II. 3rd *Imp.*)

PHILOSTRATUS: IMAGINES; CALLISTRATUS: DESCRIPTIONS. A. Fairbanks. (2nd *Imp.*)

PHILOSTRATUS and EUNAPIUS: LIVES OF THE SOPHISTS. Wilmer Cave Wright. (2nd *Imp.*)

PINDAR. Sir J. E. Sandys. (8th *Imp. revised.*)

PLATO: CHARMIDES, ALCIBIADES, HIPPARCHUS, THE LOVERS, THEAGES, MINOS and EPINOMIS. W. R. M. Lamb. (2nd *Imp.*)

PLATO: CRATYLUS, PARMENIDES, GREATER HIPPIAS, LESSER HIPPIAS. H. N. Fowler. (4th *Imp.*)

PLATO: EUTHYPHRO, APOLOGY, CRITO, PHAEDO, PHAEDRUS. H. N. Fowler. (11th *Imp.*)

PLATO: LACHES, PROTAGORAS, MENO, EUTHYDEMUS. W. R. M. Lamb. (3rd *Imp. revised.*)

PLATO: LAWS. Rev. R. G. Bury. 2 Vols. (3rd *Imp.*)

PLATO: LYSIS, SYMPOSIUM, GORGIAS. W. R. M. Lamb. (5th *Imp. revised.*)

PLATO: REPUBLIC. Paul Shorey. 2 Vols. (Vol. I. 5th *Imp.*, Vol. II. 4th *Imp.*)

PLATO: STATESMAN, PHILEBUS. H. N. Fowler; ION. W. R. M. Lamb. (4th *Imp.*)

PLATO: THEAETETUS and SOPHIST. H. N. Fowler. (4th *Imp.*)

PLATO: TIMAEUS, CRITIAS, CLITOPHO, MENEXENUS, EPISTULAE. Rev. R. G. Bury. (3rd *Imp.*)

PLUTARCH: MORALIA. 14 Vols. Vols. I.–V. F. C. Babbitt. Vol. VI. W. C. Helmbold. Vol. VII. P. H. de Lacy and B. Einarson. Vol. X. H. N. Fowler. Vol. XII. H. Cherniss and W. C. Helmbold. (Vols. I.–VI. and X. 2nd *Imp.*)

PLUTARCH: THE PARALLEL LIVES. B. Perrin. 11 Vols. (Vols. I., II., VI., VII., and XI. 3rd *Imp.* Vols. III.–V. and VIII.–X. 2nd *Imp.*)

POLYBIUS. W. R. Paton. 6 Vols. (2nd *Imp.*)

PROCOPIUS: HISTORY OF THE WARS. H. B. Dewing. 7 Vols. (Vol. I. 3rd *Imp.*, Vols. II.–VII. 2nd *Imp.*)

PTOLEMY: TETRABIBLOS. Cf. MANETHO.

QUINTUS SMYRNAEUS. A. S. Way. Verse trans. (3rd *Imp.*)

SEXTUS EMPIRICUS. Rev. R. G. Bury. 4 Vols. (Vol. I. 4th *Imp.*, Vols. II. and III. 2nd *Imp.*)

SOPHOCLES. F. Storr. 2 Vols. (Vol. I. 10th *Imp.* Vol. II. 6th *Imp.*) Verse trans.

STRABO: GEOGRAPHY. Horace L. Jones. 8 Vols. (Vols. I., V., and VIII. 3rd *Imp.*, Vols. II., III., IV., VI., and VII. 2nd *Imp.*)

THEOPHRASTUS: CHARACTERS. J. M. Edmonds. HERODES, etc. A. D. Knox. (3rd *Imp.*)

7

THEOPHRASTUS : ENQUIRY INTO PLANTS. Sir Arthur Hort, Bart. 2 Vols. (*2nd Imp.*)

THUCYDIDES. C. F. Smith. 4 Vols. (Vol. I. *5th Imp.*, Vols. II., III., and IV. *3rd Imp. revised*)

TRYPHIODOBUS. Cf. OPPIAN.

XENOPHON : CYROPAEDIA. Walter Miller. 2 Vols. (Vol. I. *4th Imp.*, Vol. II. *3rd Imp.*)

XENOPHON : HELLENICA, ANABASIS, APOLOGY, and SYMPOSIUM. C. L. Brownson and O. J. Todd. 3 Vols. (Vols. I. and III. *3rd Imp.*, Vol. II. *4th Imp.*)

XENOPHON : MEMORABILIA and OECONOMICUS. E. C. Marchant. (*3rd Imp.*)

XENOPHON : SCRIPTA MINORA. E. C. Marchant. (*3rd Imp.*)

IN PREPARATION

Greek Authors

ARISTOTLE : HISTORY OF ANIMALS. A. L. Peck.

PLOTINUS : A. H. Armstrong.

Latin Authors

PHAEDRUS. Ben E. Perry.

DESCRIPTIVE PROSPECTUS ON APPLICATION

London   **WILLIAM HEINEMANN LTD**

Cambridge, Mass.   **HARVARD UNIVERSITY PRESS**